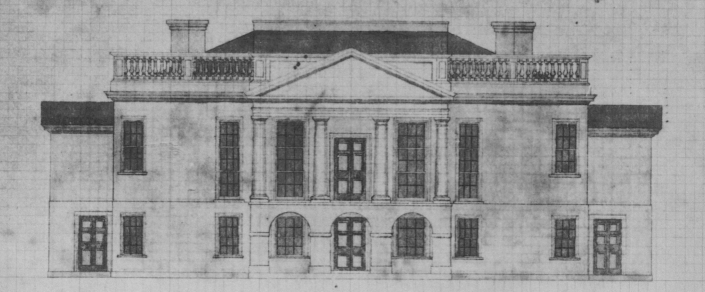

Th: Jefferson

To

GEORGE T. STEWART

friend of Poplar Forest, admirer of Thomas Jefferson

POPLAR FOREST

& ——

THOMAS JEFFERSON

THOMAS JEFFERSON · ARCHITECT OF DEMOCRACY

1743
250
1993

S. ALLEN CHAMBERS, JR.

Published for
The Corporation for Jefferson's Poplar Forest
in commemoration of the 250th anniversary
of the birth of Thomas Jefferson

To Jefferson, the landscape was an integral part of the overall design plan. Poplar trees at the front of the house survive from Jefferson's time. Archaeologists continue to research the original landscape design.

Jefferson crowned his villa retreat with a balustrade edging the roof and a Chinese railing surrounding the skylight above the center cube room. A fire in 1845 led to alterations in the original Jefferson roofline, which was reconstructed by The Corporation for Jefferson's Poplar Forest in 1998.

(Unless otherwise noted, all color plates of Poplar Forest are by Robert C. Lautman, 1998, for The Corporation for Jefferson's Poplar Forest)

Frontispiece;
Thomas Jefferson, by Rembrandt Peale.
Jefferson sat for this portrait in January 1805.
Later that year he began preparations for his house at Poplar Forest.
(Collection of the New York Historical Society)

First Edition 1993
Second impression 1998

Library of Congress Catalog Card Number
93-90066

ISBN 0-9667169-0-6

Chambers, S. Allen, Jr.
Poplar Forest and Thomas Jefferson

Designed by Donald G. Paulhus

Printed in the United States of America

CONTENTS

Archaeological excavations in 1989-91 uncovered ▶ brick and stone foundations and floors of Jefferson's service wing, east of the main house.
(*The Corporation for Jefferson's Poplar Forest staff photo*)

◀ Jefferson's dining room at Poplar Forest epitomizes his desire to create light, open spaces and a rotunda house. A perfect cube, the space measures 20 feet all around. It is believed that the 16-foot long skylight was one of the largest of its kind in America at the time of construction. The photo shows the perspective looking westward from the granddaughters' bedroom to Jefferson's room.

◀ Jefferson's intricate landscape design included two necessaries symmetrically aligned on an axis on either side of the two mounds flanking the house. The eight-sided necessaries and house reflect Jefferson's fascination with octagons.

The back of Poplar Forest features Jefferson's trademark neo-classical portico with its lunette window as well as Tuscan columns, brick arcade, faux grain mahogany doors, and triple sash windows. The upper level door on the east stair pavilion of the building originally opened onto the roof of a wing of service rooms that Jefferson added in 1814. Restoration plans call for reconstructing the wing.

"MY OTHER HOME"

"I am just returned from one of my long absences, having been at my other home for five weeks past."[1] So Thomas Jefferson (1743–1826) wrote to John Adams in 1814. Adams and a small number of friends with whom Jefferson corresponded in a similar vein were among the privileged few who ever knew of Poplar Forest, his "other home," in Bedford County, Virginia. Fewer still of his acquaintances were ever invited to visit him there. Poplar Forest was a private place for its owner-builder and his family, but even when Jefferson was otherwise involved in his many state and national engagements, it was never far from his mind. In late November 1821, he wrote his friend and protégé William Short that he had just returned to Monticello from Poplar Forest, which he had "visited four times this year." He also informed Short that he had "an excellent house there" and that he was "comfortably fixed and attended, have a few good neighbors, and pass my time there in a tranquility and retirement much adapted to my age and indolence." Years later, one of his granddaughters recalled in similar terms what his Bedford retreat meant to him: "At Poplar Forest he found in a pleasant home, rest, leisure, power to carry on his favorite pursuits — to think, to study, to read — whilst the presence of part of his family took away all character of solitude from his retreat."[2]

The most famous feature of Poplar Forest is the remarkable house that Jefferson built there. "Architecture is my delight, and putting up and pulling down one of my favorite amusements," he is reported to have said, and Poplar Forest beautifully illustrates that delight.[3] Unlike Monticello, which was the product of several building operations, Poplar Forest was essentially conceived as a whole (fig. 1). Although Jefferson continued to embellish and improve the house during his many visits, by and large those improvements were more in the nature of finishing touches and refinements to his original conception; it never received the full-scale alterations that he undertook at Monticello. As a unified whole, Poplar Forest has been termed "Jefferson's most brilliant domestic design." Even its usually modest creator once proudly told his son-in-law John Wayles Eppes: "It is the best dwelling house in the state, except that of Monticello; perhaps preferable to that, as more proportioned to the faculties of a private citizen."[4]

Jefferson's first known reference to his plan to build at Poplar Forest is in a letter that he wrote in 1806 to Elizabeth Trist, an old friend of long standing. His letter apparently crossed in the mails with one she wrote him. Both missives told well, if briefly, what his idea for Poplar Forest was all about, though Mrs. Trist didn't have it quite right. Jefferson stated: "I am preparing an occasional retreat in Bedford, where I expect to settle some of my grandchildren." Mrs. Trist, having been informed by her niece that he was "building on one of your plantations . . . and that you mean to pass your summers there," thought it "a good plan to avoid being run down with company."[5]

At the time the two corresponded, Jefferson was just beginning the second year of his second term as president of the United States. By 1809, when the house at his Bedford retreat was sufficiently complete to receive him, that term was over. Thus, the house he built at Poplar Forest never served as Jefferson's Camp David during his presidency. Still, a comparison between the two is not inappropriate. Perhaps more than for any former chief executive before or since, Jefferson's retirement from the presidency was anything but the calm twilight years that term generally connotes. He needed a place to escape from the crowds and worries that constantly plagued him at Monticello, and although getting there was seldom half the fun — it generally took him from two-and-a-half to three days to travel the ninety-mile distance between his two homes — he found the time he needed at Poplar Forest; the time to think, to study, to read.

Long before he built his "retirement" retreat, though, Poplar Forest had been of importance to Jefferson in another dimension; as a huge tract of land, divided into several plantations, or farms, each with its separate work force. Plantation operations had begun long before Jefferson acquired the land, and had continued under his aegis for many years before he planned the house that was to crown its red-clay hills. As a working plantation, Poplar Forest was an essential part of Jefferson's economic portfolio, and the income derived from it — albeit sometimes less than it might have been under better supervision — helped support its frequently absent landowner throughout his adult life. Jefferson once called the property "the most valuable of my possessions," and predicted (wrongly, as it turned out) that it would "become the residence of the greater part of my family."[6] During his many visits he oversaw the planting and harvesting of crops, conversed with his overseers, saw to the housing and clothing of his slave work force, and experimented with new methods of plowing and crop rotation. And while it was a retreat from the *uninvited* hordes who swarmed at Monticello, he always found time to see his "few good neighbors" in Bedford, and on more than a few occasions invited them over to partake of "plain plantation fare."[7]

Fig. 1 Thomas Jefferson's two homes: Poplar Forest (above) and Monticello (below). The photograph of the north (entrance) facade of Poplar Forest was taken in April 1943, that of the east (entrance) facade of Monticello dates from 1992. (*The Corporation for Jefferson's Poplar Forest; Robert C. Lautman, for Monticello, Thomas Jefferson Memorial Foundation, Inc.*)

How has Poplar Forest remained such a secret? Over the intervening years since Jefferson bragged about it to one of his sons-in-law, it has remained almost unknown except to those in its neighborhood, while Monticello has come to be known and seen by admirers from all corners of the globe. Part of the reason is that it was in private hands until 1984, although by then efforts were well under way to acquire it and open it to the public. As late as 1979, however, Poplar Forest was still lived in as it had always been: almost without exception by families who appreciated it as their home.

In part because of Poplar Forest's obscurity, the few sporadic references published about the house over the years have been largely inaccurate. One of the earliest historians to mention it was Henry Howe, who wrote in 1845 that it "was originally the property of Jefferson and occasionally his residence in the summer months. It is an octagonal brick edifice, built by him on the same plan with Monticello, although much smaller." One of the most recent misconceptions dates from a 1991 description of the plan as having the "distinctive shape of a square surrounding an octagon."[8] Regarding Howe's reference, the two houses definitely do not follow the same plan, no matter what their relative sizes; regarding the latter reference, the octagon surrounds a square, not the reverse.

In 1951, one of Jefferson's biographers stated: "Unfortunately, the building is no longer in existence; it burnt down in 1845." Yes, there was a fire in the mid-nineteenth century; indeed it was in 1845, but the house was not completely destroyed. Even so, the conflagration was sufficiently serious, and the changes made in the rebuilding were sufficiently drastic, that a writer who had stated in 1930 that Poplar Forest was "still in a perfect state of preservation" was equally misinformed.[9]

Just as unfortunate as the statements concerning the house itself are the misconceptions regarding its use and what it meant to Jefferson. By all odds the most persistent is the thought, promulgated by Mrs. Trist, Henry Howe, and countless others since, that it was simply his summer house. Jefferson never said so, and the careful records he kept of his many visits prove that this was never the case. During a *February* visit he once wrote that he had "seen the face of no human being for days but the servants." He then went on to explain one of the reasons why: "We have had seven snows since I came, making all together about 10 1/2 inches."[10]

As might be gathered from the number of quotations I have used so far, letters were all-important to Thomas Jefferson. In his later years he unequivocally declared that "the letters of a person . . . form the only full and genuine journal of his life."[11] Certainly letters comprise the primary journal of Poplar Forest during his lifetime. Jefferson built the house somewhat as an absentee contractor, and an amazingly complete body of correspondence between him and the many individuals who contributed their various talents to the building process survives. In fact, spelling and grammar notwithstanding, the epistolary records left by the builders, giving their progress reports along with their complaints (a fairly consistent one being requests for payments), are among the most complete for any major house of the early American republic. Variations in spelling even the most familiar words were perhaps more common then than now, and in the many quotations that will follow, I have chosen for the most part to let the writers spell for themselves, rather than inserting [*sic*] after every change from the norm. While what follows will not be precisely an epistolary history, in many ways it will come close.

This is not to say that the letters contain all there is to know about any of the varied aspects of Poplar Forest. Not at all. Regarding the house, they contain tantalizing references to drawings, plans, and instructions that in all-too-many instances have not survived, or at least have not yet surfaced. Fortunately, several drawings remain that illustrate the evolution of the design, as do an elevation of the south facade and a first-floor plan that show the house in its original condition, or at least as it was originally intended to be. Long attributed to the hand of Jefferson's granddaughter, Cornelia Randolph, these last two — reproduced as the endpapers of this volume — are now credited to John Neilson, one of his master builders at Monticello and at the University of Virginia. Neilson was only peripherally involved in the construction of Poplar Forest, however, and probably never saw it. Nor is it known just why or when his elevation and plan were drawn, and recent investigations have demonstrated that they are not as accurate as had been thought previously. Also surviving is a written specification in Jefferson's hand, giving instructions to his builders for an alteration in the roof structure and skylight, made necessary after a disastrous hailstorm (see figs. 80 and 81). Fortunately, this specification describes features that later disappeared altogether, and its survival ensures that accurate reconstructions of them can be made.

The story of Poplar Forest does not end with the death of Thomas Jefferson, and, fortunately, papers also remain from those whose association with the property and the house followed his. Jefferson's will devised Poplar Forest to his grandson, Francis Eppes, who had already begun living there before his grandfather's death in 1826. Eppes, the one notable exception to all the owners who have appreciated the property, at least kept rudimentary records during his short tenure. When he sold Poplar Forest in 1828, after holding title for only two years, he terminated a 64-year ownership by one family that had begun with his great-grandfather, John Wayles. The next family held it almost twice as long. The 118-year tenure of the Cobbs-Hutter family, from 1828 to 1946, was the longest period of single-family ownership of Poplar Forest. Members of this family wrote frequently and at length, and a great number of their letters have been preserved. In addition, they farmed the land and earned their livelihood from it — at least during the first two generations of their ownership — and they, like Jefferson, kept extensive farm records.

During the long ownership of the Cobbs-Hutter family, Poplar Forest began to be known and appreciated — by scholars and dedicated amateurs if not by the general public — as the "other home" of Thomas Jefferson. Throughout their tenure, the Cobbses and Hutters were aware of the importance of the house as Jefferson's, and they generously shared the information that they had gleaned (and sometimes embellished) to those who showed an interest. Their story is an important one and deserves more extended treatment than can be given here.

In 1946, the Watts family followed the Hutters, and followed them as well in their appreciation of Poplar Forest's history and significance. They began a partial restoration of the house, and were as generous as the Hutters had been in allowing those who found their way to Bedford to come and see it. During their ownership as well, Poplar Forest was not in the least degree a tourist attraction or a historic house museum. It was a family home.

In 1984, after an unbroken chain of private ownership, the estate was acquired by the Corporation for Jefferson's Poplar Forest, a nonprofit foundation organized expressly for the purpose of protecting and restoring the house and grounds and opening them to the public. At the outset, it was hoped that enough information could be gleaned concerning the property to effect a restoration to the condition that its creator knew, but this was by no means a given. Early in its ownership, the Corporation began to plan an exhaustive research effort, and one of the first priorities in this program was to undertake a thorough documentary investigation. It has been my pleasant task to conduct that phase of the research.

Documentary investigation, however, is only one phase of a much broader research program currently underway. Archeological investigations are being conducted and the house itself has undergone as thorough an analysis as current state-of-the-art restoration technology permits. Under the expert hands in charge, more has been revealed of the original condition than any layman would have thought possible. The landscape and the slave work force are only two of many other subjects that are being studied. While the results from these investigations will be discussed where appropriate in the text to follow, the actual work currently under way will not be my major focus. Each of these is a subject worthy of separate and lengthy treatment by the individuals responsible for undertaking it. Suffice it to say here that the results of all the varied arenas of investigation to learn the history and to gauge the feasibility of restoration have been more positive than we dared hope. While many questions remain, both on specific details and on larger issues of preservation philosophy, whatever restoration is carried out will be firmly grounded in the facts revealed through the research.

It is not only the story of the building of a house that unfolds in Jefferson's many letters, account books, memoranda to his overseers, and other surviving written documentation. The story of Poplar Forest is the story of Thomas Jefferson. It is the story of a man full of life, love, and concern for his fellow Americans. It is the story of his amazing talent and knowledge in so many fields of human endeavor. It is the story of family and friends, land and crops, and, as is well known, the story of a man who owned a number of his fellow human beings. It is a story of Jefferson's aspirations, but also one of realities that continually prevented him from reaching his goals. The story of Poplar Forest is vital to a complete understanding of Jefferson, just as an understanding of the man is obviously necessary to comprehend the place. The story of the two is a dual biography of a special place and an extraordinary human being. It is a story well worth the telling and, I hope, a story that will be worth the reading.

"THE POPLAR FOREST"
(1745–74)

What's in a name? Usually, quite a lot. The very name Poplar Forest tells much about the original nature of what became Thomas Jefferson's property in Bedford County, Virginia, or at least tells much about its condition when someone first gave it that name sometime in the early eighteenth century. Poplar Forest was then an uncleared woodland, dominated by a handsome deciduous native tree, the *Liriodendron tulipifera*. The tulip poplar, a relative of the magnolia, grows tall and full in the Virginia woods, and its blossom obviously reminded transplanted Europeans of a flower with which they were familiar when they named it. Harkening back even further in the corporate memory, Jefferson once alluded to the tulip poplar as "the Juno of our groves"[1] (fig. 2). Names these early colonists gave to other natural features when they first explored the area around the Poplar Forest also tell much about what they found. Bear Branch (or Bear Creek) and Tomahawk Creek flow through the tract. Jefferson would later name his two plantation operations at Poplar Forest after them. Buffalo Creek and Wolf Branch are on the extremities of the original land grant, and Elk Creek is not far away.

Topographically Poplar Forest was, and is, a gently undulating expanse of Virginia's Piedmont, lying at the foot of the Blue Ridge mountains. The Blue Ridge (also named for obvious reasons) had presented the first substantial natural barrier for the Virginia colonists to conquer in their inevitable trek westward from Tidewater. Speaking of names, among the individual peaks that can be seen from Poplar Forest is one whose name conjures up the wilderness and two whose names tell just as eloquently of the expanding early settlement and cultivation of the Piedmont: No Business Mountain on one hand; Apple Orchard and Tobacco Row on the other fig. 3).

By the mid-eighteenth century, colonial Virginians had long since mastered the challenges of the mountains, no matter what names they gave them, and were beginning to survey, patent, settle, and farm land on both sides of the Blue Ridge: in the Piedmont to the east and in the Valley of Virginia to the west. In the vanguard of the settlement of the colony's frontier were a number of Tidewater entrepreneurs who obtained vast tracts for speculation and profit. Although they continued to live

Fig. 2 Poplar Forest, looking toward the house from the northwest, April 1943. The large poplars date from the mid-to-late eighteenth century. *(The Corporation for Jefferson's Poplar Forest)*

in the more settled flatlands along the navigable rivers to the east, they placed tenants and slaves on these rolling uplands farther west. These tenants and slaves in turn cleared the lands and planted tobacco on them. When the time was deemed right, or when demands made it necessary, the grantees would sell these tracts, or at least portions of them, to others. In other instances, the speculators died in possession of their tracts, firm in the belief that their heirs would benefit from the trouble they had taken to secure them a proper inheritance. Poplar Forest, over the years, illustrated both situations.

The name Poplar Forest first appears in the record, somewhat breathlessly, on June 13, 1745, when the Council of Virginia granted William Stith "leave to join two Tracts of Land at the Poplar Forest in the said County of Albemarle the one Containing 1172 Acres and the other 939 and to take in the land round his Bounds so as to make up the Quantity four thousand Acres passing the Ridge between the Waters of James River and Roanoak all to be taken into one inclusive Patent including likewise 200 Acres which he proposes to purchase of Francis Callaway." A year after that initial grant, Stith was again

given leave to "take up and ad" land to increase his Poplar Forest holdings to 4,000 acres. In 1749, he was authorized to increase it to "Six thousand Acres, to be included in one Patent, and taken up any where round the Bounds of his present Land in Albemarle or Lunenburg County."[2] Also during 1749, a survey of Stith's 1745 grant was made and recorded in the Surveyor's Book at the Albemarle County Courthouse (fig. 4).

Virginia's counties were divided time and again during the eighteenth century, as settlers on the frontier found it inconvenient, if not impossible, to attend court at existing county seats far to the east. Albemarle County had been formed in 1744 from Goochland County, its progenitor to the east. Lunenburg County, only created in 1746, was of course not mentioned in the 1745 grant of Poplar Forest, but it was referred to in Stith's 1749 patent. Not until the next decade, with the formation of Bedford County — named in honor of John Russell, fourth Duke of Bedford — would Poplar Forest be removed from the jurisdiction of its two original parent counties, Albemarle and Lunenburg.[3]

One of the first orders of the day for the magistrates of

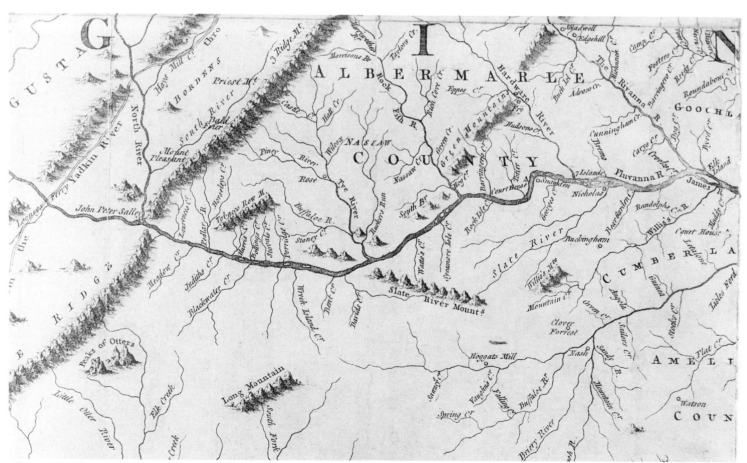

Fig. 3 Detail, Frye and Jefferson's map of Virginia, second edition, 1775. Thomas Jefferson's father, Peter Jefferson, and Joshua Frye prepared this map. Poplar Forest (not shown) is located between the Peaks of Otter and Blackwater Creek, seen to the lower left of center. Jefferson's birthplace, Shadwell, is shown at the extreme upper right. (*Geography and Map Division, Library of Congress*)

a newly established county was to select a site for, and to give a name to, the new seat of justice. William Callaway made the site selection of the Bedford County seat easy by donating fifty acres of land near Poplar Forest. After providing for the land to be laid out in lots, the justices ordered "that the said town be called by the name of New London." What's in a name? Sometimes not much. New London was destined to fall far short of the obvious expectations of those who named it.

William Stith (1707–55), the original patentee of Poplar Forest, invested heavily in Virginia's expanding frontier, and though his speculations in real estate occupied only a small portion of his time and talent, he had amassed an enormous number of acres at the time of his death. In Bedford County, in addition to his Poplar Forest tract, he also held land on Judy's, or Judith, Creek, and on Blackwater Creek.[4] Stith cut quite a figure in his time. Born in Virginia, educated at Oxford, and

ordained a minister, he returned to his native colony in 1731, where he became chaplain to the House of Burgesses and, toward the end of his life, served briefly as the third president of the College of William and Mary. He was also a historian, and his chronicle *The History of the First Discovery and Settlement of Virginia*, published in Williamsburg in 1747, was one of the first important histories of the Old Dominion.[5] Thomas Jefferson didn't think much of it, even though it was apparently among the first of many books he purchased. Writing his own history of Virginia some thirty years later, he characterized Stith in his *Notes on the State of Virginia* as "a man of classical learning, and very exact, but of no taste in style. He is inelegant, therefore, and his details often too minute to be tolerable, even to a native of the country, whose history he writes."[6] Given the penchant of Virginians for loving things Virginian, Jefferson could hardly have spoken harsher words. Whether Stith first named Pop-

Fig. 4 Poplar Forest Tract. William Stith's 4,000 acre tract, as surveyed and recorded in 1749. *(Courtesy, Clerk of Albemarle County Court, Charlottesville, photograph by Mike Bailey, 1991)*

lar Forest is not known; the wording of the grant suggests that the tract was known as such earlier. At any rate, it is certain that — contrary to popular belief—Thomas Jefferson did not name the property. Although he was in Albemarle County at the time Stith received the grant, he was then all of two years and two months old.[7]

When William Stith patented Poplar Forest, Thomas Jefferson's father, Peter Jefferson (1707/8–57) was speculating in western lands himself. Like Stith, he found the red soil of what became Bedford County to his liking. In fact, in more than one instance the two obtained patents on lands that were in close proximity to each other, if not actually adjoining. Both men received grants on Blackwater Creek at the same June 13, 1745, council meeting at which Stith was given leave to join the two tracts at the Poplar Forest. Peter Jefferson also acquired property on Judith Creek, where Stith also held land, and he soon added to his holdings in the area with a patent for acreage

Fig. 5 The road to Poplar Forest. At the time Jefferson made his first trip to Poplar Forest, and for years afterward, most "roads" in Piedmont Virginia were little more than trails through the woods. On more than one occasion, Jefferson had to hire a guide to show him the way. (*Tom Graves, Jr., 1991*)

on the same Tomahawk Creek that flows through Poplar Forest.[8] Years later, Thomas Jefferson's daughter, Martha Jefferson Randolph, told her daughter, Ellen Coolidge: "You know that he [Thomas Jefferson] recieved a great estate from his own father. I should suppose at least 10,000 acres of land here [Monticello] and at Poplar Forest where his and my Mother's lands were contiguous."[9]

A convenient record of the chain of title to Poplar Forest is provided in a letter that Jefferson wrote his Bedford neighbor William Radford in 1822: "The title to the Pop. For. is short. It was patented by parson Wm. Stith descended on his youngest and only surviving daughter and child Mrs. Pasteur who sold it to Col. P. Randolph who sold it to Mr. Wayles."[10] "Col. P. Randolph" was Peter Randolph, a kinsman of both Stith and Jefferson's, who held the title until July 3, 1764, when he conveyed "unto the said Wayles or his assignees two Tracts of Land viz Poplar Forest and Judys Creek containing about 5800 acres."[11]

"Mr. Wayles" was John Wayles (1715–73), who, more than either of his contemporaries William Stith or Peter Jefferson, was a land speculator and entrepreneur par excellence. He would also become Thomas Jefferson's father-in-law, and it was from his land books, "in which are recorded the title papers of all the lands he owned, from the patent thro all the subseq. conveyancies down to himself," that Jefferson was later able to reconstruct the chain of title for William Radford.[12] In addition to the Poplar Forest and Judith Creek properties that he purchased from Peter Randolph, Wayles bought adjoining tracts to enlarge his Poplar Forest holdings. Jefferson provided a convenient summary of these transactions in 1794 and 1810, when he jotted down his land holdings in his Farm Book, noting the original Stith holdings, Wayles's later acquisitions, and some of his own purchases (see figs. 12 and 46).

John Wayles died on May 28, 1773, and bequeathed Poplar Forest to his daughter Martha Jefferson. As her husband recalled in his 1822 letter to William Radford: "On his death and the partition of his estate . . . between his 3 daugs. Mrs. J. Mrs. E. and Mrs. S., the Pop. For. was, among other lands, allotted to Mrs. Jefferson."[13] Among those other lands allotted to Martha Jefferson was the Judith Creek tract, and her husband listed the acreage of these two Bedford County holdings in his Memorandum Book: at the time of the inheritance, Poplar Forest contained 4,819 acres and Judith Creek 2,042, for a total of 6,861 acres.[14] The Bedford property represented only a portion of the total acreage Martha Jefferson inherited from her father. She also received 135 slaves, and a huge debt.[15]

Before the estate was actually settled, in fact only months after his father-in-law's death, Jefferson made his first recorded trip to Poplar Forest (fig. 5). As was his custom, Jefferson recorded payments made along the way in his Memorandum Book. On September 7, 1773, he and his servant Jupiter crossed James River, where he "pd. ferriage at Davies's ferry." On the eighth he recorded that he "pd. Smith at Poplar Forest 7 1/2d," and the next day paid for entertainment at New London. Less than a week later, on September 13, Jefferson and Jupiter recrossed James River, downstream from Davies's, on their return journey. This time Jefferson noted that he "pd. ferrge. at Lynch's."[16]

As John Wayles's estate was not finally settled until January 1774, and as Jefferson was one of the executors, his 1773 trip may well have been taken to see how the land lay and, depending on his impressions, to secure it as part of Martha's share in her father's inheritance. If that was the scenario, he obviously liked what he saw. Soon after the settlement of the estate, Jefferson had to sell much of the property (including the Judith Creek lands) bequeathed to Martha to help alleviate the debt that went along with the inheritance. Only Poplar Forest was kept entire.

Just as the origin of its name is unknown, we also do not know under whose ownership the lands at Poplar Forest were first cultivated (fig 6). By the time Jefferson visited in 1773, plantation operations were well under way, and he was soon to increase both the operations and the number of slaves working there. His Farm Book, which he began keeping at the time the Wayles estate was settled and which he maintained until just over a month before his death, records many of the plantation activities at Poplar Forest and lists the slaves who worked there. In an entry titled "A Roll of the slaves of John Wayles which were allotted to T. J. in right of his wife on a division of the estate Jan. 14, 1774," Jefferson listed and named six at Poplar Forest, five at Wingo's, and nine at "Judith's creek, or Dun lora."[17] Wingo's was the westernmost section of the Poplar Forest tract, which at this time was apparently being operated as a separate plantation. Three of the six slaves at Poplar Forest were children, and two of the adults, Guinea Will and Betty, presumably their parents, were recorded as "labourers in the ground." These five were bracketed into a family group. The sixth was "Billy boy," the smith, or blacksmith. Later the same year, in a Farm Book reference titled "Location of Slaves for 1774," Jefferson named twelve at Poplar Forest, fifteen at Wingo's, and eighteen at Dun lora.[18] He had transferred one family of four to Poplar Forest from Indian Camp, another of John Wayles's properties, in Cumberland County. Will and Judy were the adults; and Jemmy and York, the children. Again, the adults were listed as "labourers in the ground," as were the two other transferees to Poplar Forest: Tom Shackleford and Amy. That same year, Jefferson recorded in his Farm Book that he provided new beds and blankets for many of these slaves.[19]

For the most part, the slaves at Poplar Forest listed as

Fig. 6 Poplar Forest, distant view of the house from the northwest, showing orchard and livestock in foreground, ca. 1911. (*The Corporation for Jefferson's Poplar Forest*)

"labourers in the ground" were workers in the tobacco fields. In addition to the slaves already at his Bedford plantations, Jefferson noted in his Memorandum Book on October 12, 1774, that he had "hired of Mr. Eppes in Bedford last year" seven additional laborers.

Tobacco was literally the cash crop of colonial Virginia; not only did it serve as the colony's chief export, it was also a medium of exchange. It also wore out the land, and provided nothing in and of itself for either the laborers or owners of the land. Writing at Poplar Forest in 1781, Jefferson condemned tobacco as "a culture productive of infinite wretchedness. Those employed in it are in a continued state of exertion beyond the powers of nature to support. Little food of any kind is raised by them; so that the men and animals on these farms are badly fed, and the earth is rapidly impoverished."[20] Time and again Jefferson sought to supplant tobacco with other crops on his several plantations, but the economics of the time prevented him from ever eliminating it. Throughout his lifetime and later, the fields of Poplar Forest continued to produce tobacco, which, as for many of his contemporaries, remained Jefferson's main source of income.[21]

Jefferson hoped to replace tobacco with crops that demanded less of the soil and that were of more immediate benefit and use to the laborers and property owners. Wheat was chief among such crops, and, again writing at Poplar Forest, he contrasted it with tobacco as "the reverse in every circumstance. Besides cloathing the earth with herbage, and preserving its fertility, it feeds the labourers plentifully, requires from them only a moderate toil, . . . and diffuses plenty and happiness among the whole."[22] Though it never supplanted tobacco, wheat eventually became an important crop at Poplar Forest. Flour was milled nearby and was used for bread to feed Jefferson's slaves both in Bedford and in Albemarle.[23]

Over the years, Jefferson, his overseers, and their slave laborers at Poplar Forest would grow many other crops in addition to tobacco and wheat, both for use on the plantations and for sale in the marketplace. In addition, cattle, hogs, and sheep would play an increasingly important role in his farm operations and as a source of revenue. He would even establish cottage industries at Poplar Forest, again both to serve his own needs and to provide income. As time went on, Jefferson would rely more and more on the income his Bedford County plantations produced as his expenses and the interest payments on his debts increased. In time, he would direct the clearing of new fields and pastures, and he would obtain additional slaves to work them. Even now, at the very outset of Jefferson's ownership, however, one thing was obvious. The name Poplar Forest told far less accurately the nature of the land and the activities it supported than it had when William Stith first took up his patent just over a quarter century earlier (fig. 7).

Fig. 7 Poplar Forest, view from south, 1990. This aerial view shows the relation of the house to its grounds and, in the distance, the Blue Ridge mountains. (*The Corporation for Jefferson's Poplar Forest*)

"Better Acquainted with My Own Country"
(1774–84)

When John Wayles's estate—with its legacy of lands, slaves, and debts—was settled in 1774, Martha Wayles Skelton Jefferson was twenty-five years old and her husband was thirty-one. They had been married less than a year and a half, and had one child, a daughter named after her mother. Martha's first husband, Bathurst Skelton, had died in 1768, and their son had died three years later. Jefferson was then already well along in his career of public service. In 1760, at the age of seventeen, he had gone to the College of William and Mary in Virginia's colonial capital, Williamsburg. Two years later, also in Williamsburg, he began to read law under the direction of George Wythe, and in 1767 he was admitted to the Virginia bar. In 1769 the voters of Albemarle County elected the young lawyer to represent them in the Virginia House of Burgesses, where he served until 1775. His career advanced when the Virginia Convention, meeting in Richmond in March of that year, elected him a deputy to the Continental Congress. (It was at this same Richmond meeting that Patrick Henry delivered his famous challenge: "Give me liberty, or give me death," and helped propel England's American colonies on their way toward becoming a nation.) By this time Jefferson had virtually abandoned his private law practice. Instead, his legal training would stand him in good stead in the services he would soon render to a much larger constituency. On June 11, 1775, he noted in his Memorandum Book: "set out from Wmsburgh. for Philadelphia." The shot heard round the world had been fired at Concord, Massachusetts, in April, and upon his arrival in Philadelphia, Jefferson began to play a pivotal role in the formation of the new nation. A year to the day after his recorded departure from Williamsburg, he was appointed the head of a committee of five to prepare a declaration of independence, which was adopted on July 4, less than a month after it was begun.[1]

While in Philadelphia, Jefferson also found time to draft a proposed constitution for his native Virginia, but as adopted, it was far more conservative than he had hoped it would be. Soon after he returned to Virginia in September 1776, he took his seat in the House of Delegates, the successor to the colonial House of Burgesses, in Virginia's General Assembly. There, at a more leisurely pace, he proceeded to launch his proposed reforms by introducing a number of bills. One of those he submitted called for removing the seat of government from Williamsburg to the more centrally located Richmond. That same bill also provided for the construction of buildings to serve the commonwealth, to be "built in a handsome manner with walls of brick, or stone & Porticos where the same may be convenient or ornamental, and with pillars and pavements of stone."[2]

All these activities kept the young Jefferson from personally attending to the Poplar Forest property he had inherited from his father-in-law and likewise prevented him from attending to building and landscaping at his beloved Monticello. His trips to Philadelphia in 1775 and 1776, and numerous journeys in the years immediately following, both to Williamsburg and to Richmond, also left him little time to be with his family. After his daughter Martha, two more children had been born: another daughter in April 1774 and a son in May 1777. Neither child survived infancy, but in August 1778 a third daughter, Mary, was born. She and Martha would prove to be the only two of Jefferson's six children to reach adulthood.

Throughout these and his later years of public service, Jefferson regularly expressed the wish to be at home, among his family and friends. Less than a month after he became governor of Virginia, on June 1, 1779, he wrote: "The hour of private retirement to which I am drawn by my nature with a propensity almost irresistible, will be the most welcome of my life."[3] Of all the duties that he assumed in service to his state and country, his short span as Virginia's wartime chief executive was the most frustrating. The commonwealth's recently adopted constitution gave its executive few powers, and the governor's chief duties were to implement the wishes of the General Assembly. He spent the first year of his incumbency in Williamsburg, but on April 1, 1780, the government, including the governor, moved to Richmond. Although Jefferson made no effort to campaign for another term, he was reelected on June 1, 1780, for a second one-year administration. He served until the end of that term a year later.

After his first recorded visit to Poplar Forest in 1773, Jefferson apparently did not return until 1781.[4] This second visit was for a far longer time than he had anticipated, but in fact the entire trip was unanticipated until the last moment. During his first year and well into his second term as governor, Jefferson and the General Assembly remained in relative safety outside the theater of war. America's struggle for independence had been waged both north and south, but the Old Dominion had thus far escaped its ravages. After the disastrous defeat of colonial troops at Camden, South Carolina, in August 1780, the situation soon changed for the worse. In October, the British sailed into Chesapeake Bay and captured Portsmouth, Virginia. Continuing their foray, they took Richmond on January 5, 1781. Jefferson had received reports minimizing the impending danger, and therefore had not called out the militia to defend the capital, a non-action for which he would later be called to task. The enemy retired in a few days, but this raid, led by Benedict Arnold, was only a harbinger. In May 1781, less than a month before Jefferson's second term as governor was to end, the British once again attacked Virginia. Their campaign was now under the direction of Gen. Charles Cornwallis, who intended both to disrupt the government and to capture the governor. Early in May, the Assembly and Jefferson retreated from Richmond to Charlottesville, where they planned to reconvene in a less vulnerable location, and again Jefferson's action would be called into question. In Charlottesville, on May 28, the General Assembly resolved to elect Jefferson's successor on June 2, the day on which his term would end, but on the appointed day they decided to postpone the vote until Monday, June 4. As it turned out, they were not able to vote until a week later, and then, still in retreat from the British, not in Charlottesville, but across the Blue Ridge in Staunton. There, on June 12, they finally elected as Jefferson's successor his friend and compatriot Thomas Nelson, Jr. On that same day, the members of the legislature also passed an ominous resolution: "*Resolved*, That at the next session of Assembly an inquiry be made into the conduct of the Executive of this State for the last twelve months."[5]

Long before then, Jefferson was at Poplar Forest, having barely escaped capture at Monticello by the British troops under the direction of Lt. Col. Banastre Tarleton. Had it not been for Jack Jouett — who happened to be at the right place at the right time — Tarleton's raid might have succeeded. The right place was Cuckoo Tavern in Louisa County and the right time was Sunday, June 3. Jouett overheard Tarleton's dragoons, during a brief stop at the tavern, discussing their plan to capture the governor, and he then rode through the night to give his warning. Jefferson first saw to his family's escape from Monticello and then followed them on Monday, June 4, after bundling up a number of papers to take with him. He and his family, then consisting of his wife, Martha, and their two young daughters, were joined on the trip by William Short, whom Jefferson regarded as something of "an adoptive son," and Jupiter.[6]

Jefferson had undoubtedly intended this visit to Poplar Forest to be a short one. There was no adequate dwelling to house his family, and the health of his wife was also a consideration. Entries in his Memorandum Book record the progress of his sojourn and bear witness to the rampant inflation that the war had wreaked on Virginia's currency. On June 11, he recorded having paid £2,400 for 160 pounds of brown sugar, the same day he noted the payment of £300 for twenty-five pounds of coffee. Throughout the visit he recorded exorbitant payments to several slaves for chickens. Judy was the chief supplier, and on one occasion Jefferson paid her £40.10. He reimbursed Betty £26.8, while Pat and Dinah both were given £12 for their chickens. On June 30, Jefferson gave a Dr. Brown £600 for two visits. That, presumably, was in connection with an accident that he had suffered that day. While riding his horse, Caractacus, Jefferson had a fall, and he was unable to travel for several weeks thereafter.[7] He took the occasion to work on a project that he had begun sometime earlier, and for which he had carried his notes from Monticello. It was a task to which

he turned with obvious delight.

Jefferson explained the circumstances of the project in his "Autobiography," written twenty years after the fact: "Before I had left America . . . I had received a letter from M. de Marbois, of the French legation in Philadelphia, informing me he had been instructed by his government to obtain such statistical accounts of the different states of our Union, as might be useful for their information; and addressing to me a number of queries relative to the state of Virginia."[8]

On November 30, 1780, Jefferson had written the French vice-consul in Virginia that he was "at present busily employed for Monsr. Marbois, . . . and have to acknolege to him the mysterious obligation for making me much better acquainted with my own country than I ever was before."[9] The events of war soon prevented him from continuing that busy employment, and on March 4, 1781, he had to write Marbois to say that he had been able to accomplish very little, but hoped to be able to do more soon.[10] His unexpectedly lengthy stay at Poplar Forest gave him the perfect opportunity to return to his task, and *Notes on the State of Virginia*, first published in 1785, was the fortuitous result. Jefferson would protest in his advertisement to the 1787 English edition of *Notes*: "The subjects are all treated imperfectly; some scarcely touched on." A more objective contemporary called the work: "a most excellent natural history not merely of Virginia but of North America and possibly equal if not superior to that of any country yet published."[11] Because some of the information given in *Notes* relates to activities that Jefferson would undertake on later visits to Poplar Forest — not to mention the fact that so much of it was composed there — it deserves to be discussed in some detail.

Notes on the State of Virginia is far more than "a most excellent natural history." Organized into twenty-three chapters (labeled Queries), each in response to a specific question posed by Marbois, it also treats of religion, manners, and manufactures, and much else besides. In answer to query 15, whose subject was "Colleges, Buildings, and Roads," Jefferson took the occasion to enlarge upon the subject and to pen a diatribe against Virginia's architecture. Regarding public buildings, he had a few kind words to say about the Capitol in Williamsburg, and although he found the Governor's Palace "not handsome without," he conceded that it was "spacious and commodious within." Having lived there during his first term as governor, he obviously was qualified to offer those comments. On the other hand, he declared that the college and hospital in Williamsburg were "rude, mis-shapen piles, which, but that they have roofs, would be taken for brick-kilns." Part of the problem, Jefferson felt, was that "a workman could scarcely be found here capable of drawing an order."[12] He could certainly do that, and although he would not decide the final form of his new

Virginia Capitol in Richmond for several years, he had in all likelihood already begun planning for the building, even to the determination of its Ionic order, by the time this passage in *Notes* was written.[13]

If he had little good to say about Virginia's built environment, Jefferson had nothing but good to say about its scenery and natural wonders. He acknowledged that "the height of our mountains has not yet been estimated with any degree of exactness," and then continued: "The mountains of the Blue ridge, and of these the Peaks of Otter, are thought to be of a greater height, measured from their base, than any others in our country, and perhaps in North America. From data, which may found a tolerable conjecture, we suppose the highest peak to be about 4000 feet perpendicular"[14] (fig. 8). That was a bit of an exaggeration, but it would be a while before he could prove or disprove it. Years later, while visiting Poplar Forest, he took his theodolite with him to Bedford to measure the Peaks, and he then found them to be considerably less lofty than he had supposed in 1781 (see chap. XII).

About Virginia's Natural Bridge, he minced words not at all. Not surprisingly, Marbois's inquiries did not include one on this unique phenomenon, about which he had probably never heard. Working conscientiously within the outlines his inquirer had furnished, Jefferson decided to include his discussion of the bridge under "Query 5: Cascades," realizing full well that "though not comprehended under the present head, [it] must not be pretermitted." Natural Bridge was, he unequivocally declared, "the most sublime of nature's works.... It is impossible for the emotions arising from the sublime, to be felt beyond what they are here; so beautiful an arch, so elevated, so light: and springing as it were up to heaven, the rapture of the spectator is really indescribable"[15] (fig. 9). He also furnished figures on the height and width of the bridge, and here he was on surer ground than he had been in discussing the Peaks of Otter. He had owned Natural Bridge since 1774, and would visit it a number of times during his trips to Poplar Forest.[16]

While the fields of Poplar Forest could not compare to the Peaks of Otter or the Natural Bridge in scenic wonder, they must have had an influence on the panegyric that he composed in general on the subject of farming and farmers in Virginia. His feelings on tobacco versus wheat — which he discussed in Query 20 — have been mentioned. As for farmers, he declared that "those who labor in the earth are the chosen people of God, if ever he had a chosen people, whose breasts he has made his peculiar deposit for substantial and genuine virtue." Urban dwellers did not fare so well: "The mobs of great cities add just so much to the support of pure government, as sores do to the strength of the human body." Fortunately, Virginia had "an immensity of land courting the industry of the husbandman," and "while we

have land to labour then, let us never wish to see our citizens occupied at a workbench, or twirling a distaff."[17] In espousing such views, Jefferson was echoing classical agronomists from Cato to Pliny: "The rural tribes who possessed farms were the most highly regarded, while it was a disgrace to be transferred into a city tribe because of the disapproval of inactivity."[18]

Of course, the cultivation of land in Virginia in Jefferson's time depended on the institution of slavery, which he detested, though he participated fully in it. Again, the headings of Marbois's queries didn't allow for an individual treatment of this subject, so Jefferson chose to deal with it under "Query 8: Population." He stated that the proportion of free inhabitants to slaves in Virginia was nearly eleven to ten, and that "under the mild treatment our slaves experience, . . . this blot in our country increases as fast, or faster than the whites." He added that during "the very first session held under the republican government, the assembly passed a law for the perpetual prohibition of the importation of slaves. This will in some measure stop the increase of this great political and moral evil, while the minds of our citizens may be ripening for a complete emancipation of human nature."[19] He was too modest to add that he had a large part in the decree prohibiting further importation of slaves. As for "the mild treatment our slaves experience," however, an event that happened two or three days after he left Poplar Forest in 1781 proved that this was not always the case. A July 28, 1781, entry in the Bedford County Order Book tells the tale. Jack, "a Negroe Man Slave the property of Thomas Jefferson Esq." and his cohort Will had been found guilty of breaking into a millhouse belonging to John Thompson, Jr., and then stealing whiskey, leather and other goods that had been stored in it. For his felony, Jack took "25 Lashes on his Bare Back well laid on," and Will received thirty-nine. At that, Jefferson's slaves fared better than Peter, who belonged to John Thompson, Sr., the father of the owner of the millhouse. Apparently Peter had been the ringleader, and the court commanded the Sheriff to "carry him to the Pillory and nail his Ears thereto & cut off his Right Ear, & from thence to the Whiping Post and give him 40 Lashes save one on his Bare Back well laid on."[20]

One question that may never be answered regarding Jefferson's prolonged 1781 visit to Poplar Forest is where he and his entourage stayed. Obviously there had to be houses on the property for the overseer and the slave work force, but as far as is known no manor house had yet been built during Stith's, Wayles's, or Jefferson's ownership. At the time, Thomas Bennet was Jefferson's Poplar Forest overseer, and the group most likely lodged with him. On a later trip to Poplar Forest, taken before he built his own house, Jefferson is said to have stayed "in one of the two rooms of an overseer's house," and it is doubtful if any better accommodations would have been

Fig. 8 The Peaks of Otter, Bedford County, Virginia. At the time Jefferson wrote of them in his *Notes on Virginia*, he and many others thought these were the highest mountains in the United States. *(Tom Graves, Jr., 1991)*

available before then.[21] On the other hand, a 1790 plat of the property notes a building labeled "old plantation," which, both by its name and its very existence, indicates that some sort of headquarters existed only nine years earlier.[22] Later still, while giving directions to an overseer, Jefferson may have been referring to an earlier house in directing him to put some material in "the log house near the dwelling house."[23]

By late July 1781, Jefferson and his entourage were back at Monticello. In August he received an appointment to go to Europe as a peace commissioner, but he refused. As he wrote Edmund Randolph, then attorney general of Virginia: "I have retired to my farm, my family and books from which I think nothing will evermore separate me. A desire to leave public office with a reputation not more blotted than it deserves will oblige me to emerge at the next session of our assembly and perhaps to accept a seat in it, but as I go with but a single object, I shall withdraw when that shall be accomplished."[24]

In December 1781 Jefferson attended the Virginia General Assembly and was vindicated when both the House of Delegates and the Senate concurred in a resolution directing that "sincere thanks of the general assembly be given to our former governor Thomas Jefferson, esquire, for his impartial, upright and attentive administration whilst in office." The resolution noted that "pop-

Fig. 9 Natural Bridge, Rockbridge County, Virginia. Oil painting by Frederick Edwin Church, 1852. Jefferson owned this "most sublime of nature's works" and visited it on several occasions while staying at Poplar Forest. *(Courtesy University of Virginia Art Museum)*

ular rumours, gaining some degree of credence, by more pointed accusations, rendered it necessary to make an enquiry into his conduct, . . . but that conduct having become the object of open scrutiny, ten fold value is added to an approbation founded on a cool and deliberate discussion."[25] Although now officially exonerated from the accusations of the assembly's resolution of June 12, 1781, Jefferson would never forget the wounds brought about by what he considered a completely unjust and unfounded criticism of his conduct during his second term as Virginia's governor.

Early in 1782, Poplar Forest was again on Jefferson's mind. On February 12, he made the first entry relating to it in his Garden Book, an ongoing journal in which he had been keeping records since 1766: "Sent to Poplar For. 6 Apricot trees, 2 large Morellas, 2 Kentish cherries, 2 May Dukes, 2 Carnations, 2 Black hearts, 2 White hearts, 2 Newtown pippings, 2 Russetins, 2 Golden Wildings, & some white strawberries."[26] Jupiter, who had been to Poplar Forest at least twice before, took the plants to Bedford, and in his Memorandum Book, Jefferson noted on February 12 that he gave money to "Jup for ferrge. to Popl For."

The fact that Jupiter's stock was primarily fruit trees and the fact that he was sent to Poplar Forest so soon after Jefferson's protracted visit are surely related. Jefferson's visit had been during the season when such fruits would have been ripening, had they been available. He was undoubtedly planning for the future. As it happened, it was eighteen years before he was finally able to return to Poplar Forest, and by then the fruit trees would undoubtedly have matured to provide welcome sustenance.

It was as a private citizen rather than as an official of the commonwealth that Jefferson furnished another service to the colonial effort during the Revolution. Along with other farmers and planters, he supplied livestock and food from Poplar Forest for the revolutionary cause. In April 1782, the Campbell County clerk recorded that "Thomas Jefferson proved that he furnished . . . three hundred and twenty five pound of Beef for which he is allowed at the rate of sixteen shillings and eight pence per Hundred Weight and two pecks of corn for which he is allowed the sum of one shilling."[27] He fared less well financially from the county coffers than had his Poplar Forest slaves from his own pockets when he paid them for chickens the year before.

Though he seldom mentioned the fact in his letters during these years, Jefferson's wife's health was continually declining. Their fifth child, a girl, had been born in November 1780, but survived only until April of the following year, just before the family's unintended trip to Poplar Forest. She had been named Lucy, and was followed by a sixth infant in May 1782, who was given the same name. Martha Jefferson never fully recovered from this last birth, and throughout the spring and summer she continued to grow weaker. On September 6, 1782, she died, leaving her husband with three young daughters, Martha (Patsy), Mary (Polly), and Lucy. In his Memorandum Book, he recorded "my dear wife died this day at 11:45 A.M."

After a period of intense grief, Jefferson once again turned from his private affairs to those of the public, this time with relief. As one of his biographers has sagely observed, he "welcomed for once the chance to get away from Monticello" after his wife's death.[28] In November 1782, Jefferson accepted the appointment, which had been renewed, to become a member of a commission to negotiate the terms of peace following the Revolution. Before going north to prepare for his trip abroad, he placed his two younger daughters, Mary and Lucy, with their aunt and uncle Elizabeth and Francis Eppes at Eppington, their plantation in Chesterfield County, Virginia. Martha, then ten, was deemed old enough to accompany her father. When he reached Philadelphia late that December, Jefferson, along with James Madison and others, lodged with Mary House and her daughter, Elizabeth Trist. It was the beginning of a long and lasting friendship. As it turned out, it would be a long time before Jefferson actually set sail for Europe, as Congress decided the climate was not then propitious to send a delegation. In the interim, on June 6, 1783, Virginia elected him a delegate to the Continental Congress, and he spent the fall months in Princeton, Annapolis, and Philadelphia, each in its turn the seat of the peripatetic new government.

Almost a year after his election to the Continental Congress, an event that would dramatically change Jefferson's career and direction took place. As he recalled it: "On the 7th of May [1784] Congress resolved that a Minister Plenipotentiary should be appointed in addition to Mr. Adams & Dr. Franklin for negotiating treaties of commerce with foreign nations, and I was elected to that duty."[29] Leaving Philadelphia with Martha, he journeyed to New York and then to Boston. On July 5, 1784, at 4 A.M., father and daughter embarked from Boston on the Ceres for France.[30] Jefferson carried with him more than a score of commissions authorizing the ministers to negotiate treaties, and also took his manuscript of Notes on Virginia. Among the bon-voyage wishes he received, a letter from John Tyler, then speaker of the Virginia House of Delegates, and a friend since college days, was particularly felicitous: "God send you safe to the destined port, continue there in health and happiness, as long as you choose to stay, and waft you back to your native country, where you will always be acceptable to the good and virtuous."[31]

"LABOURING WITHOUT PLEASURE... OR PROFIT"
(1784–93)

Thomas Jefferson, then a forty-one year old widower, and his eldest daughter, Martha, almost twelve, arrived in Paris on August 6, 1784. Martha, or Patsy as she was then known, was soon placed in school in the Abbaye Royale de Panthémont, where her sister Mary would join her after she arrived in Paris from Virginia, by way of England, in 1787. Lucy, Jefferson's youngest daughter, died late in 1784 at Eppington.

In the spring and summer following Jefferson's arrival in Paris, the positions of the several American ministers there changed radically. As he told it years later: "Mr. Adams being appointed Min. Pleny. of the U. S. to London, left us in June, and in July 1785 Dr. Franklin returned to America and I was appointed his successor at Paris." He also observed that following in Benjamin Franklin's footsteps "was an excellent school of humility."[1] The ministers of the new nation negotiated and concluded several treaties of commerce with the older European powers, but questions of their authority, coupled with the frustratingly long time it took to receive instructions from across the Atlantic, clouded their success. When the Constitution replaced the weaker Articles of Confederation in 1788, the task of the ministers was made clearer, but by then, Jefferson would be ready to return home.

In the meantime he had made good use of his time abroad in other venues. He saw to the printing of his *Notes on Virginia*; found time to immerse himself in two of his favorite subjects, architecture and gardening; corresponded and visited with men of letters and science; and constantly bought books, both for his American friends and to add to his growing personal library. Few of his endeavors were made solely for his own benefit. As he wrote James Madison: "You see I am an enthusiast on the subject of the arts. But it is an enthusiasm of which I am not ashamed, as its object is to improve the taste of my countrymen, to increase their reputation, to reconcile to them the respect of the world, and to procure them its praise." Jefferson alluded here to the continuation of one of his earliest architectural projects — a new capitol for his native state. Having received a letter from two of the "directors of the public buildings, desiring I would have drawn for them, plans of sundry buildings, and, in the first place, a capitol," Jefferson informed Madison that he had "engaged an architect of capital abilities in this business." The architect was Charles Louis Clérisseau, and the two had taken "for our model what is called the *Maison Quarré* of Nismes, one of the most beautiful, if not the most beautiful and precious morsel of architecture left us by antiquity."[2]

Jefferson sent the plans on Jan. 28, 1786, and in his covering letter bragged that the designs were "simple & sublime, more cannot be said, they are . . . copied from . . . the most perfect model of antient architecture remaining on earth; one which has received the appro-

bation of near 2000 years."[3] Jefferson also got Clérisseau to provide "a model of the building made in stucco, only changing the order from Corinthian to Ionic, on account of the difficulty of the Corinthian capitals."[4] The capitol that emerged on its acropolis in Richmond is generally regarded as the first American expression of the Classical Revival in architecture, a movement that would sweep the country in the next century[5] (fig. 10).

In the spring of 1787, on a trip to the south of France, Jefferson was able to see for the first time the building he had used as his model. He described the effect it had on him in a letter to Madame de Tessé, Lafayette's aunt: "Here I am, Madam, gazing whole hours at the Maison Quarée, like a lover at his mistress. The stocking weavers and silk spinners around it consider me a hypochondriac Englishman, about to write with a pistol the last chapter of his history." And if she might think it strange that he had fallen in love with a temple, he had something still worse to confess. A private house in Paris had affected him similarly. He had been "violently smitten with the Hôtel de Salm, and used to go to the Thuleries almost daily to look at it."[6]

Prior to leaving America for Paris, Jefferson had placed his plantation affairs in the capable hands of Nicholas Lewis, who was assisted in his work by Jefferson's brother-in-law Francis Eppes.[7] Lewis served in the capacity of supervisor, or manager, of all Jefferson's plantations in Albemarle and Bedford counties, while Thomas Bennet remained as overseer at Poplar Forest at least until July 1783. During the years Jefferson was abroad, Lewis and Eppes were directed to apply any and all profits they realized from the plantations to the payment of Jefferson's debts, but this was not always possible. In September 1784, Eppes reported that he had "seen Mr. Lewis since you left America. He gives me a very bad account of crops at Monticello as well as Bedford."[8]

A possibility that Jefferson considered, then rejected, to pay his debts was to sell several parcels of land. He had, he wrote Lewis in 1787, "sold too much of them already, and they are the only sure provision for my children." He had also considered selling slaves, but decided against this too, "as long as there remains any prospect of paying my debts with their labour. In this I am governed solely by views to their happiness." In his correspondence with Lewis, Jefferson also suggested opening more land at Poplar Forest, and sending more slaves to work there, as "the lands in Bedford are much better for tobacco than those of Albemarle."[9]

Late in November 1788, Jefferson requested permission to return home for five or six months, feeling that he had accomplished all he could for the time being in his position abroad. Not until August 1789 did he learn, from John Jay, secretary for foreign affairs, that his request had been granted. William Short, who had served as Jefferson's secretary in Paris, and who would remain there to act in his stead as chargé d'affaires, bet him a beaver hat that he would return. As it turned out, Short lost his bet, for Jefferson was never to go back to Europe.

Jefferson and his two daughters left Paris in September 1789, sailed across the channel to England, and boarded the *Clermont*, bound for Norfolk, on October 22. When they disembarked on November 23, he had been away from Virginia for over five years. He described the events that transpired so rapidly upon his return:

On my way home I passed some days at Eppington in Chesterfield, the residence of my friend and connection, Mr. Eppes, and, while there, I received a letter from the President, Genl. Washington, by express, covering an appointment to be secretary of state. I received it with real regret. My wish had been to return to Paris, where I had left my household establishment. . . . I then meant to return home, to withdraw from Political life, into which I had been impressed by the circumstances of the times, to sink into the bosom of my family and friends, and devote myself to studies more congenial to my mind[10] (fig. 11).

The time was not yet ripe for that, and on the first of March 1790, he left Monticello for New York, then the capital of the country. Not surprisingly, he did not go to Bedford during that brief winter stopover. Before leaving Virginia, however, he did find time to attend to a certain matter regarding Poplar Forest.

On February 23, 1790, Martha Jefferson and Thomas Mann Randolph, Jr., were married at Monticello. His daughter's choice of husband was entirely to Jefferson's liking, as he told her future father-in-law: "The marriage of your son with my daughter cannot be more pleasing to you than to me." He also expressed his pleasure "that the bond of friendship between us, as old as ourselves, should be drawn closer and closer to the day of our death."[11] Jefferson and the senior Randolph had spent several years of their youth together at Tuckahoe, the Randolph family home in Goochland County, and Randolph was a cousin of Jefferson's wife. In anticipation of the event, and to provide the customary dowry a bride then brought to a marriage, Jefferson also told the senior Randolph: "I propose to give to my daughter immediately my best plantation in Bedford, of 1000 acres of the Poplar Forest tract, & 25 negroes little & big." His "best plantation" was the tract known as Wingo's, at the westernmost end of Poplar Forest. Ultimately, Jefferson would give the Randolphs 1,441 1/2 acres, almost half again as many as the 1,000 first intended.[12] In addition to the land, Jefferson also deeded Martha and her heirs twenty-seven slaves and "all the stock of work horses, cattle, hogs & sheep & the plantation interests now on or belonging to the plantation called Wingo's."[13]

Martha later recalled the gift of her dowry in a letter to her daughter Ellen, and also noted that it was done "at a time when he thought himself not only perfectly solvent but rich enough to provide well for myself and his other grandchildren."[14] In that assumption, she was incorrect. Stopping in Richmond on his way to New York, Jefferson had to arrange for a loan and also had to make further provisions with his creditors regarding the inherited Wayles debt.

Fig. 10 Virginia State Capitol, Richmond; Thomas Jefferson, architect. This engraving, published in London in 1831, shows the capitol as originally designed, though the steps to the front portico had not yet been built. (*Virginia Historical Society*)

As he had done before he left for Paris, Jefferson again engaged Nicholas Lewis to manage his plantation affairs while he was away from Virginia, managing the affairs of the new nation. Soon after he arrived in New York, he received good news from Lewis's wife, Mary: "We have now intelligence from Bedford by a letter from Clark — and also from Mr. Meriweather who informs us that they are in great forwardness and every preparation for a crop and the overseers are managing uncommonly well. The wheat there commands 5/6 now at Richmond and the rise which terms Mr. Lewis has directed Clark to sell for he has refused 28/ for his shear of tobacco at Linchborge." Her only bad news was "the measles is among your Negroes at Bedford, but they have lost none." The Clark mentioned in Mrs. Lewis's letter was Bowling Clark (or Clarke, as Jefferson generally wrote his name), who seems to have begun his duties as overseer in Bedford around 1788, and who would continue in Jefferson's service there until 1801.[15]

Likely in response to Mary Lewis's April letter, Jefferson wrote her husband from New York on July 4, 1790, taking no note at all of the fact that he was writing on the anniversary of the adoption of the Declaration of Independence. Instead, his thoughts were on his farms and their cultivation: "In Albemarle I presume we may lay aside tobacco entirely; and in Bedford the more we can lay it aside the happier I shall be. I believe it cannot there be entirely discontinued, for want of open lands." In addition, he expressed the wish to get "under way with our domestic cultivation & manufacture of hemp, flax, cotton & Wool" for his workers.[16]

Jefferson's twelve-year-old younger daughter — who after her sojourn in Europe was more often known as Maria than as Mary — had gone back to Eppington to live with her aunt and uncle when her father left for New York. She too was in Jefferson's thoughts on the Fourth of July, 1790: "How many chickens have you raised this summer? . . . Tell me what sort of weather you have had, what sort of crops are likely to be made."[17] If that inquiry stopped ever so short of actually declaring his homesickness, he was more overt in other letters he wrote during his stint as secretary of state in George Washington's cabinet.

Fig. 11 Eppington, Chesterfield County, Virginia. It was at this handsome Georgian manor, dating from the 1760s, that Jefferson learned of his appointment as secretary of state in Washington's cabinet. (*Virginia Department of Historic Resources*)

In May 1791, writing from Philadelphia, which had now replaced New York as the nation's capital, he thanked his new son-in-law for replacing some trees at Monticello, and lamented: "I long to be free for pursuits of this kind instead of the detestable ones in which I am now labouring without pleasure to myself, or profit to others." Several months later he was even more vocal in his lament, if a letter to an Albemarle County friend can be taken as proof: "I am in an office of infinite labour, & as disagreeable to me as it is laborious. I came into it utterly against my will, and under the cogency of arguments derived from the novelty of the government, the necessity of its setting out well etc. But I pant after Monticello & my family. I cannot let it be long before I join them."[18] At least his Philadelphia sojourn was made more pleasant than it might otherwise have been with the company of one of his nephews. John Wayles Eppes, nicknamed "Jack," the son of Francis and Elizabeth Eppes, was there studying law under his uncle's watchful eye.

As during his previous governmental stints, Jefferson saw much of men and morality that only confirmed and increased his desire to return to private life. His entire term as secretary of state was made insufferable by his constant differences of opinion with Alexander Hamilton, Washington's secretary of the treasury. As ardent a Federalist as Jefferson was a Republican, Hamilton clashed with him on matters foreign and domestic, though at first their relationship as coequals in Washington's cabinet seemed surprisingly cordial. It soon became obvious, though, that anyone who believed that "a public debt is a public blessing" and in "the necessity of either force or corruption to govern men" would hardly agree with anything that Jefferson espoused.[19]

While in Paris, Jefferson had expressed the hope that he would not have to sell slaves to help clear his debts. Upon his return to America, with a clearer picture of his finances, he was forced to change his mind. He ordered a sale of twenty-nine slaves from Poplar Forest, which was held at New London on December 15, 1791. He realized only £1302.15, and complained that his proceeds were "miserable enough, the negroes having averaged only £45 apiece."[20] Almost a year later, he wrote Thomas Mann Randolph, Jr., that, because of "the short proceeds of my sale the last year, . . . I therefore, while at home, sent orders to Bedford to sell a dozen [more] negroes from thence taking the opportunity of some sale in the neighborhood to carry them to."[21]

Those "orders to Bedford" doubtless referred to a letter that Jefferson had written a few weeks earlier to his overseer, Bowling Clark. In it, he commenced rather abruptly by stating: "The following are the slaves which I have concluded to sell from Bedford." Jefferson then listed eleven men, women, and children, among whom

were "York & Jame boy sons of old Will & Judy." He also advised Clark that the purchaser could "receive the two old people for nothing should they chuse to go with their sons. this, as they please." Because there were so few to be sold, and because "I do not (while in public life) like to have my name annexed in the public papers to the sale of property," Jefferson concluded that "it will be best to carry them to some other sale of slaves in that part of the country to be sold." According to records in his Farm Book, this sale took place on December 14, 1792, and the eleven slaves brought a total of £560.2, an average of about £5 more per person than the earlier sale had realized.[22] Old Judy and Old Will, who had been at Poplar Forest since 1774, opted to remain there.[23]

Early in 1792, Jefferson wrote Martha on "no particular subject," but while recalling "the various scenes thro which we have passed together, in our wanderings over the world," told her of his desire "of being at home once more, and of exchanging labor, envy, and malice for ease, domestic occupation, and domestic love and society; where I may once more be happy with you, with Mr. Randolph and little Anne, with whom even Socrates might ride on a stick without being ridiculous." Anne was Anne Cary Randolph, the first of Martha and Thomas Mann Randolph's many children. She was born at Monticello on January 23, 1791, and was Jefferson's first grandchild. In March 1792, in another letter to Martha, he continued his refrain: "The ensuing year will be the longest of my life, and the last of such hateful labors; the next we will sow our cabbages together."[24] To ensure that he really would be able to sow his cabbages in Virginia, he wrote to Washington on May 23, 1792, tendering his resignation from the office of secretary of state after his first term expired. Washington reluctantly accepted his resignation, but coaxed him to remain in office until the end of 1793. In May 1793, James Madison joined the president in pleading with him to remain: "I feel for your situation but you must bear it. Every consideration private as well as public requires a further sacrifice of your longings for the repose of Monticello."[25] Jefferson's response gave little indication that he would change his mind, but ultimately he did agree to remain the length of time that Washington had urged. By the end of that time his desire to return home had only increased. Even after two hundred years, the excitement of his anticipation shines through in a letter he wrote to Angelica Church, a friend from his time in France, who happened to be Alexander Hamilton's sister-in-law: "I am going to Virginia. I have at length become able to fix that to the beginning of the new year. . . . I am then to be liberated from the hated occupations of politics, and to remain in the bosom of my family, my farm, and my books. I have my house to build, my fields to farm, and to watch for the happiness of those who labor for mine."[26]

"TRANQUILITY IS NOW MY OBJECT"
(1794–1800)

When Jefferson returned to Virginia in 1794, at the end of his stint as Washington's secretary of state, he was fifty years old. Years later, his great-granddaughter Sarah Randolph would comment knowingly on the way things were upon his return:

He now owned in his native State over ten thousand acres of land, which for ten long years had been subject to the bad cultivation, mismanagement, and ravages of hired overseers. Of these large landed estates, between five and six thousand acres, comprising the farms of Monticello, Montalto, Tufton, Shadwell, Lego, Pantops, Pouncey's and Limestone, were in the county of Albemarle; while another fine and favorite estate, called Poplar Forest, lay in Bedford County, and contained over four thousand acres. Of his land in Albemarle only twelve hundred acres were in cultivation, and in Bedford eight hundred — the two together making two thousand acres of arable land.[1]

Jefferson left Philadelphia on January 5, 1794, and upon his arrival at Monticello on the sixteenth of the month, he would remain in Virginia for three years. At long last he was able to spend a relatively uninterrupted time seeing to his family, attempting to get his affairs in order, beginning the remodeling of Monticello, and especially attending to the lands he loved (fig. 12). He wrote George Washington in a burst of enthusiasm soon after his return: "I return to farming with an ardor which I scarcely knew in my youth, and which has got the better entirely of my love of study."[2]

At the time of Jefferson's return, his family consisted of Martha and her husband, Thomas Mann Randolph, Jr.; their two children, Anne Cary and Thomas Jefferson Randolph; and Maria, now returned from Eppington to live at Monticello. Martha was only twenty-one years old; her husband twenty-five; and Maria, just sixteen. Anne Cary Randolph was almost three, and her brother, Jefferson's namesake, not yet two years old. Born on September 12, 1792, he would become a source of constant pride and help to his grandfather. Later in 1794, a third child would be born to the Randolphs, but would not survive infancy. Though he would have liked them to be, the Randolphs were not always at Monticello during this period of Jefferson's life. They continued to spend a great deal of time at Varina, a Henrico County plantation that had been given them by Thomas Mann Randolph's father upon their marriage.

After a year of doing what he claimed to like most, Jefferson was even more enthusiastic than he had been in his 1794 letter to Washington. In late spring of 1795 he wrote Gen. Henry Knox, who had been his colleague as secretary of war in Washington's cabinet: "I am become the most ardent farmer in the state. I live on my horse from morning to night almost. . . . I rarely look into a book, and more rarely take up a pen."[3] In addition to his agricultural pursuits, Jefferson tried his hand at manu-

Fig. 12 Land Roll. In 1794 Jefferson listed his many properties in his Farm Book. Poplar Forest contained 4,627 1/2 acres at the time (cf. fig. 46). *(Thomas Jefferson's Farm Book, Coolidge Collection, Massachusetts Historical Society)*

52. Land-Roll: in 1794.

acres. — acres

1052 3/4. Monticello. viz. 1000. patented by Peter Jefferson. 1735. July 19.
27 1/2 recd. in exchange by T. Jefferson from N. Lewis.
25 1/4 purchd by T. Jefferson from Richard Overton

(571 3/4) 571 3/4 Montalto. part of 483. acres purchased by T. Jefferson from E. Carter
12 1/2 the residue were conveyed by T. J. to N. Lewis in exchange
571 3/4 61 1/4 purchased by T. Jefferson from Benjamin Brown
40 purchased by do. from T. Wells

1924 1/2 300. Tufton. viz 150. called Tufton, pat. by T. Jefferson, 1755. Sep. 10.
150. called Portobello. patd. by P. Jefferson. 1740. Sep. 16
300.

400. Shadwell. purchased by P. Jefferson of William Randolph.

819 1/4 Lego. purchased by T. Jefferson of Thomas Garth.

819 1/4 Pant-ops. viz 650. purchased by P. Jefferson of the Smiths.
169 1/4 purchased by T. Jefferson of Walter Mousley.
819 1/4

2768 1/2 730. viz. 485. surveyed in the name of T. Jefferson.
245. an undivided moiety of 490. survd. for J. Harvie
730.

400. Pouncey's. viz 300 part of the 400. patd. by P. Jefferson. 1756. Aug. 16
100. residue thereof devisd. by P. Jefferson to Speirs
400. and repurchased by T. Jefferson from Speirs

404. 4. Limestone. purchased by T. Jefferson from Robert Sharpe.
66 2/3 66 2/3 Limestone. an undivided sixth of 400. acres on the waters of Hardware. patd. by Philip Mayo. Sep. 1. 1749
222. on Mc. Gehee's road patd. by T. Jefferson 1788. Apr. 12.

418 196. on waters of Buckisle. patd. by T. Jefferson 1788. Apr. 12.

5591 2/3 in Albemarle.

4627 1/2 Poplar Forest. viz. 3000. part of 4000. patd. by Stith.
1000. thereof conveyed to M. & M. Randolph.
3000.
256. patd. by Danl. Robertson
380. patd. by Callaway.
183. patd. by J. Robertson.
800. survd. for J. Wayles 1770. Oct. 25.
8 1/2 acres patented by T. Jefferson
4627 1/2

474. Tullos's. viz. 374. patd. by Tullos.

5101 1/2 in Bedford & Campbell. 100 purchased by J. Wayles of Richd. Stith pat.d by T. J.
474.

157. in Rockbridge. Natural Bridge. patd. by T. Jefferson 1774. July 5.

10,647 acres.

4. lots in Beverley town. viz. No. 57. 107. 108. 151. this last being the Ferry lot.

part of lot 335. in Richmond, containing 825. square yards, purchd by T. J. of Wm. B[...]

facturing upon his resignation from public office. In May 1794, he established a nailery at Monticello. Not only would it provide nails for his own extensive building operations, its products were sold to neighbors. Early in the next century, he would direct that nails from the Monticello nailery be used in building the house at Poplar Forest.[4]

During the first summer following his return to Virginia, Jefferson planned a long-overdue trip to Poplar Forest. He had been absent so long, in fact, that he couldn't actually recall just how long it had been since his last trip. On August 16, 1794, he wrote his old friend James Steptoe, who lived near New London: "I shall certainly be in Bedford this fall. Since last there (now 12 years ago) I was fully determined to have visited it once or twice a year." Twelve days later, he wrote his brother-in-law Francis Eppes: "I shall be obliged . . . to take a journey to Bedford, to which place I have not had it in my power to go for fourteen years past." No matter if it was twelve or fourteen, Jefferson was ultimately unable to go to Bedford in 1794. Nor did a trip planned for the next year, which he mentioned to several friends, ever take place.[5] As it turned out, six more years would pass before he was able to find time to visit Poplar Forest. During that long interim he continued to administer its operations from a distance, through his overseers. An excessively rainy summer in 1795 destroyed his corn and tobacco crops to such an extent that in writing to his son-in-law, Jefferson stated, "I fear to hear from Bedford." But, if his crops were destroyed, his livestock flourished. In his Farm Book, he noted that eighty-three hogs were slaughtered at Bedford in December 1795. Ten were reserved for Bowling Clark, who continued as overseer at Poplar Forest, and the slaves received the same number. After two other small provisions, the remaining sixty were sent to Monticello to augment the food supply there.[6] The close relationship between operations at Poplar Forest and Monticello is also indicated by an advertisement that Clark placed in a Lynchburg newspaper two years later (fig. 13).

On Sept. 29, 1796, Jefferson received a letter from John Wayles Eppes, asking for his daughter Maria's hand in marriage. Not only did Jefferson approve of "Jack," who was Maria's half first cousin, he later wrote Martha that he could not have found anyone more suitable for a son-in-law "if I had had the whole earth free to have chosen a partner for her." He also told her: "I now see our fireside formed into a group, no one member of which has a fibre in their composition which can ever produce any jarring or jealousies among us." To ensure that the fireside would remain close, he noted, "in order to keep us all together, instead of a present provision in Bedford, as in your case, I think to open and resettle the plantation of Pantops for them." Pantops, one of Jefferson's many

Fig. 13 Even though one of Jefferson's horses had run away from his "seat in Albemarle" four months earlier, Bowling Clark, the overseer at Poplar Forest, placed a notice in the *Lynchburg Weekly Museum* on August 16, 1797, stating that he would give "a generous reward" for the return of the horse to either of Jefferson's homes. *(Courtesy Jones Memorial Library, Lynchburg; photograph by Tom Graves, Jr., 1991)*

Albemarle County properties, consisted of two tracts, totalling 819 1/4 acres, part of which had been purchased by Jefferson, and part by his father. It was in clear view of Monticello and would have put the Eppes family close at hand. Jefferson closed his letter to Martha with yet another variation on his habitual refrain: "When I look to the ineffable pleasure of my family society, I become more and more disgusted with the jealousies, the hatred, and the rancorous and malignant passions of this scene, and lament my having ever again been drawn into public view. Tranquility is now my object."[7]

That object was not to be realized just yet — or, in fact, any time soon, as Jefferson's Virginia pastorale came to a grinding halt. Through no fault — much less effort — of his own, he had been elected to the office of vice president of the United States. In November 1796, electors in the various states of the union were chosen to cast their ballots for the next president and vice president. Under the system then prevailing, each elector voted for two contenders; the one receiving the most votes was chosen president, and the runner-up, vice president. There was no separate ballot for each office, nor any "ticket" drawn along party lines. Given his penchant for private life over public, the fact that the letter in which it appears was written to his son-in-law before he knew the outcome of the election, and the fact that it was not intended for publication, Jefferson's November 28, 1796, remark to Thomas Mann Randolph, Jr., has the definite ring of truth: "Few will believe . . . that I do sincerely wish to be the second on that vote rather than the first. The considerations which induce this preference are solid, whether viewed with relation to interest, happiness, or reputation. Ambition is long since dead in my mind. Yet even a well-weighed ambition would take the same side."[8] In the same letter, Jefferson noted that he had made a good sale on his wheat from Bedford, but didn't mention the newest addition to their family. The Randolphs had presented him with his latest grandchild over a month earlier. Born on October 13, 1796, Ellen Wayles Randolph would become one of his favorites, and would journey with him to Poplar Forest many times in the future. She would also, in her many letters and reminiscences, become an invaluable and reliable source of information on both the house at Poplar Forest and the life that went on within its walls.[9]

Jefferson's wish regarding the election of 1796 was granted. When the results were tallied, he placed second behind his fellow patriot, John Adams, who was elected president. Then as now, the office of vice president of the United States was ill-defined, and during his term Jefferson was able to spend far more time in Virginia than he had during his years as secretary of state. He set out from Monticello on February 20, 1797, and arrived in Philadelphia, then the nation's capital, on March 2. The next day, which was the day before he was to be inaugurated as

vice president of the United States, he was made president of an organization whose meetings were far more enjoyable than the Senate sessions over which he was required to preside. In fact, he acknowledged *this* election as the most flattering incident of his life. The organization was the American Philosophical Society, of which no less a luminary than Benjamin Franklin had served as president. Jefferson had been a member for many years and would continue as its chief executive until 1815, long after he had given up most other offices.

On October 13, 1797, a year after their engagement was announced, Maria Jefferson and John Wayles Eppes were married at Monticello. The day before, the bride's father deeded Pantops to them, along with thirty-one slaves.[10] Soon after his return to Philadelphia in December 1797, Jefferson provided Maria with yet another present. Writing Thomas Mann Randolph, Jr., on March 22, 1798, he announced that, along with a number of plants that he wished Randolph to have planted at Monticello, he had "just put on board the sloop *Sally* . . . for Richmond, a harpsichord for Maria," and had instructed his Richmond factor to then forward it "up the river without delay."[11] That the harpsichord arrived safe and almost sound was confirmed by Martha, who wrote her father on May 12: "I dined at Monticello a fortnight ago and saw Maria's harpsichord which arrived safe except for the lock and 1 or 2 pieces of the molding which got torn off someway." She added: "it is a charming one I think tho certainly inferior to mine."[12] As of the end of that month, the intended recipient still had not learned of its arrival, safe or otherwise, and as late as 1801 Maria was asking for time to choose between it and a piano.[13]

The fact that Jefferson had Maria's harpsichord sent to Monticello, rather than instructing his Richmond agent to keep it in Richmond, where the Eppeses could have easily picked it up and taken it to their Tidewater home, may be seen as one in the series of attempts he made to induce them to move to Albemarle. In a letter telling Maria how pleased he was to learn of her engagement, he had rather autocratically assumed the newlyweds would live at Monticello, at least at first: "As in the case of your sister, . . . we shall all live together as long as it is agreeable to you, but whenever inclination convenience or a curiosity to try new things shall give a wish to be separately established, it must be at Pantops." He also suggested that she could ride over to Pantops from Monticello "to superintend the spinning house, dairy, etc. You might even have a room there to be in comfort if business or variety should induce a short stay." That was but the gestation of an idea. Six months later the idea of a room had grown into the idea of a house. On December 2, 1797, Jefferson wrote Maria from Monticello: "Tell Mr. Eppes that I have orders for a sufficient force to begin and finish his house during the winter after the Christmas holidays; so that his people may come safely after New Year's day."[14] The newlyweds had other ideas. Beginning their married life at Eppington, the home they had both known as children, they eventually lived at several other Eppes family properties in Tidewater. In spite of Jefferson's efforts, they were never to live at Pantops, much less at Monticello.

During the time he was attempting to get his family close about him, Jefferson was regularly traveling between Albemarle and Philadelphia, tending to his duties as vice president. Also during these years, he became more and more the leader of the Republican faction, as partisan lines came to be drawn between them and the Federalists in American politics. On May 15, 1800, the day after Congress adjourned, Vice-President Jefferson left Philadelphia and arrived home at Monticello on May 29, having visited John Wayles and Maria Eppes on his way. He remained in Virginia until he resumed his official duties in November, and during that time he was at long last able to visit Poplar Forest. Although it was his first visit in eighteen years, it lasted less than a week.[15]

Though short, the visit was extremely important in light of what apparently transpired during it. Henry S. Randall, in his *Life of Thomas Jefferson*, published in 1858, was more than likely relaying information he received from Jefferson's granddaughter Ellen Randolph Coolidge when he wrote:

It was towards the close of his Presidency that Mr. Jefferson began to think seriously of building a house at Poplar Forest. But the first idea was conceived much sooner, and he used to say from his having been confined there for three days, in one of the two rooms of an overseer's house, during a great rain storm. Finding nothing but an almanack to read, he finally, in despair, fell to computing how long it would take to pay the national debt. The usual pocket-book of logarithms chanced to be absent, and he had slowly to run over interminable masses of figures. But he persisted and finally ascertained to his satisfaction that the internal taxes could be abolished, and the debt still be paid in eighteen years by the increase of revenue and a proper retrenchment in expenditures. This occurred in 1801, and it led him to introduce the original of the passage in his first message, commencing with the words, "Other circumstances, combined with the increase of numbers," etc.... The three days among the overseer's dogs and children, were therefore not unfruitful ones. And they suggested a more convenient resort from long rain storms, and an uninterrupted retreat for the solitary study of high problems[16] *(fig. 14).*

From that account it is not entirely clear if Ellen meant that the trip to Poplar Forest took place in 1801 or that the message (his first annual message to Congress, delivered on December 8, 1801) was given then. If the former, her otherwise remarkable memory was off a year on the date. Jefferson visited not in 1801, but in 1800. What he chose to do with his time during those rainy days at Poplar Forest makes one wonder how much he truly desired tranquility, or if he would ever be able to actually achieve it. Even in 1800, any time spent on planning how to balance the federal budget was about as far removed from tranquility as could be imagined. But that other project that he conceived at the same time, "of building a house at Poplar Forest," was to provide many more pleasant hours.

Fig. 14 Jefferson's notes and doodles. Whether or not this page of various drawings and figures has anything to do with Poplar Forest is unknown. In light of the statement by Henry S. Randall that Jefferson first thought of building a house there during his confinement at an overseer's house, and that he also calculated how to pay the national debt at the same time, it is interesting to note that the figure at the lower right-hand corner is accompanied by the words "to draw 3 sides of an Octagon," and that the countries listed above are among those to which the new United States was in debt at the time. *(Coolidge Collection, Massachusetts Historical Society)*

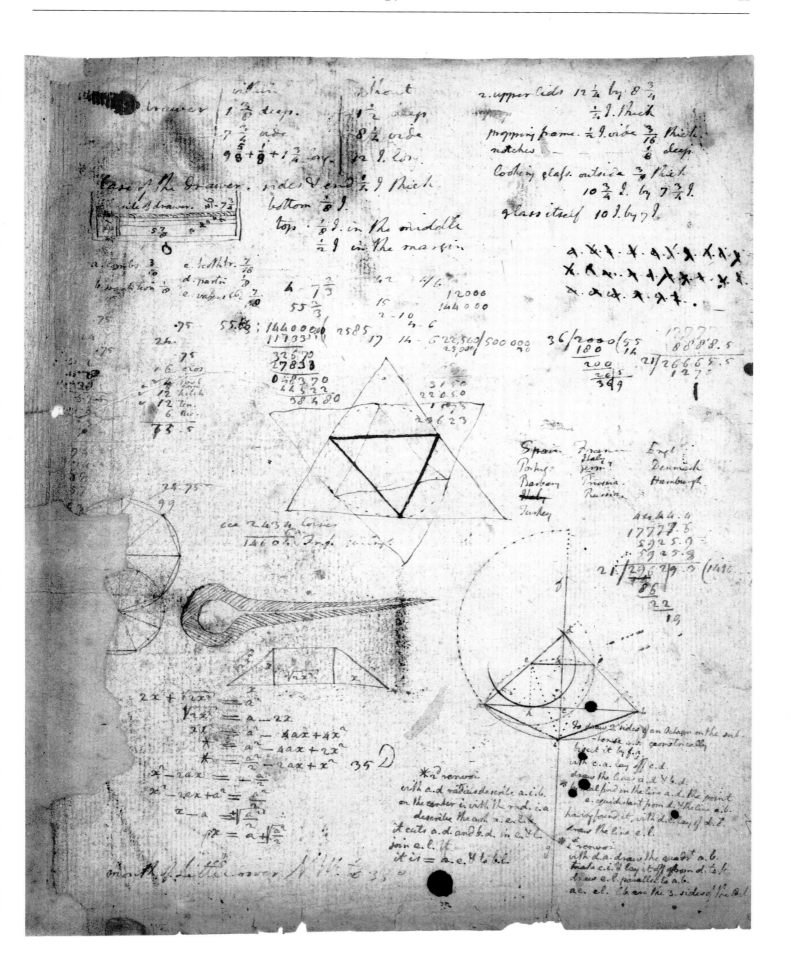

"DESTINED FOR A DWELLING HOUSE"
(1800–1805)

Instead of returning to Philadelphia when he left Virginia in November 1800 to complete his term as vice president, Jefferson went to Washington, the new Federal City on the banks of the Potomac. As secretary of state during George Washington's administration, Jefferson had played a great part in locating, planning, developing, and even naming the new capital.[1] The affairs and machinery of government had moved there in June, and by the time Jefferson arrived, the people of the United States had cast their ballots for a new president, or at least had cast their votes for the electors, who would then vote for the president. Jefferson and Aaron Burr, the two Republican candidates, were pitted against John Adams and Charles Cotesworth Pinckney, the two Federalists.

The contest that opened the new century remains one of the fiercest ever waged in American politics. Charges of atheism (for the benefit of the New England states), liberal views on slavery (which played to southern emotions), and personal immorality (intended to hurt him throughout the nation) were only three of the many indictments hurled against Jefferson. On February 11, 1801, in his role as presiding officer of the joint session of the two houses of Congress, the vice president opened the electors' ballots. The result, which by then had been long expected, was a tie. It was not, however, a tie between the Republicans and the Federalists, but between Jefferson and Burr. As prescribed by law, the decision then became the prerogative of the House of Representatives, where the tie between the two candidates persisted. Only on the thirty-sixth ballot, taken on February 17, 1801, was Thomas Jefferson elected third president of the United States. His inauguration on March 4 was the first to be held at the new capitol building, still far from finished, and his inaugural address helped heal the schism that had developed between proponents of a strong central government and one less centralized. "We are all republicans — we are all federalists," he declared, and wondered aloud that any patriot would try to alter the government then "in the full tide of successful experiment." During his presidency, he would more than double the extent of what he termed "the rising nation, spread over a wide and fruitful land" and would guide its course as he saw best. Even so, as he realized and stated at the outset of his presidency, "it will rarely fall to the lot of imperfect man to retire from this station with the reputation and favor which bring him into it."[2]

On March 19, Jefferson moved from his boarding house on Capitol Hill to the still-unfinished President's House a mile away.[3] Abigail Adams had complained about the uncompleted state of the house during her short tenure there, but Jefferson, having only recently finished his roof at Monticello, felt completely at home. In fact, he soon initiated a number of changes of his own. The East Room, where Mrs. Adams had hung her laundry, was partitioned to provide quarters for his private secretary, Capt. Meriwether Lewis. Other changes he made included alterations to the entrance and a great deal of embellishment in the interiors.[4] As he had just done at Monticello, he also added service wings to either side of the main block. At the President's House, the land sloped to the south, so that the wings could be built into the hill, allowing them to appear as low walls from the formal, north front, while on the south they were fully exposed and above grade. Individual rooms opened on the south into Tuscan colonnades, which extended the full length of the wings (fig. 15). The wings were covered with shallow, sloped roofs, which in turn were covered with railed platforms, serving as walkways entered from the main floor of the house.[5] Though these wings were called offices, the uses to which the rooms were put were far different from the connotation that term now has. Contained within them were servants' bedrooms, privies, a smokehouse, and a coach house. Although Jefferson had planned to have the wings built during his first term, it was not until his second that they were completed, under the direction of Benjamin H. Latrobe, whom he had appointed surveyor of the public buildings. By the time the wings were finished, Jefferson had also seen to the replacement of the original slate roof of the President's House — which not only leaked but was beginning to cause the walls to buckle — with a lighter one of sheet iron.

If the President's House was unfinished during Jefferson's incumbency, the grounds around it, almost totally barren of landscaping, were a perfect match. Again, though he was unable to do all that he wished, and though much of what he planned and planted only reached maturity in later administrations, Jefferson was assiduous in attempting to develop the grounds in an appropriate fashion (fig. 16). The northern half of the President's Park was, for the most part, formally planned, with tree-lined vistas extending the visual lengths of L'Enfant's grand diagonal avenues that ended at the grounds. In between the formal lines of trees were other plantings. The approach to the main, north entrance was a drive, extending straight toward the house, and ending in a circular carriage turnaround, with a fifty-foot outer radius. To the south, the grounds were generally less formal, though a rigidly rectangular lawn, some 200 feet wide, and bordered by trees and flowers, extended 400 feet straight to the south, toward the Potomac River and the view beyond.[6] Farther south, on either side of the rectangular space, Jefferson supervised the building of two earthen mounds that became known as "the Jefferson mounds." In addition to being important components of the landscaping, these helped screen the environs of the President's House and gave them privacy.[7] Such mounds were important elements of pleasure grounds at the time. At nearby Mount Vernon, which Jefferson visited, George Washington had them on either side of the bowling green and planted them with willow trees. The work that Jefferson supervised in both the President's House and the grounds of the President's Park would soon find "striking similarities" in Bedford County, Virginia.[8]

While his two terms as president allowed him far less time away from office than his previous duties as vice president had, Jefferson nevertheless still found time to cross the Potomac for frequent and lengthy stays in Virginia. During the summer months, he, in effect, took the office with him. As he wrote his secretary of the treasury, Albert Gallatin: "I consider it as a trying experiment for a person from the mountains to pass the two bilious months on the tide-water. I have not done it these forty years, and nothing should induce me to do it."[9]

In 1800 Jefferson paid taxes on 4,000 acres of land in Bedford County, and for the first time, the amounts were stated in dollars rather than pounds: on an assessed value of $9,840, his tax was $47.25. On August 17, 1801, he noted in his Memorandum Book that he "gave Jame Hubbard for expences to Poplar Forest 1. D." Hubbard, or Hubard, was one of Jefferson's slaves, and while no details remain to explain the purpose of this particular

trip, in all likelihood it was connected to the hiring of a new overseer. On August 12 Wilson Cary Nicholas, an Albemarle County friend, congressman, and business associate, had written Jefferson: "I have informed B. Griffin that you are disposed to employ him to manage your estate in Bedford, he desires me to inform you that he will be at your house by the 16th. instant. I have told him that you are willing to give the 12th. part of the crop, which I think full enough for twenty five hands."[10] Hubbard probably accompanied Griffin on his trip to his new place of work. Griffin would serve, with mixed reviews, as the Poplar Forest overseer until 1811.

Although Griffin replaced Bowling Clark as overseer at Poplar Forest in the fall of 1801, Clark was soon engaged to perform another service. On October 8 and 9, 1801, writing from Washington, Jefferson penned almost identical letters to his two sons-in-law, proposing gifts of certain portions of the Poplar Forest lands to each. "Sometime since," he informed them, "I . . . wrote to Bowling Clarke, who is honest, judicious & intimately acquainted with the tract to have two parcels of 800, or 1000 acres laid off" for each. Inasmuch as the Randolphs had already been given a portion of land to the northwest of the core tract, Jefferson proposed that their new

Fig. 15 The President's House, Washington, D.C. This ca. 1830 view shows the west wing—fronted by a Tuscan colonnade added by Jefferson during his presidency — to the left of the main block. A matching wing to the east is not seen in this picture. (*Prints and Photographs Division, Library of Congress*)

tract would be in the same quadrant, and would adjoin their earlier holding, while Eppes would receive a tract to the southeast. Acknowledging that "the land in the S. E. end is not as rich as to the North," Jefferson had consequently authorized Clark "to equalize the two by a difference in quantity." He also advised Randolph and Eppes that if they would each hire ten laboring men and "employ them in clearing lands within your respective parts," he would pay for them, and suggested that the two men might "both visit the place and see the allotment Clarke has made."[11]

Jefferson always regarded land as "the only sure provision for my children," and the timing of these gifts to his two sons-in-law was more than likely prompted by their growing families. Martha's fifth child, Cornelia, had been born two years earlier, on July 26, 1799, and her sixth, Virginia, on August 22, 1801. On September 20, 1801, Maria gave birth to a son at Monticello. Named Francis Eppes, in honor of his paternal grandfather and several generations before that, he was the seventh to carry the name, and would ultimately inherit Poplar Forest.

By May 1803, Randolph had been to Poplar Forest, where he "had an opportunity of seeing the land which has been laid off there for Maria." He reported to Eppes that it "contains 900 acres and that 350 of it is prime Tobacco land." The proposed division allotted only 450 acres to Randolph, but as all of it was considered prime land, the immense difference in actual acreage was deemed equitable by the two brothers-in-law.[12] In spite of his elaborate preparations, nothing came of Jefferson's proposed gifts of Bedford land to his sons-in-law. The subject, however, would come up time and again, at least between Jefferson and Eppes.

In the same October 9, 1801, letter to John Wayles Eppes announcing his proposed gift of Poplar Forest land, Jefferson took the occasion to urge the couple once again to make their permanent home in Albemarle: "Understanding that you thought of building some time ere long on the upper Pantops I mentioned to Maria (I do not recollect whether I did to you) that I thought it indispensable that the ground should be first levelled as that of Monticello is, and that if you would be at the trouble of hiring hands & having the work done, I would pay their hire: and this I recommend to you." The work involved at Pantops, in combination with arrangements to be made

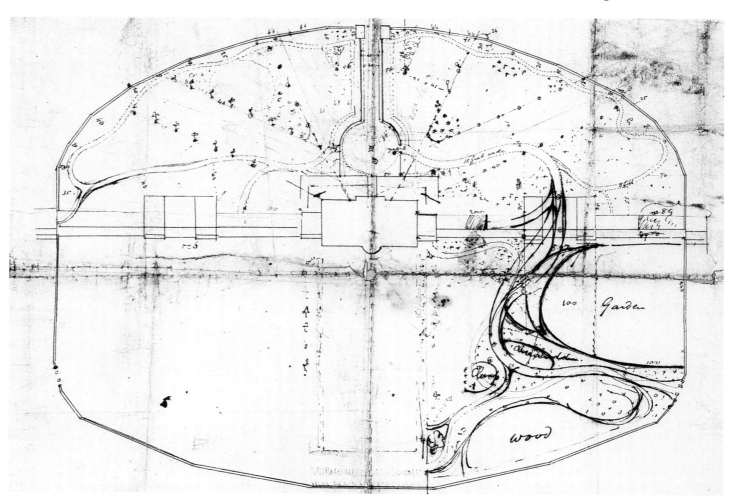

Fig. 16 Grounds of the President's House, Washington, D.C., ca. 1807. Probably drawn under Jefferson's supervision, this plat shows a rectangular parterre to the south of the house and a circular carriage turnaround to the north, features that would soon appear at Poplar Forest. (*Geography and Map Division, Library of Congress*)

at Poplar Forest, Jefferson advised, "would give you so much to do in the upper country that I should think you and Maria had better make Monticello your head quarters for the next year as Central to all your concerns." If they would only move to Monticello, Jefferson wrote Maria later in the month, "it might induce me to take flying trips by stealth, to have the enjoyment of family society for a few days undisturbed."[13] Jefferson did not tell Eppes in this letter, nor apparently in the many others that he wrote urging him and Maria to move to Albemarle, that in addition to providing the property and leveling the site, he also planned to provide the design for their house at Pantops. Perhaps they all understood that such would be the case.

In addition to planning for Pantops, Jefferson was also beginning to think of building a house at Poplar Forest during his years as president. Just when he began to take pen to paper to begin his designs is not known. His granddaughter Ellen's contention that, although he "began to think seriously of building a house at Poplar Forest" toward the end of his presidency, he had conceived the idea "much sooner"— coupled with her remembering that the idea was connected with his 1800

(or 1801) stay in Bedford — seems as logical a beginning point as any. Inasmuch as actual work is known to have started soon after his second term as president began, it must have been sometime during his first term that he began actively planning it. At any rate, a number of extant drawings in Jefferson's hand show different, but related, plans, which are apparently preliminary drawings for the house he originally intended to build there.[14] None are dated, but one has a penciled notation "plan for Bedford" in Jefferson's handwriting (fig. 17). The others, though not so labeled, are obviously variations on the same theme. All have a completely octagonal room, most have porticos, alcove beds, and inconspicuous stairways, all favorite and familiar features in Jefferson's domestic architecture.

The drawing shown in figure 17 is one of the more complex versions, and is probably the fourth in the scheme of development, if indeed there was a discernable evolution. It shows two rooms in a central block, flanked by rooms to either side. One of the central rooms, presumably the salon, is a complete octagon, with one end projecting into a columned portico, much as the salon at Monticello does. The other central room,

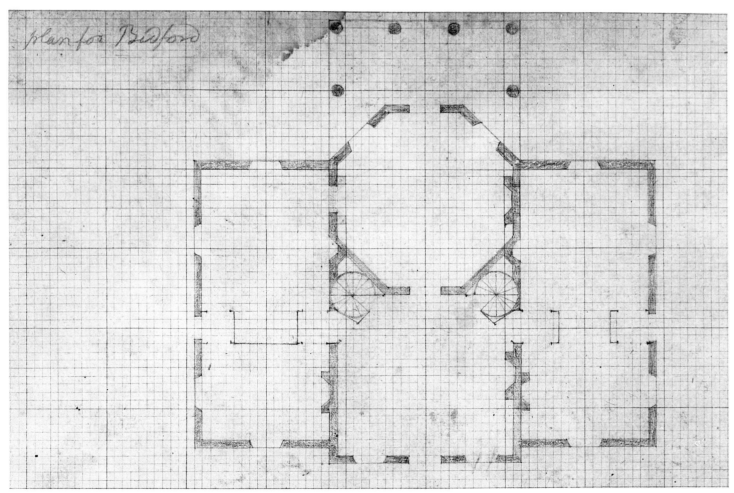

Fig. 17 "Plan for Bedford," inscribed in Jefferson's hand in the upper left-hand corner, indicates he once considered using this floor plan for his house at Poplar Forest. *(Coolidge Collection, Massachusetts Historical Society)*

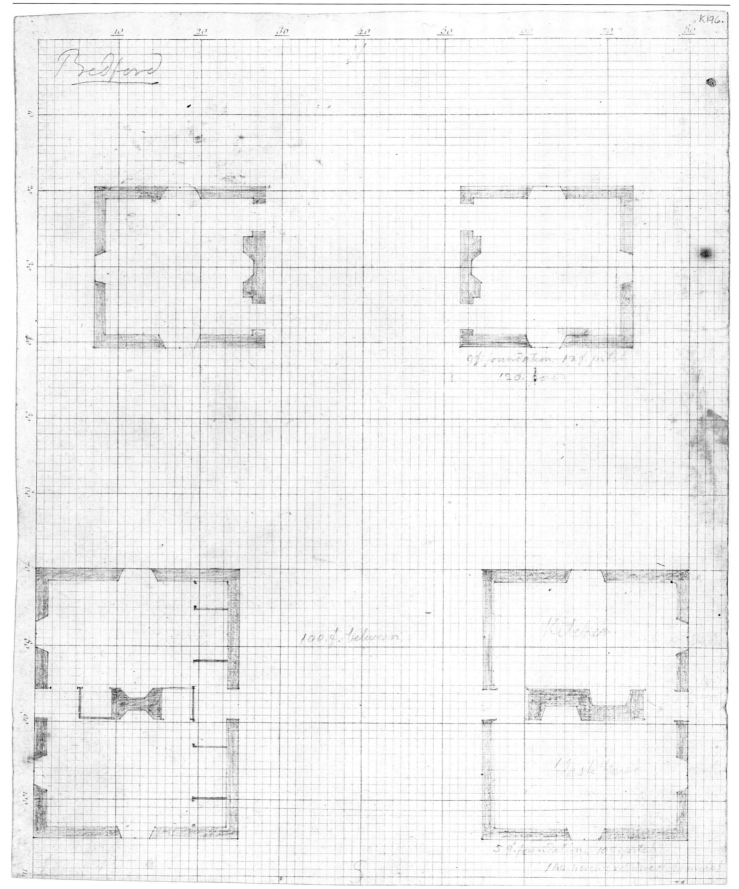

Fig. 18 Poplar Forest, outbuildings. As in the illustration shown as fig. 17, this otherwise unlabeled drawing has the word *Bedford* in the upper left-hand corner. *(Coolidge Collection, Massachusetts Historical Society)*

in the same relative location as the entrance hall at Monticello, is not octagonal, but does have a polygonal bay opposite the entrance. Set within the angles formed by these walls and the inner walls of the octagonal room are matching circular stairways. On either side of these central spaces is a chamber-dressing room, with an alcove bed centered in each. Jefferson learned about alcove beds while in France, and used them in his domestic designs whenever he could. He had introduced them in the house he occupied during his stay in New York in 1789, and in 1793, in providing suggestions to James Madison on a house Madison's brother was building, he admitted: "I am much attached" to them.[15] Essentially, alcove beds were built-in features, either set within a wall, or constructed in the center of a room, with walls built at head and foot. The final Poplar Forest plan would have two alcove beds, each centering one of the two main bedrooms.

Two related drawings for outbuildings are associated with Jefferson's early plans for Poplar Forest (figs. 18 and 19). Figure 18 has the word *Bedford* penciled in the upper left-hand corner, and the plan shown in the lower right-hand corner (labeled kitchen-wash house) is obviously a less polished version of the same building shown in figure 19. The kitchen-wash house and a building that apparently was intended to be its twin on the exterior, judging from their somewhat unusual and mirror-image fenestration patterns, were to have been built a hundred feet apart, with the main house between them, as a note on the plan in figure 19 suggests: "Having driven a pin in the center of the spot destined for a dwelling house hereafter, measure 50 f. due East from that pin, and there make the center of the door as at a." The fact that Jefferson wrote "destined for a dwelling house *hereafter*" in his instructions would seem to indicate that he may have planned to build only the two dependencies at first. In fact, the other dependency (shown at the lower left in figure 18) could have served quite adequately as a temporary lodging. Its plan shows two bedrooms, each with an alcove bed and a fireplace, and — luxury of luxuries for the time — each bedroom would apparently have had two closets. The proposed locations of the other two buildings shown in figure 18 are not given, nor are the uses for which they were intended indicated. It may be that Jefferson planned them as temporary living and dining spaces, which the ensemble otherwise would have lacked. As with the larger buildings, each was a mirror image of the other, and each was equipped with a fireplace. Apparently none of these outbuildings was built at Poplar Forest, just as the manor house itself was not to follow the form shown in Jefferson's early sketches.[16]

Jefferson's loneliness in Washington was abated during his first term of office when Martha, accompanied by two of her children, and Maria spent several weeks with him in the winter of 1802–03. During that same winter,

Jefferson set in motion two endeavors that would culminate in two of the most memorable accomplishments of his career as president. On January 11, 1803, he nominated James Monroe as minister extraordinary to negotiate with the French concerning the Louisiana question, a perplexing situation involving navigation along the Mississippi, access to the port of New Orleans, and the westward expansion of the United States. A week later, Jefferson requested from Congress a $2,500 appropriation to finance "a western expedition in which commercial, scientific, and military objectives would be conjoined."[17] Though the two endeavors were ostensibly unconnected, the timing of each was fortuitous in relation to the other. The first would result in the Louisiana Purchase, news of which was published in the *National Intelligencer* on July 4, 1803. The night before that announcement, Meriwether Lewis had written his mother: "Day after tomorrow I start for the West."[18] Lewis was about to begin his famous expedition, whose command he shared with William Clark.

Even with these accomplishments, Jefferson continued to pine for retirement and his return home. That same January, he wrote his good friend Madame de Tessé that while he might return to Monticello in 1805, he would surely do so by "1809 at the latest (because then, at any rate, I am determined to draw the curtain between the political world and myself)."[19]

In 1803 both of the president's sons-in-law served in the Eighth Congress as representatives from Virginia, and both spent the winter of 1803–04 with him in the President's House. They were not joined by their wives, though Jefferson had written Maria that he had hopes that Eppes's election would also "secure me your company next winter."[20] Although he constantly wrote Martha and Maria of his loneliness, his younger daughter must have thought otherwise. After her visit the year before, when she saw how many people constantly surrounded the president, she feared that "it will always be the case now in your summer visits [to Monticello] to have a crowd."[21] That would prove to be a very accurate prediction, and the situation she prophesied had much to do with Jefferson's plans for a retreat. Unfortunately, Maria was not to enjoy those summer visits, crowds or not.

On January 29, 1804, still trying to convince the Eppeses to move to Albemarle, Jefferson wrote Maria that "we will begin the levelling and establishing of your hen-house at Pantops" in March, or soon thereafter.[22] His allusion to the proposed new house as a hen-house was in reference both to some bantam fowls he had just acquired and which he planned to distribute in the family, and to the fact that Maria was soon to have another child. In February Maria gave birth to a daughter, but by the middle of March, Jefferson worriedly wrote her husband: "Your letter of the 9th has at length relieved my spirits; still the debility of Maria will need attention, lest

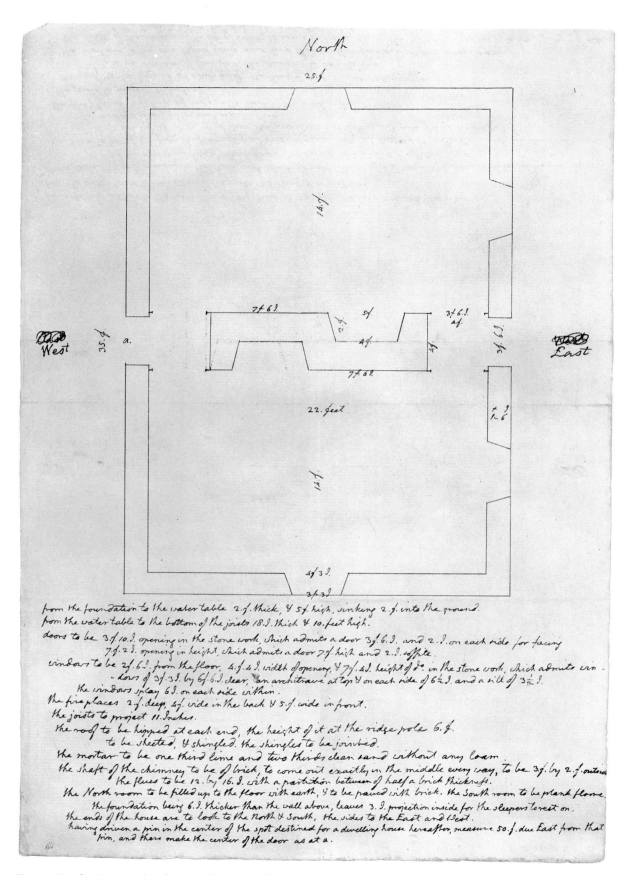

Fig. 19 Poplar Forest, kitchen-wash house. This larger-scale drawing shows a building whose plan matches the one seen in the lower right corner of fig. 18. *(Coolidge Collection, Massachusetts Historical Society)*

a recurrence of fever should degenerate into typhus." As her condition worsened, Jefferson returned to be with her at Monticello, where she had been taken "on a litter by hand, so weak as barely to be able to stand." On April 16, the day before her death, her brother-in-law, Thomas Mann Randolph, Jr., wrote a moving and perceptive letter: "How the President will get over this blow, I cannot pronounce. I will not conjecture from my knowledge of the firmness of his mind or the recollection that he has passed 40 years in the constant practice of a rigid control over his feelings; for I do not believe his understanding has strengthened at the expense of his heart. I can tell you how he bears it now. He passed all last evening with her handkerchief in his hand. I begin to feel the want of mine."[23]

All that Jefferson himself wrote on April 17, 1804, was a notation in his Memorandum Book, echoing poignantly a similar note he had penned there some twenty-two years earlier: "This morning between 8. & 9. oclock my dear daughter Maria Eppes died." On June 4, he composed what was apparently the first letter written to her widower after Maria's death: "While I live, both of the children will be to me the dearest of all pledges: and I should consider it as increasing our misfortune, should we have the less of your society. It will in no wise change my views at Pantops, and should considerations which ought not to be opposed by me in the actual state of things induce you to change the purpose of your residence at Pantops, I shall still do there what I had always proposed to you, expecting it will some day become the residence of Francis. I may only take more time for it."[24]

In response, Eppes, who had moved back to Eppington, mournfully replied: "The period I fear will not soon arrive when I shall be able to feel any comfort in a home of my own." In the meantime, he would keep Francis and the infant (who would survive only a short while) at Eppington, and unselfishly told his father-in-law: "When you retire from public life if it shall be your wish to have either of the children with you or both I shall consider your claim assuaged to my own. They will be to you I hope as dear as to myself, and between your house and Eppington my heart will never I hope learn to draw a line." He also told Jefferson to "act as you think best for the welfare of my children" in regard to Pantops, but as far as the house that Jefferson had promised to build was concerned, hoped that he would give "Francis the value of it in land adjoining Pant-Ops." He now doubted that he would ever live at Pantops, as he confessed that his feelings did not "at present point to that spot as all the ideas of happiness I had formed for that place would in turn present to my view the miserable wreck that is left me." Eppes concluded by assuring Jefferson: "While my heart remains what it now is I shall always feel for you as a second father and in passing with you as much of my time as circumstances will permit, shall be following only the

impulse of my own feelings."[25]

In November 1804, Jefferson was elected to his second term as president. Between his election and his inauguration on March 4, 1805, he sat for what has come to be one of his best-known, and best-loved, likenesses, the famous Rembrandt Peale portrait done in January 1805 (frontispiece). So proud was the artist's father, Charles Willson Peale, that on the eve of Jefferson's inauguration, he displayed the portrait "at a special illumination" at his Philadelphia museum.[26] As Jefferson had speculated to Madame de Tessé early in 1803, "the curtain between the political world and myself" would now definitely not be drawn until 1809. His reelection gave eloquent testimony to his popularity, as he carried all the states except Connecticut and Delaware. Vice-president Aaron Burr had effectively cut himself out of a future in politics after his infamous duel with Alexander Hamilton that summer, and in Burr's stead, George Clinton, former governor of New York, was elected to be Jefferson's new vice president.

As Jefferson had predicted at the beginning of his first term, he was ultimately not destined "to retire from this station with the reputation and favor" that he had brought into it. His second term as president was one of trials and tribulations, and his letters to his family and his friends speak eloquently of the torments he was enduring. Not the least of his problems was a growing realization that he would leave the office of president with his finances still in arrears, even though he had at long last managed to eradicate what he termed "Mr. Wayles's great debt."[27] Toward the end of his second term, he would calculate that he would leave Washington with a debt of "about ten thousand Dollars" that had accumulated during his presidency.[28] In his plans for the eventual payment of his debt, the income from the Poplar Forest fields, which he estimated at $2,500 annually, figured prominently.[29] To ensure the greatest productivity, and consequently the greatest income, from his lands would necessitate firsthand supervision of the farm operations upon his retirement from public office. That, in turn, would mean numerous and lengthy visits to Bedford, and by extension, logical or otherwise, it would certainly be beneficial to have more comfortable lodgings than those that had previously existed at Poplar Forest. Of course there were many other considerations (including the one hinted in Maria's 1802 letter regarding crowds) that went into the decision to build the house that was to crown his Bedford property. Given these possible reasons, there is something both appealing and appalling in Jefferson's completely irrational plan to achieve financial independence while building a house that would eventually cost as much, if not more, than the amount of the debt he sought to erase. By the time he left the presidency, not only had such a house begun to take shape, it was almost ready to receive him.

"CHISOLM GOES TO BEDFORD"

(1805–8)

Three weeks after the inauguration to his second term as president of the United States, Jefferson turned his attention to a personal project. Having "searched my papers," he found the plat that Bowling Clark had prepared, drawing boundaries for the Bedford tracts he had promised his two sons-in-law four years earlier. Clark's proposed division of the property was not to his liking, he wrote John Wayles Eppes on March 25, 1805, as it left some 500 acres of land "in a long narrow useless belt cut off from the body of my tract which would have been injurious to me, and useless to you." Two months later, Jefferson informed Eppes that he would leave Washington "perhaps by the middle of July," and would "proceed almost directly to Bedford," where he would get Mr. Clay and Mr. Clark to help him lay out new boundaries. Jefferson assured Eppes that "the tenderest considerations ensure a conscientious performance of this duty."[1] Although he did take the promised trip, which extended from July 26 through July 31, still nothing came of the proposed gifts of land.[2] In fact, though he did not mention it to Eppes, there was apparently another reason that Jefferson went to Bedford at this time. On September 29, 1805, two months after his visit, he noted in his Memorandum Book: "Pd. Chisolm 10. D. Chisolm goes to Bedford to work at 20. D. pr. month. Hhd. exp. 10. 50. set out from Monticello."

The story of the construction of the house at Poplar Forest begins with that short note. Hugh Chisolm, "one of Jefferson's most trusted workers, [was] a bricklayer, a carpenter, and a man of all trades." He began working at Monticello in 1796, and continued in Jefferson's employ as late as 1824. In addition to his work on Monticello and Poplar Forest, Chisolm worked on the University of Virginia and, between his projects for Jefferson, helped James Madison in the remodeling of Montpelier. In recommending him for that work, Jefferson told Madison that he was "a very good humoured man."[3] His letters, reporting the progress of work at Poplar Forest, attest to this. Unfailingly encouraging and optimistic, he was honest as the day is long, and always looked out for the interests of his employer.

Two days after Chisolm set out for Bedford, Jefferson set out from Monticello for Washington. There the winter of 1805–6 was made pleasant by having Martha, her husband (who was still serving in Congress), and their children with him. By this time the Randolph's seventh child, Mary Jefferson, had been born, and she was joined by their eighth on January 17, 1806. The first child to be born in the President's House, he was named James Madison Randolph. The Randolphs remained in Washington until the following spring, and on April 27, 1806, Jefferson wrote Elizabeth Trist, his old friend from Phil-

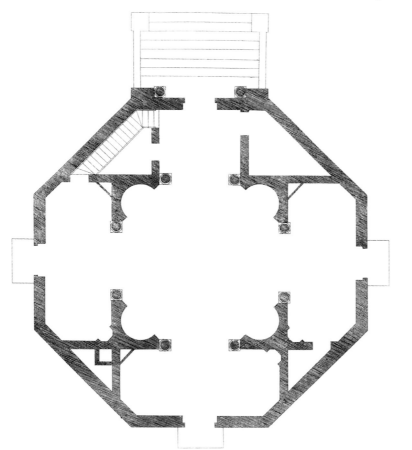

Fig. 20 Plate 20b from Wilhelm Gottleib Becker's *Neue Garten-und-Landschafts-Gebaude* (1788–89) shows a plan for a garden temple that has great similarities to Jefferson's plan for Poplar Forest (cf. fig. 21). *(Print Collection, Miriam & Ira D. Wallach Division of Art, Prints and Photographs, New York Public Library, Astor, Lenox and Tilden Foundations)*

adelphia, giving her the latest news: "My daughter & her family are with me & well. They will set out for Albemarle in 2 or 3 days." From Albemarle, he confessed, "I can give you no news, having nobody there now who writes me." Even so, he concluded: "I am looking to my final return there with more desire than to any other object in this world. It is yet three years distant. This summer will entirely finish the house at Monticello & I am preparing an occasional retreat in Bedford, where I expect to settle some of my grandchildren."[4]

Just what, if anything, had been accomplished on that "occasional retreat" by this time is impossible to ascertain. Chisolm had been there seven months when Jefferson wrote to Mrs. Trist, and had probably spent his time preparing the site, assembling stones, excavating for the foundation, digging clay for the bricks, and obtaining sand for mortar. Jefferson's use of the present progressive tense, *am preparing*, in reporting his new project, was probably as good a choice of verb as could be made.

Meanwhile, the question of building on the land at Pantops surfaced again. On May 24, 1806, Jefferson answered a letter John Wayles Eppes had written to him on the sixteenth of that month, in which he had announced both his intentions to remarry and, in spite of what he had written earlier, his wish to spend most of his time at Pantops with his new wife. Jefferson assured

Eppes again that if he, Eppes, would hire help to level the site for the proposed house, he, Jefferson, would pay for them, as he had promised earlier. But, as far as actually *paying* for the new house was concerned he now confessed: "With respect to a house, my former purpose had in view an object the most desireable for my comfort in this world. That has become impossible, and the object ceasing, I had retained nothing more than an indeterminate idea, if our dear Francis should live, to be doing such things there at convenience hereafter as might tempt him to make it a residence." Even "doing such things there at convenience" was now in jeopardy. As Jefferson continued: "Another circumstance renders it impossible now for me to do anything beyond the levelling. I have gotten so into arrears at Washington, as to render it necessary for me not only to avoid new engagements, but to suspend every expence which is not indispensable: otherwise I shall leave that place with burthens contracted there, which if they should fall on my private fortune, will doom me to a comfortless old age."[5]

What he might have called his current building project at Poplar Forest, if not a "new engagement," is hard to fathom, but there was another reason — even beyond the good excuses he cited in his letter to Eppes — why Jefferson was now loath to build at Pantops. He

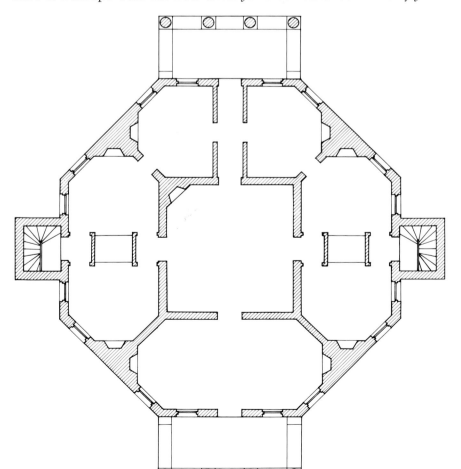

Fig. 21 Poplar Forest, reconstructed floor plan showing the house as built. The two doors of communication that Jefferson added at the last moment on the first floor, and which are not seen in the Neilson plan (endpaper), are those connecting the large east and west bedrooms (shown with alcove beds) to the small rooms on either side of the narrow entrance hall. *(Tim Buehner, delineator, 1991)*

would reveal to Eppes some years later that the house at Poplar Forest was "exactly on the plan once thought of for Pantops."[6] Considerations of costs aside, it is unlikely that even someone who was as fond of building as Jefferson was would have wanted two identical houses going up at the same time.

Jefferson's several preliminary plans for a house in Bedford, discussed in Chapter V and exemplified in figure 17, had been interesting enough, but they showed little advancement over his domestic plans as they had developed during past years and in other projects. The plan for Pantops (if indeed the house built at Poplar Forest was the one originally intended for Pantops) was far more innovative and daring, and if he could only build one house, it should come as no surprise that he chose to build from that plan.

The origins of that plan have been discussed often, and every suggestion postulated as Jefferson's possible inspiration has been met with a corresponding argument to disprove it. Jefferson's penchant for octagonal and polygonal *rooms* is well known, as his preliminary designs for the Bedford house demonstrate and as numerous rooms at Monticello and other houses he designed well prove. It could be argued that a completely octagonal *house* is but a logical culmination of Jefferson's infatuation with a shape that, heretofore, he had used only in rooms. In fact, even before Poplar Forest was begun, Jefferson had already designed free-standing octagonal rooms, as well as buildings that were completely octagonal. One of his early proposals for Monticello included one-room octagonal pavilions as part of the overall scheme. In that same designed-but-not-built category were plans for an octagonal chapel and one for an octagonal structure to be built of logs.[7]

Even those plans for what were admittedly simpler and smaller buildings could not have sprung full blown from Jefferson's mind. Octagonal plans had been published in many architectural books before his time, for structures as diverse as garden temples, baptisteries, churches, and, on occasion, houses. In 1727, British architect William Kent had shown an octagonal house in his *Designs of Inigo Jones*, a volume that Jefferson owned by 1779.[8] That design is for a far larger building than Poplar Forest, and the plan, though encased in an octagon, has none of the logical arrangement of spaces developed in Jefferson's plan.

Other possible sources for the Poplar Forest plan that have been cited over the years are Andrea Palladio's Villa Rotonda, dating from the sixteenth century, and a plate from Robert Morris's *Select Architecture*, published in 1755. In the first instance, Jefferson's fondness for things Palladian is well known. He was quoted in his later years as saying that, in architecture, Palladio "was the Bible."[9] In the second instance, Robert Morris was a disciple of Palladio, and Jefferson apparently based

other designs on plates shown in his *Select Architecture*. Neither of these suggested sources is truly convincing as the source of the Poplar Forest plan except for general ideas they may have furnished.

Recently, an expert on Jefferson's landscape architecture has uncovered a plate in a German book on garden structures that shows a plan for an octagonal garden temple bearing an uncanny resemblance to the fully realized Poplar Forest plan, both in basic room arrangement and in size (fig. 20).[10] The book is Wilhelm Gottlieb Becker's *Neue Garten-und-Landschafts-Gebaude*, published in 1798–99. Its connection, if any, with the plan for Poplar Forest, is not known, but it is intriguing to note that Jefferson purchased his copy in June 1805, only a few months before he sent Chisolm to Bedford to begin preparations for the house.

The plan of Poplar Forest (fig. 21) demonstrates a refinement and logical development of spaces implicit in the octagonal form that the German model still failed to achieve, no matter how close in appearance the two seem at first glance. Each plan shows a square central space — both were lit from above, though neither plan indicates this — flanked on three sides by rooms whose shapes are elongated octagons. On the fourth, or entrance side, a short hall leads from the front door, and is flanked by smaller spaces in each plan. In the German version, a staircase occupies a portion of one of these spaces, while in Jefferson's plan each space is a small, separate room. Where Jefferson's plan soars above the other is in its full realization of the octagonal and polygonal shapes inherent in the form. The elongated octagon of each of the three major rooms surrounding the central, square space of his plan is formed simply by the expedient of having four diagonal walls extend at forty-five-degree angles from the four corners of the central space to the centerlines of the four angular outer walls. The four chimneys of the house are located at the intersections of these walls, and the chimney breasts at each end of the three large outer rooms provide the flat end walls required to make the rooms octagonal. Jefferson's three elongated octagons are far more logical in arrangement than their equivalents in the German plan. Becker did not incorporate any structural diagonal walls *inside* his octagonal house, and the manipulation necessary to create octagonal rooms resulted in several awkwardly shaped subsidiary rooms, if not plain waste space. On the other hand, the central room of the German building was given an octagonal form by the surrounds of the niches in each of its four corners, and was a far more "architectonic" space than Jefferson's central room, where the chimney breast, situated in one corner, resulted in a somewhat awkward angular wall in an otherwise square room.

Just as Jefferson's use of the octagonal form for the envelope of the Poplar Forest house must have had some precedent, so his eminently satisfactory solution of division of spaces within that envelope, which Becker had not fully developed, did not spring full blown. In addition to the preliminary plans labeled "Bedford," Jefferson also drew at least two preliminary plans for the house at Pantops — or for the house that was eventually built at Poplar Forest (fig. 22). These shed no light on any evolution of the exterior form, as both sketches already show a complete octagon, but they clearly demonstrate the progression of Jefferson's thoughts on the refinements and arrangement of spaces within. The earlier of the two, shown on the right in figure 22, is an incomplete sketch, and seems to indicate that — instead of the central square room that was ultimately built — Jefferson originally intended to have two equally large rectangular rooms in the center of the house. Four small triangular spaces would then have been formed by the "leftover" spaces between the central, rectangular rooms and two

elongated hexagonal rooms to either side. These spaces could conceivably been utilized as closets or stairways, or for other subsidiary purposes, but whatever their intended uses, the overall plan did not take ultimate advantage of the octagonal form. At best, this plan was a dead end, and could hardly have been satisfactorily developed further along the lines begun. The more completed drawing to the left, except for minor changes, shows the house essentially as built, and the possibility exists that it was at this point, while Jefferson was struggling with the arrangement of the interior, that he saw Becker's plan, with its central, square room, and realized it offered a more logical and sensible point of departure than the proposal he had been considering.

Jefferson's fully-realized plan for Poplar Forest makes wonderful use of light, air, and space. The dark, narrow entrance hall (only four feet wide), contrasts effectively with the central room, bathed in light from the skylight

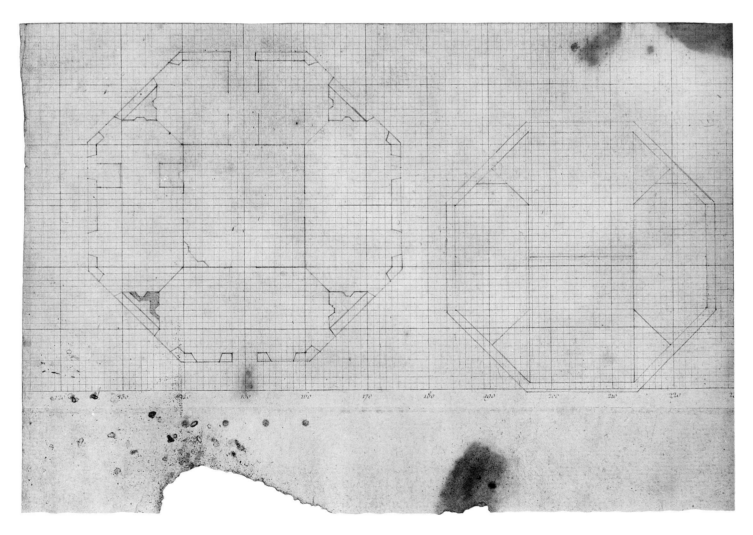

Fig. 22 Pantops/Poplar Forest, preliminary plans. These two sketch plans indicate the evolution of Jefferson's thinking on the arrangement of spaces within an octagonal shell. *(Coolidge Collection, Massachusetts Historical Society)*

above. Dimensions of this room, which served as the dining room, are twenty feet by twenty feet, which, with its twenty-foot height, made it an exact cube, a favorite shape of classically-minded architects such as Jefferson (see fig. 94). Beyond, and on the main north-south axis, was the drawing room, or parlor. With four triple-hung windows, extending from the floor almost to the entablature, and facing southeast, south, and southwest, it was as light and airy a room as could be desired. Centered in the south wall of the parlor was a door leading to the south portico. When it, the front door, and the two dining-room doors in line with them were open, direct ven-

tilation and a vista were provided along the north-south axis of the house. The dimensions of the parlor are basically rectangular, approximately fifteen feet by thirty feet, though, as was mentioned, the overall shape is that of an elongated octagon. The parlor, along with the other rooms on the perimeter of the house, had an ample ceiling height of over twelve feet. To the east and west of the dining room were the two main bedrooms, the one on the west being Jefferson's own. Though divided into two sections by the alcove beds, these chambers have the same overall dimensions and shape as the parlor.

On June 16, 1806, almost nine months after Chisolm

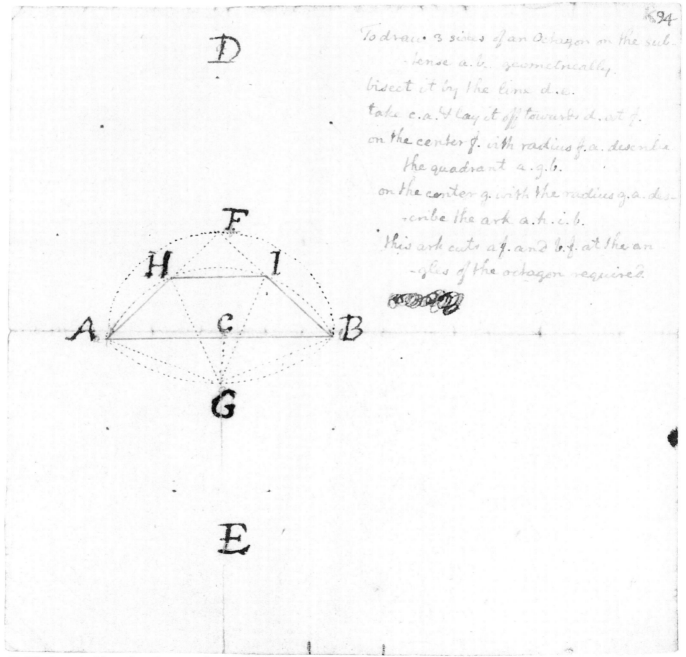

Fig. 23 "To draw 3 sides of an Octagon," an undated drawing from Jefferson's notes, is a clearer example of the procedure also shown in the small sketch seen as part of figure 14. *(Coolidge Collection, Massachusetts Historical Society)*

moved to Bedford, Jefferson wrote Martha from Washington: "I find by a letter from Chisolm that I shall have to proceed to Bedford almost without stopping in Albemarle. I shall probably be kept there a week or 10 days laying the foundation of the house, which he is not equal to himself, so that it will be near the middle of August before I shall be fixed at Monticello."[11]

Chisolm's letter has not been located, and it may seem strange that a master builder who had certainly laid foundations before was "not equal" to this one. But this was no ordinary house. While Jefferson's answer does not state the exact problem, the likely assumption is that Chisolm needed help in laying out the octagonal form upon which everything about Poplar Forest would depend. Certain inconsistencies in the angles of the walls in the basement of the house may, or may not, be evidence that this was indeed the problem. As Jefferson's own drawings of octagons indicate, determining the proper angles and wall lengths of a regular octagon was a sophisticated geometric exercise, dependant on arcs, radii, and quadrants (fig. 23). Perhaps Chisolm could have laid out a small-scale octagon on paper, but enlarging it some fifty feet in diameter, and laying it out on a hillside in Bedford County may well have been beyond his ken.

Chisolm also had to mold special bricks to form the forty-five degree angles at the eight corners of the walls of the octagonal house. These pentagonal bricks, known more formally as squint bricks, are similar to normal stretchers except at one end, where they have a specially formed angle (fig. 24). In addition to using them on the walls, Chisolm found another use for many of these squint bricks. The cellar below the central dining room at Poplar Forest was designed and built to serve as a wine cellar and for dry storage of other perishable items. In order for its temperature to be kept as constantly cool as possible, its walls were built of stone, and its floor, set four feet lower than those of the rooms surrounding it, was of brick. As this room was not a public space, the paving bricks of the floor were not laid in any particular pattern. In fact, an inordinate number of the pavers used here are squint bricks — some of them misshaped, but all similar to those that form the angles of the walls of the house.

As so often proved to be the case, Jefferson's proposed trip to Poplar Forest was delayed in the summer of 1806. His visit to Virginia began on July 24, and in spite of what he had written Martha, he went directly from Washington to Monticello. Finally, on August 17, he "set out for Bedford," accompanied by his young grandson Thomas Jefferson Randolph, then almost fourteen years old.[12] Unlike his trip the year before, this visit is well documented, primarily because of a letter that Jefferson wrote Hugh Chisolm on September 7, 1806, after his return to Monticello. It is, in fact, one of the most illuminating of the many letters that passed between the architect-owner and his builder:

It occurred to me after leaving Poplar Forest that there ought to be some more doors of communication in the rooms of the house below, than what I had marked in the plan given you. I therefore sketched them with a pencil and sent the sketch to you by Mr. Griffin. I now send you a sketch in ink, wherein you will find the following alterations:

1. 4 doors of communication between the rooms below.
2. 2 " between the rooms above.
3. The two porches which I told you I should add.
4. Two stairways necessary for communication between the upper and lower floors without going from under cover.

The porticos & stairways will require some more digging. You must make the space between window & window on the East & West sides, exactly 10 ft. so that the stairway may be placed between without blocking up the windows. Everything is drawn so plainly that no further explanation is necessary. Take care of the drawings as they will be necessary for Mr. Perry, & I do not reserve another copy for him. Accept my best wishes.[13]

Unfortunately, the drawings Jefferson referred to have not been found. The two doors "between the rooms above" that he listed as his second proposed change allowed direct communication between the two main bedrooms and the smaller rooms on either side of the entrance passage (cf. endpapers and fig. 21). Changes 3 and 4 are far more important and show well the transformation going on in Jefferson's thinking at this time. Essentially they show an abstract architectural theoretician becoming a practical housebuilder and owner. Before these two changes were made, the plan of Poplar Forest was a perfect octagon. With them it no longer was. If anything, the overall form now resembled a modified Greek cross as much as anything else. But whatever compromises these changes entailed in the overall form

Fig. 24 To form the forty-five-degree angles required in building an octagonal structure, specially molded squint bricks were necessary. A number of them were used to pave the floor of the wine cellar under the dining room at Poplar Forest. *(Tom Graves, Jr., 1991)*

were more than compensated for by the practical advantages they gained, and although the basic form was changed, the proposed alterations made no changes at all to the original and clever arrangement of spaces within. With change number 3 the front door would now be protected from weather by the front porch, and an auxiliary living space would be provided by the south porch. In addition, that south porch would keep the parlor from being flooded with too much direct sunlight in the summer. Change number 4 was perhaps even more practical. Now the two stories would be connected internally by the two stairways, and now food could be brought to the dining room without being transported through the front door. Without these alterations, Poplar Forest would have remained a perfect octagon. It also would have remained a totally impractical house in which to live.

Even with these changes, as later owners were to find out, Poplar Forest was not the most practical house in which to live. Fiske Kimball, perhaps the first authority on Jefferson's architecture to address the issue, observed that "the use of the central, distributing room as a dining room is an instance of freedom which would not have been admissible had the life at Poplar Forest been less simple." A more recent scholar has stated: "Poplar Forest, for all of its light and air, must have been inconvenient, like all excessively rational buildings: nearly every room was a passageway, either to other rooms or to the stairways."[14]

Jefferson was not designing just a house, however. He was designing a villa, a particular type of structure that has been described in terms that fit Poplar Forest almost perfectly: "A villa is a building in the country designed for its owner's enjoyment and relaxation. Though it may also be the center of an agricultural enterprise, the pleasure factor is what essentially distinguishes the villa residence from the farmhouse and the villa estate from the farm. The farmhouse tends to be simple in structure and to conserve ancient forms that do not require the intervention of a designer. The villa is typically the product of an architect's imagination and asserts its modernity."[15] From classical times forward, such villas have served their owners as places of retreat, places where they could leave the practical requirements, and perhaps some of the responsibilities, of their year-round homes, places where they could indulge in less practical approaches to design. Under the aegis of later owners, Poplar Forest would become a farmhouse soon enough, but in its original conception and design, it was far from that.

Work continued on Poplar Forest during the fall of 1806, and on September 25 Jefferson noted in his Memorandum Book that he had "inclosed to Hugh Chisolm 20. D. to pay for digging & on account." To further assist in the digging and disposal of the dirt, he wrote Edmund Bacon, his overseer at Monticello, on September 29:

"Jerry and his wagon are to go to Bedford before Christmas, and to stay there till they have done all the hauling for my house there." In addition, he told Bacon to have Jerry, who was one of his slaves, take both a bull calf and a young ram with him, and "a pair of fowls, some clover seed, and some cow-peas."[16]

Jefferson returned to Washington the first week in October of 1806, and within the month was already longing to be back home in Virginia. On the twentieth of the month he wrote Martha: "The loneliness of this place is more intolerable than I ever found it. My daily rides too are sickening for want of some interest in the scenes I pass over: and indeed I look over the two ensuing years as the most tedious of my life."[17]

Fortunately, within the week news arrived that alleviated his malaise, if only temporarily. On October 24 Jefferson received a letter that Meriwether Lewis had written a month earlier, announcing that he and William Clark had returned to St. Louis from their westward venture. By the time Lewis arrived back in Washington (most likely on December 28, 1806), he had been away from the President's House a full two-and-a-half years.[18]

In addition to listening to Lewis's tales of his journey after the explorer returned in triumph to Washington, Jefferson found time to compose a letter on a far more mundane subject. Writing James Dinsmore on December 28, he advised: "The window frames at Poplar Forest may be of poplar dug out of the solid, with locust sills; tho' I do not know why the sides and top might not also be of locust dug out of the solid."[19] Whether poplar or locust — or, as it turned out, whether walnut or pine — the fabrication of the window frames was in good hands. James Dinsmore, a native of Northern Ireland, had been with Jefferson almost as long as Hugh Chisolm, having come to Monticello from Philadelphia in 1798. Jefferson had paid for his tools and for his expenses from Philadelphia to Albemarle, and had put Dinsmore in charge of building operations at Monticello. Again like Chisolm, he worked on many other projects in addition to Jefferson's buildings, including James Madison's Montpelier and John Hartwell Cocke's Bremo.[20]

On January 11, 1807, Jefferson noted in his Memorandum Book that he had "inclosed to Burgess Griffin 15. D. to pay stone mason 13.33." That same day he also sent Bacon $245 to be distributed to various workmen, $50 of which was to go to Chisolm. These payments, and the consequent drain on his cash reserves, may have prompted his response that same day to the Reverend Charles Clay, one of his Bedford neighbors, thanking him for letting him know that a parcel of land adjacent to Poplar Forest was for sale. Although he had always wished to purchase the property in question, as it "would straiten the lines of the Poplar Forest," he had to pass up the opportunity. As he had confided to others before, Jefferson told Clay that he had hoped "to keep the expences of my office within the limits of its salary, so as to apply my private income entirely to the improvement and enlargement of my estate," but had been unable to do so.[21]

Jefferson's January 1807 letter to Clay had news of a more worldly sort as well. Aaron Burr's conspiracy to set up a new nation west of the Mississippi still remains a mystery in many respects. Though Jefferson's attempt to explain it to Clay may perhaps be exaggerated, it gives a fine sense of the confusion and threat the incident raised: "Burr's enterprise is the most extraordinary since the days of Don Quixot. It is so extravagant that those who know his understanding would not believe it if the proofs admitted doubt. He has meant to place himself on the throne of Montezuma, and extend his empire to the Allegany seizing on N Orleans as the instrument of compulsion for our Western States."[22] Ultimately, Burr's conspiracy was crushed, but in attempting to have him prosecuted, Jefferson experienced one of the most frustrating episodes of his presidency. The trial, held in Richmond, and presided over by Chief Justice John Marshall, extended from March to September of 1807. Much to the president's regret, it resulted in Burr's acquittal on all charges, both of treason and of misdemeanor.[23]

Throughout the period of the Burr trial, work was going on at a furious pace at Poplar Forest, as shown by the several letters that Jefferson and Chisolm exchanged at the time. Given the frustrations he was simultaneously experiencing as president in Washington, Jefferson probably enjoyed the relief his favorite occupation of "putting up and pulling down" afforded him during this period as much as at any time in his life.

On June 1, 1807, Chisolm wrote: "I thought proper to inform you of my progress made hear since I see you," and proceeded to tell his employer:

The walls are all leavel except the squar room the stone masons is not come to do them yet tho they say that they will be hear in a few days. The south piazer is up to the wartertable the starway I have not done any thing to nor do not intend to do them untill the walls of the house are finished as I had reather put them up after them than to bild them with the out walls of the house as the angles where the join interfear so much with the Line that I work by. I am now ready for the window and door frames[24] (fig. 25).

Chisolm, a bricklayer, apparently didn't want to lay the stone walls of the "squar room" in the basement. Perhaps still smarting from his apparent inability to lay out the octagonal foundation, he also didn't want anything to obstruct the proper angles of the exterior walls of the house until they were completed. Hence his reluctance to start construction on the "starway" that would "interfear so much with the Line that I work by."

Fig. 25 Poplar Forest, arcade under the south portico. On June 1, 1807, master-builder Hugh Chisolm reported to Jefferson that "the south piazer is up to the wartertable." *(Jack E. Boucher, 1986, for the Historic American Buildings Survey, Prints and Photographs Division, Library of Congress)*

Fig. 26 Poplar Forest, south view. To make the house appear as a two-story pavilion from the south, or rear, Jefferson instructed his builder on June 5, 1807, to have the slaves "dig and remove the earth South of the house, 90 feet wide." This view also shows the trees that once lined the upper levels of the sunken lawn. *(C. O. Greene, 1940, for the Historic American Buildings Survey, Prints and Photographs Division, Library of Congress)*

Chisolm also reported that Jerry (who had come back to Poplar Forest from Monticello with his wagon in April) had "done halling for Mr. Perry and is at this time Halling of sand which is a very tegerous Job."[25] Until now, Chisolm and his assistants had been staying with the overseer, Burgess Griffin, and his family, but that situation was to change. Chisolm had just found out that "with a respect of sacking us they charge you a shilling a night which never I knew untill a few days pass." To save his employer what he regarded as an unwarranted expense, he suggested that he could "get ozenburgs for a tick and fill with straw." As far as Jefferson's own accommodations for his next trip were concerned, Chisolm optimistically suggested: "If it be possible for to get a room finished for you agin the time you told me you wood come to see us it shall be certenly done and I think if I go on uninterruptly I shall have it ready, You will please to send me thirty dolars as soon as it is covenient. Except my best wishes."[26] "Ozenburgs" was Chisolm's way of spelling *oznabrig*, or *osnaburg*, which was a coarse linen frequently used for clothing for slaves. In this instance Chisolm planned to used it as a covering for his straw mattress.

Jefferson replied promptly from Washington on June 5, enclosing the thirty dollars Chisolm had requested. He approved Chisolm's plan of "fixing up a bed for yourself," which he felt would "give Mr. Griffin's family as little trouble as possible." He refrained from entering any controversy over Griffin's charge of a shilling per night for "sacking," but offered to pay for "oznabrigs for a straw bed & 2 pr. of sheets, and striped blankets," if Chisolm would purchase them. In fact, he suggested that if Chisolm could perhaps "fix yourself a snug lodging place in the barn I should think it would be more agreeable." Jefferson also expressed the hope that Chisolm "will have finished at Poplar Forest in time to work at Monticello in Aug. and Sep." Regarding the builder's readiness "for the window and door frames," he reminded him: "With respect to door frames, you should recollect that I never have any in my buildings. You are to work up the proper opening for them which you will find in your instructions, & if the window frames are ready it is better to put them up & work the wall to them, but if not ready, they are not to be waited for. They can be put in afterwards, tho' with more trouble."[27]

As a postscript to this letter, Jefferson made a plea and a suggestion. His plea was simply to urge Jerry to hurry his work along, as "we are in great distress for [his] waggon at Monticello." His suggestion was far more involved, and may be regarded as the first reference to landscaping at Poplar Forest. It also provides a remarkable insight into Jefferson's relations with his slave work force:

If you would engage the negroes to dig and remove the earth South of the house, 90 feet wide, down to a foot below the lower floor, and descending from thence due south 1 inch in every 10 ft. till it gets clear out of the ground, I would gladly pay them for it. But it is only with their own free will and undertaking to do it in their own time. The digging and removing is worth a bit a cubic yard. You might lay off separate slipes from the house south till it clears the hill and of such widths as each person or gang chose to undertake: & Mr. Perry may make wheelbarrows sufficient for them, & charge them to me[28] *(fig. 26).*

Apparently Chisolm didn't start right away on the digging. The first notice he seems to have given Jefferson of having engaged anyone to work on this project would not appear until just over a year later, in the summer of 1808. At any rate, what Jefferson described in his postscript was the sunken lawn, a very distinctive feature of the grounds at Poplar Forest. Also referred to as a bowling green, parterre, or swale — to list a few of the names it has been given over the years — the sunken lawn extends from the rear of the basement level of the south facade and enables the house to appear as a full two-story building on that elevation. Though Jefferson didn't suggest in his letter to Chisolm where the dirt that was to be removed in the excavation was to be placed, it is almost certain that it was used in forming the two mounds, one to the east and one to the west of the house, that are also such distinctive features of the Poplar Forest landscape. The mounds may have been started earlier, using earth dug out for the cellar, but it is doubtful that the excavation there would have produced sufficient earth to construct them (fig. 27).

The mounds and the formal south lawn at Poplar Forest recall with unmistakable clarity the landscaping at the President's House, which Jefferson was supervising at about the same time. As was noted above, the formal south lawn at the President's House, which was bordered by flowers and trees, measured approximately 200 feet by 400 feet. Its counterpart at Poplar Forest, which also was planned to be bordered by flowers and trees, was almost exactly half as large, measuring approximately 100 feet (if the five-foot slopes are included as part of it) by 200 feet.[29] Both lawns obviously share the same proportional relationships to the houses they embellish. At Washington, "Jefferson's mounds" were located to the southeast and southwest of the formal lawn, and though they were a conspicuous enough part of the landscaping scheme there, they were not integral to the overall design as their equivalents at Poplar Forest are. The Poplar Forest mounds, which are almost directly east and west of the house, are among the major features of the landscape, and undoubtedly were conceived almost as appendages to the house itself.

Chisolm's June 15 response to Jefferson's June 1, 1807, letter conveyed the message that he was apparently idle "at this time" waiting for another workman, perhaps the stonemason. In response to Jefferson's request to hurry

Jerry in his work, he informed his employer: "Jerry is still hauling sand and as he is to hall all for me I don't expect that he will come down [to Monticello] as soon as you look for him. For there is the water and wood that I never thought of at the time that see you and Griffin says that he will not haul anything."[30] Apparently the stonemason arrived soon afterwards, for on July 6, Jefferson entered in his Memorandum Book the fact that he had "inclosed to Burgess Griffin 100.D. for lime & stonework." It also seems apparent that the relationship between Chisolm and Griffin had not improved since the oznabrig affair.

Jefferson seldom mentioned affairs of state in his correspondence with Chisolm, but he made an exception in a letter he wrote from Monticello on August 5, 1807: "I arrived here yesterday, having been detained at Washington longer than I expected by the extraordinary occurrences in the Chesapeake. A post comes here to me every day to inform me of the daily proceedings of the British, so that I am tied here, as it were, and am altogether uncertain when I can proceed to Poplar forest."[31]

The occurrences in the Chesapeake were indeed extraordinary, and brought to a climax problems that had been festering throughout his presidency. On June 22, 1807, while Aaron Burr's trial was being adjudicated in Richmond, the American ship *Chesapeake* was fired upon and boarded by the captain and crew of H.M.S. *Leopard*, just off Cape Henry, Virginia, in an illegal search for British seamen who had deserted the Royal Navy. This affair and the continuing negotiations it prompted plagued Jefferson's second term, and were in part responsible for his imposition of an embargo on December 22, 1807. The embargo, in addition to being ultimately unsuccessful, was by all odds the most unpopular act Jefferson ever sponsored or approved during his presidency. It was particularly detested in New England, whose whole economy depended on maritime interests.

Not all the news on the national scene was bad that year. On June 8, 1807, Jefferson had enclosed a payment to Chisolm in a note to his Bedford friend James Steptoe, and along with the payment added: "Supposing that Lt. Pike's journey up the Mississippi & his map may be acceptable to Mr. Steptoe, he incloses him a copy of each, and salutes him with friendship & respect." Zebulon Pike, whose two western expeditions followed those of Lewis and Clark, wrote to the president on October 29, 1807, that he had collected skins of various animals and "various examples of the Industry and advancement of the Arts amongst the spanish missions, or civilized Indians."[32] As with the Lewis and Clark expedition, the journeys of Lieutenant Pike added immeasurably to the store of knowledge about the people and resources of the lands to the west of what was then America's frontier.

In August 1807, John Wayles Eppes wrote a note to Jef-

ferson that contained what must have been welcome news: "I have recently passed a few weeks at my new purchase. I find it a very pleasant situation.... It is about four miles from Wilis's Mountain of which I have a fine view." Eppes's new purchase, to which he moved permanently several years later, was Millbrook, or as he generally wrote it, Mill Brook, in Buckingham County. In November 1810 he wrote his former father-in-law that he was "now occupied in fixing a permanent residence here," and invited Jefferson to visit "in some of your trips to Bedford."[33] Millbrook was to remain his home, or at least his home base, for the rest of his life, and Jefferson would find the time to visit on several of his trips between Monticello and Poplar Forest. Eppes's move provided a final answer at last to the questions of clearing the land, grading the site, and building a house at Pantops. It did not, however, resolve the question of the land itself.

When he was finally able to make his fall trip to Poplar Forest in 1807, Jefferson did "proceed to Bedford almost without stopping in Albemarle," as he had planned to do when Chisolm needed him so desperately the year before. Leaving Washington on September 8, 1807, he was on his way to Bedford on the eleventh. One of the first orders of business on his arrival was to send Jerry and the wagon back to Monticello, and he noted in his Memorandum Book on September 15 that he "gave Jerry for his expenses home 1. D." He was home in record time himself, arriving back at Monticello on September 17. Chisolm may well have accompanied him, for he was soon reported to be at work at Monticello. Little is known of Jefferson's activities during this extremely short stay in Bedford, but work had at least progressed to the extent that he could begin to think of furniture for his new house. On September 26, just before he left Monticello to return to Washington, he wrote William Couch, owner of a fleet of river boats at the hamlet of Warren in Albemarle County, asking him to see to the shipment "by your boats" of certain items, among them "3 dozen chairs to be sent for me from Richmond to Lynchburg, where they will be received by the house of Wm. Brown and noted to Burgess Griffin my overseer at Poplar forest."[34] As it turned out, that shipment was apparently never attended to, for two years later Jefferson had to repeat the order with a different merchant — the second time with more success (see chap. XI).

On October 16, 1807, James Dinsmore reported to Jefferson that Chisolm was working at Monticello, but he was still concerned about the window sash for Poplar Forest: "You expressed a wish to have the sashes for Poplar Forest made of walnut. If you still desire it you will please to let me know that we may have the walnut got to kiln dry along with the plank. I would beg leave however to observe that I am afraid there is none to be had about here but what is so much given to warp that it will render it very unfit for that purpose." Jefferson responded to his inquiry on October 25: "I should certainly prefer walnut for the Bedford sashes, because well rubbed on the inside and unpainted it has a richer look than a painted sash, and I believe no wood is more durable but if you cannot get it good, then certainly good pine will be preferable to bad walnut. It must therefore depend on your being able to get good walnut and without delaying the work. The sashes for the lower rooms may be of pine."[35]

By this time Jefferson was making additional arrangements not only for the building of Poplar Forest, but for its use. He had already ordered chairs, and on November 7, 1807, he sent a letter to George Jefferson, his cousin and partner in the Richmond firm of Gibson and Jefferson, agents and factors who would handle an increasing workload for the former president when he moved back to Virginia for good. His letter advised his cousin to expect some boxes that he was having shipped to Richmond, one of which contained "crockery ware for my use in Bedford, & specially directed on a card on the top to be sent up by Mr. Couch's boats belonging to Warren, as he will see to the stage conveyance to Lynchburg."[36]

On December 11, John Perry, another of Jefferson's builders, had written a note from Monticello informing him that "the ruff of the Bedford house is framed and will be sheeted by Christmas." Four days later, Jefferson wrote Chisolm, still at Monticello, with instructions concerning the work he wished performed there "before you go to Bedford" in the spring.[37] About the same time he was corresponding with Chisolm and Perry, Jefferson sent a memorandum to Edmund Bacon at Monticello. Among the many tasks he wanted Bacon to attend to during the ensuing year, was to "get from Mr. Perry and Mr. Dinsmore, an estimate of all the nails we shall want for the house in Bedford; and when you have no orders to execute for others, let the boys be making them, and keep them separate from all others; and when the wagon goes up at Christmas, send what then shall be ready."[38]

Two days after Christmas 1807, Jefferson again wrote Elizabeth Trist, informing her of the health of his family and friends, and direly predicting that "the ensuing year will be the longest year of my life."[39] The ensuing year would, at any rate, be the last full year of his term of office as president, but whether he recalled it or not, Jefferson had complained almost verbatim to his daughter Martha in 1792 when he had been secretary of state in Washington's cabinet. Whether 1808 would seem to be the longest year of his life or not, it would at least soon be over. Throughout that year, as he had during the last, Jefferson would continue to find respite from his duties as president by overseeing the construction of the new house that he would come to enjoy so much in the future.

Fig. 27 West mound, with necessary, 1943. Presumably, the mounds on either side of the house were constructed from dirt taken from the excavations of the south lawn. *(The Corporation for Jefferson's Poplar Forest)*

"A Very Great Improvement to Look of the House"
(1808)

Early in January 1808, Jefferson wrote his daughter Martha, assessing his financial situation, and speculating on the future. He was "retiring from office loaded with serious debts, which will materially affect the tranquility of my retirement." Those debts, he confided, would also prevent him from assisting her husband in paying off some of the Randolph family debts, as he had planned to do. Still, he was hopeful that if the Randolphs, who were then living at Edgehill, near Monticello, would live with him, income from her husband's estate could then be "employed for meeting his own difficulties." Their income from the crops would see them through, and at least they had their lands, which, "if we preserve them, are sufficient to place all the children in independence."[1]

Martha's response to her father's letter proved her mettle: "The subject of your last letter has cast a gloom over my spirits that I can not shake off. The impossibility of paying serious debts by crops, and living at the same time, has been so often proved, that I am afraid you should trust to it. If by any sacrifice of the Bedford lands you can relieve your self from the pressure of debt I conjure you not to think of the children, your own happiness is alone to be considered. Let not the tranquility of your old age be disturbed and we shall do well."[2]

No matter his precarious financial situation, nor the increasingly onerous duties of his last year as president. Neither affected progress on his newest architectural engagement. Throughout the year a flurry of letters passed back and forth between Jefferson and his workmen, both at Poplar Forest and at Monticello, attesting to the work going on. Just before the close of the previous year, on December 29, 1807, Jefferson had written Dinsmore again from Washington, asking if window glass had been obtained yet "for the Bedford sashes," and requesting him to "let me know by the return of post, that I may immediately provide for it." On the first day of the new year, Dinsmore informed him that "there has not been any glass got, for the Bedford sashes," and sent a list of the number of panes and sizes needed for both Monticello and Poplar Forest. Toward the end of the month, Dinsmore followed that note with another: "We must make the sashes for P. Forest so soon as it is dry that Mr. Barry may get them glazed before he quits here."[3] Mr. Barry was Richard Barry, who had arrived at Monticello on March 28, 1805, and was employed by Jefferson for several years as a painter and glazier.[4] Jefferson responded to Dinsmore's letters on February 6, 1808, with bad news. The glass for the Poplar Forest sashes couldn't leave Philadelphia until the ice-bound Delaware River thawed in the spring. He had better news late in March. On the eighteenth of that month, he had sent eight boxes of glass "from [Washington] to Alexandria to be forwarded by the first vessel to Richmond." He wisely sent more than Dinsmore had requested, "in order to have a supply for breakage."[5]

Hugh Chisolm had spent the winter at Monticello, and on February 17, 1808, he wrote his employer concerning preparations for brickmaking there and at Poplar Forest: "We have got the earth turned up the second time for the bricks and are now prepare the yard to lay them on. I wanted to propose to you for the bricks to be maid at Poplar Forest at the same time of making things here for it is not necessary for both of us to attend to making bricks at one place. I can send my Brother to Bedford or can go myself, and then the brickmaking will all be finished at both places in the same time. I hope it will suit you in this way, and pleas to let me now next post."[6]

In his answer, Jefferson authorized Chisolm to carry "on the brickmaking at Poplar Forest at the same time as at Monticello." According to notes Chisolm made later that year, his brother, John, started work at Poplar Forest on March 10. Chisolm did not join him until some time later.[7] On March 19, Edmund Bacon informed Jefferson in a somewhat garbled manner that Chisolm was not quite on schedule with his work at Monticello:

You directed Sir I should send the waggon with Mr. Chisholm to Bedford in February. But Mr. Chisholm did not go and I considered as he was not ready to go to Bedford, it was not worth while to send the waggon as Mr. Chisholm said it was to haul for him. And I have thought it best to let you no of the waggons not going as perhaps you would wish me to send the load it was to carry (without waiting any longer for Mr. Chisholm). I am informed the wirk man in Bedford is in want of more nails which I dont know whether you would wish me to send or for Mr. Griffin to send for them. I sent to Bedford By Jerry 700 pounds of nails last year.[8]

Jefferson responded to Bacon's letter on March 22: "The waggon must not go to Bedford before Mr. Chisolm goes. It will not be wanting there till they are proceeding to burn the brick kiln which must not be till Mr. Chisolm is there himself. Whatever nails are wanting in Bedford must be sent. If you can deliver them at Warren to Mr. Couch he will deliver them to Mr. Brown my merchant at Lynchburg." Once again he had to add a postscript: "Pray expedite Mr Chisolm in his brickmaking etc. at Monticello as much as you possibly can."[9] As it turned out, the wagon was to go long before Hugh Chisolm did.

A week later, on March 29, Jefferson corresponded with John Perry about the flooring at Poplar Forest, sharing the benefit of knowledge that he had acquired in

Europe, as well as his own familiarity with the characteristics of various woods: "The floor at Poplar forest being intended for an under floor must be laid with oak. Poplar would not hold the nails, and pine is too distant & dear. All the floors of Europe are of oak, so are the decks of ships. Good nailing will secure it against warping. Perhaps it may be easier done in herring bone, as the hall floor at Monticello was. In that case your sleepers should be but 14. I. from center to center, in order that the plank may be cut into two feet lengths."[10]

In April, Jefferson received good news and bad news: the former from Dinsmore, the latter from Bacon. Dinsmore reported the glass had arrived in good condition, though Jefferson had sent the wrong sizes for "the inner window of the dining room [at Monticello]." Bacon recounted that he had been "constantly pushing M. Chisolm with his work but he is rather slower than he might be."[11]

Jefferson visited Monticello in May 1808, but intended to wait until his longer summer visit to go to Poplar Forest. Upon his return to Washington in June, he wrote both Bacon and Dinsmore. To Bacon he suggested: "As soon as the sashes are ready for Bedford, furnish Mr. Randolph 3 of your best hands, instead of his waterman, who are to carry the sashes, tables, and other things up to Lynchburg, and to give notice of their arrival to Mr. Chisolm, who will then be in Bedford, and will have Jerry's wagon there, which he must send for the things to Lynchburg. In the mean time, they must be lodged at Mr. Brown's, at Lynchburg. Jerry is to go to Bedford with his wagon as soon as Mr. Chisolm goes." To Dinsmore, he recalled that he had "observed about a dozen gutters of sheet iron lying out in front of the kitchen" during his recent visit to Monticello. Supposing these were not needed there, he asked: "Would it not be well to send 8 of them to Bedford for the gutters of the two porticos?" Dinsmore answered on June 24. The window sashes were still not ready, but everything else was:

I have packed up to go with the waggon this day for P. F. 4 tables 2 mattresses 2 oznaburg beds 2 bolsters & pillows, 2 pair of sheets, 2 stoves, 57 metal sash wts and 12 pieces of sheet iron and a small piece of sheet lead for the gutters. We concluded it best to send the tables and beds by the waggon — as the sashes will not be ready before harvest. I have sent all the sheet iron that was left from John Perrys roof which will be sufficient for 4 gutters 17 feet long each which I hope will do as I could not venture to send any of the wide sheets that were for the gutters of the ballustrade.[12]

Bacon responded to Jefferson with an abbreviated message giving essentially the same information, and added that "Jerry left heare last satterday set of for Bedford with a load of the articles you directed to go by him. The Boat has not started yet. The window sashes are not done glaseing."[13]

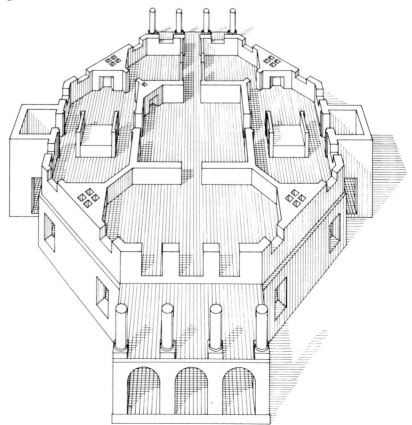

Fig. 28 Poplar Forest, perspective plan. The alcoves for the beds, which were built in 1808, are seen in the middle of the two bedrooms to either side of the central room. (*Tim Buehner, delineator, 1991*)

Still worried about the windows, Jefferson asked Dinsmore on June 27: "You mention no window cord sent to Poplar Forest. If none is gone, and you have it not, let me know it by return of post and how much, & I will get it here and forward it on." On July 1, Dinsmore assured him: "We have three twists of sash cord to spare from here which will be sufficient for twelve windows and will nearly do all the weights." He had not mentioned them because "the waggon was obliged to leave the sash weights behind being overloaded so that we must send them and the cord along with the sashes, which will be ready in a fortnight." He added: "Mr. Chisolm will start for Poplar Forest in a few days."[14]

According to his own records, Chisolm completed his work at Monticello on July 6, 1808.[15] Two weeks later he wrote Jefferson from Poplar Forest, proudly listing all that he had accomplished since that time. Though he did not mention his brother by name, he at least referred to him in using the plural *we* in his report. As John Chisolm had by then been at Poplar Forest more than four months, as opposed to Hugh's two weeks, the lion's share of credit should be accorded him:

It is my wish to inform you, how we are coming on with our work at this place. We have burnt the bricks, and a finer kiln I never burnt in my life, it contains seventy five thousand. We made the bricks for the basis and capts. of the columns as I thought it would make a better job than to have them of wood. We are at this time runing the starways, as for the diging what I showed you at Monticello was a fact. I brought my boys from Albemarle, and made laborers of them, and I set fill [sic] to diging, and I mean to keep him at it as long as I am hear, for I think it as necessary job as can be done to the Building. I hope you will approve of it. When the starways are done, I mean to run the columns next. Mr. Perry has laid the flow in west room and is now studing the alcove, as soon as he is done that I shall bricknog and plaster it for your reception. With a respect to lasths I can get good pine for ash [?] and it will be a very good exchange for that purpose and the pine is very convenient, if you approve of this exchange you will please to let now. I hope to see you at Poplar Forest as soon as you make it convenient[16] *(fig. 28).*

The decision—which Chisolm claimed as his own—to make the bases and capitals of the columns of brick was certainly a wise one, but it would hardly seem that Jefferson would have directed the bases and capitals to be of wood if the shafts themselves were to be of brick. In fact, Chisolm's letter recalls correspondence four years earlier between Jefferson and Benjamin Henry Latrobe concerning the columns for the House of Representatives in Washington. In 1804, Jefferson had inquired of Latrobe:

Would it not be best to make the internal columns of well-burnt brick, moulded in portions of circles adapted to the

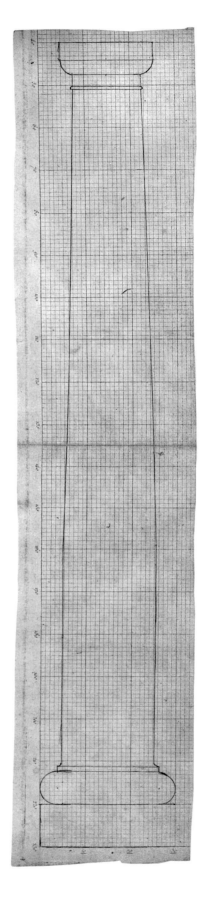

Fig. 29 Tuscan column. Jefferson drew this elevation of a column for the University of Virginia. It is of the same order as those in the porticoes at Poplar Forest. *(Thomas Jefferson Papers, Manuscripts Division, Special Collections Department, University of Virginia, Charlottesville)*

diminution of the columns? Burlington, in his notes on Palladio, tells us that he found most of the buildings erected under Palladio's direction, and described in his architecture, to have their columns made of brick in this way and covered with stucco. I know an instance of a range of six or eight columns in Virginia, twenty feet high, well proportioned and properly diminished, executed by a common bricklayer. The bases and capitals would of course be of hewn stone.[17]

Obviously Jefferson felt the state of architecture in the commonwealth had improved since the time he had written in his *Notes on Virginia* that "a workman could scarcely be found here capable of drawing an order." At Poplar Forest, not only the shafts but also the bases and capitals, as Chisolm informed Jefferson, are of molded brick, which, like the shafts, were then stuccoed. Whether Chisolm could *draw* an order or not, he could at least build one.

Perhaps it is not surprising that Chisolm made no mention of the particular order that he was using for his "basis and capts. of the columns," but it is certain that he had specific instructions from Jefferson on that score. In classical architecture, every proportion of a building is properly dependent upon the column and its diameter. The accurate dimensioning and positioning of the columns establish modules, and these in turn define the proportions throughout the rest of the building; not things that Thomas Jefferson would have left to the discretion of his builder.[18] Exact proportions for each classical order, however, were not universal. They depended on which particular book of classical architectural sources an architect-builder might use.

Jefferson chose the Tuscan order, the simplest of the Roman orders, to govern the proportions of Poplar Forest (fig. 29). That in itself is somewhat surprising, as he was later quoted as having said "the Tuscan order was too plain — it would do for your barns, etc., but was not fit for a dwelling House."[19] As evidence that — even in architecture — Jefferson didn't always practice what he preached, he more than once employed the Tuscan order for buildings other than barns. He used it in his contemporary work on the offices at the President's House (see fig. 15), and was also to choose it for the colonnades connecting the pavilions on the Lawn at the University of Virginia (see fig. 73). Perhaps he selected it for Poplar Forest because it was one of the easiest orders to execute, a consideration of some importance as he was having to supervise the building operations from a distance.

Which of his several architectural volumes Jefferson consulted to decide on the particular model for the Tuscan order at Poplar Forest is unknown. He could have turned to several editions of Palladio that he owned, and may well have chosen Giacomo Leoni's *The Architecture of A. Palladio; in Four Books* (London, 1715), the same book that he used for the exterior Doric order at Monti-

cello.[20] In fact, the proportional relationships in the Tuscan Order established in that volume comport more closely with those at Poplar Forest than do the proportions in other known sources that Jefferson might have used. Freart de Chambray's *Parallele de l'Architecture antique avec la modern* (Paris 1766) is another possibility, or he could have consulted Charles Antoine Jombert's 1764 *Architecture de Palladio*, which he is known to have used later at the University of Virginia (fig. 30). As this latter edition was relatively small and easily transported, it would have had its advantages as an on-site guide for Chisolm to follow. In fact, the year before Chisolm went to Bedford, Jefferson had lent it to James Oldham in Richmond: "I send you my portable edition, which I value.... it contains only the 1st book on the orders, which is the essential part."[21]

In their present state, the columns at Poplar Forest are not correctly proportioned according to any published source that Jefferson is known to have owned, as their

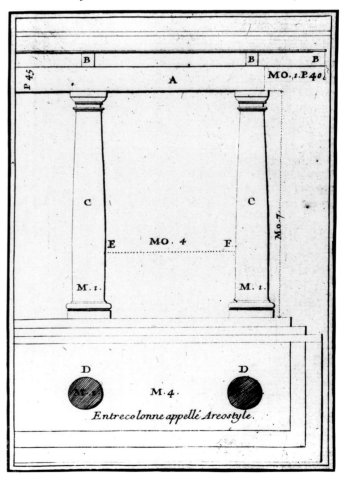

Fig. 30 Tuscan columns. Plate 2 from Charles Antoine Jombert's *Architecture de Palladio* (1764) shows the spacing and proper proportions of the Tuscan order. *(Rare Books Division, Special Collections Department, University of Virginia Library, Charlottesville)*

diameters are too short for their height (figs. 31 and 32). Only with a thicker coating of stucco, or rendering, than is now present would the proportions be correct according to the dictates of Leoni's *Palladio*. At Monticello, the brick columns of the west portico have extremely thick coatings, and more than likely those at Poplar Forest were similarly treated originally. As Jefferson noted in his letter to Latrobe concerning the capitol in Washington, such had been the generally accepted method used by the master, Palladio, himself.

Chisolm followed his July 22, 1808, progress report with one on September 4, in which he summarized a phenomenal amount of work accomplished during the interim:

I think proper to inform you how we come on with our work, I have done both of the stairways and one of the necessary, and in the course of this week I will have the other done, we have also run the columns for the South portaco and I think they will, when finished be elegant. The west room is finished in the manner which you told me. I still keep fill [sic] at the diging, and give him all the assistance that I possible can, it seem to go on tolerable smooth but slaugh, tho they is a very great improvement to look of the house besides the benefit by what digging, is already done. I woud be glad to see you hear if it is not in your power to come soon it would be necessary for you to give me some instructions about the kitchen as I shall be ready for it in eight or ten days from this time.[22]

Fig. 31 Poplar Forest, north (left) and south (right) portico elevations, as they appeared in the late twentieth century. The columns survived the fire of 1845, but the pediment was not replaced in the subsequent rebuilding of the south portico. *(Drawing, 1985, Historic American Buildings Survey, Prints and Photographs Division, Library of Congress)*

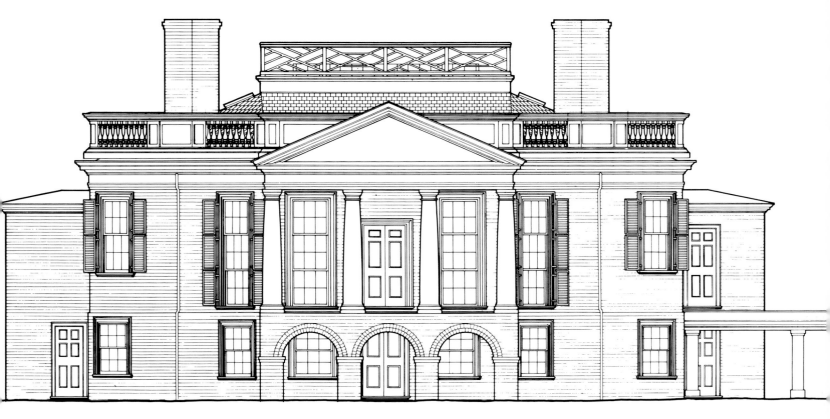

Fig. 32 Poplar Forest, south elevation. This drawing, based on actual measurements of the existing fabric and using proportions derived from the Tuscan order, shows the south facade as it would have appeared when originally completed under Jefferson's aegis. This drawing differs in several respects from the drawing of the same elevation attributed to John Neilson (see endpaper). *(Courtesy Mesick-Cohen-Waite, Architects, 1992)*

Chisolm's reports of July 22 and September 4, 1808, are among the most important records that remain to chronicle the actual construction of Poplar Forest. The earlier of the two gives verbal confirmation of the existence of the alcove beds, or at least one of them, and his announcement that as soon as Perry had finished the framework for the alcove, he [Chisolm] "shall bricknog and plaster it for your reception" reveals that this feature was of far more durable construction than might otherwise have been supposed. Chisolm's stating in his second report that "the west room is finished in the manner which you told me," along with his earlier notation that he would finish its bed alcove "for your reception," strongly hints that the west bedroom was to be Jefferson's own, a fact that later correspondence seems to prove as well. Chisolm's letters also report the construction and finishing of the stairways, which, he had informed Jefferson the previous summer, he had not intended to work on "untill the walls of the house are finished" because their projections would interfere with the lines he worked by.[23] Obviously, that was no longer a problem, as the main walls had by now been completed (fig. 33).

In addition to construction on the house itself, Chisolm's 1808 summer reports tell of other work as well. In the same sentence in his September 4 letter in which he announced the completion of both stairways, he told Jefferson that he had finished "one of the necessary, and in course of this week I will have the other done."[24] This is the only reference yet found that documents the building of two of the most exceptional features of the Poplar Forest complex, and two of the least changed — the delightful, matching privies that echo, on a much reduced scale, the shape and form of the main house (fig. 34). Having mastered the fine art of laying octagonal foundations on the main house (thanks to Jefferson's help), Chisolm must have laid the foundations of these greatly reduced versions with ease. That their construction moved along swiftly is certainly evident from the timing indicated in his report.

The design heritage of these two necessaries, as privies were generally called at the time, is far more sophisticated than the uses for which they were constructed would suggest. Other examples of garden "temples" or ornaments that combine architectural form with utilitarian function can be found throughout European landscapes of the eighteenth and early-nineteenth centuries. While rarer, American examples can be cited as well, among them the two octagonal necessaries which serve as focal points in the gardens at George Washington's Mount Vernon. Later residents and observers have generally assumed that the mounds at Poplar Forest were specifically located to hide the necessaries from view from the house, but that contention is easily refuted

Fig. 33 Poplar Forest, west facade, 1912. Hugh Chisolm reported finishing the stairways, meaning the stair pavilions, on September 4, 1808. This, one of the earliest known photographs of the house, shows the west pavilion with its lunette window that originally lit the stairway inside. *(The Corporation for Jefferson's Poplar Forest)*

by the sophistication of their design (fig. 35). If, indeed, the necessaries were meant to be hidden from view, there was no need to expend the talent, time, or money on them that Jefferson obviously did. Located as they are, close to the house and the mounds, they should be regarded primarily as integral parts of Jefferson's overall design for his retreat. And, as recent investigations at the house have suggested, they may not even have been quite as "necessary" as once supposed. In addition to these outdoor facilities, Poplar Forest was apparently equipped during Jefferson's time with an indoor privy, located at ground level, under the stairway of the western pavilion.[25]

In his letter of July 22, Chisolm somewhat cryptically informed Jefferson that another phase of work, digging out the sunken lawn, had begun, and in his September 4 letter, that it was continuing. While he never specifically referred to this operation, his mention in the first that he had "set fill to diging" and in the second that he "still keep fill at the diging"— coupled with his observation in both missives that the work was both necessary and beneficial — certainly points to this as the work involved. In the postscript of his letter of the previous summer to Chisolm, Jefferson had suggested that his slaves could excavate and grade the sunken lawn, had offered to pay them for the work, and suggested that Mr. Perry could provide the necessary wheelbarrows. Apparently only one of the slaves, Phill (a.k.a. "fill") Hubbard, had taken

him up on the offer, and presumably the fill that Phill obtained from his digging was used to construct the mounds between the house and the necessaries. If so, Phill must not have gauged the placement of his wheelbarrow loads very well, as the two mounds do not align on the east-west axis of the house as Jefferson undoubtedly intended (fig. 36). Their nonalignment consequently seems to have thrown Chisolm off in positioning the foundations of the necessaries as well. Though each necessary at least occupies an identical position in relation to its adjacent mound, the two are not in line with each other, nor do they align with the cross-axis of the house.

Although Chisolm, his brother John, and their workers had accomplished what they had set out to do on the house, outbuildings, and lawn in a remarkably short time, they were far from finished. According to Chisolm's September 4 report, they would be ready "in eight or ten days" to build another important outbuilding, the kitchen. The location of this first kitchen that served the house then being built at Poplar Forest is a matter for speculation. As was noted above (see chap. V), Jefferson had drawn a plan for a kitchen-wash house, along with other outbuildings, in an earlier scheme for Poplar Forest, and had written instructions for it to be fifty feet east from the center of the dwelling house (see figs. 18 and 19). Whether that specific location was chosen in 1808 may never be established. A wing that Jefferson built later,

Fig. 34 West necessary. As in the main house, specially molded bricks were used to form the angles of this diminutive octagonal structure and its twin to the east. *(Jack E. Boucher, 1986, for the Historic American Buildings Survey, Prints and Photographs Division, Library of Congress)*

and which included a kitchen among its suite of rooms, extended a distance of 100 feet to the east of the main house. Grading that was undertaken in preparing for that wing eliminated any evidence that may have existed of an earlier kitchen on a portion of that spot (see Chap. X).

Jefferson did not respond to Chisolm's letter of July 22 until September 8, 1808, nor had he by then received Chisolm's report of September 4. His delay in writing was probably due to the fact that he had planned to be at Poplar Forest long before then. Unfortunately, "a hurt which [he] recieved in riding" at Monticello not only prevented that, it had confined him "to the house a considerable time," and ultimately kept him from going at all during this visit to Virginia. Assuming that this might prove to be the case, he implored Chisolm:

Should I not [visit Poplar Forest], I must pray you to leave your part of the work compleat, and to have all rubbish from the cellar and round about the house within the terrases removed. I wish to know what progress Phill has made in the digging, and would have him continue at it under your direction and Mr. Perry's as long as either of you are at work there, and then to come home. If I do not go to Bedford I will send you the 20 D. you desired. I hope you made the exchange of the laths you mentioned without waiting for my approbation. As soon as you have finished at Poplar Forest, Mr. Madison desires to employ you in making bricks this fall at his house, which I presume he will want laid next spring. Whether by

time or the job, I know not. You had better write to him stating your own terms. Mr. Dinsmore goes to work for him about Christmas. I shall have a small job for you here in the spring.

P.S. I think I desired you to plaister the South & East rooms below for Mr. Griffin's family to go into when they chuse.[26]

Jefferson had written Madison three days earlier regarding Chisolm's proposed future employment there, and gave him a well-deserved round of praise: "Mr. Dinsmore informs me you wish to employ Hugh Chisolm, a bricklayer now working for me in Bedford, if I have no occasion for him. He will probably finish for me this month; after which I shall have nothing more for him the present year. I will write to him on the subject of your desire. He is a very good humored man, works as well as most of our bricklayers, and has had the benefit of becoming familiar with many things, with which they are unacquainted."[27] He was kind enough not to mention Chisolm's occasional lapses with schedules.

In addition to his injury, there was another event that prevented Jefferson from going to Poplar Forest before returning to Washington late in the summer of 1808. On September 17, his eldest grandchild, Anne Cary Randolph, and Charles Lewis Bankhead were married at Monticello. On the wedding day, her parents presented her with her dowry: "One full third part in quantity of the tract of land held and owned in fee simple by the said [Martha] in the county of Bedford and containing by estimation 1450 acres . . . being part of the larger tract of

Fig. 35 West necessary, rear view. This view also shows the mound beyond that rises between the house and the privy. *(Jack E. Boucher, 1986, for the Historic American Buildings Survey, Prints and Photographs Division, Library of Congress)*

land known by the name of The Poplar Forest."[28] It was a portion of the land that Jefferson had given Martha upon her own marriage, and the gift marked the third generation of the Jefferson family that had inherited part of the original Poplar Forest tract. By November Jefferson reported to Martha that the Bankheads "think of settling ultimately at Poplar Forest. It is a fine establishment & good neighborhood."[29]

On September 23, 1808, six days after the wedding, Hugh Chisolm stopped by Monticello on his way to see Secretary of State James Madison at Montpelier before he left Virginia for Washington. Jefferson provided him with a letter of introduction to his new employer, announcing that "the bearer is Mr. Chisolm the bricklayer who wished to see you before your departure," and also offered several suggestions, which he credited to Dinsmore, for improving Montpelier.[30] Jefferson himself departed for Washington several days later, while Chisolm returned to Poplar Forest to finish up before beginning his work for Madison. He stayed in Bedford only a short while, and on October 20, from Montpelier, sent Jefferson his final progress report, at last giving proper credit to his brother, John, and abandoning his phonetic approach in spelling Phill Hubbard's name:

I left Poplar forest the 7th of this month and likewise told Phill what he was to do and left my brother there to plaister the too rooms that you wanted done, as the floors was not laid

and the season for brickmaking so far advanced I could not wait myself for the carpenters work, and my Brother will work as fast as the carpenters, my not waiting for the plaistering I hope will make no difference. I look for him now every day from there and if you have not sent the money on to Poplar forrist that I ast, you will please to send $35 dollars there and stop $10 for me at Orange Court House and you will much oblige your friend and well wisher. You will send it to John R. Chisolm at Poplar Forest.[31]

According to a note Hugh Chisolm made of the dates he and his brother had worked at Poplar Forest, John had begun on March 10 and had finished on November 4. Including the work Hugh had done at Monticello that year, he tallied his own time as "7 months & 24 days." John had clocked in almost as much, working "7 months & 20 days." Each of the brothers had received twenty dollars per month, the figure that Jefferson and Hugh had agreed upon in September 1805. The Chisolms had also had the help of "too Boys from february 9th to oct. 2d," who together had labored "201 days at 4/6 per day." In addition to his salary, Chisolm also charged Jefferson for "16 gallons of whiskey at Poplar forrest at 3/6 per gallon"[32] (fig. 37).

Though he was not in charge at Montpelier, where he worked under the supervision of James Dinsmore, Hugh Chisolm would perform equally well there, and was responsible for brickmaking, underpinning the house,

Fig. 36 Poplar Forest, site plan, 1985. The sunken lawn, or swale, to the south of the house is shown in this drawing, as are the two mounds, to right and left, that were presumably created from the excavation. The mounds are not in an axial alignment with the house. (*Historic American Buildings Survey, Prints and Photographs Division, Library of Congress*)

and many other tasks.[33] Even before he rendered his final account to Madison in January 1814, he had returned to Jefferson's employ, to work again at Poplar Forest.

With all the time and energy Jefferson spent on seeing to the progress at Poplar Forest, not to mention the work still under way at Monticello, it seems remarkable that he had any time at all to attend to his official duties during his last year as president of the United States. Though his habitual loneliness was abated during the winter of 1807–08 when John Wayles Eppes, who was serving in Congress, and his son Francis stayed with him at the President's House, there was hardly anything else pleasant about his last year in Washington. The embargo had completely failed to achieve its purpose, and a resolution to repeal its main provisions was passed late in his administration, to take effect soon after the end of his term. In the very last week of his presidency, the Senate unanimously rejected Jefferson's nomination of William Short as minister to Russia. The day that happened, he once more took refuge in a letter to Martha, declaring yet again how he looked "with infinite joy to the moment when I shall be ultimately moored in the midst of my affections, and free to follow the pursuits of my choice."[34] At least he could take comfort in the fact that James Madison, his able secretary of state, had been elected his successor as the nation's fourth president, with a margin of 122 electoral votes to 49.

At long last, after the trial of Aaron Burr and the tribulation of the embargo, Jefferson's second term was over. In writing to Madame de Corny, a friend from his long-ago days in Paris, just before his term ended, he prophesied a fitting, peaceful finis to his many years of public service: "I at length detach myself from public life, which I never loved, to retire to the bosom of my family my friends, my farm and books, which I have always loved. I retire in hearty affection with the world, because indeed the world has been kinder to me than I claimed." He was a bit more graphic in a letter he wrote the same day to another French friend, Pierre Samuel duPont de Nemours. His postscript added a definite prosaic note to his poetry: "Within a few days I retire to my family, my books, and farms & having gained the harbor myself, shall look on my friends still buffeting the storm, with anxiety indeed, but not with envy. Never did a prisoner, released from his chains, feel such relief as I shall on shaking off the shackles of power. P. S. If you return to us, bring a couple of pair of true-bred Shepherd's dogs. You will add a valuable possession to a country now beginning to pay great attention to the raising [of] sheep."[35]

The "longest year of his life" was over. While tranquillity may have eluded Jefferson during his years of public service, now, on the eve of what he considered his retirement, he would begin to do his best to achieve it. At Poplar Forest, more than anywhere else, he would come closest to that goal, even to the raising of sheep.

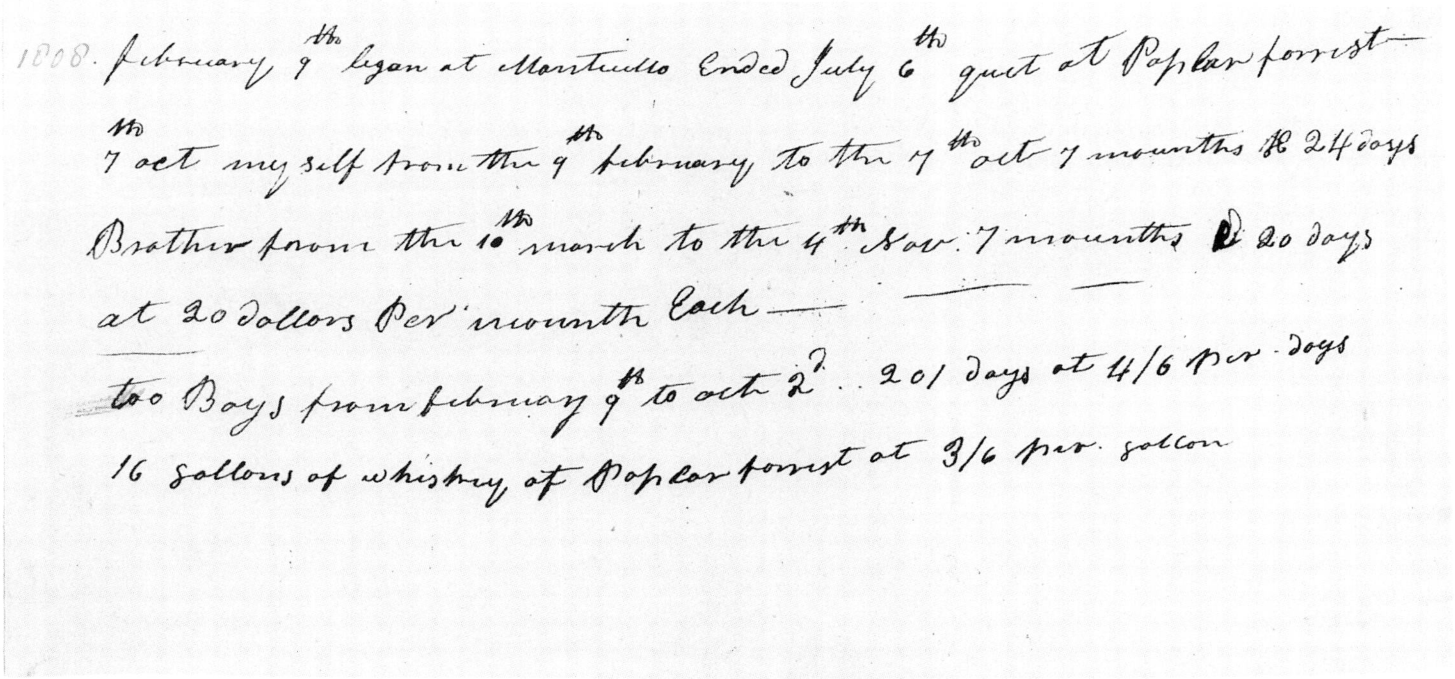
1808. february 9th began at Monticello Ended July 6th quit at Poplar forrest—
7th oct my self from the 9th february to the 7th oct 7 mounths & 24 days
Brother from the 10th march to the 4th Nov. 7 mounths & 20 days
at 20 dollors Per mounth Each—
too Boys from february 9th to oct 2d.. 201 days at 4/6 per. days
16 gollons of whiskey at Poplar forrest at 3/6 per. gollon

Fig. 37 Hugh Chisolm's note recording the time he and his brother worked at Poplar Forest in 1808. Notice the last item.
(Coolidge Collection, Massachusetts Historical Society)

"QUITE AT LEISURE"
(1809–11)

By the time Jefferson left the presidency, a great deal of work had been accomplished on the house, the outbuildings, and the grounds at Poplar Forest. Just as much remained to be done, however, and in truth, the house could have been described as nothing more than a shell. The walls were up, and the roof was sheathed but not shingled. Some flooring had been laid, but that work was far from complete. None of the rooms on the main floor had been plastered. Doors were yet to be hung, trim had not been applied, the lunette windows lighting the stairways had not yet been installed. Perhaps needless to say, no painting of walls, or of any woodwork that might have been in place, had been accomplished.

Hugh Chisolm had departed, but Phill Hubbard, the excavator extraordinaire, who had been in Bedford at least since July 1808, was still at work in the yard, digging out the sunken lawn, filling his wheelbarrow with the dirt he excavated, and depositing it on top of the ever-heightening mounds. In fact, Phill was to remain at Poplar Forest far longer than Jefferson had intended. The original plan was for him to assist in a job of sawing at Monticello during the fall and winter of 1808–09, but on December 29, 1808, the Monticello overseer, Edmund Bacon, informed his employer that Phill "had not come down from Bedford yet" and would be awhile "digging about the house." In his response to Bacon, written on January 3, 1809, Jefferson "directed that Phill Hubbard should come home whenever Reuben Perry should leave Poplar Forest. This you can learn from John Perry."[1]

Once the brothers Chisolm completed their initial work at Poplar Forest, another sibling team took up where they left off. Actually, both of the brothers Perry had already been involved in the building during the time Hugh Chisolm was in charge of the on-site operations, though Jefferson's occasional references to "Mr. Perry," without further identification, often make it difficult to ascertain whether he was referring to John or Reuben. As a builder of fine houses throughout Piedmont Virginia, John was to become the more prominent of the two, but Reuben did his share, if not more, at Poplar Forest.[2] His forte was carpentry, and both he and John had worked for Jefferson at Monticello as early as 1800. In December 1812, Jefferson described Reuben as a "housejoiner at Lynchburg," and in other correspondence he asked him "to be in readiness to come the moment of my arrival at Poplar Forest"—both references giving evidence that he was not solely in Jefferson's employ during the time he worked there.[3]

In addition to getting his Bedford house in order, Jefferson attempted once again to get his financial house in order before leaving the presidency. If anything, the picture was even bleaker than it had been a year earlier. Now, as he had then, he assessed his situation, planned ways to correct it, and wrote home about it. One means of reducing the debt, he told Thomas Mann Randolph, Jr., would be to sell "a detached tract in Bedford near Lynchburg of about 400 a[cres]. . . . rich, very hilly and extraordinarily timbered, which the demands of Lynchburg for building render of consequence." This was the tract known as Tullos, which he had listed in his 1794 land roll (see fig. 12). He told Randolph that he "would rather avoid selling [it] if I can, altho it is too small for one of the children. My idea is that if your lands and mine adjacent to one another in Albemarle and Bedford will ensure of competent provision to all the children, and if by selling our detached parcels we can clear ourselves of debt, it will enable us to enjoy an easy situation in tranquility." To Martha he again suggested that the entire family would be able to live "within the income of my Albemarle possessions," and that after his debt had been paid, the "Bedford income, about 2000 to 2500 [annually] would then be free to assist the children as they grow up and want to establish themselves. . . . My own personal wants will be almost nothing beyond those of a chum of the family."[4] Just before her father arrived back at Monticello, Martha came to stay, as did her husband and their family, moving from nearby Edgehill.

On Saturday, March 4, 1809, James Madison was inaugurated as the nation's fourth president, and Thomas Jefferson, then sixty-five years old, became for the first time in forty years, a private citizen. He was also a very happy man. Less than a month after he left Washington, Elizabeth Trist reported to her grandson Nicholas Trist from Albemarle County: "Mr. Jefferson called last week, and dined here yesterday. I never saw him look better nor appear so happy." In a letter written to John Barnes, his Georgetown factor and friend, several weeks later, Jefferson admitted that "the total change of occupation from the house and writing table to constant employment in the garden and farm has added wonderfully to my happiness. It is seldom and with great reluctance I even take up a pen. I read some, but not much."[5]

On June 12, 1809, he wrote George Jefferson that he would probably go to Bedford "towards the end of this month, but am not bound to any fixed time."[6] As it turned out, it was not until November 1809 that Jefferson was finally able to set out for Poplar Forest. The trip was his first in over a year and it is thought that this was the first time he actually stayed in his new house.

Apparently his Lynchburg neighbors must have realized that this was a special trip, or perhaps they wanted to show their appreciation for all he had done for them and his country over the years, or perhaps it was a little of both. At any rate, the invitation they offered him in November 1809 certainly showed how glad they were that he would be their new neighbor (fig. 38). Although Jefferson modestly stated in a letter written the next year that "as yet I am personally a stranger among the neighbors here as I have never had the opportunity of making myself personally acceptable to them by any particular service," in time a number of his Lynchburg acquaintances would become his valued friends.[7] And, as might be expected, he also renewed his acquaintance with a number of friends from former years who were now his neighbors in Bedford.

Two of them have been mentioned in passing. Except for James Steptoe, Jefferson had probably known Charles Clay the longest of all his Bedford neighbors. Before the Revolution, as rector of St. Anne's parish in Albemarle County, Clay had performed the funeral services for both Jefferson's sister Elizabeth and his great childhood friend Dabney Carr. Upon Jefferson's retirement from the presidency, after which he was able to visit Poplar Forest more frequently than before, he and Clay resumed their friendship, as Clay's Bedford home, Ivy Hill, was only a short distance from Poplar Forest. The

two men would almost invariably find the occasion to meet and visit during Jefferson's trips. Clay was the only individual singled out by Jefferson's granddaughter Ellen Randolph Coolidge when she reminisced years later about her visits to Poplar Forest: "I remember among these neighbors a certain 'Parson' Clay, as he was called, who must have been an Episcopal clergyman before the Revolution, to whose four sons my grandfather used to lend books and who astonished me with their names of Cyrus, Odin, Julius and Paul."[8] The facade of Clay's house, which burned early in the twentieth century, was centered with a two-tiered portico, but the building otherwise made little attempt at architectural distinction (fig. 39). As with the majority of the houses in the vicinity, the plain, straight, unembellished lines of Ivy Hill contrasted strongly with the obvious architectural refinements and carefully wrought proportions with which Jefferson embellished Poplar Forest.

James Steptoe (1750–1826), to whom Jefferson had sent Lieutenant Zebulon Pike's map, was commonly known as "Jemmy" Steptoe. He and Jefferson were contemporaries, and had first met each other as students at the College of William and Mary. A native of Westmoreland County, Steptoe was appointed second clerk of Bedford County in 1772, and in 1782 he built his house, Federal

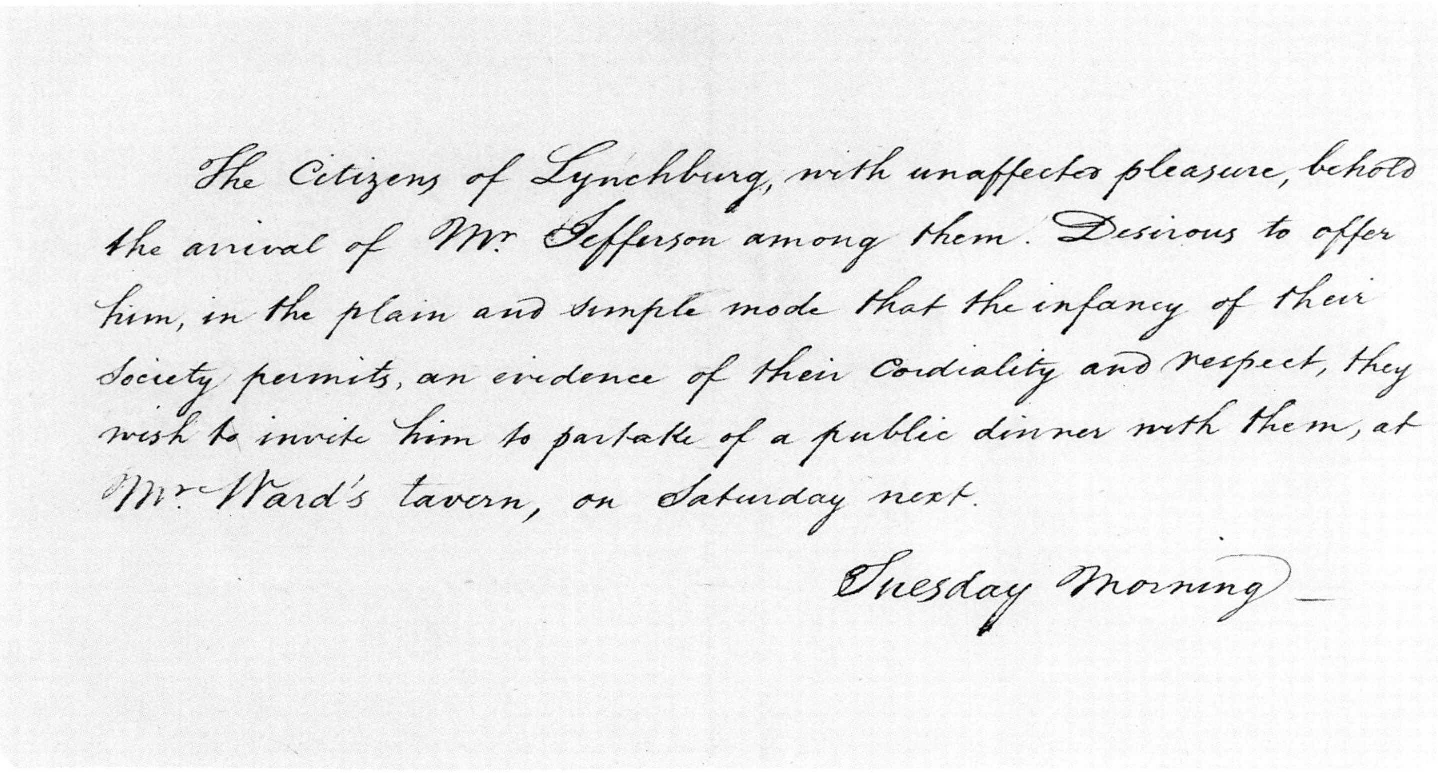

The Citizens of Lynchburg, with unaffected pleasure, behold the arrival of Mr Jefferson among them. Desirous to offer him, in the plain and simple mode that the infancy of their society permits, an evidence of their cordiality and respect, they wish to invite him to partake of a public dinner with them, at Mr Ward's tavern, on Saturday next.

Tuesday Morning —

Fig. 38 Invitation from "the Citizens of Lynchburg," November, 1809. *(Coolidge Collection, Massachusetts Historical Society)*

Hill, near New London (fig. 40). The exception that proves the rule, Federal Hill was architecturally quite sophisticated for its time and place. Its two-story, pedimented central section, flanked by one-story wings to either side, evidenced an architectural lineage that can be traced back to Palladio. Jefferson himself had used this arrangement in his first designs for Monticello, and may even have had some influence at Federal Hill. According to tradition it was Jefferson's custom to always let Steptoe know when he was in the neighborhood so that they could visit. Whether that was always observed or not, on one occasion he sent a note asking, "Thursday if the weather is fine will James Steptoe have soup with a friend?"[9] In 1826, the year both he and Jefferson died, Steptoe had his portrait painted, and behind him the artist painted a map; not Lieutenant Pike's map, but the Frye-Jefferson map of Virginia that Jefferson's father and Joshua Frye had prepared. In addition, he instructed

his portraitist to include a small reproduction of a portrait of Jefferson on an adjacent wall (fig. 41).

For the most part, Jefferson's November 1809 visit to Poplar Forest was a working trip. Among other things, he attended to the sale of the year's tobacco crop and authorized James Martin, whose property adjoined the Tullo's tract, to sell that and another parcel of his property in Bedford and Campbell counties. In connection with the second parcel, he wrote James Steptoe, asking him to "search his records for an entry that had been made by Richard Stith, formerly surveyor of Bedford for 98 acres of land on Ivy Creek or its waters."[10]

He also checked on the progress of Reuben Perry's work. On December 23, after Jefferson had returned to Monticello, Perry wrote him: "I received yours of the 9th. Nov. in which was inclused three pounds on acct. of money advanced for nails for you. Also your directions to have the cellar cleaned out by Phill. But as he is to go

Fig. 39 Ivy Hill. "Parson" Charles Clay and his family lived near Poplar Forest in this house, which was built in 1790. His grave remains on the property. Like James Steptoe's Federal Hill, (fig. 40), it was fronted by a handsome two-story portico. *(Courtesy Mrs. R. Gene Goley)*

away at Christmas he will not have the chance to do it as Mr. Richardson can't possibly git done by that time. He has had a good many laths to get and it will be as much as he will git the lathing done this week." Mr. Richardson was John, who apparently had replaced Chisolm's brother, John, as the plasterer. As it turned out, Richardson was not to finish plastering "by that time," or by any other time. Neither Perry nor Jefferson knew this yet, and in closing his letter, Perry was every bit as confident and enthusiastic as his predecessor, Hugh Chisolm, had ever been: "I will attend to everything here that concerns the Building most certainly."[11]

Soon after his return to Monticello, Jefferson also heard from James Martin, who reported that he had received offers for the land. At the same time he was corresponding with Martin, Jefferson asked Charles Clay and James Steptoe if they would value the property, and informed them that the letters requesting their assist-

ance would be handed them "by my son-in-law, Mr. Randolph, with the integrity and honor of whose character you are already acquainted," and whom he had authorized to "make sale of any portion of my Poplar Forest lands." For his part, Jefferson pledged to "oblige myself to confirm the same and to convey a title accordingly."[12] Samuel J. Harrison, a wealthy Lynchburger who would become another of Jefferson's good friends, bought the property for £1,200, but Jefferson's pledge to confirm the title was easier said than done. There was another claimant to part of it, and toward the end of the month Jefferson's overseer, Burgess Griffin, informed him that the individual had "duly commenced clearing and building of negroes houses on Stithes entry. Mr. Harrison says he expects us to keep him from injuring of the law until he can get possession." Griffin's report was soon confirmed by James Martin, who wrote that the claimant was cutting timber on the tract "at a most dreadful rate

Fig. 40 Federal Hill, James Steptoe's house near New London, was probably begun in 1782. (*Archives, Virginia Department of Historic Resources*)

and says he means to keep full propulsion." The individual was Samuel Scott, who proved to be such a thorn in Jefferson's flesh that he later referred to him in a letter as "the old drunkard Scott."[13] Only after Scott brought suit, to which Jefferson brought a counter-suit, was the issue of ownership finally settled, in 1814, in Jefferson's favor.[14] That Jefferson was not alone in his opinion of Scott was demonstrated by the testimony of a witness in the suit, who recalled: "I thought him extravagant on the subject of the people of Lynchburg when he spoke of them as a set of fops, whores, rogues and rascals."[15] Although somewhat modified since his time, Scott's house, Locust Thicket, still stands — a well-proportioned, frame farm house, with a handsome, pedimented central bay projecting from its facade (fig. 42).

Thomas Mann Randolph, Jr., obviously stayed at his father-in-law's new house when he went with his letters of introduction to Messrs. Clay and Steptoe in December 1809, but it must have been more like a camping trip than anything else. Griffin's letter of December 27 certainly hints that this was the case: "The table clothe and towels was found since M. Randolph went from heer." Neither the problems with Scott nor the news that the towels had been found was the main thrust of Griffin's letter, which was both to inform Jefferson about the corn and tobacco crops, and to tell him of the work then going on in the house: "Mr. Richerson thinks it will take him 2 weeks yet to finish the plastering he has never lost one day since he began there was not more than halfe lathes suffisant for the work I think by keeping good fiers thare will not be any danger of the plastering."[16]

John Richardson's own report, given two weeks later, told an entirely different story:

My being desirous to inform you in wrighting, my fulfilment, in complying with your direction that you left with Mr.

Fig. 41 James ("Jemmy") Steptoe, 1826 oil painting by Harvey Mitchell. In addition to the Frye and Jefferson map shown on the wall in the background, Steptoe directed that his portrait include one of his friend as well. To the left is seen a copy of the familiar portrait of Jefferson by St. Mémim, originally drawn in 1804. Through the open window, the Peaks of Otter are shown. *(Courtesy Clerk of Bedford County Court, Bedford; photograph by Tom Graves, Jr., 1991)*

Perry, I have used every exertion to finish the plastering before this date but finding it ought of my power it being solely from bad management in Mr. Griffin I had no other assistance but Phill, which he had everything to put in place, and put in order before I could do anything. Mr. Griffin gave himself no trouble about nothing when he was not interested, as he has frequently told me when I would make application to him, his answer to me would be that if I did not make my man Phill do what I want done, it mought go undone, on Munday we had some words respecting his conduct to me, which I am confident will be disagreable to you when you hear it, but as disagreable as it is, I am in hope you will excues me if I should mention some of them.

After reciting a veritable litany of problems with Griffin, Richardson concluded: "Lastly I cannot persuade Mr. Griffin to get lime, had there been lime I should have finished if I had to bord myself until it was com-

pleted. There is nothing more I can do until further orders from you, the center room to plaster and the west room, I remain your devoted and very humble servant. John Richardson."[17] It is not known with whom Jefferson sided in this dispute, but some three months later he gave $126 to Griffin, of which $51 was to go to "John Richardson for plaistering."[18] This was the last payment that Richardson would receive, while Griffin would remain as overseer for another year.

In addition to the costs associated with his new house at Poplar Forest, there was another expense that added to Jefferson's already overloaded account during the years of his retirement. But, like the house, this expense was self-inflicted and one that he was happy to undertake. It was the education of his grandson Francis Eppes (fig. 43). John Wayles Eppes, disappointed in his plans to remarry in 1806, had better luck in 1809, when he married Martha Burke Jones, of Halifax, North Carolina. He

Fig. 42 Locust Thicket. The home of Samuel Scott, with whom Jefferson had a prolonged dispute over property boundaries, still stands on Old Forest Road in Lynchburg. *(Tom Graves, Jr., 1991)*

wrote to his former father-in-law on July 10 of that year on the subject of his son's education, which he offered to leave in Jefferson's hands.[19] At first Francis, who was then almost nine years old, was tutored at Monticello, dividing his time between there and his father's home. On Christmas Day 1809, after a half year of supervising his grandson, Jefferson wrote the senior Eppes that "a boy of finer dispositions, & more easily governed, I have never seen. I have had no occasion to exercise any restraint towards him, but as to his appetite." A year and a month later, on January 24, 1811, he reported that "Francis enjoys perfect health, and is on his first Latin declension. I shall turn him over to Jefferson [Thomas Jefferson Randolph] during my absense in Bedford."[20] That summer, on a visit to Millbrook, Francis wrote to his grandfather, and Jefferson's fond response indicates that his student had apparently mastered more than his first declension:

I am glad to learn you are becoming a Roman, which a familiarity with their history will certainly make you. The putting you into qui, quae, quod, was only to strengthen your memory, which you may do quite as well by getting pieces of poetry by heart. Jefferson & myself intend you a visit in November, and it will then be a question for the consideration of your papa and yourself whether you shall not return with us & visit your cousins. This will be acceptable to us all, and only deprecated by the partridges and snowbirds against which you may commence hostilities. Adieu my dear Francis, be industrious in advancing yourself in knolege which with your good disposition, will ensure the love of others, & your own happiness, & the love & happiness of none more than of

    Yours affectionately
    Th. Jefferson [21]

Fig. 43 Francis Eppes, pencil and crayon sketch, 1805. At the time this drawing was made, Jefferson's grandson was four years old. Several years later, Jefferson undertook the supervision of his education. *(Monticello, Thomas Jefferson Memorial Foundation, Inc.).*

As in so many of their dealings, Jefferson and the senior Eppes would have disagreements over the ensuing years in arranging and providing for Francis's education, but both men regarded it as an important duty, even if each had his own ideas about how best to accomplish it.

In his December 1809 trip to Bedford to see about the sale of his father-in-law's land, Thomas Mann Randolph, Jr., also tended to the sale of his own. The Randolphs, now firmly established in Albemarle, had no need of their Bedford land, but, like Jefferson, always had need of cash. In addition to their debts, there were also more than enough mouths to feed. Benjamin Franklin Randolph, the ninth of Martha and Thomas Mann Randolph's brood, had been born on July 14, 1808. On Jan. 31, 1810, their tenth child, Meriwether Lewis Randolph, was born. Less than a month later, on February 19, 1810, for the sum of $8,400, Anne Moseley purchased from them

"all that part of the tract of land in the County of Bedford which was conveyed by Thomas Jefferson to the said Thomas Mann & Martha by deed" twenty years earlier. It was the property that had been Martha's dowry, and according to the deed contained 840 acres.[22] Anne Moseley, recently widowed at the time of her purchase, gained a reputation as one of the best farmers of the area, and though no letters are known to have passed between her and Jefferson, he did on occasion have to buy corn from her to supplement his own supply.[23] Ashwood, the house Mrs. Moseley built on her new purchase, was a straightforward, Federal-style, brick structure, as uncompromising in its architectural severity as any of those built by Jefferson's neighbors on their extensive farms adjoining Poplar Forest (fig. 44). Though its design has occasionally been credited to Jefferson, and though it has also occasionally been identified as the

Fig. 44 Ashwood. Anne Moseley, who in 1810 purchased the portion of the Poplar Forest tract that Jefferson had given Martha upon her marriage, built this house on it. A discernable vertical line in the brickwork to the right of the second-floor doorway indicates that it may have been a three-bay house originally, rather than the five-bay building shown here. The house, much altered since this photograph was taken, remains. *(Courtesy Mrs. R. Gene Goley)*

dwelling he occupied at Poplar Forest before building his own house, no documentary or architectural evidence exists to support either claim.[24]

A day before the deed between the Randolphs and Anne Moseley was signed, sealed, and delivered, Jefferson wrote one of his Bedford County neighbors: "Mr. Burgess Griffin informs me that he has sold you my crop of tobacco made at the Poplar forest the last year, for which you will make payment there." The recipient was Charles Johnston, who had just recently moved into his new house, Sandusky, near Poplar Forest (fig. 45). A wealthy merchant and planter, formerly of Richmond, Johnston paid a total of $2,005.11 for the tobacco, just within the range of the estimate that Jefferson had made to Martha a year earlier that the income from his Bedford lands was "about 2000 to 2500."[25]

Jefferson started on the first of his three visits to Pop-

lar Forest in 1810 on March 27 and stayed until April 12. Another bright financial note was sounded when he noted in his Memorandum Book on April 7 that he had "recd. from Saml. Jordan Harrison an ord. on Gibson & Jeff. for £300. & £100. cash, being the 1st. of 3. paiments for my lands on Ivy cr. sold to him, to wit, Tullos's and Stith's." Before his visit, he had prepared another roll of his landholdings, and while in Bedford he took the time to prepare a roll of his slaves there, noting their birth dates and to which of his two separate plantation operations they belonged (figs. 46 and 47). If the number of slaves can be taken as any indication, the operations at Poplar Forest (or Tomahawk), where he listed fifty-six slaves, were precisely twice as large as those at Bear Creek, where he counted twenty-eight. The last slave named at Poplar Forest was "Old Judy," whose birth date was given as "abt 1728."[26]

Fig. 45 Sandusky. Built ca. 1808 by Charles Johnston, and named by him in commemoration of a Shawnee Indian camp in Ohio where he had been taken prisoner after being captured on a trip to Kentucky, this well-preserved dwelling is an early example of a formal, five-bay, Federal-style house in the Lynchburg/Bedford area. *(Author's collection)*

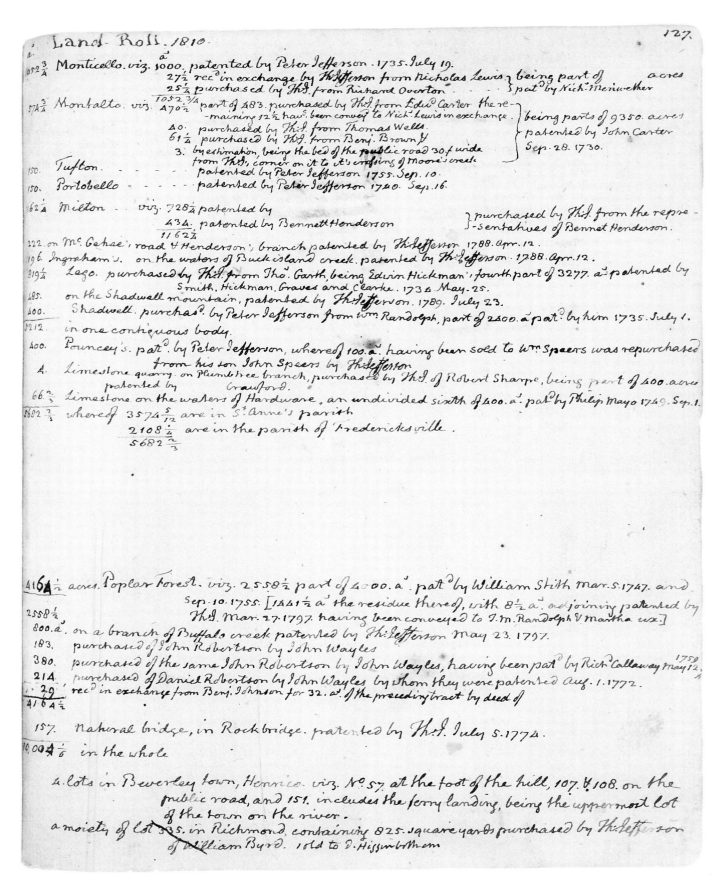

Fig. 46 Land Roll. In 1810, as he had done in 1794, Jefferson took stock of his real estate holdings in his Farm Book. Poplar Forest, still composed of many separately acquired tracts, now contained 4,164 1/2 acres (cf. fig. 12). (*Thomas Jefferson's Farm Book, Coolidge Collection, Massachusetts Historical Society*)

Before setting out on his second trip to Bedford in 1810, Jefferson submitted the first of what would become almost standing annual orders to a Richmond merchant, Joseph Darmsdatt, for food supplies for himself and his work force at Poplar Forest: "In the years 1796 and 1797 while living at home I had considerable dealings with you in the article of salt fish, and recollect that I was well satisfied with those dealings. . . . I will begin by asking the favor of you to send me a dozen barrels of herrings of the last season, one half of them to Milton, and the other half to Lynchburg to the address of Messrs. Brown and Robertson, merchants of that place."[27] "Messrs. Brown and Robertson" was one of the leading Lynchburg commercial firms of the early-nineteenth century. William Brown had opened the first dry-goods store in Lynchburg, and had become "a banker and agent for nearly the entire country trading here." His association with Jefferson was short-lived as he was killed the next year in the Richmond theater fire of December 1811.[28] His partner, Archibald Robertson, who carried on the firm, would come to be a friend and confidant of Jefferson's, and would undertake practically all of his dealings requiring the services of a commission merchant in the area. He would also become one of Jefferson's patient and long-suffering creditors.

Upon his arrival at Poplar Forest, Jefferson formalized his arrangements with Reuben Perry, and recorded in his Memorandum Book on August 30 that "Reuben Perry agrees to work for me @ 4/6 a day always, allowing the same for his assistant." Charles Bankhead, Jefferson's grandson-in-law, accompanied him on this trip to look over the land he and Anne had received from her parents, and Jefferson happily reported that "he is so pleased with the place & neighborhood that his settlement here is decided on. He brings his people here this winter, and his family in the spring." Jefferson conveyed his pleasure at this prospect to William A. Burwell, who had served as his private secretary during part of his first term as president, and who was now living in Franklin County, to the southwest of Bedford. "Should chance or business direct your steps to Lynchburg . . . you know we shall be happy to see you," he told his young friend, and if their paths were not to cross at Poplar Forest, "that pleasure must be adjourned to Monticello where we shall count on seeing Mrs. Burwell & yourself." Jefferson also had a favor to ask. He recalled that Burwell had told him of a quarry that could provide millstones, and as he was now about to build "a small mill here to save my toll and to grind my plaister which the mills of the neighborhood refuse," he wished to know where it was, and what the stones might cost.[29]

After jotting down a payment of $4.81, which he identified as "debts for duck, chickens, vegetables, etc.," in his Memorandum Book on September 6, Jefferson left Poplar Forest and arrived back at Monticello on September 9. Later that month, obviously pleased with what he had seen, he wrote that Poplar Forest was "the most valuable of my possessions and will become the residence of the greater part of my family," the last statement probably spurred on by the hope that the Bankheads would soon settle there.[30] He also began to make additional arrangements for more work to be done on his new house. On September 26, 1810, he wrote James Dinsmore, then in charge of the remodeling that James Madison was undertaking at Montpelier: "Johnny Hemings is just entering on a job of sash doors for the house at Poplar forest, and tells me he cannot proceed without his sash planes and the templet belonging to them in your possession. They may come safely in a box by the stage to the care of Mr. Higginbotham. If you could send them by Sunday's stage you would oblige me."[31] David Higginbotham was Jefferson's merchant-factor in Milton, a small town on the Rivanna River near Monticello, but as far as the Poplar Forest story is concerned, the other name mentioned in Jefferson's communiqué to Dinsmore is far more significant.

Much has been said and written over the years about the remarkable Hemings family of Monticello.[32] They were Jefferson's slaves, and Johnny, or John, born in 1776, was the son of Betty Hemings, herself the daughter of a slave who had belonged to John Wayles, Jefferson's father-in-law. John was a carpenter and joiner, and examples of his considerable skills are still evident at Monticello. The job of making sash doors is the first known commission Jefferson gave him for work on the house at Poplar Forest, but it would by no means be the last. In April 1811, Jefferson gave him "15.D. to wit the wages of one month in the year which I allow him as an encouragement." This was the first of what became annual gratuities that he gave both Hemings and Burwell, who was Jefferson's butler and John's nephew.[33]

While at Monticello in the autumn of 1810, Jefferson received the information he had requested from William Burwell, his correspondent in Franklin County. The stone quarry was on the Pigg River, about forty-five miles from New London. Burwell discouraged Jefferson from building his own mill at Poplar Forest, primarily because of the difficulty of finding good millers, but, if he did decide to go ahead and build one, his friend urged him to have it "*cheaply* constructed." Also while at Monticello, Jefferson requested Hugh Chisolm to come from Montpelier to "do the small job wanting here," which

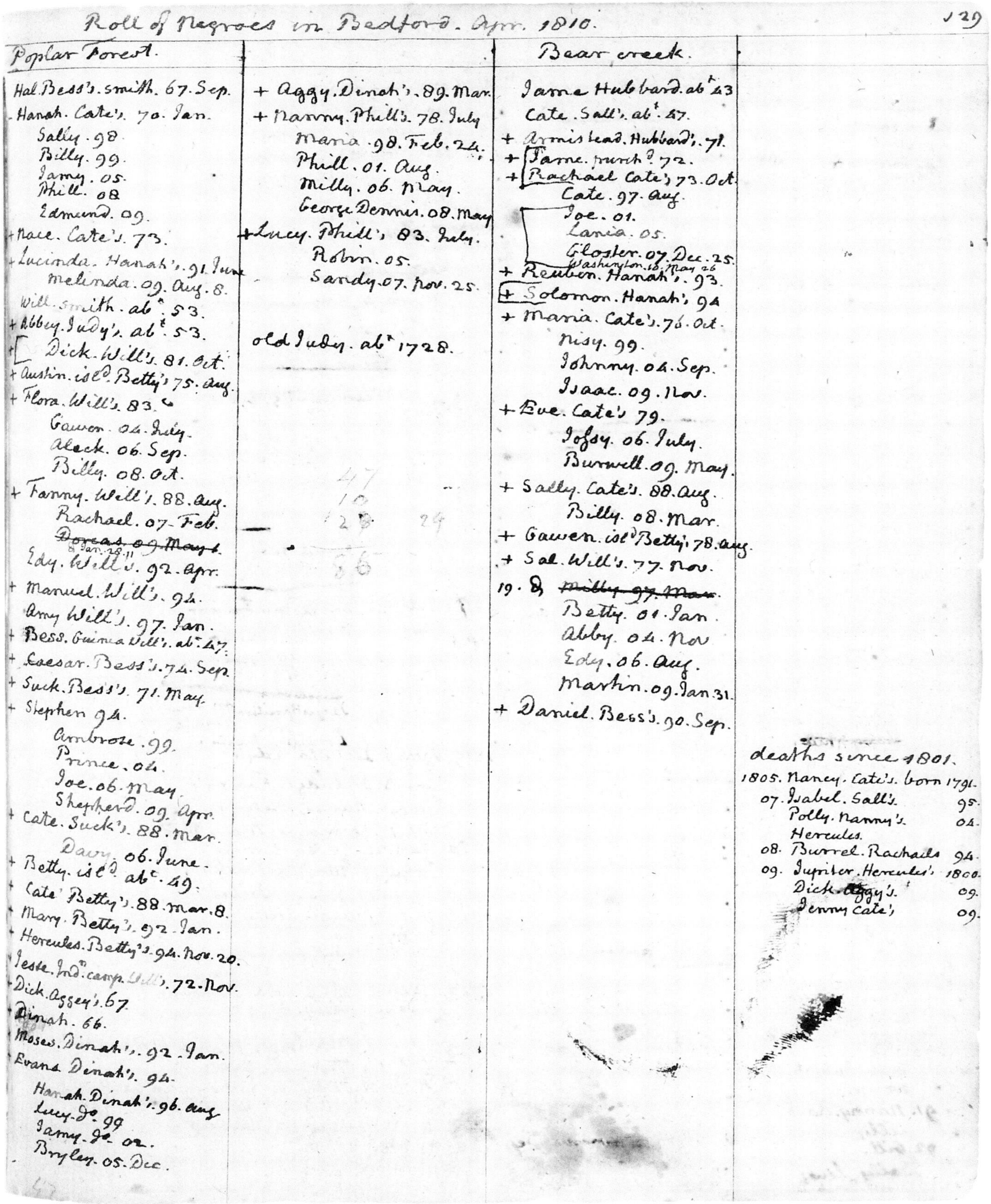

Roll of Negroes in Bedford. Apr. 1810.   129

Poplar Forest.

Hal. Bess's. smith. 67. Sep.
Hanah. Cate's. 70. Jan.
   Sally. 98
   Billy. 99
   Jamy. 05.
   Phill. 08
   Edmund. 09
+ Nace. Cate's. 73.
+ Lucinda. Hanah's. 91. June
   Melinda. 09. Aug. 8.
+ Will. smith. ab.t 53.
+ Abbey. Judy's. ab.t 53.
+ [Dick. Will's. 81. Oct.
+ Austin. isd. Betty's. 75. Aug.
+ Flora. Will's. 83.
   Gawen. 04. July.
   Alick. 06. Sep.
   Billy. 08. Oct.
+ Fanny. Will's. 88. Aug.
   Rachael. 07. Feb.
   Dorcas. 09. May.
   Edy. Will's. 92. Apr.
+ Manuel. Will's. 94.
   Amy. Will's. 97. Jan.
+ Bess. Guinea Will's. ab.t 47.
+ Caesar. Bess's. 74. Sep.
+ Suck. Bess's. 71. May.
+ Stephen. 94.
   Ambrose. 99.
   Prince. 04.
   Joe. 06. May.
   Shepherd. 09. Apr.
+ Cate. Suck's. 88. Mar.
   Davy. 06. June.
+ Betty. isd. ab.t 49.
+ Cate. Betty's. 88. Mar. 8.
+ Mary. Betty's. 92. Jan.
+ Hercules. Betty's. 94. Nov. 20.
+ Jesse. Ind.n camp Will's. 72. Nov.
+ Dick. Aggey's. 67
+ Dinah. 66.
+ Moses. Dinah's. 92. Jan.
+ Evans. Dinah's. 94.
   Hanah. Dinah's. 96. Aug.
   Lucy. do. 99
   Jamy. do. 02.
   Bryley. 05. Dec.

+ Aggy. Dinah's. 89. Mar.
+ Nanny. Phill's. 78. July
   Maria. 98. Feb. 24.
   Phill. 01. Aug.
   Milly. 06. May.
   George Dennis. 08. May
+ Lucy. Phill's. 83. July.
   Robin. 05.
   Sandy. 07. Nov. 25.

old Judy. ab.t 1728.

47
12
128   29
—
86

Bear creek.

Jame. Hubbard. ab.t 43
Cate. Sall's. ab.t 57.
+ Armistead. Hubbard's. 71.
+ Jame. purch.d 72.
+ Rachael. Cate's. 73. Oct.
   Cate. 97. Aug.
   Joe. 01.
   Lania. 05.
   Gloster. 07. Dec. 25.
   Washington. 10. May 26
+ Reuben. Hanah's. 93.
+ Solomon. Hanah's. 94.
+ Maria. Cate's. 76. Oct.
   Nisy. 99.
   Johnny. 04. Sep.
   Isaac. 09. Nov.
+ Eve. Cate's. 79.
   Jossy. 06. July.
   Burwell. 09. May.
+ Sally. Cate's. 88. Aug.
   Billy. 08. Mar.
+ Gawen. isd. Betty's. 78. Aug.
+ Sal. Will's. 77. Nov.
19.   Milly. 99. Mar.
   Betty. 01. Jan.
   Abby. 04. Nov.
   Edy. 06. Aug.
   Martin. 09. Jan 31.
+ Daniel. Bess's. 90. Sep.

deaths since 1801.
1805. Nancy. Cate's. born 1791.
   07. Isabel. Sall's.   95.
   Polly. Nanny's.   04.
   Hercules.
   08. Burrel. Rachael's   94.
   09. Jupiter. Hercules'. 1800.
   Dick. Aggy's.   09.
   Jenny. Cate's.   09.

Fig. 47 Roll of Negroes in Bedford. In addition to recording his land holdings in 1810, Jefferson also listed his slaves and the two plantations (Poplar Forest and Bear Creek) to which each was assigned. (*Thomas Jefferson's Farm Book, Coolidge Collection, Massachusetts Historical Society*)

was to work on the cistern. He hoped that his asking in advance would enable Chisolm "to put the President's work into such a state as not to suffer by a short absense."[34] That letter was dated September 10, and on the seventeenth, Jefferson noted in his Memorandum Book that "H. Chisolm begins to work." On November 17, 1810, while at Monticello, Chisolm finally received final payment for the work he had done at Poplar Forest, for which he had submitted his bill in February 1808.[35]

Although Jefferson had planned to return to Poplar Forest in October 1810, it was not until December that he was able to find time to take his third and last trip that year. Though he made no mention of it, this was apparently the only time that he ever spent Christmas at Poplar Forest. Soon after his return, he wrote to John Barnes in Georgetown: "I continue in the enjoyment of good health, take much exercise, and make frequent journies to Bedford, the only journies I now take, or ever expect to take."[36] That did not prove to be exactly the case, but it is a fact that Jefferson, formerly an inveterate traveler, never left the state of Virginia after he retired from the presidency. Though he would travel elsewhere in the state, and in fact had already done so, for the most part his future trips would be between his two homes.

The next trip was soon enough. On January 25, 1811, he hastily penned a note to James Monroe: "I am just on the wing to Bedford to which place my affairs call me suddenly." Although he actually didn't "wing" it to Bedford until two days later, this uncharacteristically early-in-the-year trip was indeed prompted by a sudden call, which apparently prevented Anne Bankhead, who was to have accompanied him on his first visit of the new year, from going. A flood had breached the dam at the mill where his wheat was waiting to be ground, and he had to make other arrangements to have the grain ground into flour before it was transported to Richmond for sale. Upon his arrival Jefferson found that the dam had been breached a second time, and that he would have to remain longer than he had intended. Obviously and justifiably feeling sorry for himself, he wrote to Martha on February 24:

I have wished for Anne but once since I came here, and that has been from the moment of my arrival to the present one. The weather has been such that I have seen the face of no human being for days but the servants. I am like a state prisoner. My keepers set before me at fixed hours something to eat and withdraw. We have had seven snows since I came, making all together about 10 1/2 inches. The ground has been now covered a fortnight. I had begun to prepare an Asparagus bed, and to plant some raspberry bushes, gooseberry bushes etc. for Anne, but it has been impossible to go on with it, the earth is so deep frozen, and I expect to leave it so.[37]

The ground thawed late in February, and just before leaving Poplar Forest, Jefferson recorded planting the items he had been unable to get into the ground earlier. In addition to the raspberries and gooseberries for Anne, as well as several ornamental shrubs, he noted the planting of "50 cutting of Athenian poplar. Nursery next N. fence between 2. stables" and "25. cuttings of Weepg. willow along side of the Ath poplars." That this was not to be their permanent location is proven by the note that followed: "Memom. plant on each mound 4. weeping willows on the top in a square 20 f. apart. Golden willows in a circle round the middle. 15. f. apart. Aspens in a circle round the foot. 15.f. apart. plant 6. weeping willows round each Cloacinal."[38] Obviously Jefferson intended the mounds to be covered with dense, thick shade. As was mentioned, George Washington had given his ornamental mounds at Mount Vernon a similar treatment, and had also utilized willows to created the effect he wanted. The weeping willows Jefferson planted "round each Cloacinal," were probably intended to afford privacy. Cloacina, or cloacinal, derived from the Latin verb to cleanse, was Jefferson's classical term for a necessary, or privy.

Unfortunately, not only was Anne Bankhead unable to accompany her grandfather on this trip, she was never to enjoy the fruits of the raspberries and gooseberries that Jefferson planted. During this winter visit he still had every assurance that the Bankheads would become his close neighbors, settling on the property her parents had given them, but by June, if not before, that hope had to be abandoned, as her husband told him they were planning to sell the land.[39] Jefferson's hopes that his Poplar Forest lands would "become the residence of the greater part of my family" were growing dim.

Early in February 1811 Jefferson and Reuben Perry entered into an agreement that involved one of Jefferson's slaves. Jame Hubbard was a brother of Phill Hubbard; both were sons of Jame and Cate, who were among the most important and trusted of the Poplar Forest slaves. While Phill continued in Jefferson's service as a valued worker, Jame had run away time and again. Although by now Jefferson had definitely given up on him, Perry still had hope, even though at the time he agreed to purchase him Jame was "at this time absconded from his habitation in Albemarle." Perry agreed to pay Jefferson $300 whether Jame was recovered or not, and an additional $200 whenever he was apprehended from his latest attempt at freedom. Instead of paying cash, though, it was agreed that Perry "or his assigns will accept of such work to those amounts in Carpentry or House joinery, to be performed by the sd. Reuben [Perry], and on such part of the lands called the Poplar Forest in Bedford, as the said Thomas [Jefferson] or his assigns shall indicate." Perry was to be given six months to "commence any parcel of work so to be indicated, and continue at it steadily, and with all his force until compleated." So that there would be no dispute between the two parties, it was decided that the value of the work "shall be estimated at the prices which have been settled by agreement or practice for similar work done between John Perry brother of the sd. Reuben & the said Thomas."[40] During the late winter and early spring of 1811, Perry attempted to locate and capture Jame and took out a long-running advertisement in the *Richmond Enquirer*, describing the runaway as being about six feet tall, having "stout limbs and strong made, of daring demeanor bold and harsh features, dark complexion," and adding that he was likely to drink and would attempt to pass himself off as a freeman.[41] It would be almost a year before Jame was apprehended and turned over to Perry, but in the meantime Jefferson was anxious that his builder commence his work. John Hemings had finished the sash doors, and it was time for Perry to install them. On May 10, Jefferson wrote Perry: "My boat will start to Lynchburg as soon as it has got all my flour down from hence; which will be in about one trip more. She will carry the 4. pair of glass doors with their jambs & soffites, & the semicircular windows, all ready glazed for hanging. I must pray you to be in readiness to come the moment of my arrival at Poplar Forest to put them all up, that it may be done while I am there. I shall not set out from hence till the boat has started for Lynchburg."[42]

Although Jefferson had planned to go early in July, an attack of rheumatism, which kept him "to the house & mostly to the bed for a fortnight," delayed the visit until August. That delay kept him from dealing personally with a change of management at his Bedford plantations. On August 4, 1811, while still at Monticello, he recorded that he had "agreed with Jeremiah Goodman to serve me next year as overseer in Bedford over a plantation & 16. hands, for which I am to give him 200.D. a year, & all other articles to stand as by our original agreement."[43] That original agreement apparently referred to Goodman's previous employment as overseer at Lego, one of Jefferson's Albemarle County farms. Goodman became overseer at the Poplar Forest (Tomahawk) plantation, while Nimrod Darnell was placed in charge at Bear Creek later in the year.[44]

Unfortunately, though Jefferson thought he had gotten over his rheumatism before he undertook the August trip, soon after his arrival at Poplar Forest he complained that he had "suffered much coming, staying, and shall returning. If I am not better after a little rest at home I shall set out for the warm springs."[45] Perhaps because of this attack, which kept him in his new house a great deal

of the time, he took the occasion to catch up on his correspondence. Two of the best-known letters that he ever penned from Poplar Forest date from this visit. The first was to Benjamin Rush, a famous Philadelphia doctor and fellow signer of the Declaration of Independence. Though he had now been in the habit of coming to Bedford on a regular basis for only two years, Jefferson afforded Rush the clearest statement he ever made of what he did and enjoyed on his visits to Poplar Forest:

I write to you from a place, 90 miles from Monticello, near the New London of this state, which I visit three or four times a year. I stay from a fortnight to a month at a time. I have fixed myself comfortably, keep some books here, bring others occasionally, am in the solitude of a hermit, and quite at leisure to attend to my absent friends. I note this to show that I am not in a situation to examine the dates of our letters, whether I have overcome the annual period of asking how you do? . . . I take moderate rides without much fatigue, but my journey to this place on a hard-going gig, gave me great sufferings, which I expect will be renewed on my return, as soon as I am able. . . . I find friendship to be like wine, raw when new, ripened with age, the true old man's milk and restorative cordial.[46]

Three days later, on August 20, he wrote another Philadelphia friend of long standing, Charles Willson Peale:

It is a long time, my dear sir, since we have exchanged a letter. . . . I shall still be anxious to hear from you sometimes, and to know that you are well and happy. I know I have heard that you have retired from the city to a farm & that you give your whole time to that. Does not the museum suffer? and is the farm as interesting? Here, as you know, we are all farmers, but not in a pleasing stile. We have so little labor in proportion to our land, that altho perhaps we make more profit from the same labor we cannot give to our grounds that stile of beauty which satisfies the eye of the amateur. Our rotations are corn, wheat & clover, or corn, wheat, clover and clover, or wheat, corn, wheat, clover and clover, preceding the clover by a plaistering, but some instead of clover, substitute mere rest, and all are slovenly enough. We are adding the care of merino sheep. I have often thought that if heaven had given me choice of my position and calling, it should have been on a rich spot of earth, well watered, and near a good market for the productions of the garden. No occupation is so delightful to me as the culture of the earth, and no culture comparable to that of the garden. Such a variety of subjects, some are always coming to perfection, the failure of one thing repaired by the success of another, and instead of one harvest, a continued one through the year. Under a total want of demand except for our family table, I am still devoted to the garden, but tho an old man, I am but a young gardener [47] *(fig. 48)*.

He also did something else, something that no one but Thomas Jefferson would have thought of, and one has to wonder just what Parson Clay must have thought when he received this message, written the same day he wrote Peale:

While here, & much confined to the house by my rheumatism, I have amused myself with calculating the hour lines of an horizontal disk for the latitude of this place, which I find to be 37 22' 26". The calculations are for every 5 minutes of time and are always exact to within less than half a second of a degree. As I do not know that any body here has taken this trouble before, I have supposed a copy would be acceptable to you. . . . Williamsburg being very nearly in the parallel of Poplar Forest, the calculations now sent would serve for all the counties on the line between that place and this, for your own place, New london, and Lynchburg in this neighborhood.[48]

When he returned to Poplar Forest for the third time in 1811, Jefferson was accompanied by his grandson Thomas Jefferson Randolph, and on the way the two stopped by Millbrook to see the Eppeses.[49] After his arrival at Poplar Forest, he composed a lengthy memorandum to guide Jeremiah Goodman in his work for the next year. As this was the first time he had written to his new overseer, it was full of details that give a rare and complete glimpse into the affairs of an early-nineteenth-century Virginia plantation. After telling him which fields were to be planted with which crops, Jefferson introduced the slave work force to him, telling what each one's task was, from Hanah, "who cooks & washes for me when I am here" to Bess, who "makes the butter during the season, to be sent to Monticello in the winter." Jefferson directed Goodman to give special attention to "Nace, the former headman, and the best we have ever known, [who] is to be entirely kept from labour until he recovers, which will probably be very long. He may do anything which he can do sitting in a warm room, such as shoemaking and making baskets. He can shell corn in the corn house when it is quite warm, or in his own house at any time." Should any of the slaves become ill, "let our neighbor Dr. Steptoe be called in." Dr. Steptoe was William, son of James Steptoe, and he would come to be another valued Bedford friend and companion. Jefferson concluded his instructions to Goodman by telling him how many hogs were to be kept and slaughtered at Poplar Forest, and how many were to be driven to Monticello, a subject he then took up in a memorandum to his Monticello overseer, Edmund Bacon: "I find I can drive from hence 4 or 5 beeves and as many muttons as we can want; all as fat as they can be; and having to drive these I concluded to drive the hogs also and kill them at Monticello. The whole will start therefore as soon as the hogs are fat enough."[50]

In what must have been a melancholy task, he also sold the Bankhead property during this visit. Earlier in the year, Charles Bankhead had advised him that "Mr. Radford of Lynchburg has lately written me on the subject of our land in Bedford, and expresses strong desire to become a purchaser." As it turned out, William Radford and Joel Yancey, both of whom were described in the deed later that year as "of the County of Campbell" purchased the land on which Jefferson had hoped his first grandchild and her husband would settle.[51] Jefferson's apparent loss would soon become a gain. Both Radford and Yancey would come to be among the select Bedford coterie of his close friends. Jefferson would eventually hire Yancey to supervise his farming operations at Poplar Forest, while Radford, who was Anne Moseley's son-in-law, would purchase additional land from Jefferson in the years to come. Both would soon build, or add to, handsome houses on what had formerly been part of the original Poplar Forest tract (see figs. 60 and 69).

During this last visit in 1811, Jefferson wrote again to Benjamin Rush: "While at Monticello I am so much engrossed by business or society that I can only write on matters of strong urgency. Here I have leisure, as I have every where the disposition to think of my friends."[52] There was another friend he was thinking of just then besides Rush. In fact, his letter to Rush was the beginning of a reconciliation with one of his oldest friends, but one from whom he had been alienated for all too long. Jefferson had just heard that John Adams had told a friend: "I always loved Jefferson, and still love him." "This is enough for me," Jefferson declared to Rush, who had also played a part in the reconciliation: "I only needed this knowledge to revive towards him all the affections of the most cordial moments of our lives."[53] The numerous letters that the two patriots and friends subsequently wrote to each other have ever since enriched those who read them.

Jefferson's last visit to Poplar Forest in 1811 was of a month's duration; the longest sojourn he had made since his momentous trip in 1781, when he had composed the text for his *Notes on Virginia*, exactly thirty years earlier. When he departed on December 20, much remained to be taken care of in the next several years — on the house, on the land and its workers, and on his ever-increasing financial worries. Still, as his letters to Benjamin Rush and Charles Willson Peale show, only two years after he first occupied it, Poplar Forest had already become what Jefferson had planned it to be: his villa retreat. Few others would consider all that he accomplished during this and subsequent visits as coming even close to being "quite at leisure," but he certainly did.

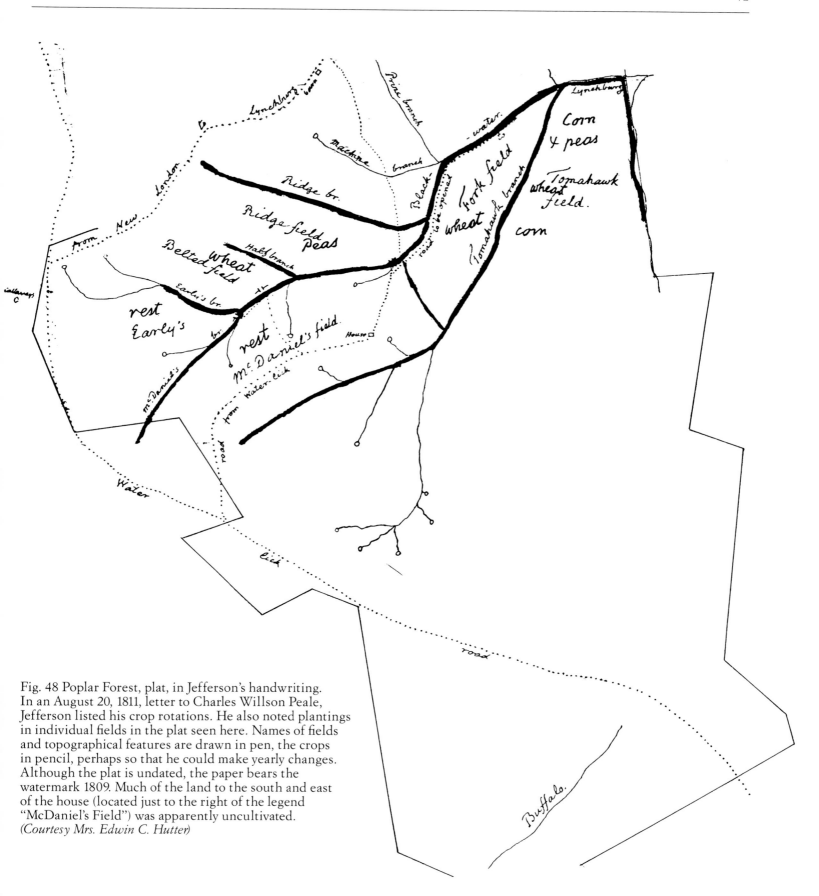

Fig. 48 Poplar Forest, plat, in Jefferson's handwriting.
In an August 20, 1811, letter to Charles Willson Peale,
Jefferson listed his crop rotations. He also noted plantings
in individual fields in the plat seen here. Names of fields
and topographical features are drawn in pen, the crops
in pencil, perhaps so that he could make yearly changes.
Although the plat is undated, the paper bears the
watermark 1809. Much of the land to the south and east
of the house (located just to the right of the legend
"McDaniel's Field") was apparently uncultivated.
(*Courtesy Mrs. Edwin C. Hutter*)

"THE BEST DWELLING HOUSE IN THE STATE"
(1812–13)

Judging from the remaining records, Jefferson's 1812 spring visit to Poplar Forest, which lasted from May 10 to May 20, was centered around matters outside, not inside, the house. On May 12, he drafted further written instructions to Jeremiah Goodman regarding landscaping:

[as] soon as the green swerd seed is ripe, have [som]e gathered by the negro children and sowed on all the naked parts [of the] mound, and then cover those parts lightly [with s]traw first, & brush laid over that.

[if m]ore seed could be gathered by the children it might be sowed in the fall or spring in the square round the house where the greensward has not as yet taken.

have strong stakes 12 f. long stuck by such of the young trees as grow crooked, and tie them up to the stake in as many places as necessary.

That the plants he had originally intended for Anne Bankhead were still thriving is indicated by Jefferson's directing Goodman to "weed the gooseberries, raspberries, strawberries & rose bushes." He also directed his overseer to "sow lettuce the 1st. of June," and informed him that he had "promised mr. Caruthers of Rockbridge to give him a ram & ewe lamb of this year, I believe if he should send, we must give him one of our rams, and a ewe lamb, and turn out another ram for ourselves the next year."[1] Thereby hung a tale.

As a later observer has noted, "from 1809 through 1813, sheep raising and sheep breeding became one of Jefferson's many passions."[2] His proposal to give a ram and ewe to William Caruthers of Rockbridge was part of a larger scheme, which was no less than to furnish "my whole state gratis, by *giving* a full blooded ram to every county as fast as they can be raised." The breed, the Spanish Merino, was prized especially for the quality of its wool, and Jefferson hoped that by giving a ram to a farmer in every county he would "see my whole state covered with this valuable race at no expence to the farmers and the moderate one to me of maintaining the flock while doing it." Jefferson's rather grandiose plans for the propagation of sheep in Virginia were never fully accomplished. As it turned out, Caruthers didn't request his sheep in 1812, and the next year Jefferson would write: "I sent my flock of them to a place I have in Bedford, where they are beginning to be known and in great demand. . . . My place is 3 miles from New London on the road to Lynchburg. On your signifying your wish on this subject I will give directions to my manager there to deliver a pair to your order."[3] Eventually, Caruthers obtained his pair from the flock at Monticello instead of Bedford.

Upon his return to Monticello from his spring visit to Poplar Forest in 1812, Jefferson learned that the Pantops situation had yet again come to a head. On June 3 he wrote John Wayles Eppes, giving him a glimpse into his

own financial situation as well as his opinion on what he had heard about the Albemarle land:

I learnt accidentally a day or two ago that you were proposing to sell Pantops, and had offered it to some persons in this neighborhood. This is done, I have no doubt, after mature consideration, and under the view that it will be most beneficial to Francis, of whose interests no one can be a more faithful depository than yourself. Candor obliges me to say that an estate so closely and constantly under my eye could not pass out of the family without sentiments of regret, which would be renewed as often as the object should meet the eye. This induces me to request that I may have the refusal of it on the same terms on which you might be willing to sell it to others. These I understand to be on payments of considerable length, and this circumstance may bring it within my means. You know of the debt brought on me by my Washington residence. I have got through more than half of it, and confide that two years more will clear me of the residue. I could then, without inconvenience, begin to set apart annually, a portion of the price, so as to make sure of the whole in time. At 10. D. the acre, the price at which I am told it is offered, it would be a very safe purchase, if brought within the term in which I could accomplish it.[4]

Later that month, Jefferson wrote Eppes again, this time with a different idea. Instead of having to buy Pantops from his son-in-law, he now proposed that "an exchange of lands in Bedford, equivalent in value to Pantops, may be the subject of future consideration, wherein we shall both be governed by the same object, the best interests of Francis."[5]

What appeared at the time to be bad news actually was to prove a turning point in Jefferson's thoughts and plans for Poplar Forest. While many details were yet to be worked out, the ultimate disposition of his Bedford property was beginning to germinate now, thanks to John Wayles Eppes's attempt to sell Pantops without bothering to let his benefactor know of his plans or even giving him the right of first refusal.

In fact, even before his next trip to Poplar Forest, Jefferson began to make arrangements that were at least in part precipitated by what he was planning. On August 9, 1812, he wrote Reuben Perry that he would leave Monticello "within about 10 days or a fortnight from this time, and have to request that you will be ready to come there on notice of my arrival and lay all the grounds for the plaistering while I am there. In this I hope you will not fail me." After that, Jefferson then hoped that Perry would come to Monticello for "a large job to be executed here, to wit a barn, which with its sheds will be 66 x 42 feet."[6]

Jefferson arrived at Poplar Forest on the second of September, and the next day sent for Perry, who came over from Lynchburg right away. On September 3, the two men added a codicil to their February 1811 agreement regarding the sale of Jame Hubbard, who had been captured and was turned over to Perry during this visit. As an inducement for Perry to work on the Monticello barn as well as other projects in Albemarle, Jefferson subtracted fifty dollars from the price they had originally agreed upon for Jame. Through no fault of his own, though, Perry was not able to start work right away at Poplar Forest. On September 12, Jefferson wrote him that he had "not been able to send for the plank during my stay here, but the waggon will go for it the next week so as to have it ready. I shall return here with Chisolm the middle of October, and shall certainly have more than a month's work for you here, and I shall be ready for you in Albemarle the moment I go back."[7]

Soon after his arrival back at Monticello, Jefferson continued his dialogue with John Wayles Eppes on the Poplar Forest-Pantops predicament. Having had the opportunity on his recent visit to Bedford to select the land he proposed to transfer in exchange for Pantops, he found that he could "lay off a parcel of between 770 and 80 acres, . . . divided from the residue of my tract by a small creek or branch, called Tomahawk which runs entirely across it and which altho wanting a few acres to be equal in quantity to Pantops, would command a higher price at market, lands being one fourth dearer there than in Albemarle. But I would at a future day engage to make it up equal in quantity also." Then, in what has become one of the most frequently quoted of his many references to Poplar Forest, he added: "Besides, if we make this exchange and Francis should settle on it, it would certainly be my intention to add to it the dwelling house I have built there. It is an octagon of 50 f. diameter, of brick, well built, will be plaistered this fall, when nothing will be wanting to finish it compleatly but the cornices and some of the doors. When finished, it will be the best dwelling house in the state, except that of Monticello; perhaps preferable to that, as more proportioned to the faculties of a private citizen." In addition, he told Eppes that he "would probably go on with the cornices and doors at my leisure at Monticello, and in planting & improving the grounds around it. I have just paid between 3. and 4000 Dollars cash for the building, besides doing all the planter's work, which is fully the half. So that it's cost may be very moderately rated at 6000 D." He closed by sending his respects to Mrs. Eppes, and his love to Francis, "whom we are expecting to come on to school room."[8]

In spite of this phenomenally generous offer, Eppes did not take Jefferson up on the exchange of lands right away. Perhaps he wondered if the offer was really serious. Although Jefferson wrote that the parcel he now proposed to exchange for Pantops was "adjacent to the one on Buffalo formerly laid off,"[9] he had never made good on that gift of land, which he had promised to Eppes in 1801, over a decade earlier (see Chap. V). The subject of

Pantops and its disposition would continue to be a bone of contention between the two men for awhile longer, but from this time on, Jefferson never wavered in his plans to leave Poplar Forest to the only surviving child of his daughter Maria. Almost everything that he henceforth lavished on the house and the property, not to mention the arrangements he was soon to make for the education of his grandson, were done with this object in mind.

On October 10, 1812, Jefferson informed Goodman that a recent fall from his horse had incapacitated him, and would prevent him from returning to Poplar Forest as soon as he had planned. In the meantime, he wrote, Hugh Chisolm, who was then at Monticello, would return to Bedford next week with Reuben Perry, who had been interrupted in his work by a summons "to attend our court" in Albemarle. Upon his return, Chisolm was to "proceed to do the plaistering of the house, or he will not finish this season." To prepare for him, and to ensure that the work would indeed proceed as soon as Chisolm arrived, Jefferson told Goodman that "100 bushels of lime must be got of Mr. Clarke, and a load of it brought home & put into the log house near the dwelling house." He further directed Goodman to obtain "about 200 bushels of very clear gritty sand." Jefferson also suggested that "Chisolm had better lodge in the large room below which should be cleaned out for him," and as he [Jefferson] could not be there, "the meat laid by for me must be used for him." Chisolm could "either have his dinner given him at his own room or with you as you please."[10] He followed this letter with one on October 18 in which he informed Goodman that although he hoped to return "the moment I can travel without too much pain," it was still uncertain if he would be able to visit Poplar Forest that fall. "In the meantime I hope you will do every thing to forward Mr. Chisolm, as the season is far advanced, and I am anxious to be done with it, and not to interrupt another year with it. Two hands will be necessary for him till he gets a stock of mortar made up. . . . Afterwards one will suffice, and that had better be Phill Hubbard because he understands the making mortar so well." Chisolm had informed Jefferson that he thought he could "do the whole in 7 weeks. This will carry it into December when plaistering becomes very precarious"[11]

On November 11, a month after he sent the first of his two letters regarding the plastering to Goodman, Jefferson noted in his Memorandum Book that he "set out for Pop. For." As soon as he got there, he found there was a problem:

I sent here from Albemarle a Plaisterer to plaister my house. I did not order on any plaister of Paris because I understood it could always be bought in Lynchburg, and the small quantity of only 5 bushels was necessary. I am disappointed

however in my expectation of buying even that quantity in Lynchburg, and being told you have some there which you had bought for the purposes of your farm, I take the liberty of requesting you to spare me 5 bushels. I will either have the same quantity brought from Richmond to replace it, or, as your communications there are so much more perfect and direct than mine if you will take the trouble I will gladly pay you the price now at whatever advance you shall suppose it to have got to by the circumstances of the war, with the transportation, etc. I am the more in hope this will not be inconvenient to you as the plaister is not usually put on the farm till spring, and there will therefore be abundant time to have it replaced. The plaistering of a house being a permanent thing, I am unwilling to have a permanent eyesore in it, occasioned by this small failure.[12]

The war to which he referred was the War of 1812, which had broken out earlier that year, and the neighbor to whom he wrote was Charles Johnston of Sandusky, who was able to provide what Jefferson needed. On November 19, he recorded in his Memorandum Book that he "pd. Chas. Johnston for 5. bush. plaister Paris 6.75."

Virginians didn't celebrate Thanksgiving in the early nineteenth century as they do today, but November was still turkey time, and on the seventeenth of the month, Jefferson recorded giving Kate $3.00 for six turkeys. Several days later Charles Clay was kind enough to send him additional provender during this late fall visit. Along with a sample of cider came the invitation to ask for more "if you think it worth putting in your bottles," as "it will give me more pleasure than any use I shall make of it." Clay's wife contributed to the cause as well, and both she and the good Parson undoubtedly shared the accompanying sentiments that he credited solely to her: "Mrs. Clay begs the acceptance of a cheese (of her own make) as a testimony of her high respect for that Patriot who had more than doubled the extent of his country with peaceful negotiations, without having ended the lives of his fellow citizens."[13]

On this, his last trip in 1812, Jefferson once again tended to matters horticultural. In fact, his November and December planting memoranda for 1812 are the most important clues remaining as to the original intent of his landscaping scheme at Poplar Forest. On November 20 he checked the nursery and found that all the saplings that had been heeled in had survived. From the twenty-fifth to the twenty-seventh he transplanted them all: "Took from the Nursery & planted in the grounds round the house 20 weeping willows. 30 golden willows. 10 Athenian poplars. 3 Lombardy poplars. 2 Monto. Aspens. 16 Calycanthuses." He also planted "12. Mont. Aspens [and] 16 paper mulberries" in the nursery on November 27th, and sometime during the month noted that he was either to plant, or had planted "clump of Athenian & Balsam poplars at each corner of house.

Fig. 49 Southwest elevation. This ca. 1930 photo shows several of the trees that once delineated the upper level of the south lawn. According to his notes, Jefferson first planted shrubs to define the banks between the two levels. This photograph also shows a windowless southwest wall, rather than the way it appeared both in Jefferson's time and after a partial restoration in the 1940s (cf. fig. 117). *(Virginia State Library and Archives)*

intermix locusts, common & Kentucky, red-buds, dogwoods, calycanthus, liriodendron." He also intended to "plant a double row of paper mulberries from stairways to the Mounds," but soon discovered a slight problem that he may not have noticed before. On December 5 he measured the distance from the house to the mounds, in all likelihood as preparation for setting out the mulberries, and realized that Phill's Hubbard's calculations, made when he was building the mounds with his wheelbarrow loads of dirt, had not been as exact as he could have wished. "From the wall of the Western Stairway to the foot of the Western mound" he found the distance to be ninety-one feet. From the eastern stairway to the foot of the eastern mound, what should have been the equivalent was only eighty-four feet; seven feet shorter.[14]

On the same day (December 5) he noted that discovery, Jefferson recorded that he had planted "Mont. Aspens from Mr Clay's. viz. 12. round the Eastern mound & 4 round West [mound]. 6. still wanting. planted also 2. European mullberies from mr. Clay's as part of the double row from the Western Mound towards the house." That these two mulberries were planted on this row might relate to his recent realization that the western row was longer than its eastern counterpart, due to the placement of the mounds. He made further calculations, and these, too, were in relation to the planting of mulberries: "From the N. door along the circular road to the gate due South from the house is 270 yds. Consqly. 540 yrds. round. Plant a row of paper mulberries on each side all around except the curve at the N. Door; at 20. f. apart. will take about 160. trees." Jefferson was obviously quite fond of "Otaheite or Paper mulberries," and regarded them as "valuable for the regularity of their form, velvet leaf and for being fruitless. They are charming near a porch for densely shading it."[15]

Jefferson's last note in his December 5 memorandum dealt with the slopes on either side of the sunken lawn: "Plant on each bank, right & left, on the S. side of the house, a row of lilacs, Althaeas, Gelder roses, Roses, calycanthus."[16] As at the President's House and in most landscapes of the period where there was a sunken lawn or parterre, this feature at Poplar Forest was meant to be defined not only by the slopes on either side but by ornamentals planted on them (fig 49).

Some of Jefferson's notations regarding his plans for planting at Poplar Forest are so abbreviated that differing interpretations are possible, and in several instances it seems that they were things he planned to do rather than things that he had accomplished. In general, though, the notations show well how much attention he gave to the landscaping of the grounds around his villa retreat, and certainly document his intentions. He obviously had kept his word, given several months earlier to John Wayles Eppes, that he would continue "in planting & improving the grounds around" the house.[17]

Jefferson soon had another job for Reuben Perry at Poplar Forest. By now he had lived in his new house long enough to realize that there was at least one serious problem that needed to be corrected. The fireplaces didn't draw, or rather some of them drew *too* much. On December 10 he wrote Robert Richardson at the Oxford Iron Works, located several miles east of Lynchburg, that he had "occasion for some iron backs for my fireplaces at this place, of a particular size and form. Mr. Reuben Perry, housejoiner at Lynchburg, has promised to make the mould and forward it to you, and, as it is probable his wood will not be well seasoned & liable to shrink, I have to request you to have 7 cast as soon as convenient."[18] He had put words in Perry's mouth, but at least he wrote his builder that same day, explaining the problem:

In addition to the jobs to be done here I must add 3. chimney screens to be made of half-inch boards, plain, to fit exactly within the grounds for the architraves of the fireplaces. They are for the West fireplace of the parlour, and the North fireplaces of the East & West rooms because these rooms having two fireplaces each, the one which has no fire in it draws the smoke of the next room down into the room. The battens are to be within and so shortened as to let the screen lie flush on the margin within the ground. . . . I have written to Mr. Richardson at the Oxford iron works to make the iron backs as soon as he receives the models from you. I find that for wanting of plumbing the grounds in the parlour, several of them will be to take down when we go to putting up the architraves & cornices. I pray you to have strict attention paid to this in the rooms still to be done. I press Mr. Goodman to get all the plank ready as soon as possible and rely on your promise to finish everything as soon as the plank is ready.[19]

He "pressed" Mr. Goodman several days later, telling him that "all the plank necessary for finishing Mr. Perry's work must be got & kilndried with as little delay as possible and notice given him to come & finish." On Dec. 26, having returned to Monticello, Jefferson had to urge Perry again to send the model for the firebacks right away, as Richardson had informed him that the furnace would not "continue much longer in blast." Perry obviously complied, and the firebacks were delivered in February 1813.[20]

On December 13, just prior to leaving Poplar Forest, Jefferson gave Goodman instructions that would, if carried out, make his visits the next year more delectable: "Sow a bed of Carrots, & one of Salsafia, each about as large as the Asparagus bed; and sow a small bed of spinach. Long haricots to be planted as usual, & Lettuce to be sown in the spring. If a thimblefull of seed could be sowed every other Monday, on a bed of 4. f. wide & 6. or 8. feet long it would be best, as I should then always find some fit for use when I come."[21]

He also, just prior to his departure, returned the favor

of the gifts the Clays had sent him. On December 14, he wrote Charles Clay: "I go certainly tomorrow, *wind* and weather permitting and both have abated considerably. I promised you some of my kale seed, which I now send. I do not remember to have seen salsafia in your garden and yet it is one of the best roots for the winter. Some call it the oyster plant because fried in batter it can scarcely be distinguished from a fried oyster." Not to be outdone in generosity, Parson Clay returned the favor as soon as he could, and ingenuously invited himself to dinner as well. Upon learning that Jefferson had arrived on his spring visit in 1813, he sent a servant to Poplar Forest with a gift and a note: "I yesterday heard of your being up and intended visiting you this day with a mess of asparagus, which grow upon us with a threatning aspect. We shall want your frequent aid in keeping it within proper subjugation; Billy brings you a mess, and I propose coming to see how you have it dressed, with the utmost respect." Jefferson cordially responded several days later: "Our spinning machine is in operation, and a piece of cloth is begun with the flying shuttle, neither goes on perfectly as yet, from the want of a little more practice: but they will give Mrs. Clay an idea of what would be their proper operation, if she can do me the favor to come and take a plantation dinner with me tomorrow. You will come of course, according to promise."[22]

In conjunction with his attempts to increase his flocks of sheep during these years, Jefferson established spinning and weaving operations at both Poplar Forest and Monticello. The effort was primarily to provide clothing for his slave work force, as the War of 1812 effectively cut off the importation of cloth. In his memorandum of December 1811 he had instructed Goodman as to which of the female slaves were to be "employed in weaving," and noted that they were to spin not only wool and cotton, but flax as well.[23] As the war escalated, these operations achieved a sense of urgency, and on February 21, 1812, Jefferson had written Goodman that he hoped "the spinning and weaving has got well under way. I am informed from Richmond that there is not a single yard of cotton or oznabrigs to be had there, nor is there another yard ordered or expected. We have no chance therefore of clothing the negroes next winter but with what we shall make ourselves." Later that year, he had directed Goodman to send "Sally & Maria [to Monticello] to learn to weave & spin." Maria took to it right away, and on March 5, 1813, Jefferson told his overseer that she was "becoming a capital spinner. . . . She learnt from a girl younger than herself in 4 or 5 days." Unfortunately, of Sally he reported, "we can make nothing at all. I never saw so hopeless a subject. She seems neither to have the inclination nor the understanding to learn."[24]

The same day that he wrote the Clays regarding his spinning operations during his spring, 1813, visit to Poplar Forest, Jefferson also reported to Martha on the same

subject: "The spinning Jenny is at work, well while with washed cotton, but very ill when with unwashed, at least this is Maria's way of accounting for the occasional difference of it's work. The flying shuttle began a little yesterday, but owing to a variety of fixings which the loom required it exhibited very poorly. We hope to see it do better to day." Operations continued to improve, at least judging from a letter Jefferson sent his brother Randolph on May 25, after he had returned to Monticello: "I shall be able to give you the spinning Jenny which I carried to Bedford. It is a very fine one of 12 spindles. I am obliged to make a larger one for that place, and the cart which carries it up shall bring the one there to Snowden on its return." He had already planned for his larger jenny at Poplar Forest in his instructions to Goodman: "In making your spinning house let the door be 4 f. 6. I. wide in the clear to let in the machine of 24 spindles."[25]

Reuben Perry had apparently continued his work on the house throughout the winter of 1812/13, and was definitely still at work during Jefferson's spring visit. In the same May 6, 1813, letter in which he told Martha of the progress in the spinning operations, Jefferson added: "I am afraid I shall be detained here in getting Reuben Perry off before I go away, if I leave him I shall have no confidence in his following me. Still I shall not fail to be at home within a week or ten days from this date."[26] On May 15 he returned to Monticello, and his confidence in his builder was restored when Perry came to Monticello to build the barn. In July Perry presented his employer with a bill for $212.87, presumably for work that he had done at Poplar Forest. Included in his itemized account were individual items for "framing, skirting & shingling, planking, shingling hips, flooring, flooring loft, making & hanging 5 dble. doors, [and] bargeboard."[27] In December 1813 he presented a second bill to Jefferson for his work at both places. The total for Poplar Forest in this second account was £63-4-7, or in dollars, $210.76. Perry included charges for preparing the plaster grounds throughout the house, as well as for fabricating window sills and "2 trap doors," which presumably led from each side of the attic above the two bedrooms to the roof. Perry subtracted from his bill "the price of Jame Hubbard," which he gave as $450, and several lesser amounts for other costs that he had incurred. In all, he received only "sixty seven dollars and 48. cents" in cash for his work at Poplar Forest and Monticello.[28]

Reuben Perry's work was now done, but it remained for Hugh Chisolm to return and finish the plastering. As it turned out, he would have far more to do than just that. By the time he arrived, Jefferson was well into planning another building operation at Poplar Forest. In fact, even before Perry finished his plaster grounds and working on the trapdoors, Jefferson had announced that he was ready to start "putting up and pulling down" once again.

"A WING OF OFFICES"
(1813–15)

On April 18, 1813, Jefferson wrote John Wayles Eppes yet another letter on the subject of Pantops versus Poplar Forest. It was in answer to one that Eppes had written, and his first sentence showed how far apart in their thinking the two men still were: "I have been in the less haste to answer your last letter because it appeared from that as if the farther we proceeded in our negociation, the wider we got apart." Not only did Eppes want Jefferson to give more land than his former father-in-law had proposed the previous September as an equitable exchange for Pantops, he wanted that extra land to be "laid off so as to include the Dwelling house" at Poplar Forest. That was the proverbial straw that broke the camel's back:

Now certainly from the moment of contemplating an exchange, with the idea of placing Francis's property in a mass together, that of annexing to it the excellent dwelling house I have built there has been associated by me with delight, and in consequence of it I have already resumed the inside finishing, which I had not before intended. I have engaged a workman to build offices, have laid off a handsome curtilage connecting the house with the Tomahawk, have inclosed and divided it into suitable appendages to a Dwelling house, and have begun it's improvement by planting trees of use and ornament. The consideration for this was to be the gratifying him by the gift of so comfortable an establishment. But your proposition goes to take from it the character of a gift, and to make it merely a part of an equivalent for property already his. Supposing the lands given in exchange to be as they are deemed, equal in quantity and value to those recieved, it is no slight proposition to throw in a house, which in its present state is of more than half the value of the land, and if finished will be nearly of its whole value.[1]

Eppes continued to press his case in a letter of May 25, but the exchange he proposed was never to take place. Francis would, of course, get Poplar Forest in good time, but not for the moment. His father would never do so, though he would try again years later. For the moment, though, there was another pressing concern of more immediate benefit to Francis than his eventual inheritance. It was his education. In his April 18 letter to Eppes, Jefferson stated that another grandson, Thomas Jefferson Randolph, "had given us reason to hope we should, ere this, have seen Francis here for the purpose of going to school," and suggested one near Monticello at Milton that he might attend.[2] Though Jefferson didn't then know it, Francis was already at school; in fact two letters that would explain things were then on their way to Monticello. On April 11, both Francis and his cousin John Wayles Baker had written him. Francis, then eleven years old, told his grandfather: "I wish to see you very

much. I am Sorry that you wont Write to me. This leter will make twice I have wrote to you and if you dont answer this leter I Shant write to you anymore. I have got trough my latin Gramer and I am going trough again. I enclose a leter in this from My Cousin Wale Baker. Give my love to all of the family." Fortunately, his cousin's letter mentioned where they were, which Francis had neglected to tell: "I am at school at Lynchburg to a gentleman of the name of Mr. Holcomb. I like him very much. He is very good to cousin and myself."[3] For his part, the senior Eppes sought to clarify matters when he wrote Jefferson on May 25. He had heard of the Milton school but had dismissed it as "it was not a desirable situation for a boy as young as Francis." Instead, he had "sent him to Lynchburg," and assured Jefferson that "the school at which he is placed is a very good one." He added that if Jefferson thought another school might be more suitable "than the one in which he is placed I shall feel pleasure in yielding on that subject of my opinions to yours."[4]

Either Jefferson had not received his letter, had ignored it, or simply hadn't opened it when he wrote Eppes a month later from Monticello: "I was in Bedford a fortnight in the month of May, and did not know that Francis and his cousin Baker were within 10 miles of me at Lynchburg." At least he had received the boys' letters by then: "I learnt it by letters from themselves after I had returned home. I shall go there early in August and hope their master will permit them to pass their Saturdays and Sundays with me."[5] Almost immediately upon his arrival at Poplar Forest that August, he wrote letters to Francis and his tutor. To his grandson he announced that he was sending "two horses for yourself and your cousin and hope your tutor will permit you both to come and stay with me." To his tutor he wrote:

Th. Jefferson presents his compliments to the Principal of the Lynchburg academy with who Francis Eppes a grandson of his is, the only child of a deceased daughter, whom he has but rare opportunities of seeing. There is with him also another connection, Master Baker. It will be a gratification if they can be permitted to come and stay with him till Monday morning when they shall be sent back again. If the principal himself could at any time make it convenient to come and take a plantation dinner with Th. J. he would be very happy to see him. He salutes him with esteem and respect.[6]

The "Principal of the Lynchburg academy" was Thomas A. Holcombe, a Lynchburg lawyer as well as a schoolmaster. Elected mayor in 1824, he achieved even more fame as "the Father of temperance in our State."[7] Even though the senior Eppes had not consulted Jefferson before sending Francis to him, both the teacher and the location of his school met with the grandfather's approval: "I was much pleased too that Francis was placed at school at Lynchburg, as, besides giving me opportunities of seeing him, it will habitualize him to the neighborhood, and give him those early attachments of friendship and acquaintance which carry their impression and value through life."[8] Though Jefferson's hopes for Francis's eventual induction into the old-boy network of Lynchburg would never be realized, at least he and his grandson did find ample opportunities to see each other often during Jefferson's subsequent visits to Poplar Forest. Unfortunately, they missed connections this time. Francis was then with his father in Millbrook, and it was not until his November trip to Bedford that Jefferson finally caught up with his grandson.

In addition to giving his views on the proposed land transfer, Jefferson's several letters to the senior Eppes during this period tell a great deal about the work then going on with the house at Poplar Forest, though on occasion he might have been more accurate had he used the future rather than the past tense in his reports. The correspondence also shows, once again, that sometimes by accident, more often by design (as it were), Jefferson was almost constitutionally incapable of living in a completed house.

Reuben Perry was still at work on the inside finishing, including the installation of the iron firebacks and preparing the plaster grounds, during Jefferson's May 1813 visit, certainly justifying the statement to Eppes a month earlier that "I have already resumed the inside finishing." On the other hand, his assertion in that same letter of April 18 that "I have engaged a workman to build offices," was premature, for it was not until almost exactly a year later that he really began to embark on this addition. Part of the reason for the delay was undoubtedly the fact that Hugh Chisolm was not yet available

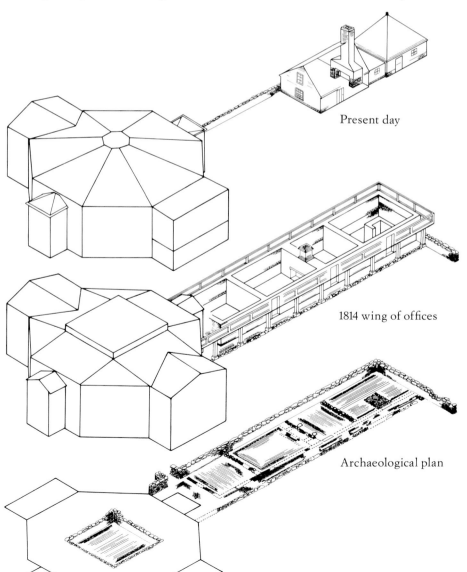

Present day

1814 wing of offices

Archaeological plan

Fig. 50 Poplar Forest, office wing, isometric drawing, 1991. The middle view shows the presumed original appearance and arrangement of rooms in Jefferson's office addition (cf. fig. 15 [The President's House] and fig. 53 [Monticello]). *(The Corporation for Jefferson's Poplar Forest)*

to do the work. On July 17, 1813, Jefferson advised Goodman that he wished "to have the work ready for Chisolm in case he gets released from military duty in time to do it."[9] That wasn't to happen until nine months later. On April 16, 1814, Jefferson wrote a note that Hugh Chisolm, now free from his military service and on his way to Poplar Forest from Monticello, hand-delivered to William Shirman, of Nelson County:

I have about 80 or 100 perch of stone work to be laid at Poplar Forest in Bedford, 10 miles from Lynchburg: and also from one to two hundred perch to lay at this place; in all of which I should be willing to employ you. . . . Mr. Chisolm, the bearer of this letter, a bricklayer of this neighborhood can give you full information of the subject. He is now on his way to Poplar Forest to do some plaistering and brickwork for me. It is while he will be there that I should want you to do the stonework at that place. I shall be there the first or second week in May, and should be glad if you could come then and let us agree on this subject.[10]

As it turned out, Shirman had other commitments, and was unable to do the work. Instead, the versatile Hugh Chisolm was once again called upon not only "to do some plaistering and brickwork" but also to do the stonework, and then to continue and ultimately finish what Jefferson referred to as "offices."

As was mentioned in connection with the offices at the President's House in Washington (Chap. V), the term *offices* in early-nineteenth-century American parlance did not mean what it does today. There, as at Poplar Forest, what Jefferson meant in using the term was a wing of service rooms. Linguistically as well as architecturally, the offices at Poplar Forest resembled both those at the President's House and at Monticello to a marked degree. Both of them, however, were larger than those soon to be built in Bedford. At both other places, two ranges of office wings were built, extending on both sides of the houses they served. At Poplar Forest there was only one wing. In all three places, the wings were built into the slope of the land. On one front, all a viewer could see was a low wall, extending only a few feet above grade. On the opposite side, the wings were fully above grade, and there a covered walkway protected the passage, with doors opening from it into the individul rooms behind. Above, the roofs were topped with plank, forming a "terras," as Jefferson generally termed it, which served as a deck or promenade for walking in good weather (fig. 50).

Jefferson had written to Mr. Shirman that he would be at Poplar Forest during the first or second week in May,

Fig. 51 In 1989–91, the original foundations and floor paving of Jefferson's 1814 wing of offices were uncovered and found to be in a remarkable state of preservation. *(The Corporation for Jefferson's Poplar Forest)*

but on May 10, 1814, he wrote Chisolm that his proposed trip had been "detained by the carriage maker at Charlottesville far beyond my expectation." He would, he felt sure, be able to be there on the twentieth, but even that generous estimate proved to be optimistic. On May 22, Chisolm wrote him in some desperation: "I have done the plaistering and have begun to lay the stone wall myself as you have maid a much longer stay in Albemarle than I expected. I have been afraid that some accident must have happened from your delay. If it should be the case I pray you would write immediately the size of the building and the openings and whether I shall build the pillars with circular brick or with square bricks. The people are all well at both places. Except my best wishes."[11] Fortunately for Chisolm, unfortunately for later-day historians who might have learned a lot had his questions been answered in writing, the day he wrote was the day Jefferson left Monticello. Upon his arrival at Poplar Forest on the twenty-fifth, he undoubtedly gave verbal answers to Chisolm's questions.

It is only in recent years, thanks to an extensive archeological excavation, that much at all is known of Jefferson's wing of offices at Poplar Forest (fig. 51). The stone wall that Hugh Chisolm laid — which now serves in part as a retaining wall and in part as the foundation for walls

of later structures built on the site — remains, as does a brick side wall and portions of the south wall, incorporated in a later kitchen. Other than that, all above-ground traces of his office wing have disappeared. The exact time and circumstances of the disappearance are not known, but it was after both Jefferson's and Francis Eppes's tenures.

The archeological investigation found the foundations and flooring of the office wing to be remarkably intact, only inches below grade in the yard east of the house. Immediately to the east of the eastern stair pavilion and adjacent to it, a passage led from the rear yard, via stone steps set in the stone wall, to the higher level of the front yard. Eastward of this passage were four rooms. The archeological investigations established the uses of two of them and provided evidence for the probable uses of the other two. The room closest to the house was almost square, measuring sixteen by fifteen feet, and was unheated, a condition that hints it was intended either as a dairy or simply as a storage room. The next room in sequence, moving east, was the largest of the four. It measured twenty-four by fifteen feet, and was the kitchen. Beyond, and sharing the same chimney, was what is thought to have been the cook's room. It was almost square, measuring fifteen feet, two inches, by fif-

Fig. 52 The 1989–91 archeological investigation of Jefferson's office wing also determined that the two brick outbuildings near its eastern end had been re-built over its foundations. (*The Corporation for Jefferson's Poplar Forest*)

teen feet. The fourth room was a smokehouse, which measured twenty-three by fifteen feet. The eastern wall of this last room was partially built into the eastern mound.[12]

The covered, stone-paved, piazza connecting the offices, and forming the southern side of the wing, was three-feet, six inches, wide (fig. 52). Along its southern, or outer, edge, both square pier bases and pie-shaped bricks were found. At present, the ultimate answer to Chisolm's question as to whether he should "build the pillars with circular brick or with square bricks" is unclear. Evidence suggests that another of his questions, concerning the openings, was answered by having a doorway every twenty-five feet from the passageway between the house and the wing to the smokehouse. Although the rooms were of varying dimensions, regular spacing of the doors leading into them would have presented a symmetrical appearance on the exterior.

On June 6, 1814, Jefferson, still at Poplar Forest, sent Martha a report on Chisolm's progress, or lack of same: "I have for some time been sensible I should be detained here longer than I had expected, but could not till now judge how long. Chisolm will finish his work in about 10 days, and it is very essential that I should see the walls covered with their plates, that they may be in a state of preservation. This will keep me 3 or 4 days longer, so that I expect to be here still about a fortnight longer." The plates — timbers laid on top of the walls, and thus covering them — would protect the still-damp walls and mortar until they finished settling. Once that was done, the plates could safely receive the heavy joists needed for framing the deck above. Jefferson's sense of urgency in making sure the plates were put on the walls before he left was probably prompted by the weather during his visit: "There have not been more than 2 or 3 days without rain since I came here," he told Martha.[13]

Just before his departure, Jefferson paid Chisolm $10.00, and on July 5, after he returned to Monticello, recorded that "Hugh Chisolm finished at Pop. For. the 1st. day of this month." He wrote John Adams that same day, and revealed that he had done far more on his recent visit than supervise Chisolm's work. Perhaps the incessant rain had contributed to this endeavor: "I am just returned from one of my long absences, having been at my other home for five weeks past. Having more leisure there than here for reading I amused myself with reading seriously Plato's Republic. I am wrong however in calling it amusement, for it was the heaviest task-work I ever went through. . . . I laid it down after to ask myself how it could have been that the world should have so

Fig. 53 Monticello, south office wing. In 1814 Jefferson wrote John Wayles Eppes that the offices at Poplar Forest were built "in the manner of those at Monticello." *(Robert C. Lautman, 1992, for Monticello, Thomas Jefferson Memorial Foundation, Inc.).*

long consented to give approbation to such nonsense as this?"[14]

A week or so after that, Jefferson went through yet another chapter, or at least another verse, in the heavy taskwork that the subject of Pantops had become. Having been thwarted in his attempt to gain more on the proposed exchange of land that Jefferson had suggested, John Wayles Eppes — once again without telling his former father-in-law — had offered Pantops for sale. On July 16, 1814, Jefferson wrote Eppes: "Mr. Estin Randolph has showed me a letter from you, proposing to sell him Pantops, in order to lay out the money in lands in your neighborhood for Francis." At the time, Randolph held the lease on Pantops, and Jefferson had consulted with him before writing Eppes the previous September. Needless to say, this proposed sale, with its concomitant proposal for Francis to move near his father in Buckingham, did not comport with Jefferson's plans for his grandson to inherit and live at Poplar Forest. It was partially to convince Eppes once again just how valuable the Bedford property was that he described the work that he had accomplished, and what he planned in the future:

I have this summer built a wing of offices 110 feet long, in the manner of those at Monticello, with a flat roof in the level of the floor of the house. The whole, as it now stands, could not be valued at less than 10,000 D. and I am going on. I am also making such improvements of the grounds as require time to perfect themselves: and instead of clearing on the lands proposed for him once in 5 years only as formerly mentioned, I clear on them every year, and by the time he comes of age, there will probably be 300. acres of open land, so that he would be comfortably and handsomely fixed at once; and in a part of the country which I really consider as the most desirable in this state, for soil, climate and convenience to market[15] (fig. 53).

Fortunately, Eppes did not go to see for himself. At the time that letter was written, the wing had not been roofed, nor were any of the rooms finished inside. In October 1814 Jefferson wrote Jeremiah Goodman, whose brother was scheduled to work on the roof: "I wrote you Sep. 27. Since that your brother has been taken ill, and is in such a situation in point of health as to render it certain he cannot go to Bedford. Consequently the job of covering the offices must lie over till the spring."[16] At least the walls had been covered with the protective plates.

By the time the wings were finally roofed, several of Jefferson's granddaughters were old enough to accompany him on his visits to Poplar Forest. The pleasure the completed terrace afforded was commented upon by one of them years afterward, and by Jefferson himself soon after the work was completed. Ellen Coolidge recalled that her grandfather habitually retired after dinner (which was about three P.M.) for some hours, "and later in the afternoon walked with us on the terrace," while Jefferson, writing his daughter Martha in August 1817, told her that "about twilight of the evening, we sally out with the owls & bats and take our evening exercise on the terras."[17]

The addition of the office wing to the east made profound changes to the house at Poplar Forest, both architecturally and sociologically. Architecturally, the wing destroyed the careful symmetry and balance, or in more abstract terms, the rationality, that had governed the original design: a central house flanked on either side by mounds, and beyond them by the octagonal necessaries reflecting the shape of the house. Of course, a companion wing to the west would have righted the symmetry again, but nothing in Jefferson's existing correspondence nor in the architectural and archeological investigations that have been undertaken gives any evidence whatsoever that he ever built, much less contemplated building, a matching western wing.

Sociologically, the addition of the office wing can be seen as a beginning step in the transformation of Poplar Forest from a villa to a farmhouse. Until this time, and indeed throughout his ownership, Jefferson enjoyed Poplar Forest in the same manner as the ancients had enjoyed their villas: as occasional retreats. But Jefferson was not building the office wing primarily for himself. It was constructed only after he had determined that Francis Eppes would make Poplar Forest his year-round home, and contained rooms that were far more essential to such use than to a villa retreat. Of course, later owners would do far more to change the nature and use of the house at Poplar Forest than either Jefferson or Francis Eppes did, but the process of transformation had begun.

In any event, the wing was not an unqualified success. John Hemings would have to repair it only ten years or so after it was built and eventually it would have to be replaced altogether (see chaps. XX and XXIII).[18] When that happened, two separate buildings, rather than a connected wing of offices, were constructed (see fig. 109). These buildings, which remain, occupy the easternmost portion of the site and were probably built in part of material salvaged from Jefferson's wing of offices. The western building, closest to the house, was a kitchen; its companion, adjacent to the mound, seems to have served, at different times, both as a smokehouse and as a dairy.

Unlike the terrace that capped Jefferson's office wing, each of the two replacement buildings has a steep roof; that on the kitchen is gabled, that on the smokehouse-dairy is pyramidal. Perhaps later owners did not have the luxury of time for (much less the conception of) a contemplative walk "about twilight of the evening . . . with the owls & bats." Certainly such a conceit is far more akin to the poetic idea of a villa retreat than to a more prosaic working farm.

"Furnished in the Simplest Manner"
AND
"The Finest Part of Virginia"
(1814–15)

After his return to Monticello from a second trip in 1814 to Poplar Forest, Jefferson wrote Jeremiah Goodman on December 10: "I am satisfied there will be peace this winter." That being the case, he urged him to "hasten therefore the getting the tobacco ready and sending it off to market when it can be handled. The great prices will be for that market the moment peace opens the bay."[1] Jefferson's confidence that the Chesapeake Bay would soon be reopened to commerce was bolstered by information he had just received from James Monroe that negotiations to end the War of 1812 were about to be satisfactorily concluded. His "insider information" was confirmed later that month, when a preliminary treaty was signed in Ghent on Christmas Day 1814. That treaty was ratified by President James Madison's signature at Washington on February 15, 1815.

For the United States, the nadir of the war had occurred when the British entered Washington on August 24, 1814, and torched the President's House and the Capitol. The destruction of the Congressional Library, then housed in the Capitol, prompted Jefferson to offer to sell his own library from Monticello to replace it. In April 1815 he received the sum of $23,950 for his collection, and the state of his finances at the time can be gauged by the fact he was able "to remit to myself" only $8,500 of the total.[2] The major part had gone to the payment of his debts.

Because of the extraordinary expenses the country had incurred during the war years, both the United States and the Commonwealth of Virginia imposed spe-

cial taxes when peace was declared. The bill that became law in Virginia was passed by the General Assembly on January 7, 1815. Items subject to the state tax were divided into various categories: from slaves to bookcases, from farm animals to dining tables and tea tables. At least, these are the items on which Jefferson paid duty at Poplar Forest, as he recorded on February 11:

Property in Bedford and Campbell taxed by the State

		D. C.
46 slaves of 12 years old & upwards	*@ 80 cents*	*. . . 36.80*
of 9 years and under 12	*@ 50 "*	*10.50*
12 horses and colts	*@ 21 "*	*2.52*
39 cattle	*@ 3 "*	*1.17*
4 bookcases with mahogany sashes	*@ 50 "*	*2.*
3 parts of Dining table mahogany	*@ 25 "*	*.75*
4 Pembroke tables, say teatables mahogany	*@ 25 "*	*1.*
3790 acres of land @ 85 cents on the 100 D. value		

Houses considered to be of less that $500 value were not taxed, but that exception did not apply to Poplar Forest, which the assessor valued at $4,000. Although he had to pay the *state* tax on his furnishings, he owed no *federal* tax on them. As he jotted down in his notes regarding the latter tax: "beds, bedding & kitchen furniture is exempt, & where the rest of the furniture of a house does not exceed 200. D. it pays nothing. I consider my furniture at Poplar Forest as under that value, but of this the assessor will judge for himself on an examination of the furniture."[3] As far as is known, the assessor agreed.

Fig. 54 Pembroke table. This mahogany table with pine and poplar secondary woods, now at Monticello, is thought to have been Jefferson's, and is said to have been acquired by the Cobbs family when Francis Eppes sold Poplar Forest. It may well be one of the four Pembroke tables on which Jefferson paid taxes in 1815. *(Monticello, Thomas Jefferson Memorial Foundation, Inc.)*

Fig. 55 Revolving table. An undisputed provenance establishes this as one of the pieces of furniture used by Jefferson at Poplar Forest. More than likely it was made at the Monticello joinery and was the table referred to in Jefferson's December 5, 1811, letter to Edmund Bacon. (See also fig. 56). *(Monticello, Thomas Jefferson Memorial Foundation, Inc.)*

Very little is known of the furnishings that Jefferson had at Poplar Forest, and in lieu of any inventory ever having been made, his comments on their total worth, as well as his list of the few items he considered taxable in 1815, provide extremely important information. In regard to furniture, the 1815 levy was something of a tax on the rich. The Commonwealth of Virginia imposed the duty only on pieces made "in whole or in part of mahogany," the most expensive of imported woods and generally the species selected only for the finest furniture in the finest houses. The four Pembroke tables were in all likelihood those made from an order that Jefferson had placed with James Oldham in December 1807 for "so much *fine* mahogany as would make me 4 Pembroke tables"[4] (fig. 54).

The three-part dining-room table, on which Jefferson paid $.75 in taxes, may be the one now owned by descendants of the family who purchased Poplar Forest from Francis Eppes. Its center part is a drop-leaf table — square when the leaves are opened — while the matching ends are polygonal. If placed together without the center section, the two end pieces form a perfect octagon, and if used with it, the ensemble forms an elongated octagon. Each of the several ways it could be used was a perfect shape for Poplar Forest.

The "4 bookcases with mahogany sashes" were a unique feature of the original Poplar Forest furnishings and were mentioned in a description of the house given years afterward:

In the drawing-room there was what Mr. Jefferson called his petit-format library, contained in four cases, each of which was perhaps between three and four feet in width and height. The books, to economize space, were generally of the smallest sized editions published. He had first made this collection for his convenience at Washington. It contained upwards of one hundred volumes of British, a considerable collection of Italian and French, and a few favorite Greek and Latin poets, and a larger number of prose writers of the same languages — all, it is unnecessary to say, in the original.[5]

Among the authors represented in the petit-format volumes, which were bound in "calf and red morocco," were "Virgil, Tacitus, Caesar, Cicero, Ovid, Horace, Aesop, and Homer." When the Poplar Forest library, including the petit-format volumes, was sold years after Jefferson's death, the auction catalog listed "three small mahogany bookcases."[6] A bookcase now in the collection of the Winterthur Museum is thought to be the sole known survivor of the original four. Jefferson's petit-format library was only a small portion (literally and figuratively) of the extensive collection of books he maintained at Poplar Forest (see chap. XIV).

In addition to the mahogany pieces taxed in 1815, letters and other records — and in one or two instances the actual artifacts — survive to give more evidence on the original furnishings at Poplar Forest.[7] In 1811, Jefferson had directed his Monticello overseer, Edmund Bacon, to "tell Johnny Hemings to finish off immediately the frame for the round table for this place that it may come

Fig. 56 Cornelia Randolph's ink-and-wash drawing on paper shows the table seen in Fig. 55, and one of a set of Windsor chairs that were at Poplar Forest (see fig. 57). The drawing is inscribed in ink at the lower left: "drawn by C. J. Randolph, Poplar Forest." *(Monticello, Thomas Jefferson Memorial Foundation, Inc.)*

by the waggon which will go with the hogs"[8] (fig. 55). This table, which was not of mahogany but of cherry, walnut, and southern pine, was not taxed in 1815. Cornelia Randolph, one of Jefferson's granddaughters, made an ink-and-wash drawing of it during one of her visits to Poplar Forest (fig. 56). Having also descended in the family that purchased Poplar Forest from Francis Eppes, it was later acquired by the Thomas Jefferson Memorial Foundation, Inc., and is now at Monticello. Something of a "lazy susan," it has a revolving top on a square base.

Cornelia's sketch of the table also shows a chair, though none of the many stick chairs that Jefferson had at Poplar Forest is known to have survived. Just before he left Washington for the last time in 1809, Jefferson had written George Jefferson in Richmond: "I must pray you to procure for me 3 dozen stick chairs of the kind marked in the margin, painted black with yellow rings & forward them for me to Lynchburg. . . . I inclose you 100 D. to cover that & other expenses, being all hurry on my departure"[9] (fig. 57). Jefferson's hasty marginal sketch matches Cornelia's drawing in every particular. Perhaps needless to say, these thirty-six stick, or Windsor, chairs were not made of mahogany.

Nor was another piece, or pieces, of furniture of which Jefferson was inordinately fond. His dumbwaiters at Monticello were of mahogany, but those at Poplar Forest were of walnut and pine. These devices, of which there were apparently at least two at Poplar Forest, were built so that the servants could put dishes on the several shelves, then retire from the dining room until the table was cleared. Jefferson much preferred this method of table service, rather than having the servants constantly in the dining room while he and his guests were eating and conversing. The dumbwaiter seen in figure 58 is another piece of furniture that descended in the family who bought Poplar Forest from Francis Eppes.

Years after her last visit, Ellen Randolph, by then Mrs. Joseph Coolidge, was asked to provide a description of Poplar Forest. Though she touched only briefly on the subject of furniture, what she said accords well with what is otherwise known: "It was furnished in the simplest manner, but had a very tasty air; there was nothing common or second-rate about any part of the establishment, though there was no appearance of expense."[10]

Actually, there was another item at Poplar Forest, made "in whole or in part of mahogany," that escaped being taxed in 1815. It wasn't strictly a piece of furniture, and the tax assessor, if he ever saw it, probably little understood just what it was, or how to classify it. Jefferson regarded it as indispensable, and once called it

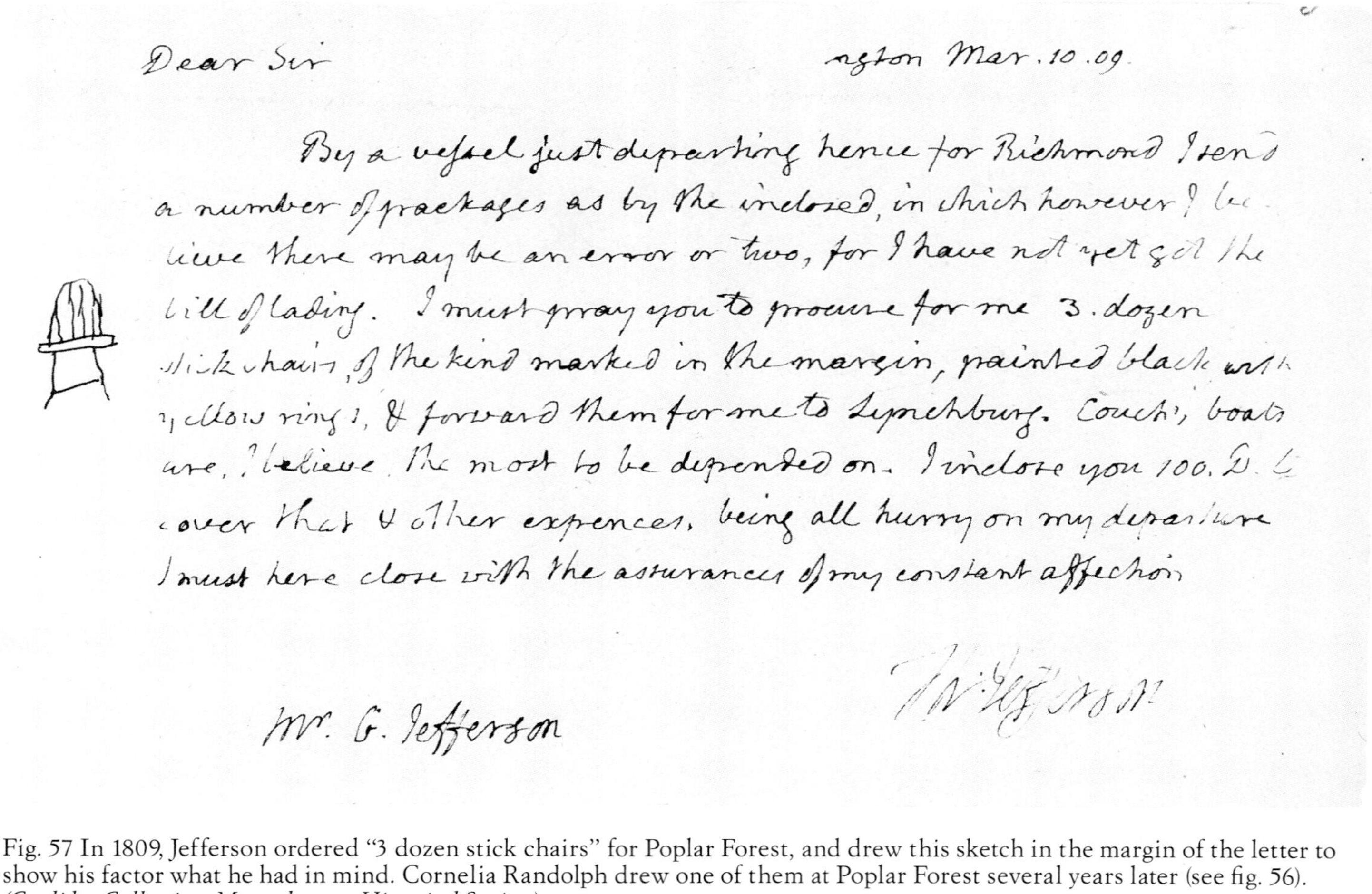

Fig. 57 In 1809, Jefferson ordered "3 dozen stick chairs" for Poplar Forest, and drew this sketch in the margin of the letter to show his factor what he had in mind. Cornelia Randolph drew one of them at Poplar Forest several years later (see fig. 56). *(Coolidge Collection, Massachusetts Historical Society)*

"the finest invention of the present age." It was a polygraph, an instrument "for copying with one pen while you write with the other & without the least additional embarrassment or exertion to the writer." The instrument had been invented in 1802 by a transplanted Englishman, John Isaac Hawkins, while he was living in Pennsylvania.[11] After Hawkins's return to England, Charles Willson Peale, acting as his agent, manufactured and sold the instrument in America. Peale and Jefferson were both enamored of the polygraph, and each contributed numerous improvements to further perfect it over the years. Jefferson owned several. The one he kept at Poplar Forest, as he noted in a letter to Peale, was a gift from the inventor: "Passing considerable portions of my time in this place, I keep for use here the portable polygraph Mr. Hawkins was so kind as to send me." That it was well used is attested to by the numerous copies of letters that he made whenever he had the "leisure, as I have every where the disposition to think of my friends."[12] The particular letter from which that quote is taken now exists in two places, at the Library of Congress and at the University of Virginia. One is the fair copy that Jefferson kept, one is the letter posted to Benjamin Rush. Before his death, Jefferson gave his portable polygraph to Nicholas P. Trist, who had become his

grandson-in-law, and who had assisted him so much with his writing in his last years. Trist in turn gave the Poplar Forest polygraph to the American Philosophical Society, where it remains (fig. 59).[13]

Following the War of 1812, Jefferson realized, if he hadn't already, that Jeremiah Goodman and Nimrod Darnell, his overseers respectively at Poplar Forest (or Tomahawk) and Bear Creek plantations, were not working out. Matters with Goodman came to a head in the winter of 1814–15. In a letter written to him on January 6, 1815, Jefferson noted that Phill Hubbard had arrived at Monticello with a complaint, which was "exactly as you supposed. He says that he and Dick's Hanah had become husband and wife, but that you drove him repeatedly from her father's house and would not let him go there, punishing her, as he supposes, for receiving him." As the two slaves lived on different plantations (Phill at Tomahawk, and Hanah at Bear Creek), Jefferson's solution was to let them go together to the latter place, while another couple from Bear Creek would be sent to replace them at Tomahawk. Jefferson also instructed Goodman to "give to Dick's Hanah a pot and a bed, which I always promise them when they take husbands at home, and I shall be very glad to hear that others of the young people follow their example." He also urged Goodman not to punish Phill for coming to Monticello, as his "character is not that of a runaway. I have known him from a boy and that he has not come off to sculk from his work."[14]

Two weeks after he wrote Goodman, Jefferson offered one of the overseer's positions to William Newby, in a letter that furnishes a capsule description both of the operation and of the sort of house he might expect if he took the job:

In Bedford I have two plantations, adjoining, of 16 hands each, uplands of the first quality, where I cultivate both tobacco and wheat. In point of soil, climate, and a substantial thrift and good neighborhood I think it the finest part of Virginia.... One of these places will be vacant the next year and I make you the first offer of it. If you chuse to undertake it, and will so inform me by answer, it is at your command. The house is uncomfortable, being a single room [with] a loft above, but I wish to add to it to make it comfortable. Another room with a passage between can quickly be added of hewn logs as is usual in that country, plaistered, with windows, stone chimney, etc. and as this would take but a very short time, I would rather leave it to be done by yourself immediately on your arrival, that you might do it to please yourself. The place is 10 miles from Lynchburg, the second town of the state as to the quantity of business, and the most thriving one in the state. I write to you this early as if you accept it, it will be satisfactory to us both to be at rest on that point, and if not, that I may have the more time to look about me. Your answer therefore is requested as soon as you can make up your mind on it. Accept my best wishes and respects.[15]

Fig. 58 Dumbwaiter. One of the Poplar Forest items on which Jefferson was *not* taxed in 1815 was this dumbwaiter, which was made of walnut and pine rather than of mahogany. It is one of several that Jefferson apparently had at Poplar Forest, all made on the same model and believed to be from the Monticello joinery. *(Monticello, Thomas Jefferson Memorial Foundation, Inc.)*

Jefferson's description of the house he planned to enlarge for Newby would have been a textbook example of a dogtrot log house. The particular log house he described has not survived, nor have many others of this type, which was among the most conventional vernacular forms in the early settlement of the Piedmont: two single-pen log houses separated by an open passageway that served as a well-ventilated living space in the summer. In later years, if the central space was enclosed to become a room usable in winter as well as in summer, the form became known as an "I House."

In addition to his shortcomings in dealing with the slave work force over which he had command, Goodman had committed another cardinal sin. He had neglected the vegetable garden, as Jefferson discovered when he arrived at Poplar Forest on May 18, 1815. Writing to Elizabeth Trist on the first of June, he griped that he had dined with friends in Albemarle "on peas the 29th of April. Here our first peas were the 29th of May, which shews the inattention here to the cheapest, pleasantest & most wholesome part of comfortable living."[16]

Jefferson had stated in his letter of January 1815 to Newby that he had planned to dismiss only one of his Bedford overseers, but when he arrived at Poplar Forest he "found [his] affairs there in so total a state of mismanagement as not only to have lost me the last year, but to threaten the loss of the present one."[17] More drastic measures were needed. Charles Clay's somewhat garbled note, dated May 23, hints at the new *modus operandi* Jefferson proposed, and obviously shows that the two had discussed the matter: "Thro' forgetfulness inattention or some other cause I am unable to hand to Capt. Slaughter the precise nature of the service for which he is wanted. Whether it is a superintendance of the business in its present form, as inspector genl. or in a more particular & pointed manner, such as I suppose Mr. Goodman now acts in — whether it is to overlook the overseers and people or the people only."[18]

Whether Joseph Slaughter (who had prepared the plat of Poplar Forest for Jefferson's proposed gift of lands to his two sons-in-law) was actually offered the position is unknown. It soon was offered to, and accepted by, someone else. Two days after Clay wrote his note, Jefferson responded: "On the subject which has been passing

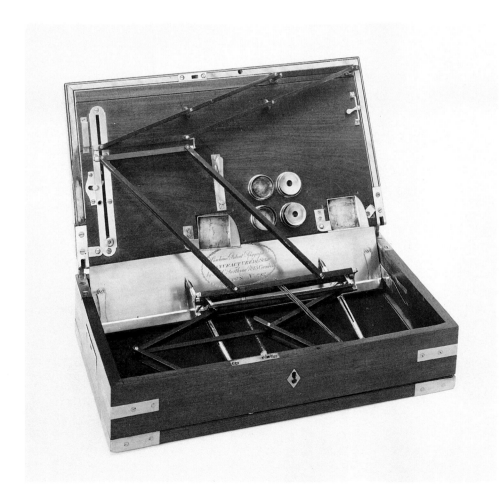

Fig. 59 Polygraph. Jefferson kept this portable instrument at Poplar Forest. It was designed to produce two copies of a letter at the same time. (*Courtesy American Philosophical Society*)

between us I have had an offer from a person who has many proper points in his character, and would see both my plantations every day." A week later he announced to Archibald Robertson: "Having found it necessary to make a change in the management of my affairs here, I have engaged Mr. Joel Yancey to undertake the direction of them and superintendance of the overseers and I have [directed] him to apply to your store for any necessaries which may be wanting for the people here or place." Robertson's response, delivered by hand, was good news indeed: "I am much pleased to hear that you have been fortunate enough to get Mr. Yancey to superintend your business in Bedford. There is no man in whom I should place more confidence than him. I think the more you are acquainted, the better you will be pleased with him."[19]

Jefferson's writing to Clay that this new person would "see both my plantations every day" and his subsequent correspondence with Robertson show that he did intend to establish a new position. Parson Clay's term for it, "inspector genl.," is as good as any. It was the position Jefferson had held himself, but that now, at the age of seventy-two, he felt someone else should assume. In addition to giving Yancey the position as overseer of both his Bedford plantations, he placed his affairs in Albemarle "under the direction of my grandson Jefferson Randolph, my activity being too much declined to take care of them myself."[20] Joel Yancey served from June 1815 to December 1821, at an annual salary of $400. He had no need of the sort of house that Jefferson had been willing to provide for William Newby. As has been noted, in 1811 Yancey and William Radford had jointly purchased the former Bankhead property. Rothsay, the house that he constructed on his portion soon after his purchase, was one of the most impressive in the area, but in concert with those built by other prosperous farmers in the early-nineteenth century in Bedford and Campbell counties, it bore little of the architectural refinements that Poplar Forest had (fig. 60). That it stood less than a mile from Poplar Forest, on a portion of its original acreage and adjoining it, made it an easy task for Yancey to see both of Jefferson's plantations every day. Of course, as might be expected, and as events would certainly prove, Jefferson himself continued to be the real inspector general at Poplar Forest.

Fig. 60 Rothsay. Built on a portion of the original Poplar Forest tract soon after his purchase in 1811, Joel Yancey's house was a handsome, substantial establishment, and might well be taken as evidence that he became Jefferson's overseer as much out of friendship as from any financial necessity. Yancey's Rothsay, seen here, burned in the early twentieth century and was replaced by another building on the site, using some of the same foundations and keeping the name. *(Courtesy Mrs. R. Gene Goley)*

"A Crowd of Curious People"
AND
"A Common Curiosity"
(Summer and Autumn–1815)

In addition to his supervisory duties with the plantation operations at Poplar Forest, Joel Yancey was called upon to help in many other ways. On July 25, 1815, Jefferson wrote to his new overseer, asking him "to give the inclosed bill to Mr. Atkinson & get him to saw it immediately so as to have it ready on the arrival of the carpenters." He added that the wood could be taken from "poplars in the cleared grounds:"

A note for Mr. Atkinson.
I shall have occasion for 600 feet, running measure of scantling 5 1/4 inches square, clear of the saw, all of heart poplar, without a speck of sap. When we use it it will be cut into lengths of 2 ft. 8 I. for ballusters. The stocks therefore must be of such lengths as to cut into these smaller lengths of 2 ft. 8 I. without waste.
For example a stock of 8 feet will give 3 lengths
          10 f. 8 I   - - - - 4 lengths
          13 f. 4 I   - - - - 5 lengths
          16 f.   - - - - - 6 lengths
to be done immediately so as to be ready on our arrival.[1]

Now that his new wing of offices was more or less complete, Jefferson turned his architectural interests again to the main house at Poplar Forest. If the addition of the wing had been more practical than beautiful, Jefferson's next "improvement" to the house at Poplar Forest, to which this order pertained, was definitely in the realm of aesthetics. Actually, it would hardly have been considered an improvement, as it was simply a finishing touch to the original design. His instructions to Mr. Atkinson were for the balusters of the balustrade encircling the roof above the entablature. Jefferson was perhaps being overly frugal in telling the sawyer just how many balusters could be formed out of specific lengths of lumber, but there was more to his preciseness than just that. He had in mind a specific height for the balusters, to be in correct proportion to the rest of the house. As the Tuscan order Jefferson used at Poplar Forest had no established rules for balustrades, Jefferson in all likelihood based his proportions on the Doric order. This was the order he had used at Monticello, and the heights of the balusters in the corresponding position there accord well with the dimensions given in his directive to Mr. Atkinson for Poplar Forest. As the Poplar Forest balustrade disappeared years ago, and is shown only in the Neilson drawing of the south elevation (endpapers), the precise dimensions preserved in this note are of paramount importance.[2] That the note was preserved is due, once again, to Jefferson's use of the polygraph. History

has not revealed what Mr. Atkinson did with the note he received; the copy that has come down to the present is the one that Jefferson made and kept for his own records.

On August 7, 1815, Jefferson's only brother, Randolph, died. As Jefferson had to journey to Buckingham Court House to give testimony on the will the following month, he decided to combine that journey with an autumn visit to Poplar Forest. He and the carpenters left Monticello on August 20, and by the twenty-fifth work was progressing rapidly, not to mention noisily: "How do you do? And when will you be able to ride this far? These are my first questions," he wrote Charles Clay. "How you like the changes and chances of the European world may be the subject of conversation. But you must come with your ears stuffed full of cotton to fortify them against the noise of hammers, saws, planes etc. which assail us in every direction." Work was continuing when he wrote Martha a week later, but by then he could tell that it wouldn't be completed anytime soon: "I see no reason to believe we shall finish our work here sooner than the term I had fixed for my return. It is rather evident we must have such another expedition the next year." He also told Martha that the arrival of the unusually large group of Monticello workmen had been noticed right away by his neighbors: "The story of the neighborhood immediately was that I had brought a crowd of workers to get ready my house in a hurry for Bonaparte. Were there such people only as the believers in this, patriotism would be a ridiculous passion."[3]

After Napoleon's defeat at Waterloo in June 1815, he had hopes that he could come to America. British authorities had other plans, but it was not until mid-July that Napoleon was informed that his new destination would be St. Helena. That news apparently had not yet filtered down to Bedford by late August. But if Jefferson's neighbors were disappointed in not seeing Napoleon, two visitors who soon arrived should have sufficed. As unlikely a pair as could possibly be imagined, they were both among Jefferson's most cherished friends. In fact, they were the very first of the select few that he ever invited to stay with him at Poplar Forest.

Jefferson described Abbé Joseph Francis Correa de Serra as "a gentleman from Portugal, of the first order of science, being without exception the most learned man I have ever met with in any country. Modest, good humored, familiar, plain as a country farmer, he becomes the favorite of every one with whom he becomes acquainted." Correa de Serra had taken holy orders in Rome in 1775 — some said to escape suspicion from the

Inquisition, as his inquiring scientific mind was already beginning to arouse doubt. Two years later he received the degree of Doctor of Laws, and he was one of the founders of the Portuguese Academy of Sciences. By the time the U.S.S. *Constitution* landed him at Norfolk on February 21, 1812, his scientific genius had been universally realized, and he had already become a member of the American Philosophical Society. When he disembarked, he carried with him a letter of introduction to Jefferson from their mutual friend, Pierre Samuel duPont de Nemours. As the Frenchman had predicted, Correa de Serra and Jefferson soon became fast friends. During his years in America, Correa de Serra made annual visits to Monticello, where a bedroom (which even came to be named after him) was always ready to receive him. In 1816, a year after his visit to Poplar Forest, he was appointed the Portuguese minister plenipotentiary to the United States.

Jefferson's praise of his other guest was only slightly less extravagant: "He is accompanied by Mr. Francis Gilmer, son of Doct. Gilmer formerly of my neighborhood, the best educated young man of our state, and of the most amiable dispositions."[4] Francis Walker Gilmer had studied at the College of William and Mary, where he became interested in botany and later read law. In all

probability, he first met Correa at Monticello during one of his visits there. In a letter to his brother, Peachy R. Gilmer (who was married to Elizabeth Trist's niece), he praised his European friend even more than Jefferson had: "He is the most extraordinary man now living, or who, perhaps, ever lived." In the fall of 1814 the two men visited Philadelphia, and in August 1815 Gilmer moved to Winchester, Virginia, to begin his law practice, a venture that was soon put on hold: "I had not cleverly fixed myself at Winchester before my old friend Mr. Correa did me the honor to visit me on his way to Monticello. He proposed that I accompany him to Albemarle, a pleasure which after such a distinguished mark of his attention I cannot forego."[5] So Gilmer informed his brother-in-law, but that was only the beginning. What the good abbé had in mind was a botanical tour of the southern states, and he was aided and abetted in that plan by his friend Thomas Jefferson.

The exact date that the two visitors came to stay at Poplar Forest is not known, but it was probably after their host returned from Buckingham Court House. Jefferson went there on September 10 and returned three days later, keeping careful records of his expenses along the way (fig. 61). The night of his return the three gentlemen (and two servants) had dinner at Hoyle's Tavern in

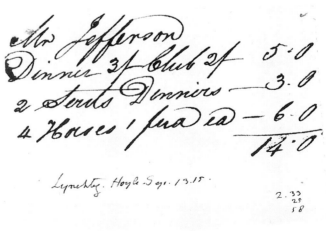

Fig. 61 During his September 1815 trip to Poplar Forest, Jefferson jotted down his expenditures on these small pieces of paper. That at left is from his stay at Henry Flood's Tavern in Buckingham County, that above from Hoyle's in Lynchburg. *(Coolidge Collection, Massachusetts Historical Society)*

Lynchburg, and the next day they were apparently joined for breakfast at Poplar Forest by Dr. William Steptoe, to whom Jefferson had written the day before[6] (fig. 62). Of all Jefferson's acquaintances in Bedford, Steptoe was the one he apparently felt had the most in common with his guests.

On the same day the group breakfasted together, Jefferson sent a note to Christopher Clark about the next phase of the visit. That letter was in part a response to one that he had just received from Clark: "A considerable diversity of opinion has persisted and still continues to persist about the height of the Peaks of Otter. The calculation generally adopted has been taken from your Notes on Virginia. Whether this standard was the result of an actual measuring is not known but I have heard that yourself have been so in doubt of its accuracy [that you] will undertake making a more correct one." Clark, or Clarke, another Bedford friend of long standing and a kinsman of Bowling Clark, the former overseer at Poplar Forest, had served in Congress while Jefferson was president. He now lived outside the Bedford county seat of Liberty at Mount Prospect (fig. 63). Whether the polygonal wing added to the main block of his house reflects any architectural advice that Jefferson may have given his friend is not known, but Mount Prospect is unique for its time and place in exhibiting such a feature. Clark's house was — and is — beautifully situated at the foot of the Peaks of Otter, and he concluded his note by inviting Jefferson to come and make it his headquarters should he decide to measure the peaks: "Perhaps no situation in the immediate vicinity of the mountain will afford as good ground for the purpose . . . as my plantation." Jefferson's response introduced his guests, and asked if they could also stay: "They would be very glad to pass two days in exploring the botany of the peaks of Otter; and I have to ask your hospitality for them those two days. They will give you no trouble but of a morning & evening, as they will be out on their rambles all day. . . . We shall dine at Liberty on Sunday and be with you in the evening in time for me to examine the grounds for measuring the height of the mountain. If I find them suitable, I should bring proper instruments with me in October or November, and make the actual measurements then." Clark wrote Jefferson that his visitors "may as well as yourself be assured that nothing will be lacking on our part to make their [visit] as agreeable as possible."[7]

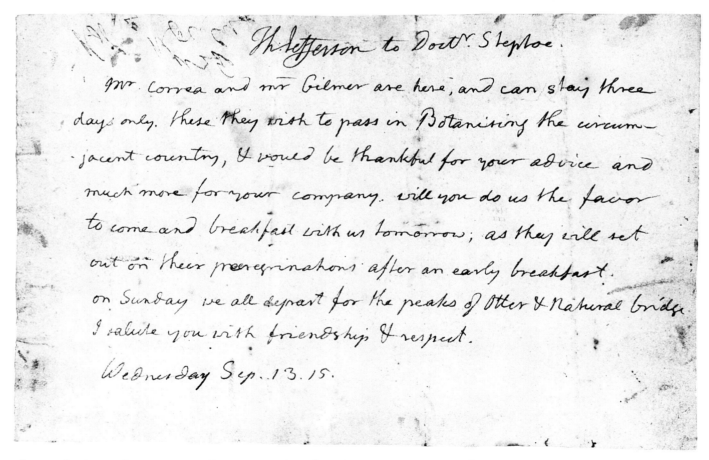

Fig. 62 On September 13, 1815, Jefferson invited his friend and neighbor Dr. William Steptoe to join him and his houseguests in a "botanising" expedition. *(Courtesy Jones Memorial Library, Lynchburg, Va; photograph by Tom Graves, Jr., 1991)*

In his Memorandum Book, Jefferson recorded paying $.93 for dinner at Liberty on September 17, which either indicates that food was a lot cheaper there than at Hoyle's at Lynchburg, where he had paid $2.58, or that he hosted his friends the first time, and they went Dutch Treat on this occasion. As planned, they spent the night at Mount Prospect, and on September 18, Jefferson climbed to the top of Sharp Top (one of the two peaks of the Peaks of Otter), and took its latitude. Presumably his friends went "botanising."

At the time the three friends visited the Peaks of Otter, Jefferson was seventy-two years old; Correa de Serra, sixty-five; and Gilmer, twenty-five. They made an extraordinary entourage; at least Peachy Gilmer and his unnamed informant thought so. Early in October he wrote his brother: "The last account I had of you was that yourself Mr. Correa & Mr. Jefferson who travelled in a vehicle much resembling a mill hopper were taking the elevation of the Peaks of Otter and the exploring the sides of them for subjects botanical."[8] One can only hope that Jefferson never heard that unflattering description of his coach. A landau, it was his pride and joy. He had designed it; John Hemings had built its wooden parts;

Fig. 63 Mount Prospect, the home of Jefferson's friend Christopher Clark, is located at the foot of the Peaks of Otter, and served as headquarters when Jefferson and his guests went there to "botanise." The brick polygonal bay seen to the left is an addition to the earlier, rectangular central block, and may well point to Jefferson's architectural influence. (Tom Graves, Jr., 1991)

and Burwell, his servant, had painted it. At the time only a year old, the carriage would subsequently be used by Jefferson on all his journeys between Poplar Forest and Monticello.[9]

On September 19 the triumvirate left Christopher Clark's and proceeded to Natural Bridge, crossing the James River at Skidmore's Ferry and staying the night at Douthat's, near the bridge. Gilmer was so impressed by Natural Bridge that he later gave a paper entitled "On the Geological Formation of the Natural Bridge of Virginia" to the American Philosophical Society.[10]

On September 20, 1815, Jefferson parted from his companions, crossed the James at Greenlee's Ferry, and spent the night at David Douglas's tavern en route to Poplar Forest. Upon his return to Bedford, aided by his polygraph, he sent identical letters to two acquaintances, Congressman John Rhea of Tennessee, and Governor John Milledge of Georgia, alerting them that Correa and Gilmer "who lately accompanied me to this place, have proceeded on a tour through the Southern country." Jefferson urged the Tennessean and Georgian to "receive them as strangers, as men of science, as my friends, and as they merit, and engage your friends to honour themselves and their state by their attentions to such men, and the facilities they can give to their enquiries." He also warned their would-be hosts that though they were "at home in every science, botany is their favorite. As every plant of any singularity stops them, their progress is of course slow."[11]

Jefferson also found time during this stay at Poplar Forest to engage in another of his favorite pursuits. On September 28, he wrote his friend and distant relative Randolph Harrison: "During a long visit to this place I have had leisure to think of your house. You seemed to require 6 rooms, neither more nor less, and a good entrance or passage of communication. The enclosed is drawn on that plan. The ground plat is in detail, and exact. The elevation is merely a sketch to give a general idea. The workman, if he is anything of an architect will be able to draw the particulars."[12] Though he took his time, Harrison eventually built Ampthill, in Cumberland County, from these plans and elevations drawn by Jefferson at Poplar Forest.[13]

Just before he left Poplar Forest, Jefferson attended again to his financial matters, asking his Richmond factor, Patrick Gibson, to arrange a loan of "another thousand dollars." He also ordered nails from Archibald Robertson in Lynchburg, presumably to use in finishing and installing the balustrade on his next visit: "Be pleased to send me by the bearer 3000 nails of the length of the longest sample sent & 3000 of the shortest. Wrought nails would be preferred, but cut ones will do." Because of the War of 1812, Jefferson had been unable to obtain iron nail-rod from Philadelphia for his nailery at Monticello. Robertson had slightly better luck, but his agent, who sent a note back with the nails, wrote that "wrought nails of the description you wanted, could not be procured, I have therefore sent cuts."[14]

On October 1, 1815, Jefferson paid $6.50 for "debts & vales at Pop. Forest" and began his return trip to Monticello. *Vales* was the word he habitually used for tips, or gratuities. That the amount this time was larger than usual reflected the extra demands he had placed on the slave work force during his lengthy stay with his guests.[15] He would return in less than a month, and from Poplar Forest he would then go back to Christopher Clark's to measure the Peaks of Otter, as he intended. Before that expedition took place, yet another visitor arrived at Poplar Forest, one who was far more of a celebrity than either Abbé Correa de Serra or Francis Walker Gilmer. It still wasn't Bonaparte, but Jefferson's Bedford neighbors might well have begun to wonder about this time just who might appear next in their midst.

Jefferson returned to Poplar Forest on the last day of October 1815 accompanied by Burwell, the carpenters, and a cart full of plants. On November 2 he sent a note to Christopher Clark:

I arrived here two days ago, and have brought with me instruments for our project at the peaks, as I presume you would like to see something of the proceedings, you must be so good as to say when your business will permit you to be at home for three or four days, for I think it will take that time. To me, after tomorrow, all days will be equal, and the sooner the better while we have such fair and moderate weather. Your earliest convenience therefore will suit me best, and you will be good enough to make it known to me by the bearer. I think I shall be obliged again to clamber to the top of the sharp peak.

Clark sent Jefferson's servant back with his answer: "I am glad to hear of your return to Bedford and if convenient to you shall be glad to see you here on next Sunday to dinner. This will give us the advantage of the early part of next week, and by which time the smoke will have probably dissipated so as to afford a fair view of the summit of the mountains." That same day, according to notes in his Garden Book, Jefferson saw to the planting of "64. paper mulberries in the nursery," the same species he had directed to have planted alongside the circular road and in the double rows between the house and the mounds in his December 1812 memorandum.[16]

On Saturday, November 4, Jefferson wrote his usual post-arrival letter to Martha, telling her that he had reached his destination "without any accident," although he had "suffered very much both mornings by cold." Thus he asked her to send his "wolf-skin pelisse and fur boots" with Billy, who was to be at Poplar Forest on the twenty-seventh to "bring the two mules to move the carpenters back" to Monticello. After writing that he planned to go "to morrow morning to Mr. Clarke's," he had to end his letter abruptly, as he was "this moment interrupted by a crowd of curious people come to see the house." It was the sort of thing that constantly happened at Monticello, but not, heretofore, at Poplar Forest. Fortunately, the sudden interruption kept him from sealing his letter, and he was later able to add a postscript explaining it: "P. S. I was most agreeably surprised to find that the party whom I thought to be merely curious visitants were General Jackson and his suite, who passing on to Lynchburg did me the favor to call."[17]

That was far from the end of it, as he was soon to find out. Later that day he was interrupted again. As he wrote Christopher Clark on Sunday, November 5: "I had everything packed and prepared yesterday to set out this morning for Mount Prospect but General Jackson called on me in the forenoon, and a committee from the citizens of Lynchburg in the afternoon to invite me to partake of a dinner they give the General on Tuesday. Respect to the citizens of Lynchburg as well as the hero of N. Orleans forbade a refusal. I will however be with you to dinner on Wednesday" (fig. 64). The committee that called on Jefferson that Saturday afternoon was apparently the "Committee of Arrangement," which had also waited "on the worthy Hero of Orleans, whilst resting himself and family at the house of his friend in Bedford, [to] invite him to partake of a Public Dinner."[18] Jackson's "friend in Bedford" was his aide and private

Fig. 64 Andrew Jackson, engraving by David Edwin, after Nathan W. Wheeler, ca. 1816. *(Prints and Photographs Division, Library of Congress)*

secretary, Major John Reid, whose family lived near New London, at Poplar Grove, where the general and Rachel stayed.

Andrew Jackson was on his way to Washington to answer charges that he had mistreated some of the civil authorities when he had declared New Orleans under martial law during the War of 1812. After his decisive victory on January 8, 1815 (after the war had officially ended), Jackson had remained in New Orleans until the spring, then returned to the Hermitage, his home near Nashville. This was his first trip beyond the boundaries of Tennessee since, and it was seized upon by a nation anxious to give him the accolades it deemed fitting following his victory. His journey to answer the trumped-up charges turned out to be more of a triumphal march than anything else.

The journey was leisurely, as towns along the way offered their tribute to the Hero of New Orleans when he passed through. John Reid wrote his mother several times on the way to Washington, giving her reports of the progress of the convoy and urging her to arrange accommodations for them when they reached Bedford: "We shall probably not reach you before the last of the month; & all I have to say is to beg that you will 'by hook or by crook' provide the means of lodging us for a few nights — after which myself & the general at least, must hasten on to the City. Betsy will remain; probably Mrs. Jackson

for a few weeks. All the beds & all the provinder in the neighborhood you must put in requisition & have in readiness by the time of our arrival."[19] His letters, supplemented by other communications, gave Lynchburg time to prepare for the general's welcome, and the celebration it held was second to none. Tuesday, November 7 was the big day, and as the *Richmond Enquirer* later informed its readers, the first order of business was a parade:

A troop of horse, with many mounted citizens, headed by Major Lynch, proceeded early in the day to meet and escort our Hero to the town. The Artillery and Rifle Companies, with their usual order and brilliacy, marched out beyond the hill to salute him as he advanced.... At length he made his appearance. The two companies in a style which would have graced veterans, performed their task, and fell in the rear of the General and his suite. — Thomas Jefferson, Esq. the great supporter of our republican institutions, added dignity to the procession. Gen. Jackson and his Aid accompanied by Gen. Leftwich and his Aid, with Mr. Jefferson in the midst, headed the procession.[20]

Eventually the procession came to Main Street, which the *Enquirer* alerted its readers, had been "swept for the occasion." After the general was escorted to his lodgings, the military companies "advanced to the eminence on the upper end of the main-street and fired a major-gen-

Fig. 65 John Jordan Cabell House, Lynchburg, photo ca. 1900. Dr. Cabell, an admirer of Jackson, decorated his house, then only several years old, in honor of Andrew Jackson's visit to Lynchburg in 1815. The house, no longer standing, was located near the site where Jackson received "a major-general's salute." *(Author's collection)*

eral's salute." Dr. John Jordan Cabell, who was "an ardent admirer of Jackson," lived near that eminence, and had just decorated the walls of his house with scenic French wallpaper in honor of the occasion. His was only one of "many private homes . . . newly decorated and furnished in [Jackson's] honor"[21] (fig. 65).

Meanwhile, preparations were going on at Martin's, Lynchburg's largest tobacco warehouse, where "a most sumptuous dinner was prepared and spread on tables sufficient for at least 300 seats." "All was order. All was social conviviality" at dinner. Afterwards the conviviality became even more social, as toasts were given, "to express the common emotions which every man felt, and was glad to utter." It took eighteen *official* toasts, each accompanied by music from a band of "20 odd musicians," to utter those common emotions. The first utterance, to "the United States of America," was accompanied by *Hail Columbia*, and the second, "to the Constitution" was attended by *Jefferson's March*. *Washington's Dirge* was the appropriate tune for a toast "to the memory of General George Washington," while *Trip to Naples* was selected to accompany the salute to "the late War." Toward the end, the toasts and their accompaniments seemed to get a bit less obvious, and perhaps a bit blurred as well. The seventeenth toast was to "the State of Vermont," with which Yankee Doodle was played, while the last, to "the American Fair," had *Rise, Cynthia* to go along

with it (fig. 66). That ended the official toasts, but the party was just beginning. Under the heading VOLUNTEERS, the Richmond press listed eleven more toasts, beginning with two offered by the two guests of honor. Jackson came first: his salute was to "James Monroe, late Secretary of War." Jefferson followed with his tribute: "Honor and gratitude to those who have filed the measure of their country's honor." These two toasts, as later observers have noted, signaled a reconciliation, and an end to any differences that may have existed between the two men and their parties.[22] After the volunteer toasts, the paper reported that General Jackson, Major Reid, and Thomas Jefferson retired, and were themselves — in absentia — the recipients of yet more toasts. That to Jefferson, "our illustrious guest," was offered by his neighbor, Charles Johnston. The paper then noted that "the evening was devoted to the performance of the last act — to pay due respect to the amiable wife of the General — A party in honor of Mrs. Jackson closed the scene."[23]

A more intimate glimpse of the proceedings was afforded by a young lady with a quintessential Virginia name: Mary Pocahontas Cabell. Factually, her account differs little from what the *Richmond Enquirer* reported. She, too, noted that "the streets were swept for the reception of the General" (which makes one wonder about the usual appearance of Lynchburg's streets), and she also remembered that the first of the musical selec-

Fig. 66 *Jefferson's March* and *Rise, Cynthia* were two of the many musical tributes accompanying the toasts at the Lynchburg banquet attended by Jefferson and Jackson in November 1815. (*Music Division, Library of Congress*)

tions at the banquet was *Hail Columbia*. But, as she was writing to an aunt in Buckingham County rather than for a newspaper audience, she could afford to be more candid in her assessments than had the *Enquirer*'s correspondent. For the rest, let her tell it like it was:

I was in town when Gen. Jackson and his suit entered. The town put on its best appearance on that day on the morning of the 7th. Nov. The streets were swept for the reception of the General. I was highly delighted with Jackson & his suit. I saw Mr. Jefferson — and old Gen. Leftwitch under whose command my Brother served a tour of duty in Maryland about this time last year. I was happy to see them all. I had no idea of going to the Ball given to the great folks but was overpersuaded by friends & acquaintances. While at the ball I was not sorry for yielding to their advice. I never heard such eloquent music in my life. 20 odd musicians composed the band which performed 3 or four marches & retreats. First Hail Columbia. Then Jacksons Grand March & then others. The majority of the Gentlemen were rather too much elated on the occasion as you may suppose — for they said to me that there was 80 gallons of 6 dollar wine drank at the dinner that day. Mr. Jefferson said it was the most extravagant dinner ever he saw. He left town that evening so he did not honor the ladies with his presence except at a distance. I had the honour of an introduction to Genrl. J. and of dancing in the first reel with him — which was the one the Ball was opened with. Mrs. J & Major Lynch opened the Ball. Genrl J. and Mrs. Coleman. Mr _____ and myself composed the other couple. . . . G. Jackson had a nephew with him the most sociable soul I ever saw. He danced . . . and laughed incessantly. The Genrl. was so liberal to me that he told me he would give me choice of nine of his nephews & invited me home with him as he will pass thru L. on his return to T. Donaldson was the name of the youth he brought to Va.[24]

The morning after the night before, Jackson and his retinue left Lynchburg for Washington. Upon his arrival there, his accusers virtually vanished, and his reception by the president and the public was as enthusiastic in the capital as it had been en route, perhaps even as ardent as it had been in Lynchburg.

For his part, Jefferson was on his way that same next morning to Christopher Clark's, making up for lost time in his attempts to measure the Peaks of Otter. Once there, as he later told a correspondent, he measured the heights from "a base of 1 1/4 mile along the low grounds of the Little Otter in the lands of Mr. Clarke & Mr. Donald." Armed "with an excellent Ramsden's Theodolite of 3 1/2 I. radius," he found the height of the "sharp peak above the bed of the river [to be] 2,946 1/2 feet, that of the flat peak 3,103 1/2 ft." The theodolite was a surveying instrument that Jefferson described as "a mathematical apparatus." He had used one for years, but in reporting this trip to an acquaintance, he observed that he may not have been completely accurate in his measurements, as his "object was only to gratify a common curiosity as to the height of those mountains, which we deem our highest."[25] More than thirty years earlier, he had conjectured in his *Notes on Virginia* that the Peaks of Otter might be higher "than any others in our country, and perhaps in North America."[26] Now, after the explorations of Lewis and Clark (not to mention those of Lieutenant Zebulon Pike of Pike's Peak fame), it was obvious that the Blue Ridge Mountains of Virginia could not claim the highest peaks on the continent.

Jefferson didn't figure the exact calculations on-site. On November 18, 1815, he wrote Charles Clay: "I was five days absent in my trip to the Peaks of Otter, and have been five days engaged in calculating the observations made. This brings me down to yesterday evening when I finished them. I am going to day to see Mr. Clarke at his new habitation, and tomorrow, weather permitting, will pay you a morning visit. In the mean time I send you a note of the result of my ten days labor, and some Otaheite or Paper mulberries."[27]

The mulberries he offered Clay were most likely part of the shipment of sixty-four that Jefferson had temporarily "heeled in" at the Poplar Forest nursery at the beginning of his trip. Now, on November 25, he transplanted thirty-eight of them, planting nineteen "in a clump between the W. Cloacina & fence & 19 do. in a clump between the E. Cloacina and fence." This dense planting of mulberries would screen the necessaries from the nearby circular road that ran almost alongside them. The same day, he also directed plantings on and about the mounds: "planted 5. Calycanthuses on each Mound. 4 Monticello aspens at the N. foot of the W. Mound & 3. do. at the N. foot of the E. Mound."[28]

When he returned to Monticello on December 15th, Jefferson was distressed to learn that he had missed a visit there from Pierre Samuel duPont de Nemours, who had recently moved to America to live. He had convinced himself that duPont, though he had said he would come to Monticello, wasn't really serious, and "had yielded therefore with the less reluctance to a detention in Bedford by a slower progress of my workmen than had been counted on." Although in his letter of November 4 to Martha, he had requested her to have Billy bring the two mules to Poplar Forest on the twenty-seventh of that month "to move the carpenters back," he only left on December 13, evidence that he had indeed tarried longer than he had originally planned. In a letter to William Short, written January 15, 1816, he observed: "of the last 5 months, 4 have been past at Poplar Forest where I am engaged in improvements requiring much of my presence."[29] Whether it was actually the slowness of the workmen or his improvements that had required his presence so long in Bedford is moot. Certainly other things — some of which he had planned, others that he definitely had not — had been at least equally responsible.

"THE MOST RISING PLACE IN THE U.S."
(1816–17)

During the mid-to-late teen years of the nineteenth century, America was at peace. Its concomitant, plenty, soon merged into prosperity, and Piedmont Virginia, especially Lynchburg, experienced it all to the fullest. Writing his friend Charles Willson Peale on May 8, 1816, Jefferson took the occasion to tell him that his "second home" was "near to Lynchburg, now the 2nd town in the state for business, and thriving with a rapidity exceeding anything we have ever seen. When I first visited that place . . . there was nothing but a ferry house."[1]

As a close neighbor to Lynchburg, Jefferson did more than just comment on its growth. He had helped it happen. In 1810, his new Lynchburg acquaintances had been bold enough to ask a favor of him. The town then had only once-a-week mail service, and the townsmen asked Jefferson if he would request twice-weekly service from Gideon Granger, whom he had appointed postmaster general in 1801. He agreed to help, and in his letter to Granger stated that "Lynchburg is perhaps the most rising place in the U.S. It is at the head of the navigation of James River, and receives all the produce of the Southwestern quarter of Virginia."[2]

In the summer of 1816, Lynchburg's common council authorized a census, and on June 27, Richardson Taylor reported that he had counted 3,087 individuals over the age of 16.[3] Two years earlier, in 1814, an extension of the town limits had been made, and three years later, in 1819, they would be extended yet again. Together these annexations more than quadrupled the original forty-five acres set off when Lynchburg was established in 1786. The increase both in population and in the extent of the town mandated a great deal of building (fig. 67).

One of Jefferson's contemporaries, John Holt Rice, passed through Lynchburg about this time, and observed that on the hills surrounding the town "quite decent houses for family residences are rising up with great rapidity."[4] One of them might have been the house that Thomas Holcombe built on the newly laid out Eighth (now Federal) Street, soon after his purchase of property there in 1814. In addition to his house, Holcombe built a wing to accommodate his school, and it was presumably there that Francis went through his academic paces.[5] Dr. George Cabell, who counted Patrick Henry among his patients, had many other enterprises in addition to his practice of medicine. His fleet of bateaux often carried Jefferson's tobacco down the James River to Richmond, and he had prospered sufficiently to build a new house during the decade. That house, named Point of Honor, was located on one of Lynchburg's surrounding hills, and incorporated in its design a pair of fashionable polygonal bays (fig. 68). As was mentioned, the use of such polygonal bays was a favorite of Jefferson's, but no documentation exists to link him with the design of Point of Honor.

Just as Mount Prospect (see fig. 63), Christopher Clark's house at the base of the Peaks of Otter, is alone in its neighborhood in incorporating a polygonal bay in its design, so Point of Honor is unique in Lynchburg. None of the other houses built in or near the town during the early-nineteenth century displayed such elaborate exterior embellishments as its polygonal bays. They were, instead, stolid, well-proportioned structures, generally two stories high and rectangular in outline, that bore unmistakable architectural resemblances to each other.

Lynchburg on James River. Va.

Fig. 67 "Lynchburg on James River, Va.," wash drawing by August Köllner, 1845. This view, one of the earliest known of the city, shows well its hilly topography. The bridge across the James River seen here replaced the one that Jefferson used. *(Courtesy Maier Museum of Art, Randolph-Macon Woman's College, Lynchburg, Va.; photograph by Tom Graves, Jr., 1992.)*

The house built by Dr. Cabell's brother and fellow doctor, John Jordan Cabell (the gentleman who had papered his walls for General Jackson's visit), was a good example (see fig. 65). Joel Yancey's Rothsay (see fig. 60) and Charles Johnston's Sandusky (see fig. 45), both near Poplar Forest, were country houses that differed little in appearance, materials, or arrangement from their town cousins. Equal in scale, but somewhat more imposing in appearance, were the frame houses built by two other neighbors — one a friend and associate, one Jefferson's adversary. William Radford's Woodbourne (fig. 69), and Samuel Scott's Locust Thicket (see fig. 42), both products of several building operations, are embellished with pedimented central bays. Obviously Samuel Scott, with whom Jefferson had a long-lasting dispute over property boundaries, wouldn't have sought architectural advice from him, but inasmuch as Lynchburg experienced such a spurt of building activity during the second decade of the nineteenth century, it seems a shame that none of his other neighbors, as far as is known, availed themselves of being able to say that they had "built upon a plan presented by Mr. Jefferson."[6]

If no one in Lynchburg ever took advantage of Jefferson's architectural talent, at least one townsman availed himself of his expertise on another subject. With all its growth, it was high time for Lynchburg to have a first-rate hostelry. That was achieved on November 1, 1817, when the Franklin Hotel, Samuel J. Harrison proprietor, opened. *The Lynchburg Press* had heralded the event on October 31, declaring that the hotel was "believed to be equal to any house in Virginia for public entertainment." Its wine list certainly was, or soon would be. On September 17, 1817, a month and a half before the hotel opened, Jefferson had met with Harrison, and the next

Fig. 68 Point of Honor. Built during the same period that Jefferson was embellishing Poplar Forest, this is Lynchburg's most elegant early-nineteenth-century mansion. *(Richard Cheek, 1979, for the Historic American Buildings Survey, Prints and Photographs Division, Library of Congress)*

Fig. 69 Woodbourne. Built in several stages from the 1780s to the 1820s, William Radford's Woodbourne achieved a remarkably harmonious facade. A near neighbor of Joel Yancey's Rothsay (fig. 60), Radford's house remains in excellent condition, and is owned by his descendants. *(photograph by Margaret Fishkin, 1991, courtesy Mrs. R. Gene Goley)*

day wrote him on one of the subjects they had discussed:

As you expressed a wish to have a note of the vines I mentioned to you yesterday, I make one on the back hereof. I can assure that they are esteemed on the continent of Europe among the best wines of Europe, and with Champagne, Burgundy and Tokay are used at the best tables there. . . . strength and flavor are the qualities which please here, as weakness and flavor do there. A first importation will enable you to judge for yourself, and should you select any on trial and wish to import them hereafter yourself either for the tavern or your own table, I will give you letters to Mr. Cathalan, our Consul at Marseilles and Mr. Appleton our Consul at Leghorn, both of them my friends and correspondents of 30 years standing. I salute you with friendship and respect.[7]

His favorite Hermitage was among the wines listed, and he gave Harrison notes on the flavor and cost of each of the many types he suggested. With Jefferson as its sommelier, the Franklin Hotel may well have lived up to the billing the local press gave it. Lynchburg had come a long way from the time, not so long ago, when "there was 80 gallons of 6 dollar wine drank at the dinner" honoring Andrew Jackson.

Unfortunately, travelers in the Piedmont, not to mention those throughout Virginia, were then more interested in tobacco than in wine. At least that might be assumed from this report: "We stopped at the Franklin Hotel . . . , which would be an excellent house, if it were kept a little cleaner; but how can a popular and much frequented house be kept clean, in a region where travelling gentlemen whilst lying in bed, do absolutely project the salivary extract of tobacco upon the walls of their chambers."[8]

Gross or not, tobacco continued as Jefferson's chief cash crop and was the very cornerstone of Lynchburg's prosperity. While Jefferson usually sold his at the Richmond market or shipped it abroad, on occasion he had his hogsheads inspected and sold at the Lynchburg warehouses. Spring Warehouse handled his tobacco more often than any other of the town's many warehouses when he chose to sell it in Lynchburg, at least if the records in its surviving daybook can be judged as proof. Unfortunately, Jefferson did not share in the prosperity enjoyed by his Lynchburg and Bedford neighbors during these years. A combination of failed crops, interest payments on preexisting loans, and of course the money he expended on his building projects conspired to continually keep him from emerging from under his staggering, and growing, burden of debt. On March 28, 1816, he wrote Archibald Robertson: "My tobacco which was all I had for market from Bedford sold very poorly," and apologized that this would prevent him from being able to reduce his debt to him that year. With his new manager,

Joel Yancey, in charge, he hoped things would soon improve, "but until then I must ask your indulgence." Unfortunately, the next year was no better, and on April 25, 1817, he again wrote Robertson: "This being the season in which the farmer recieves the fruit of his year's labor it is that also in which he is to pay attention to his debts. No debt of mine gives the more anxiety than that to your self, in which I have had great indulgence. Two years of embargo and non-intercourse, 3 of war, and 2 of disastrous drought have successively baffled my wishes to be reducing it."[9]

Although he was perhaps too young to know all the details of his grandfather's (or his father's) finances, Francis Eppes was not impressed with Lynchburg's infatuation with the dollar during these years. In 1817, when he was sixteen-years old, his father wrote his grandfather: "His great objection to Lynchburg appears to be the want of books and of persons of science. He speaks of the inhabitants as a race devoted solely to gain and having no ideas unconnected with money."[10] Francis had spent the winter of 1815–16 at Monticello, being tutored in French by his grandfather and his first cousin, Ellen Randolph, as Mr. Holcombe's school in Lynchburg had no French teacher. On December 11, 1815, Francis's thankful and somewhat relieved father wrote to Jefferson: "I fear you have undertaken a troublesome task. It is one I should certainly not have imposed on you and from which I shall feel great pleasure in relieving you whenever it becomes too weighty or whenever you suppose Francis's time can be as well bestowed elsewhere."[11] As it turned out, it was Eppes who first supposed that his son's time could be "as well bestowed elsewhere."

On March 30, 1816, Jefferson answered a letter he had received from Eppes suggesting that Francis be sent to a tutor in North Carolina of whom he had heard good reports. Jefferson had heard better reports of another teacher, one much closer to home: "At the New London Academy there is a teacher (Mr. Mitchell I think is his name) about equal to Mr. Holcomb, a young man very anxious to do what is best, and open to advice." Echoing what he had said several years earlier when he learned that Francis was at Mr. Holcombe's, Jefferson added: "I confess too I contemplate with pleasure his early familiarisation with that part of the country, having the wish to make him a comfortable future home there." Somewhat in the guise of a penitent, he then made an offer that the senior Eppes, never flush with cash himself, could hardly refuse: "I am almost afraid to propose to you to yield to me the expense and direction of his education. Yet I think I could have it conducted to his advantage." Furthermore, he had not only received recommendations of Mr. Mitchell, Jefferson had invited him to dinner during his 1816 spring visit to Poplar Forest and had found that he was "sensible, modest, anxious to improve

himself, and will conform to any desire I shall express to him." Best news of all was his price, which Jefferson said was "no more than I paid to Mr. Maury for my own education 55 years ago."[12] A month later, on April 30, he recorded in his Memorandum Book that he had given an order to his Lynchburg factor, Archibald Robertson, for $10.00 "for Mr. Mitchell for tuition from June 1." A commentary on the cost of education at the time is afforded by the fact that he paid exactly the same amount that day for Francis's "bed and washing," and a further sum of $33.33 for his board at New London Academy[13] (fig. 70).

Back at Monticello, Jefferson wrote his grandson that he had "some expectation of being at Poplar Forest the 3rd week of June, when I hope I shall see you going on cleverly and already beloved by your tutor, curators and companions as you are by your's affectionately. Th. Jefferson."[14] True to his word, Jefferson arrived at Poplar Forest during the third week of June 1816 for his second visit that year, and stayed until July 8. As the last visit had been devoted in part to making arrangements for Francis at New London Academy, this trip was timed to

Fig. 70 New London Academy. In 1816 Francis Eppes was enrolled at New London Academy, located only a short distance from Poplar Forest. This small building then served as the academy's kitchen, and is the only structure surviving from the school's first years. *(Tom Graves, Jr., 1991)*

make sure his grandson was well established there.

He wasn't. Although the session for which Jefferson paid tuition began "on Monday the 3d. of June by which day Francis should be here," he had not only missed the first day, but the first month, of classes. Not until June 24 could Jefferson write his father that he had arrived, and even then he wouldn't get to school for at least a week: "I am this moment arrived here with Ellen & Cornelia, and find Francis who arrived last night. I will take care and attend him to the Academy & see to every thing necessary for him. We will keep him with us as long as we stay (a week or ten days) and rub him up in his French."[15] Francis was soon duly enrolled at New London, but his first session there proved only a short chapter in the continuing saga of his educational career.

In his June 24 letter to the senior Eppes, Jefferson noted that Ellen and Cornelia had accompanied him to Poplar Forest. Their summer trip of 1816 was the first of many for this intrepid twosome. Ellen, Francis's language tutor, was then nineteen years old, and her sister Cornelia, sixteen (figs. 71 and 72). They seem to have written no letters on this relatively short journey, but their lengthy dispatches from subsequent visits tell vividly, accurately, charmingly, and sometimes scathingly, of the happenings and occasional mishaps they witnessed, and in which they participated. Years later, Ellen recalled this first trip and the condition of the house at the time: "The first visit I ever paid with him in what afterwards became a favorite retreat, must have been I think in the summer of 1816. The house was then unfinished, and indeed the lower or basement story was still unfinished when the property passed to my cousin Francis Eppes."[16]

Unfinished it indeed still was, but during these years there was usually at least a skeleton crew of workmen from Monticello adding some sort of finishing touch, or working on other buildings on the plantation. On July 5, 1816, just before his departure for Monticello, Jefferson noted in his Memorandum Book that he "gave Joel Yancey ord. on Gibson & Jeff. for 32.25 for so much paid by him to John Depriest for plank." On July 24, after he was back at Monticello, Yancey wrote him that, in addition to

Fig. 71 Ellen Wayles Randolph (Mrs. Joseph Coolidge, Jr.). This oil-on-canvas portrait, attributed to Francis Alexander, ca. 1836, is the only known early likeness of one of Jefferson's favorite granddaughters. (*Monticello, Thomas Jefferson Memorial Foundation, Inc., by permission of Ellen Eddy Thorndike*)

Fig. 72 Cornelia Jefferson Randolph, terra cotta bust by William J. Coffee, ca. 1819. Cornelia and her sister Ellen accompanied their grandfather on many of his visits to Poplar Forest. Coffee was the same artisan who supplied plaster ornaments for the house at Poplar Forest and for the University of Virginia. (*Monticello, Thomas Jefferson Memorial Foundation, Inc.*)

having sent "stock to the mill" to be sawn for a sawmill that Jefferson proposed to build at Poplar Forest, he had "got also the plank from Depriest for the House, but I find in putting it on, that we shall lack [some]. I sent too for 100 feet more than Goodman said it would require."[17]

On August 29, 1816, Yancey gave further discouraging information on the sawing: "Capt. Martin has disappointed me in not having your timber ready, he has already told me he could have it at any time and that you should have it time enough, but he has put it off, and now he has taken his dam down and cant tell when he can saw or grind. All your timber is lying there untouched." That information was added to his letter as a postscript; the body of the text contained more encouraging news: "Barnaby and Nace have been getting staves, building springhouse and coopers shop since harvest and will begin to set up flour barrels next week." Jefferson responded to Yancey on September 13 that he would "feel Cap. Martin's disappointment very heavily as we shall be obliged to get our stocks sawed by hand & to work them green & for outside work too. John Hemings and his two aids will set out so as to be at Poplar Forest the evening before us."[18]

Yancey's mention of the coopers shop referred to another cottage industry that Jefferson set up at Poplar Forest, in conjunction with one that was already underway at Monticello. While the distaff side of his slave work force was spinning and weaving, the males were to be kept busy, during otherwise slack periods, making barrels for storing his flour, and to sell to others. Yancey's letter of August 29, 1816, gives further information on the venture. Although Captain Mitchell "declined taking your wheat upon the terms you proposed," he had said that he would "buy your barrels at 2 a barrell and delivered in Lynchburg," a price Yancey thought too low. Though Yancey reported the coopers shop being built, and though Jefferson once advised one of his mill operators that he could "count on delivering you 4000 barels a year" from the Monticello workshop, its planned counterpart in Bedford never seems to have met his expectations.[19]

On his third 1816 visit, which occurred from late September through early October, Jefferson arrived at Poplar Forest accompanied by his daughter, Martha, and his servant Burwell. This trip was Martha's first to see her father's new house. Her daughter Ellen, who stayed behind at Monticello, congratulated her on her perfect timing, which had "saved you from many disagreeable intrusions; we have had several large parties from the springs, and a coach & four is by no means an uncommon sight at the door." She didn't mind the short call made by Baltimore architect Maximilian Godefroy and his wife and children, then on their way to Natural Bridge. Although they arrived just as she "was in the midst of my housekeeping," they "did not stay more than an hour."

Not so another group, whom she described as "imprudent and ungenteel people who behaved as if they had been in a tavern." She added that "these intruders have pretty generally expressed their regret at Grandpapa's absense, and I have rejoiced at it — on his account — not on my own God knows."[20]

Jefferson returned to Monticello on October 5, and came back to Poplar Forest for the final of his four 1816 visits on the twentieth-fourth of the same month. John Hemings was still working on the house, and on October 26 Jefferson recorded paying "his annual donation 20. D," the gratuity that he gave each year to both Hemings and Burwell. Another confirmation of ongoing work was the three-dollar payment he made to one Bradfeut for "laying a hearth and trimmer" on October 29.[21]

On this last visit in 1816, Ellen and Cornelia Randolph again accompanied their grandfather. Each had celebrated a birthday in the interim. Ellen was no longer a teenager, and the seventeen-year-old Cornelia, by now fancying herself a seasoned traveler, sagely informed her younger sister Virginia, who had been left at home in Albemarle, that the trip had been "pleasant enough" and that they had stopped for breakfast at Noah Flood's, which she found "to be the best house on the road to stop at meals & at night we were better accommodated at Hunters than anywhere else." For her part, Ellen was apparently still smarting from the crowds that had plagued Monticello and reported to her mother that "fortunately we have not been much interrupted by company." There had been a few visitors, and she then proceeded to list a number of ladies — Mrs. Yancey and Mrs. Radford among them — who had "called a few days after our arrival." Most met with her approval, and though she dipped her pen into enough vitriol to describe a later visitor as "the very quintessence of vulgarity," she observed: "upon the whole, however, I like this place and neighborhood very much and should be well pleased to pass a part of my time here every year."[22]

As he had done the previous November, Jefferson took the occasion to attend to landscaping chores at Poplar Forest during this visit. On the first of the month, he recorded planting "large roses of difft. kinds in the oval bed in the N. front. dwarf roses in the N. E. oval. Robinia hispida in the N. W. do. Althaeas, Gelder roses, lilacs, calycanthus, in both mounds. Privet round both Necessaries. White Jessamine along N. W. of E. offices. Azedaracs opp. 4 angles of the house."[23] During his visit, he also wrote Martha with a request for "some of the hardy bulbous roots of flowers," which he asked her to send with the cart that was to come from Monticello to carry their luggage back. Martha decided not to send them, as "the kinds you mentioned are all growing at present and could not be moved without destroying them, but I have sent you a number of sets of tulips and hyacinths." They were mixed, but "Cornelia knows them all," she advised.[24] Jefferson soon recorded additional plantings, presumably from stock that was already in the Poplar Forest nursery. On November 22, he wrote in his Garden Book: "planted 190 poplars in the grounds. 5 Athenian poplars. 2 Kentucky locusts near house. European mulberries in the new garden."[25]

Though Jefferson valued his privacy at Poplar Forest, there were those rare occasions when he had to accommodate some of his many admirers there rather than at Monticello. That had obviously happened the previous year when Andrew Jackson came by, and it was to happen again during this late visit in 1816. This time, though, it was not an interruption. In August, Jefferson had written from Monticello to George Flower, whom he would later identify as "the son of an English gentleman landholder, of large family connections," who had been sent by his family to America to "find an eligible situation for them."[26] Jefferson told Flower: "If you should reach this place during this month, I shall be here, happy to receive you, if later than the 1st day of Sept. I shall be gone on with my family to a possession I have near Lynchburg where I shall be glad that you become one of my family at either place."[27] As it turned out, Flower's trip had been delayed even longer than Jefferson had expected. He arrived in November from the west, entering "the State of Virginia at Abington [sic]," and came to Poplar Forest. It was a fortunate visit, at least for later-day historians. Flower left one of the few descriptions, other than those afforded by family members, of Poplar Forest as it was in Jefferson's time. While his depiction is brief, it gives an intimate glimpse of the house and its owner:

I found Mr. Jefferson at his Poplar Forest estate, in the western part of the State of Virginia. His house was built after the fashion of a French chateau, Octagon rooms, floors of polished oak, lofty ceilings, large mirrors betokened his French taste, acquired by his long residence in France. Mr. Jefferson's figure was rather majestic: tall (over six feet), thin, and rather high-shouldered: manners simple, kind, and courteous. His dress, in color and form, was quaint and old fashioned, plain and neat — a dark pepper-and-salt coat, cut in the old quaker fashion, with a single row of large metal buttons, knee-breeches, gray-worsted stockings, shoes fastened by large metal buckles — such was the appearance of Jefferson when I first made his acquaintance, in 1816. His two grand-daughters — Misses Randolph — well educated and accomplished young ladies, were staying with him at the time.[28]

Apparently young Flower, then just over thirty years old, didn't make the impression on the Misses Randolph that they did on him. If Ellen and Cornelia's letters (which failed entirely to mention him) can be taken as evidence, he was nothing to write home about. Consider-

ing Ellen's description of one of the ladies who had come to call during their visit, it is perhaps just as well for Flower that she remained silent.

On November 23, Jefferson wrote Elizabeth Trist, telling her that "Ellen and Cornelia are with me here, where we have been a month. We are all packing for an early departure tomorrow morning." Unfortunately, as he explained to Martha on December 3, they were delayed: "It began to rain that day, and we have had three regular N. E. rains successively, with intermissions of a single day between each. During the first intermission Mr. Flower left us for Monticello, but by the way of the Natural Bridge." John Hemings had finished his work for the season, and "the girls have borne [the delay] wonderfully." On December 6 the family finally left Poplar Forest for their return trip to Monticello, via Millbrook.[29]

As he had the previous winter, Francis Eppes joined his grandfather and cousins for a portion of the winter of 1816–17 at Monticello. Jefferson reported to Francis's father that he "has gone on diligently with his Spanish," apparently tutored by Ellen, as she had "the true pronunciation more perfectly than myself."[30] Instead of having Francis return to New London after his winter tutoring, Jefferson readily acquiesced in his father's plan for him to attend another school that had just opened in Richmond. Jefferson knew the headmaster, John Wood, whom he declared to be not only the "greatest Mathematician in the state," but "undoubtedly our best Grecian, and will pay particular attention to Francis." Francis went to John Wood's school as planned, but early in June, 1817, Jefferson wrote the boy's father that he had just heard that Wood "was obliged to suspend his school for four months." That may have been just as well for Francis. On May 17 his father had to chastise his son for being "capable of suspecting any person of an act of so much meanness as to enter your chamber secretly and cut your cloathes."[31] Fortunately, in an earlier correspondence, Jefferson had told the senior Eppes that, on his April 1817 trip to Bedford he would "have the opportunity of enquiring into the character lately employed in New London of whom I hear a good account."[32] Eventually, he would find the character of Alfred H. Dashiell, the new headmaster at New London, quite satisfactory. Before Francis had a chance to matriculate there again, he would attend a school that he found far more distasteful than Mr. Wood's.

Although his grandson's educational career occupied a great deal of Jefferson's time and interest, there was another project dealing with education — and architecture — that was soon to occupy far more of his energy. In fact, it had already begun to do so. Its involvement with Lynchburg and Poplar Forest would be intimate, as Jefferson embarked on yet another chapter in his distinguished career.

"THE MOST EMINENT IN THE UNITED STATES"
AND
"THE MOST SUBLIME OF NATURE'S WORKS"
(1817)

Jefferson's 1817 spring visit to Poplar Forest was brief, lasting only slightly over a week. His return to Albemarle at the end of April brooked no delay. On May 5 he attended a meeting in Charlottesville that the *Richmond Enquirer* deemed important enough to report: "On the 5th of this month, three men were seen together at Charlottesville . . . each of whom alone is calculated to attract the eager gaze of their Fellow Citizens—We mean, Thomas Jefferson, James Madison, and James Monroe. . . . The appearance of three such men together at a village where the citizens of the county had met to attend their court, is an event, which for its singularity, deserves the notice of a passing paragraph." Indeed it did. Far away in Massachusetts, John Adams also took notice and congratulated his old acquaintance, along with "Madison and Monroe, on your noble employment in founding a university. From such a noble triumvirate the world will expect something very great and very new."[1]

This gathering of two former United States presidents and the incumbent was the first meeting of the Board of Visitors of Central College. Not yet a university, it was the successor to Albemarle Academy and would be the precursor of the University of Virginia. Jefferson had already planned the "academical village" (as he called it) that would house the institution, and his suggestions were adopted at the May 5th meeting. His plan called for "a distinct pavilion or building for each separate professorship; these to be arranged around a square; each pavilion to contain a school-room and two apartments for the accommodation of the professor's family, and other reasonable conveniences." The educational aims of Jefferson's college were no less innovative and advanced than its architectural goals, and of course, the two were inseparable. As Jefferson was to state several years later: "The great object of our aim from the beginning has been to make this establishment the most eminent in the United States in order to draw to it characters of the first order . . . . and not only by their salaries, and the comforts of their situation, but by the distinguished scale of its structure. . . . Had we built a barn for a college, and log huts for accommodations, should we ever have had the assurance to propose to an European professor. . . to come to it?"[2] (fig. 73)

Jefferson sought and obtained advice from architects William Thornton and Benjamin Henry Latrobe,

among others, but the overall plan and design that emerged are his own. His academical village, eventually to be called the Lawn, is the final achievement of his architectural genius. Usually modest on the subject of his many accomplishments, even Jefferson could brag about this one, at least if Peachy Gilmer was quoting him verbatim when he reported to Nicholas Trist: "Mr. Jefferson . . . is engaged with great ardor in the superintendence of the University, which he says will when compleated be the handsomest building in the world."[3]

Just before the May 5, 1817, meeting of the Board of Visitors of Central College, John Wayles Eppes made good his long-standing threat to sell Pantops. This time Eppes's former father-in-law could hardly have been happier with the sale, as the purchaser was none other than his grandson and Eppes's nephew, Thomas Jefferson Randolph. Both Randolph and his father-in-law endorsed a note for $10,000 for the purchase.[4] Randolph, now twenty-four years old, had married Jane Hollins Nicholas two years earlier at her family's home, Mount Warren, overlooking the riverside town of Warren. Her father, Wilson Cary Nicholas, was Jefferson's friend and governor of Virginia at the time, and Jefferson and his entourage often visited Mount Warren on their trips to and from Poplar Forest.

In fact, Jefferson stopped by on his next visit to Poplar Forest, noting in his Memorandum Book on June 29 that he paid ferriage at Warren. This second visit of 1817 lasted almost two weeks, and was taken up, at least in part, with both his own financial matters and his plans for the new college. Less than a month after his return to Albemarle, he went back to Poplar Forest, arriving on August 10, for his third trip of the year. Burwell and John Hemings came along, as did Jefferson's granddaughters Ellen and Cornelia. This was their third visit to Bedford, and they were now ready to explore more unchartered territory. At least their seventy-four year old grandfather thought so. Just before leaving Monticello, he wrote their uncle, John Wayles Eppes, of his plans: "I set out for Bedford tomorrow, and shall leave this at Flood's. You will know therefore by it's receipt that we are passed on, to wit Ellen, Cornelia, and myself. Very soon after our arrival at Poplar Forest, perhaps a week, we shall go to the Nat. Bridge and be absent 4 or 5 days: and shall hope to see you & Francis soon after."[5]

The group left Poplar Forest for the bridge early on the morning of August 13, and from the first the trip was an eye-opener for Ellen and Cornelia. Only a year earlier, Jefferson had declared that he "found the road between [Natural Bridge] and Poplar Forest so trifling that I believe I shall be tempted to take it annually in autumn. It is but about 30 miles of good road and a passable gap." According to his granddaughters, he could hardly have been more mistaken. It took Cornelia two long letters to report all the happenings to her sister Virginia, at Monticello. She began her first: "We are returned from the natural bridge more anxious to see it again than we were at first because in the first place it far surpassed our expectation and in the second we saw it under many disadvantages which will be removed when we go again and grandpapa has promised that we shall, our trip was attended with disasters and accidents from time we set off until we returned again."[6]

The litany of disasters began with a delay: "We set off accordingly after Gil and Isreal [sic] had made us wait two hours," continued with the weather: "one of the hottest most disagreeable days for travelling that could be," and intensified with a near disaster: "in going over a high bridge one of the wheel horses broke through and sunk up nearly halfway in the hole." The bridge, they discovered, had "entirely gone to decay & not only several of the logs but one of the sleepers had broken through & . . . we had been in great danger of going down carriage & horses & all." Gil and Israel, two slaves accompanying the party, set things right, and the carriage was soon left at a log house, from which the entourage then proceeded on horseback. Although the house had but one room, it

Fig. 73 The University of Virginia. This engraving, published in London in 1831 from a drawing made in Jefferson's lifetime, shows the Lawn, flanked by five pavilions on each side, and the Rotunda in the distance. Pavilion 7, the first structure to be built, is the second from the left (see fig. 75). (*Virginia State Library and Archives*)

was inhabited by a large family, whom Cornelia described as "the first of that half civilized race who live beyond the ridge that we had seen." They were "as perfectly at their ease as if they had known us all their lives; the two old men entered into conversation with grandpapa at once and one of them said he had been forty three years living there [within twelve miles of the bridge] & had never seen it." Though he was described as "the most savage looking man of the two," it was the other, "with his hairy breast exposed," who shocked Cornelia more. Only one of the two men knew who Jefferson was, but when he identified their guest to the other, there ensued a discussion on where "Colonel Jefferson" lived. "He lives near Parson Clay's in Bedford," said one, "but the other one said no he did not live there he lived in Albemarle and only visited his place in Bedford call'd Poplar

Forest, sometimes." Cornelia was astounded that they "knew so much about grandpapa, . . . for he never had seen either of them before." After lunch, consisting of "cold bacon and chicken," on top of the Blue Ridge, they descended to Greenlee's Ferry on the James River.[7]

On August 30, Cornelia again took pen in hand to continue her narrative: "When we got to Greenlee's the house was an excellent brick house as well built as the houses of Lynchburg & there were three other buildings in the same yard two of brick and one of stone" (fig. 74). Unfortunately, although the interior "of the one we went into was well finished," it was filthy. Cornelia "felt exactly as if the place was polluted. I could not bear to touch anything, & at night they carried us into a very good little room, but the sheets of our bed were dirty & we were obliged to sleep on the outside that night."

Fig. 74 Greenlee's, the inn that Cornelia described as "an excellent brick house," still stands close to the banks of the James River near Natural Bridge Station. (*Tom Graves, Jr., 1991*)

Ellen, even more fastidious than Cornelia, "walked up and down the room all night and did not sleep at all," but part of her discomfort was due to a cold she had caught crossing the Blue Ridge. Their grandfather, Cornelia reported, "said he had a very nice comfortable bed but he slept in the room with two or three people."[8] He also must have gone to sleep with a smile, thinking of the liberal education he was providing for his heretofore all-too-sheltered granddaughters.

Seeing the bridge the next day more than made up for any discomforts endured along the way. Cornelia was able only to declare somewhat incoherently that "the scene was beyond anything you can imagine possibly." Ellen, writing to her mother, took a more eloquent, if less original, course by repeating exactly what their grandfather had said years earlier in his *Notes on Virginia*: that it was "the most sublime of Nature's works." Ellen was also less graphic than Cornelia in describing the previous day's journey, but did allow that "the manners and character of the people are so different from anything we are accustomed to and the scenery of the country so wild and picturesque, that we almost fancied ourselves in a new world." The party was aided in their visit by one Patrick Henry, whom Cornelia described as "a mulatto man [who] . . . generally goes with persons who go to see the bridge."[9] Henry, a freedman whom Jefferson let live on the property, assisted the party in getting to the bed of the creek below the bridge. On this trip, Jefferson gave Henry a dollar, and left five dollars with him "to be pd. to the Sher. of Rockbridge for taxes past & to come."[10]

Jefferson had been paying taxes on Natural Bridge for quite a while. In his 1794 Land Roll, he noted that he had patented it, with 157 surrounding acres, on July 5, 1774 (see fig. 12).[11] For the most part, he regarded himself "as guardian only for the public of this first of all natural curiosities," but when he left the presidency in 1809, he had almost sold it as part of his attempts to settle his debt.[12] Aware of its potential as an attraction (and that it should bring a higher price than adjacent farmland), he had then observed: "I had always believed that if there were accommodations there, the healthy part of the company which frequents the various springs, would pass the same season at the bridge of preference as their object is merely to be absent from the lower country at that season & the climate & curiosity of the bridge would render a stay there much more eligible."[13]

Instead of selling, Jefferson had leased the property in 1814 to one Philip Thornton for a shot manufactory, and in the contract made sure that the bridge would not be defaced: "The said Philip covenants on his part that he will pay the said annual rent as reserved to the said Thomas and his heirs, that he will make no erection or do any other thing which shall disfigure the said bridge as a natural curiosity; that he will commit no waste or destruction on the said bridge or lands . . . but that he will to the best of his power preserve the said bridge in its perfect natural and uninjured form."[14]

The elderly gentleman Cornelia met on her trip, who had lived within twelve miles of the bridge for forty-three years and had never seen it, was in a decided minority. Along with Niagara Falls, Natural Bridge was the great wonder of North America that all late-eighteenth and early-nineteenth-century lovers of nature, European as well as American, were expected to see.[15] Both were pictured in "Vues de l'Amérique du Nord," a French scenic wallpaper first published by the Alsatian firm of Zuber & Cie in 1834, and in other media as well.[16] Accommodations were eventually built near the bridge, and although the site never became as popular a summer resort as the Virginia springs, as Jefferson had predicted it might, Natural Bridge continues today to be a much-visited and much-appreciated scenic attraction.

Jefferson and his granddaughters stayed at the bridge until after five o'clock on the afternoon of their visit, and then returned to Greenlee's to spend the night before going back to Poplar Forest. They then remained in Bedford another month, not leaving until September 19. During this time, a great deal of work was accomplished on the house, little of it to the girls' liking. In the August 18 letter to her mother describing the bridge, Ellen also noted: "Cornelia and myself are not comfortably fixed. Our room has been pulled down and it will be some time before we get in it, probably a fortnight — in the mean time we are in that little close, disagreeable room to the right as you enter the dining room, we are so crowded we can scarcely turn. The weather hot and as Cornelia observes, we are shut up from all the breezes but the north east."[17] Ellen and Cornelia were habitually housed in the east bedroom, from which room the eastern stair descended to the ground, but they had now been relocated to the small room immediately to the right of the entrance hall as the house is entered from the front door.

The young ladies may have protested too much, for according to their grandfather, they seemed to have spent an inordinate amount of time "in that little close, disagreeable room." On Aug. 31, Jefferson wrote Martha that "Ellen and Cornelia are the severest students I have ever met with. They never leave their room but to come to meals . . . . An alteration in that part of the house, not yet finished, has deprived them of the use of their room longer than I expected, but two or three days more will now restore it to them."[18]

While it is not clear from the existing records just what the alteration was or why it necessitated the room being "pulled down," one possibility is that a connection was then being made from the main floor of the house to the terrace above the recently-built wing of offices. Evidence of a former doorway in the south wall of the eastern stair pavilion, which would have led to the terrace, has recently been confirmed in the architectural investigations. The opening of this new door would have been a sufficiently disruptive operation to necessitate the girls' being removed to another room. Another possibility is that the alterations were being undertaken to change the arrangement of the room so that one end of it could serve as a pantry. If this were the case, the alcove bed would more than likely have been changed, or at least closed in on one side. In her later remembrance of the house, Ellen stated that around the dining room were "grouped a bright drawing-room looking south, my grandfather's own chamber, three other bedrooms, and a pantry."[19] Perhaps the alteration to which Jefferson referred was a combination of the two undertakings.

Another reason Ellen and Cornelia might not have wanted to leave their room was to escape from plaster dust. On August 30, the day before he told Martha that they never left their room, Jefferson noted in his Memorandum Book that he "pd. Antrim 36. yds. plaistering 12. D." Again it is impossible to determine from the existing record if this work was undertaken in the girls' room, but it seems more than probable that it was. Antrim was Joseph Antrim, and in a letter written the next day to Hugh Chisolm, though he did not name him, Jefferson was undoubtedly referring to him in announcing that "the finest plaisterer I have ever seen in this state is anxious to undertake with us" for work at the new college.[20]

Whatever the work involved at Poplar Forest in the summer of 1817, John Hemings was in charge, and in addition to the actual construction work, he more than likely spent some of his time painting as well. In March 1817, long before the August visit, Jefferson had written Joel Yancey, enclosing "a bill of scantling which I hope Mr. Martin will be so good as to saw immediately, as it is what is to employ John Hemings in the autumn."[21] Later that month, Jefferson had reiterated the request: "The bill of scantling I sent you will not be above a day's work for Mr. Martin's mill, so I hope he will do it for me." Between those two letters to his Bedford overseer, he wrote his Albemarle supplier, David Higginbotham, on the subject of housepaint: "I shall certainly want a very great quantity in the course of the present year, as I have to renew the whole outer painting of this house [Monticello] and the terraces, and to paint that in Bedford which has never been done."[22] That particular letter was

Fig. 75 Pavilion 7, University of Virginia. The first building to be constructed at the university, this pavilion has a portico arrangement similar to the south facade at Poplar Forest. Two of its builders — Hugh Chisolm, who did much of its brickwork, and John Perry, who provided its woodwork — had worked at Poplar Forest. *(photograph ca. 1950, Virginia State Library and Archives)*

only to inform Higginbotham that he intended to paint that year, but it was not yet an order for the supplies. As his crops had failed so miserably because of a drought the last year, he had no money available then, and told his supplier that he would have to "delay my demand till towards autumn so as to bridge the time of payment within reach of the growing crop."

Ellen and Cornelia might have preferred to have remained in their room even more often than their grandfather reported. In the second of her letters to her sister Virginia describing Natural Bridge, Cornelia moaned that "tomorrow sister Ellen & myself have to put numbers on all of grandpapas books & it will take us nearly the whole day which I am very sorry for because besides wishing to write letters I should like very well to have copied a beautiful Desdimonia from Shakespeare which I am afraid I cant do now."[23] More than likely, she had planned to copy it from one of the books that Jefferson had in his Poplar Forest library. In addition to his petit-format volumes, already mentioned, the collection he maintained at his villa retreat contained a Vulgate edition of the Bible, a 108-volume series of "British Poets, from Chaucer to Churchill," a 52-volume set of Buffon's *Histoire Naturelle,* 25 volumes of Italian Poets, Bell's edition of Shakespeare, consisting of 38 volumes, and his own *Notes on Virginia,* to mention only a few.[24]

No wonder Cornelia complained about having to catalog "all of grandpapas books." It is hard to imagine how she and Ellen could have accomplished their task in "nearly the whole day." Even less wonder that in almost all his letters describing his activities at Poplar Forest, Jefferson always noted reading as one of them. In her later reminiscences of Poplar Forest, Ellen recalled the important role books played during their visits. In the evenings, her grandfather "would take his book from which he would occasionally look up to make a remark, to question us about what we were reading, or perhaps to read aloud to us from his own book, some passage which had struck him, and of which he wished to give us the benefit. About ten o'clock he rose to go, when we kissed him with warm, loving, grateful hearts and went to our rest blessing God for such a friend."[25]

Cataloging Jefferson's books was perhaps a less painful way to spend an entire day than what the Randolph siblings were next called upon to do. Sometime in September the Clays came to call, "and spent a whole day with us — from ten o'clock until near sunset." Ellen caustically suggested that Martha might well imagine "how rapidly the hours passed," but gave "the old woman the justice to say that I do not believe she intended to have paid so long a visit." She instead blamed "her savage husband [who] wholly unconscious of the ridicule and impropriety of the thing insisted upon staying all day of

it." Instead of leaving it at that, Ellen added insult to injury by telling her mother that "he is much more uncivilized than any Indian I ever saw, and indeed I doubt whether the wild Hottentots described by Peron are as bad — They certainly cannot be more savage in voice and manners, or more entirely ignorant of the rules of good breeding."[26]

During this long stay in Bedford, one of the slaves, Cretia's Johnny, made a number of trips with the cart between Jefferson's two homes. His departures from Poplar Forest took letters back to Monticello, while his arrivals brought letters, supplies and equipment for John Hemings and, on one occasion, a "head of Christ," which Ellen noted was "a great curiosity. Grandpapa is almost as much pleased with it as we are, and considers it extremely ingenious & original."[27] Nothing further is known of what was apparently a religious painting, or bust, but the fact that Jefferson had something of the sort at Poplar Forest should come as no surprise. Monticello, too, had its share of religious paintings.[28]

While his young charges were laboring over their books after their return from Natural Bridge, Jefferson was, among other things, attending to plans for his new college outside Charlottesville. On August 24, he sent Latrobe "a very ragged sketch of the [pavilion] now in hand." He was referring to the first of the professor's houses, Pavilion 7, as it has come to be known. Its facade is fronted by a five-bay portico on the second-floor level, which is supported by an arcade with six plastered piers on the first-floor level. Although wider by two bays, and of the Doric rather than the Tuscan order, its basic disposition and appearance are not unlike the original arrangement of the south portico at Poplar Forest (fig. 75).

In addition to drawing plans, or elevations, Jefferson also made arrangements for the work that was commencing on the college. In his August 31, 1817, letter praising the plasterer Joseph Antrim, he also informed Hugh Chisolm that not only was Antrim "anxious to undertake with us," but that he had "offers from some of the best workmen in Lynchburg" as well. Jefferson had every intention of hiring them, as he considered "it as the interest of the College, the town [Charlottesville] and the neighborhood to introduce a reform of the barbarous workmanship hitherto practiced there, and to raise us to a level with the rest of the country." He added: "On a trip to the Natural Bridge, I found such brickwork and stonework as cannot be seen in Albemarle."[29] Presumably he was thinking of Greenlee's, on which Cornelia had also commented favorably.

During the last weeks of his visit, Jefferson even found time to attend to another educational venture. On September 9, 1817, he wrote Joseph Cabell, a fellow member of the Board of Visitors at the Central College and a member of the General Assembly: "I promised you that I would put into the form of a bill my plan of establishing the elementary schools, without taking a cent from the literary fund. I have had leisure at this place to do this and now send you the result." The "result," sent as a bill that he proposed be submitted to the Virginia General Assembly, provided not only for primary, or elementary, schools for all, but also for "establishing a college in every district of about eighty miles square, for the second grade of education; and for the third grade, a single university, where the sciences shall be taught in their highest degree."[30] It was Jefferson's plan that his Central College would become the nucleus of the proposed university.

Just before the end of his visit, Jefferson went into Lynchburg on a shopping spree, and recorded in his Memorandum Book on September 17 paying for several items, among them three dollars for the watchmaker, and a "pr. shoes 2.75." That last item, he soon found out, was a mistake. A day later, on September 18, he returned them with this note: "Th. Jefferson begs leave to return to Mr. Newhall the shoes he got of him yesterday, which he can barely get on and find it would be impossible to wear. He will ask another pair instead of them whenever Mr. Newhall has any of the same soft quality, but a good size larger and longer." According to an early-day history of Lynchburg, James Newhall "kept for many years a shoe-store, and we well remember the intense admiration with which his sign was contemplated—a man as large as life having his boots pulled off by a colored boy."[31] An advertisement that Newhall placed in the *Lynchburg Press* was far less graphic (fig. 76).

On September 19, 1817, the day of his departure, Jefferson noted in his Memorandum book the payment of $12.05 for "debts and vales" at Poplar Forest. Again, this was a larger-than-usual sum, and reflects both the length of the stay and the fact that he had called upon his Bedford servants to look after an unusually large group; in addition to himself, his two granddaughters, Burwell, John Hemings, Cretia's Johnny, Gill, and Israel.

John Hemings would remain at Poplar Forest, continuing his work on the house until Jefferson's next visit, but by September 21, the others were back at Monticello. Three days after their return, Martha wrote her daughter Virginia, who had yet to make her first visit to Poplar Forest, and who had been sent instead to Warm Springs, perhaps as something of a compensation: "There is nothing new, nothing to prevent animal spirits from stagnation; and our Bedford party have returned so stupid from their long rustication that we have all dozed away life together since their return. We expect the Stevensons to morrow, perhaps it will be a little better with us when we have seen some body to put a few ideas in our heads."[32]

Perhaps she was being somewhat facetious, but if not, Martha had seldom seemed so far off the mark — at least if she meant to include her father in her observation. Not only had Jefferson taken his granddaughters to visit Natural Bridge during his long rustication, he had continued to supervise the ongoing construction at Poplar Forest, had composed for the General Assembly his bill for the educational system of the Commonwealth of Virginia, had sketched the design of one of the pavilions of his college, and had begun arrangements for workers to build it. In a few days, he would attend the ceremony of laying its cornerstone and would then make plans to return for his fourth visit to Poplar Forest that year.

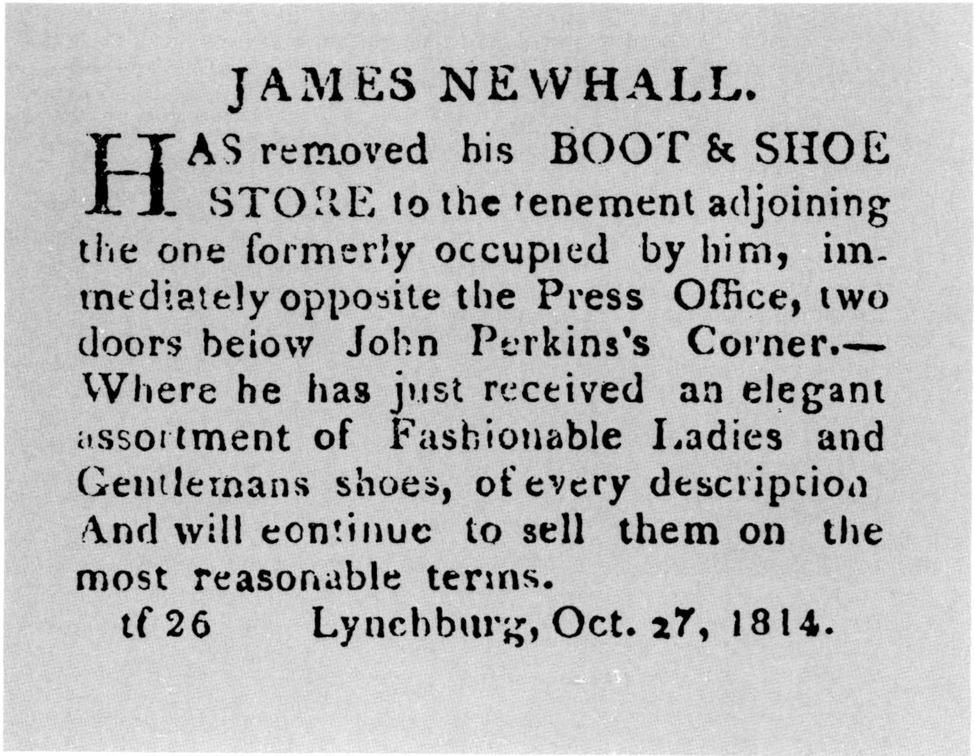

JAMES NEWHALL.

HAS removed his BOOT & SHOE STORE to the tenement adjoining the one formerly occupied by him, immediately opposite the Press Office, two doors below John Perkins's Corner.— Where he has just received an elegant assortment of Fashionable Ladies and Gentlemans shoes, of every description And will continue to sell them on the most reasonable terms.

tf 26   Lynchburg, Oct. 27, 1814.

Fig. 76 James Newhall advertised his "elegant assortment" of shoes in the *Lynchburg Press* in 1814. Elegant they may have been, but Jefferson, who bought a pair from Newhall several years later, did not find them very comfortable. *(Courtesy Jones Memorial Library, Lynchburg, Va.; photograph by Tom Graves, Jr., 1991)*

"A Babling of 40 Years Birth and Nursing"
AND
"A Clap of Thunder"
(1817–19)

On October 6, 1817, the cornerstone of the first pavilion at Central College in Charlottesville was laid. Jefferson was there, of course, and had planned to return to Poplar Forest at the end of the month, once he was assured that construction was on schedule. Unfortunately, as he wrote his overseer on November 3, he had been delayed by "the difficulty of keeping our workmen at College together so as to ensure the finishing it. This depends on their diligence for one fortnight more within which time the walls may be finished, and during which time it is probable I shall be obliged to see them every day or two, or risk the entire failure in what we have given the public a right to expect. About this time fortnight therefore I expect to be with you." He had written Joseph Cabell a week earlier in a more desperate vein: "Our Central College gives me more employment than I am equal to."[1]

Jefferson left Monticello on November 17 and arrived at Poplar Forest two days later. It wasn't the usual easy trip, and in his November 22 report to Martha he started with the bad news, then finished with the good: "I arrived here, my dear daughter after a disagreeable journey, one day shut up at Warren by steady rain, the next travelling thro a good deal of drizzle and rain, and the last excessive cold, the road being full of ice. But all well in the end. Johnny Hemings has made great progress in his work. His calculation is that he may possibly finish by this day fortnight but possibly and almost probably not till this day three weeks." Mrs. Trist and Mr. Burwell, he reported, had spent a day and night with him, and were "now starting off after an early breakfast." Jefferson's estimation of the time needed to complete the work on the house proved more accurate than Hemings's, and a week later he again wrote Martha, telling her that "the calculations in my former letter of the time when Johnny Hemings would be done was made on a guess of his own. By what he has since done I can estimate the time it will take him more exactly, and I find the cart need not leave Monticello till Thursday the 11th of December, on which day therefore I wish it to be dispatched."[2] Once again the exact nature of Hemings's work is unknown. More than likely much of it was a continuation of the work he had been doing all fall, in all probability trim work and whatever else was included in the "bill of scantling" that Jefferson had ordered in the spring from Mr. Martin, "to employ John Hemings in the autumn." Hemings, or someone under his supervision, was also painting. That the paint Jefferson had ordered from David Higginbotham was insufficient to complete the work is evidenced by Jefferson's noting in his Memorandum Book on December 3 a payment to "Dr. Humphries [for] paint

& oil. 9.05." Dr. Thomas Humphries, according to an advertisement in the *Lynchburg Press* earlier that year, had "just received from London, by the ship Averick, and from Liverpool, by the William and Ekra, a general assortment of Medicine, Paints and Painters Materials."[3]

As he also informed Martha in the second of his two letters, Jefferson had "been two days engaged from sunrise to sunset with a surveyor in running round my lines, which have never before been run round. I find that one neighbor (Cobbs) has cleared one half of his field on my land, and been cultivating it for 20 years chiefly in corn, having cut down the line trees so as to leave it nearly impossible to find out the lines. They are by no means unravelled as yet."[4] John Organ was the surveyor, and on November 29 Jefferson recorded in his Memorandum Book paying him $8.00 for "running land lines of Pop. For." Perhaps Cobbs should be excused for his trespass. In 1812, Jefferson had written of the awkward property lines between them: "There is a handsome little tract of 100 or two acres, belonging to Cobbs adjoining this part of my land, and elbowing into it disagreeably."[5]

As would be expected, Jefferson also found time during this sojourn at Poplar Forest to continue his efforts on behalf of the new college. On December 19, just prior to his departure, he wrote Joseph Cabell: "I have only this single anxiety in this world. It is a babling of 40 years birth and nursing, and if I can once see it on its legs, I will sing with sincerity and pleasure my nunc dimittis." He also told Cabell that he had "been detained a month by my affairs here, but shall depart in three days, and eat my Christmas dinner at Monticello."[6]

Jefferson left Poplar Forest in good time for his Christmas dinner, arriving at Monticello on December 23. Among the parcels and letters waiting for him there was a missive from John Wayles Eppes, written on December 11 from Washington, where he was serving in Congress. Once again, Francis and his educational career were in a state of flux, or at least in a holding pattern. Jefferson had written the senior Eppes in August 1817 that he thought Francis would be better situated at the Central College than anywhere else, but added "this is a subject for conversation when we see you at Poplar Forest." What was subsequently discussed on that visit is only a matter for speculation, though it was obvious that Central College would not open as soon as Jefferson had then hoped. Now Eppes told Jefferson: "I have put Francis to school in Georgetown. I have engaged a Spanish gentleman here to give him lessons in Spanish every Saturday evening."[7] As had so often been the case in previous attempts, this latest venture into providing a meaningful educational experience for Francis was not to prove successful. On December 28, Francis wrote his "dear grandpapa:"

I am now though not permanently fixed at school. I expect to quit this place the ensueing spring and if the central college is not ready my Father intends to place me in some school in Virginia until it goes into operation. There are a great many objections to this Georgetown College in the first place they are bigoted Catholics extremely rigid and they require the boys to observe all the regulations of their church which makes a great interruption in the course of our studies. We rise at six o'clock and go into the chapell to mass we study about two hours and three quarters in the whole of the day the rest of the time being taken up with reciting lessons and church, an hour and a half excepted for recreation. but it would be tedious and unnecessary to inumerate all the particulars suffice it is to say that they are very strict and punish for the most trivial offence[8] *(fig. 77).*

Jefferson responded to his grandson on February 6, 1818, his delay occasioned by "the daily hope of being able to speak with more certainty of the time when our Central college will be opened." As that was still undecided, "the only question is how to dispose of yourself" until that time. He had a familiar suggestion: "There is now at the N. London academy an excellent teacher, and that place is on a better footing than it ever has been. Indeed I think it now the best school I know."[9] If not the best, it was at least still the closest to Poplar Forest.

In the meantime, educational concerns on a broader scope continued to occupy Jefferson's time and talents.

On February 21, 1818, the Virginia General Assembly approved a bill authorizing the establishment of a university for the commonwealth. It was not the bill Jefferson had sent to Cabell, which had been defeated, but was a substitute. The language concerning the choice of a site was equivocal, calling simply for one that was "convenient and proper." The final decision on location, as well as the plan, organization, and branches of learning to be taught, were to be made by a board of twenty-four commissioners.[10] Thanks to Joseph C. Cabell, Jefferson was made a member of that board. The meeting in which all these decisions were to be made was set for August 1, 1818, and would be held at Rockfish Gap in the Blue Ridge Mountains, deemed to be as central a meeting spot as could be found.

On April 5, just before leaving for the first of two visits he would make to Poplar Forest in 1818, Jefferson wrote Wilson Cary Nicholas, telling him of his proposed trip, and announcing that "Mr. Coffee arrived here this morning. He represents his process as little troublesome." William J. Coffee was a sculptor and plaster worker, originally from England, and this was the first of his many associations with Jefferson. The "process" that Coffee represented as little troublesome was the making of terra-cotta busts of members of the family. On April 12, the day he left Monticello for Poplar Forest, Jefferson drew $105.00 on one of his accounts "in favr. of Mr. Coffee . . . to pay for the originals of 3. busts, to wit Mrs. Randolph's Ellen's & mine."[11] Coffee was to do other members of the family as well, but only those of Anne Bankhead and Cornelia Randolph are known to have survived to the present (see fig. 72). At least one observer

Fig. 77 Georgetown University, early-nineteenth-century view. Partially because of delays in opening Central College (now the University of Virginia), Francis Eppes attended classes here in 1817–18. The building to the left ("Old South") was completed by the time Georgetown opened in 1791; "Old North," to the right, was begun the next year. *(Prints and Photographs Division, Library of Congress)*

didn't think much of them, and if her comments are accurate, neither did Jefferson's daughter, Martha. Elizabeth Trist, writing from Monticello, told her grandson Nicholas Trist, then at West Point: "Indeed I don't think they are worth the expence except Cornelias. There is not a likeness among them all. Mrs. Randolphs has some semblance but as she says it looks like an Irish washerwoman."[12]

Again accompanied by two of his granddaughters, Jefferson arrived at Poplar Forest on April 14, 1818, in time for "an eleven o'clock breakfast," having spent the night before at Hunter's Tavern.[13] Ellen was accompanied on this trip not by her sister Cornelia, but by their younger sibling, Virginia Randolph, then sixteen years old. Virginia's first visit to Poplar Forest may have been arranged as something of a consolation to her for having missed the journey to Natural Bridge the year before. The first order of the day was to unpack, and in writing her mother on the day of their arrival, Ellen noted: "The chest of drawers is such a convenience that I no longer regret its being brought from Monticello, especially as I hope we shall be able to worry grandpapa into having more of them made. V and myself intend to be very industrious during our short stay, as it seems fated that we shall never do anything at home."[14] Apparently Jefferson was not the only member of the family who, plagued by the constant stream of visitors and the attendant confusion at Monticello, depended on visits to Poplar Forest to think, to study, and to read.

On May 1, 1818, while at Poplar Forest, Jefferson penned an entry in his Memorandum Book: "Endorsed for Wilson C. Nicholas 2. notes of 10,000 D. each to the bank of the US. at Rchmnd." As Nicholas had recently endorsed one of *his* notes and was the father-in-law of Jefferson's grandson and namesake, Thomas Jefferson Randolph, he could hardly refuse returning the favor. Even so, the note he sent Nicholas along with the endorsement shows a premonition that was all too soon to be realized: "You well know that a Virginia farmer has no resources for meeting sudden and large calls for money. The unskillful management of my farms has subjected me to some temporary uneasiness, which better management and better seasons will, I trust, require not more time to relieve than I may yet suspect, and spare me the only pain of unreadiness which I could feel at the hour of departure."[15]

Earlier in the year, Jefferson had written his Richmond factor, Patrick Gibson, that his "tobacco has sold with so little credit in Richmond for some years that at the earnest request of Mr. Yancey my manager in Bedford, I have permitted him to try it this year in the Lynchburg market where it's quality is better known."[16] This was done, and on May 2 he noted in his Memorandum Book that "the proceeds of tobo sold lately for me at Lynchburg by Mr. Yancey were 887.34 purchased by Arch. Robertson." Jefferson was not alone in his uneasiness regarding his farm and the dwindling prices that his

crops realized. Much of his concern was due to forces beyond his control. During these years Piedmont Virginia's farmers were beset by many problems, among them the exhaustion of their once-fertile fields, the expense of keeping a growing supply of slaves — just as the crops, and their marketability, were plummeting — and forces of nature. Among other disasters, the "Hessian fly" wreaked havoc on wheat, which a number of farmers had planted in hopes that it would counter the ravages wrought on the land by tobacco.[17]

On May 3, 1818, the day before he left Poplar Forest to return to Monticello, Jefferson wrote John Wayles Eppes that he had made arrangements for "Francis's board at New London with Mr. Dashiell [the headmaster] himself, who takes only three others. Francis will be much pleased with the family, which is a very genteel one, and they live well as I saw by going in upon them at their dinner unexpectedly." As Francis would have to furnish his own bed, he had directed "Mr. Yancey to have a trussel bedstead made . . . and to let it be only 3 feet wide that he may not have to take in a bedfellow which is so apt to render the progression of the itch so general at schools." He added that the school was then on vacation, but would recommence on June 1, "by which day Francis should be here." Yancey had the bed made by Reuben Perry, who submitted his bill near the end of June. For "one bed trussel," Perry charged $6.00.[18]

Jefferson's visit to Poplar Forest in the summer of 1818, which extended from July 4 to July 16, was made at a crucial time for his fledgling university. Originally, he had planned to "pass the months of Aug. and Sep. in Bedford," but went earlier so that he would be able to attend the August 1 meeting at Rockfish Gap that would decide the location of the new state university.[19] One of the first orders at that meeting was to elect a chairman. Jefferson was chosen, and on Monday, August 3, the decision was made. Central College won over its rivals, Lexington and Staunton, and would be recommended to the legislature as the site for the University of Virginia. In anticipation of the favorable outcome, a deed conveying the property had already been drawn and recorded by the Albemarle County clerk.[20] There remained the report, which it was Jefferson's duty as chairman to prepare, and, of course, favorable action by the General Assembly in due course.

After the meeting, Jefferson went to Warm Springs in an attempt to seek relief in the healing waters from his increasing bouts with rheumatism. It was a visit he deplored ever after, as it not only failed to cure him, it added to his woes. On September 11, 1818, he wrote Yancey:

I am lately returned from the Warm Springs with my health entirely prostrated by the use of the waters. They produced an imposthume and eruptions, which with the torment of the journey back reduced me to the extremest weakness. I am getting better, but still obliged to lie night and day reclined in one posture, which makes writing all but impossible. The visitors of the college meet the 1st week of October, as soon after which as I shall have strength enough, I shall be with you. . . . I enclose a letter for my grandson Francis.

In the enclosed letter, he told Francis that he would not be able to get to Poplar Forest "till the middle of October." Even if he had been able to be there in October, he wouldn't have seen his grandson. The headmaster, Rev. Alfred H. Dashiell, had resigned, and as John Wayles Eppes wrote Jefferson on October 17th, "Mr. Dashiell's leaving New London renders it necessary again to seek out some place for Francis."[21]

By November 10 Jefferson realized that he would be unable to return to Poplar Forest at all in 1818. In a letter written that day to Yancey, he began: "When I wrote to you on the 11th of Sep. I confidently hoped to recover my health and strength to be with you long before this. But I am not yet able to go out of the house: and altho' recovered, I shall not have strength for the journey until it will be too cold to undertake it. I shall not therefore see you until April." He then went on to direct his overseer "to act in all things for the best according to your own judgement, and without waiting to consult me." He did, however, send certain instructions, including a list of the slaves who were to be given blankets that winter, and those who were to be given beds. In addition, he noted that "Maria having now a child, I promised her a house to be built this winter. Be so good as to have it done. Place it along the garden fence on the road Eastward from Hanah's house." He concluded by requesting Yancey to "get Mr. Martin to saw for me the stuff stated on the next page, and to have it hauled home and stowed away in time. I shall carry up Johnny Hemings & his two assistants early in the year and they will work there till the fall."[22] Hanah, or Hannah as she spelled her name, the slave who would soon have Maria and her child as her new neighbor along the garden fence, had heard of her master's illness, and took it upon herself to send him a note on November 15. Jefferson preserved the letter, which is a rare item for its time and place [23] (fig. 78).

Throughout December 1818 and early 1819, Jefferson and Yancey corresponded as the Monticello cart wound its way between Bedford and Albemarle, carrying supplies and letters back and forth. On Christmas Eve, Yancey sent the slave Dick to Monticello with a load of pork, butter, lard, and "1 bag dried peaches weighing 45 [pounds]." On January 4, Jefferson apologized to Yancey for keeping the cart at Monticello so long. It was now on its way back, carrying up "some doors for the house which should be put in one of the rooms where they will be kept dry, and a box of wine to be put into the cellar, as it requires a cool place." He also noted, in a postscript, that "a small box of books is sent to be put into one of the rooms."[24] On January 9, 1819, Yancey answered, telling him that Jerry "delivered his load safe and I had the doors and books put in one of the rooms in the house and the wine in the cellar." He promised that "the sowing of peas

shall be attended to," and suggested that if Jefferson could "send us a plough or two by Dick it would be of great service to us." On January 17, Jefferson wrote that "the waggons arrived here on Wednesday a little after the middle of the day," and would start on their return trip "tomorrow morning (Monday)," carrying three new ploughs. He also confided to Yancey that he thought "Dick had delivered all his articles safe, . . . but I learnt afterwards that he did not deliver a bag containing a bushel of dried peaches which he said had dropped thro a hole in the bottom of his waggon; altho no hole was seen which could have let such a mass drop. This year his soap weighs 30 lbs instead of 45 lbs, and the basket of apples is a little more than half full. These repeated accidents cannot but excite suspicions of him, sufficient to make us attentive in future." Jefferson also asked Yancey "to send by Jerry the Athenian poplars in the nursery of the garden." The old bacon, he advised, "may remain as I shall pass a great proportion of the ensuing year there."[25]

In addition to his physical condition, perhaps another reason Jefferson was unable to return to Bedford in the fall of 1818 was the fact that he had to finish the report from the meeting on the university, which he submitted to Joseph Cabell on November 20. Late in December, still not sure what the outcome would be, he composed two letters that showed his continued anxiety. To John G. Jackson he wrote: "I may do for our University what others would do better were I away. My vicinity to the place alone giving me prominence in its concerns. As to everything else, I am done, enfeebled in body, probably in mind also, in memory very much and all those faculties on the wane which are the avenues to life's happiness." He read, he stated, "with avidity, but have the sensations of the gallows when obliged to take my pen." His letter to John Adams, written on the last day of the year, was far more cynical: "We are all here in the hourly expectation of hearing what our legislature decides on the Report. Being a good piece of a century behind the age they live in, we are not without fear as to their conclusions."[26]

All's well that ends well. The bill authorizing Charlottesville as the location of the University became law on January 25, 1819. Elizabeth Trist announced the effect it had three days afterwards: "Mr. Jefferson seems to be getting quite strong and the certainty now of the University being established here will add to his longevity."[27]

He needed to be strong to cope with another situation that soon developed. Later that winter Jefferson took stock of his finances and again found them to be in an increasingly perilous state. Along with other debtors throughout the country, he had received alarming news the previous summer when the Bank of the United States announced it would require a twelve-and-a-half-percent curtailment on notes renewed after the first Wednesday in August 1818. As he had become habitually addicted to renewing his notes, rather than paying down any of the principal, this regulation, which meant that he would now have to pay twelve and a half cents on each dollar of his existing loans, came "like a clap of thunder to me, for God knows I have no means in this world of raising money on so sudden a call."[28] He sent that message to Patrick Gibson, his Richmond factor who had informed him of the new policy, and who correctly predicted that this restriction of credit would cause a great deal of trouble throughout the country.

By February 1819, Jefferson had to borrow another $1,500, and at the same time he decided that the only way he could ever clear his debts would be by a method he had used before, however unwillingly. Along with the note for $1,500 that he sent to Gibson, he wrote: "These operations are so disagreeable to me that instead of waiting to relieve myself and my friends from them by annual profits, I have determined to do it by the sale of some detached lands which I have long held unimproved and

unemployed. I have given orders accordingly in Bedford and shall pursue the same object here." As soon as this could be done, he optimistically vowed that he would "be able to wipe off the whole [debt] at once. This done, I shall be for ever at ease, because I know that my income is more than the double of my expenses, if once cleared of interest."[29] His "orders in Bedford" were contained in the letter he wrote the same day to Yancey, along with his assessment on why his affairs were in such disarray, at least at Poplar Forest:

On settling up the affairs of the year I find I shall again be mortifyingly deficient in meeting the demands which 3 years of war, and 4 years of Goodman and Darnell have accumulated on me. An unwillingness to break in on the monetary provisions made for my family has hitherto prevented my relieving myself, by some sale of property from the pain of witholding the money of others which they would rather

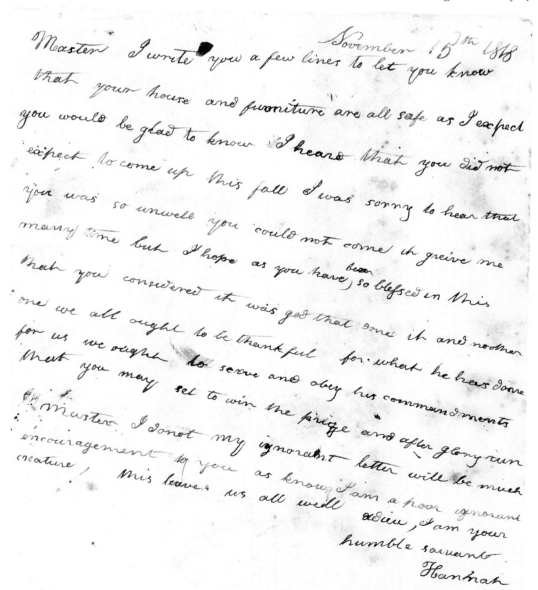

Fig. 78 Hannah, a slave whom Jefferson once described as the person "who cooks & washes for me when I am [at Poplar Forest]," sent this letter to him after learning of his illness in 1818. *(Coolidge Collection, Massachusetts Historical Society)*

recieve at the same time. The advantageous state in which I have been able to place my property here and the entire confidence I have that you will be able to do as well for me in Bedford, have nourished the expectation that 1 or 2 years of improved productiveness would liberate me from uneasiness, but I conclude now to relieve myself more speedily, if I can, without sacrifice, dispose of property which may be spared without present inconvenience. The little tract of 214 acres, called Daniel Robertson's, which runs like a dog's ear from the NE corner of Poplar Forest, might be lopped off without much injury to the main body; & if I could get for it such prices as have been given, offered, and refused for land not superior on the whole, it would produce a sum which would make my latter days happy, by owing not a cent in the world.[30]

Jefferson's eternal optimism — often bordering these days on self-delusion — kept his spirits high. Again Mrs. Trist offered her observations and comments to her grandson, having seen Jefferson soon after he had written Gibson and Yancey: "Mr. Jefferson, when I last saw him about ten days since look'd as well as he did 10 years ago, and to day the wind is blowing a perfect Hurricane he road through Charlottesville to visit the College to morrow he proposes to set out for Poplar Forest to spend a month neither of the young ladies accompany him this trip."[31] Writing on March 9, 1819, she was incorrect on the timing, and on speculating that Jefferson would go alone, but one assumes, and hopes, her impressions of his well-being were correct.

It was not until April 13, 1819, that Jefferson recorded in his Memorandum Book: "Set out for Poplar Forest." Three days before, Joel Yancey had written a letter that, had he received it before his departure, would have dampened his hopes for selling his Bedford lands at their full value: "A great many country gentlemen is almost ruined by indorsing for merchants, . . . In short there is nothing like the gloom and destruct that hangs almost upon all the people in this place and the neighborhood." As it turned out, Jefferson soon saw for himself the state of things, and reported to Patrick Gibson from Poplar Forest: "I am urging the sale of some detached parcels of land which I have here and in Albemarle. But there is at present an entire stagnation of purchase here, occasioned by the crisis of bank engagements which suspends business in Lynchburg and its vicinity for the present."[32] The Panic of 1819 was in full force, and Lynchburg, which had participated all too fully in the financial excesses that had brought it about, was as hard hit as any place in the country. Samuel J. Harrison was to lose both the Franklin Hotel and his own house. Reuben Perry was unable to meet his financial obligations, and he and his creditors agreed that "a sale of his property for cash in the present unexampled pecuniary *embarress-ment* of the country would be productive of said ruin to [him] and of probable Injury to [them]."[33] He consequently mortgaged his real estate, slaves, and personal property — including the tools of his trade and his architectural books — as security, and promised to pay his

debts over a three-year period. Little wonder that an observer was later to recall: "About the year 1819, Lynchburg was the abode of many distinguished loafers and beggars, some of whom would have been considered eminent in their profession, even in these days of progress."[34]

After sending his tobacco and flour from Bedford to Richmond, where he had decided to sell them instead of in Lynchburg in 1819, and after overseeing the planting "in the garden under the N. wall of the stable 20. cuttings of Balsam poplars from Mr. Radford," Jefferson returned to Monticello, having stayed from April 15 through April 29. Mrs. Trist was as good reporting his comings as his goings, and on May 2, 1819, informed her grandson that "Cornelia and James accompanied their Grand Father to Poplar Forest and they returned yesterday."[35] James was James Madison Randolph, then thirteen years old. He was now the older brother not only to Benjamin Franklin Randolph and Meriwether Lewis Randolph, but also to Septimia Anne and George Wythe Randolph. Septimia, the seventh daughter, had been born on January 3, 1814, and George Wythe followed four years later, on March 10, 1818. He was the last of the Randolph children, and rounded out their number to an even dozen.

Upon his return to Monticello, Jefferson informed Joel Yancey that the prices realized on his tobacco and flour at the Richmond markets were so miserable that he now looked "wistfully to the accomplishment of the sale" of his detached parcels of land to help reduce his debt. In addition to offering Daniel Robinson's tract, which he hoped might bring $50 or $60 an acre, he added "if you or Mr. Radford would give me 100 D. an acre for the 50 a. beyond Bear Branch on the west side of the road, I believe I should take it, letting my debt to you go in part for the payment." He closed his letter with the poignant statement that "to owe what I cannot pay is a constant torment."[36]

For a moment, though, Jefferson once more conveniently forgot about the state of his finances. The week after he returned from his spring trip to Poplar Forest in 1819, he sent an order to Smith and Riddle, hardware merchants in Richmond: "I must ask the favor of you to supply me with the window glass below stated, of the best quality. I wish it divided into two parcels packed in separate boxes, the one being wanting here, the other at my place near Lynchburg." For Poplar Forest he requested "25 panes 12 I. square; 50 ditto 12 x 18 I."[37] Whether the order was to replace glass that had been broken, or for glazing that had never been done — or for both — is not known. At any rate, an event was soon to occur that would necessitate a far larger shipment of glass. It would also give Jefferson the occasion to spend a great deal of time in Bedford, would afford him the opportunity to again disregard his financial plight, and would, most importantly of all, give him the chance yet again to focus his architectural attention and talents on Poplar Forest.

"GREATEST HAIL STORM EVER SAW"
(Summer 1819)

On June 13, 1819, Joel Yancey wrote what must have been the most dramatic letter he ever penned. He was still distraught in describing the catastrophic event three days after it happened:

I wrote you on the morning 10th. inst. and on the same evening about 3 o'clock there was greatest hail storm ever saw. Your house appears to have been in the center of it. The damage is immense. . . . The garden is entirely destroyed and 77 panes of glass broken to atoms and the house is flooded with water. You may form some idea of destruction when I assure you that the yard was covered, and the hail stones generally larger than partridge eggs. I have been told that some were 3 inches round. The damage in my letter cannot be less 1000 D. short. . . . I do not know what is to become of us. The glass, if to be procured in Lynchburg, I will have put in, but I have never seen any there as large panes, as those in your windows and doors.[1]

Yancey soon informed Jefferson that, as he predicted, the stores in Lynchburg had no glass "the size of that in your house here. The surest chance will be for you to order it from Richmond, to be here, to be put in during your visit. The house is very much exposed without it." On June 25 Jefferson responded. He would "be able to leave this for Poplar Forest about the 7th of July, and shall bring with me glass of one kind to repair the damages to the house, while two boxes of another kind will go up from Richmond by the first boat for Lynchburg. Johnny Hemings and his assistants will go when I do. The other carpenters something later. I hope Capt. Martin will consider what a loss and disappointment it will be to me if these people have to return for want of the stuff desired, & trust he will exert himself to compleat the bill." The glass that was to be sent from Richmond was that which Jefferson had ordered from Smith and Riddle in May, and on June 18 Andrew Smith billed him $34.00 for it. Captain Martin, who seems never to have been ready on time, once again disappointed Jefferson, as Yancey reported on July 1: "Capt. Martin has completed the first bill of timber, but will not be able for want of water to do any thing with the other this season."[2]

On July 17, Jefferson arrived at Poplar Forest, accompanied again by the inveterate travelers, Ellen and Cornelia. That day he sent a request to Bernard Peyton in Richmond:

We are here, Ellen, Cornelia and myself for two months to come, and living on plantation fare. This may be considerably improved if you can send us by a Lynchburg boat, addressed to Mr. Archibl. Robertson a keg of tongues & sounds, a small keg

of crackers, a small box of raisins, and a good cheese, to which be pleased to add a barrel of shad from my old friend Mr. Darmsdatt, who has supplied me for these 30 years. Perhaps the first 4 articles had better be put into an outer case or barrel, for greater safety. Gibson as usual will have the goodness to pay for these.[3]

Cornelia and Ellen, as usual, wrote home to give the news. As was their habit, Cornelia wrote to her younger sister, Virginia, and Ellen to their mother, Martha, though it really didn't matter who wrote to whom, as Cornelia rather ungraciously announced in her letter: "I suppose Sister Ellen will of course write to mama this time, and as therefore it would be useless for me to write also to her, I will address my letter to you." She then informed Virginia:

We arrived here yesterday to dinner after one day of the hottest sun I ever felt in my life, and one of rain, which however we nearly escaped the whole of, as we stopped at Hunters to breakfast and waited until the hardest showers were over. We found that the hail storm had shattered two of grandfathers windows, in one there was not left a single pane of glass unbroken, which was the case with several of those in the other rooms, and a gust of wind since that has done nearly the same mischief to the folding doors on one side of the dining room by blowing them to suddenly. Nothing is left of the sky light but the sash.[4]

Ellen disagreed with Cornelia in her count of the windows destroyed in their grandfather's room, and in addition to the harm caused by the hailstorm, she noted that the house and grounds had obviously suffered from neglect long before:

On arriving here we found our windows uninjured by the hail, and our room clean and pretty well aired by Eugenia's care. All the glass on the north side of the house is demolished but Grand Papa's room has lost but one window, which will soon be repaired. . . . Poplar Forest looks rather more dismal than usual; the long absence of the family appears to have . . . encreased the wildness and desolation of everything around. The weeds grow to the very door of the kitchen, as high as your head, the planks of the terrace torn up in places by the violence of the winds, the front of the house offering nothing but the sashes of its windows, except where they were protected by the portico, the dining room darkened by the boarding up of the skylight, and the floors stained . . . by the entrance of the rain-water; add to this the close musty smell which a house long shut up continues for some time to retain.[5]

Recovering from that gloomy description, she then proceeded to produce a delightful pen picture of what Poplar Forest meant to her:

— and yet in spite of all this, I have felt no depression of spirits. To the contrary, there are associations and recollections, which combined with hopes for the future give me a sensation of cheerfulness and animation — I remember how profitable my former visits have been, how much more I have always carried away, than I have ever brought, how usefully my time has been uniformly spent. I go from room to room and there are particular recollections attached to each. Here, every day for six weeks at a time I have devoted from seven to eight hours to my latin, and laid a solid foundation which gives its full value to the most trifling addition. There hour after hour, I have poured over volumes of history, which I should in vain have attempted to read at Monticello, and which were perhaps necessary to give regularity and uniformity to a shapeless mass of ideas accumulated without method or order by habits of hurried & desultory reading.[6]

Ellen also reported to their mother on her sister's drawing efforts: "Cornelia does not appear to have remarked the additional gloom in the appearance of our dwelling, but has been fretting all the morning over the loss of the sky-light, which darkens the dining room so much that she cannot draw in it — and the glare of light which falls on her beggar and his dog shows the nose of the latter in so unseemly a place, that it shocks me to look at it." Cornelia's "beggar and his dog" seems not to have survived, but other drawings that she made during her visits to Poplar Forest have (fig. 79; see also fig. 56). The news that must have gladdened Martha most of all was Ellen's reporting that her grandfather was "so little fatigued by his journey as to have ridden to see his old friend Mr. Clay this morning."[7]

The next day Jefferson sent a letter to Edmund Meeks, his chief carpenter at Monticello. Captain Martin had now finished his sawing, and as soon as Meeks and the "three carpenters under you" finished their work at Monticello, they were to come to Bedford. As it was so inconvenient for "the little mule and cart" to be away from Monticello, and as so few tools would be needed for their work at Poplar Forest, Jefferson suggested to Meeks that "they may bring them on their shoulders. They will need 2 hand saws, 2 jack planes, 2 pair chisels broad and narrow, some augers for common framing, a foot adze, and one of the narrow adzes which were made here to dig gutters in the joists. These things divided among three will weigh little."[8]

Before the carpenters arrived, Jefferson proceeded with other work on the house, work that was not dictated by the effects of the storm. On July 29 he wrote to Arthur Brockenbrough, now in charge of building operations at

Fig. 79 Whether Cornelia made this drawing during her long visit in 1819 is not known, but it, along with another that has survived (see fig. 56), illustrates the sort of furnishings at Poplar Forest during Jefferson's time. *(Monticello, Thomas Jefferson Memorial Foundation, Inc.)*

the university, giving him the bad news that marble from a quarry near Lynchburg that he had hoped would be suitable for the capitals of columns at the university "would not bear the chisel for delicate work, and is of so deep a blue as would not do with our white pillars." He told Brockenbrough that he got his "information from a Mr. Gorman who has worked in the quarry a year and a half. He is now here doing a job for me in polishing and laying some marble I had for hearths." On August 17 Jefferson wrote Brockenbrough that "Gorman will be with you within not many days. He has worked here under my eye about 3 weeks."[9] Jefferson's employment of John Gorman at Poplar Forest may have been something of a practice run for the stonecutter, who well justified the recommendation he sent to Brockenbrough. At the university, Gorman was to cut "all the stone caps, bases, sills, wall copings and newel blocks for the Rotunda, all 10 pavilions and five of the six hotels."[10]

Before the carpenters appeared at Poplar Forest, a tragedy almost ensued. Burwell, Jefferson's faithful body servant, had accompanied the group to Poplar Forest, and soon after their arrival had an attack that left him prostrate. Jefferson, Cornelia, and Ellen tried to help, but to no avail. Ellen reported to her mother on July 28 that the three of them composed "as complete a tribe of ignoramuses as I do know, and I do not believe our three heads combined contain as much medical knowledge as would save a sparrow." Nor was Dr. William Steptoe, to whom Jefferson had applied for medical help, of much assistance. In fact, his response might give pause to any patient: "My syringe is so often lent and sent about the neighborhood that I am sorry to say I do not know who had it last. However I will dispatch a boy after it, and when found send it over to Burwell, thinking it would answer a very good purpose in his case." Burwell's recovery was apparently due to the ministrations of John Hemings as much as to anyone else. In her letter of August 4 to Virginia, Ellen relayed a message from Hemings to "Aunt Priscilla to say he was doing well but *mighty tired* of the Forest and wished himself at home. Any message that she may send him it will give me great pleasure to receive from you—for Johnny is one of my favorites and more so, now than ever since I have witnessed his kind attentions to Burwell." By that time, Burwell had recovered, and had started "glazing again, although he cannot do much [of] any thing as yet."[11] Israel, the servant who had accompanied the party on their trip to Natural Bridge, was also along on this visit, and acted as major-domo during Burwell's sickness.

Cornelia also reported on Burwell's illness, and in her letter, again addressed to her sister Virginia, also gave information on the first of many social calls that she and Ellen were to make during this lengthy summer sojourn in Bedford: "We went to pay Mrs. Radford & Mrs. Yancey a visit yesterday. I saw Miss Yancey for the first time. She is an exceedingly pretty girl & has the sweetest countenance & the finest eyes I ever saw. To morrow we go to dine with Mrs. Walker a neighbor we never have seen & who has more kindness and willingness to pay us some attention than knowledge of the forms & ceremonies usually observed in proceeding to do so. I am very much obliged to her for her good will but hope my stiff neck may keep me at home."[12] Unfortunately, as she and Ellen soon found out, this trip was not one in which they were long able to pursue their studies uninterruptedly.

On July 28 Bernard Peyton reported that he had procured the items Jefferson had requested on the seventeenth of the month, and had sent them up the James River "addressed to the care of Archibald Robertson Esq. Lynchburg."[13] Pending the arrival of his groceries from Richmond, and throughout the visit, Jefferson noted in his Memorandum Book frequent payments for food. On July 31 he paid $2 for sixteen chickens, and on August 5 purchased three watermelons, six ducks, and fourteen chickens. Ten days later he bought two dozen chickens. Little wonder that Ellen soon clucked in a letter to Monticello: "We have lived altogether on chickens." In addition, she reported that they got "snow enough from Mr. Radford's (for which we send every other day) to give us hard butter and cool wine." However, "whilst Israel Cornelia and myself were butlers Grandpapa insisted on our using that cooler (refrigerator, I believe he calls it) which wasted our small stock of ice, and gave us butter that ran about the plate so that we could scarcely catch it, and wine about blood heat."[14] Presumably this refrigerator was the one — or one like it — that Jefferson had bought during his presidency.[15]

Perhaps the refrigerator simply couldn't cope with the heat that particular summer. Early in August, Ellen rhetorically asked Virginia: "Have you ever in your life known such hot weather. . . . Yesterday it reached 99 degrees. Grandpapa thinks that such a degree of heat has never before been known in this State." Reminiscing years later, she recalled this "very long [visit] during which we saw the thermometer or perhaps heard of it in the neighborhood, as high as 98 degrees Fahrenheit — higher than it was ever known at Monticello."[16]

Fortunately, the neighbors rallied round and kept them from depending altogether on poultry. Ellen particularly appreciated the attentions of Mrs. Walker, who

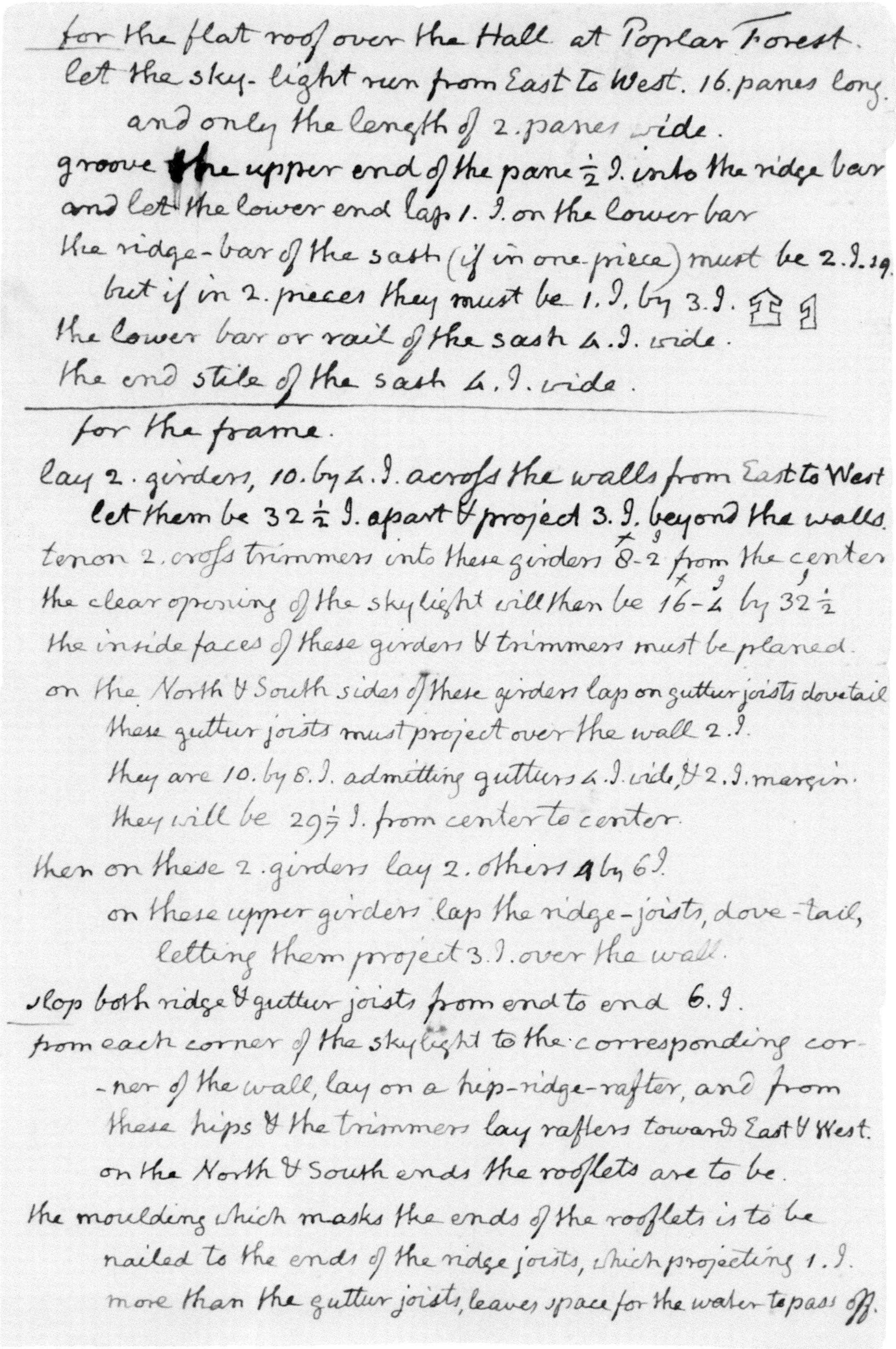

for the flat roof over the Hall. at Poplar Forest.
   let the sky- light run from East to West. 16. panes long.
      and only the length of 2. panes wide.
groove the upper end of the pane ½ I. into the ridge bar
and let the lower end lap 1. I. on the lower bar
the ridge- bar of the sash (if in one piece) must be 2. I. sq.
     but if in 2. pieces they must be 1. I. by 3. I.
the lower bar or rail of the sash 4. I. wide.
the end stile of the sash 4. I. wide.

   for the frame.
lay 2. girders, 10. by 4. I. acrofs the walls from East to West
   let them be 32½ I. apart & project 3. I. beyond the walls.
tenon 2. crofs trimmers into these girders 8-2 from the center
the clear opening of the skylight will then be 16-4 by 32½
the inside faces of these girders & trimmers must be planed.
on the North & South sides of these girders lap on gutter joists dovetail
   these gutter joists must project over the wall 2. I.
    they are 10. by 8. I. admitting gutters 4. I. wide, & 2. I. margin.
    they will be 29⅞ I. from center to center.
then on these 2. girders lay 2. others 4 by 6 I.
   on these upper girders lap the ridge- joists, dove- tail,
    letting them project 3. I. over the wall.
slop both ridge & gutter joists from end to end 6. I.
from each corner of the skylight to the corresponding cor-
  -ner of the wall, lay on a hip-ridge-rafter, and from
   these hips & the trimmers lay rafters towards East & West.
   on the North & South ends the rooflets are to be.
the moulding which masks the ends of the rooflets is to be
   nailed to the ends of the ridge joists, which projecting 1. I.
   more than the gutter joists, leaves space for the water to pass off.

Fig. 80 This, the only known specification in Jefferson's hand relating to Poplar Forest that survives, instructed the builders on the replacement of the skylight that was destroyed by the 1819 hailstorm. *(Thomas Jefferson Papers, Manuscripts Division, Special Collections Department, University of Virginia, Charlottesville)*

"is constantly sending us little presents. About once a week we see a tidy mulatto girl, with an apron as white as snow, & a nice little basket with a napkin thrown over it, in her hand. Sometimes fruit of different kinds, melons, apples, ripe peaches, etc. Then again vegetables, and on one occasion cake and sweet meats." She also noted that "in spite of all interruptions, I have done about four times as much as I have ever been able to do in the same space of time at Monticello. . . . if I only had a piano, that I might not whilst improving in other things, be falling off there."[17]

During all the heat, the carpenters were busy repairing the damage from the hailstorm. Chief among their labors was a new skylight, and in replacing the old one, Jefferson made what he considered great improvements in its design. His one-page specification for rebuilding the skylight is the only such item known to remain in his hand for construction at Poplar Forest. "John Heming," penciled in on its reverse, seems to indicate that he was once again in charge of the work (figs. 80 and 81).

Jefferson was so pleased with the results of his new roof at Poplar Forest that he directed the same system of roofing be used at the University. On September 1, 1819, he proudly wrote Arthur Brockenbrough:

I have taken off the rafter roof of the middle part of my house here, 22. f. square, and covered it with ridge & gutter rooflets, a more compleat and satisfactory job I have never seen done. Timber being plenty here I had my ridge joists 10 by 4. I. & the gutter joists 10 by 8 I. but 10 by 3 & 10 by 6 would do, because 6 I. allows a 3 I. gutter and margins of 1 1/2 I. The joists are 15 I. horizontally apart, & a single course of shingles 18 I. long reach from the ridge into the gutter, and another course over these, breaking joints, and mitring at top, are more secure than plank. The shingles are of equal thickness at both ends, and in laying on the terras, a broad plank is first nailed over the mitre to prevent water from ever entering that, & the intervals then covered with other planks. Sheet iron unquestionably endangers leaking, and will rust out sooner than the gutters, well pitched, will rot. Let all the dormitories be thus done, & without sheet iron.[18]

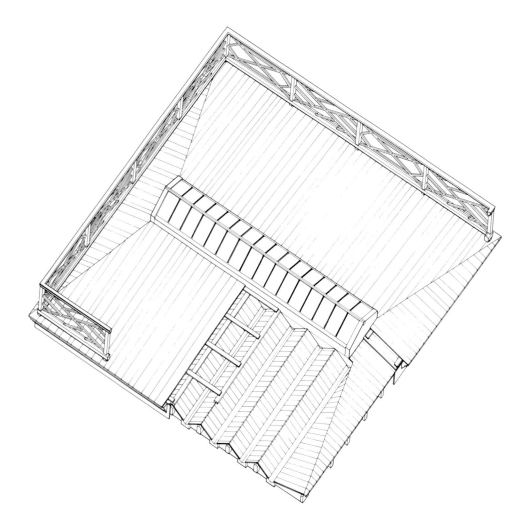

Fig. 81 Reconstruction of the skylight and deck, based on Jefferson's specifications shown in fig. 80. (*Courtesy Mesick-Cohen-Waite, Architects*)

Even before the actual skylight and roof deck surrounding it were completed, Jefferson had arranged for Joseph Antrim to return to Bedford and do the necessary plastering around the new construction. On August 8, 1819, he wrote:

I am making a change in my central room here which will require the plaistering of the ceiling to be done anew, contains say about 30 or 40 square yards. It is extremely desirable to have this done immediately on our closing the roof, which will be about the latter end of this present week. Can you do me the favor so to arrange your business as to come and do it immediately on notice? When ready, I will send a cart to bring the lime, plaister, hair, and any tools you may have occasion for, and will be in the hope of your accompanying them.[19]

Almost a month later, on September 4, he recorded in his Memorandum Book that he "gave Joseph Antrim order on A. Robertson for 19.91 for plaistering cieling of Dining room." Four days later, Edmund Meeks had also finished his work and was ready to return to Albemarle.

On September 8th, Jefferson noted in the Memorandum Book that he gave him an order "on A. Robertson for 10.D. for his expences coming & going."

In a letter written on August 9, 1819, Jefferson told Thomas Mann Randolph, Jr., that "nothing can exceed the desolation which the Lynchburg banks have produced in this country."[20] Whether or not the Lynchburg banks had anything to do with it, his own financial condition was certainly nothing short of desolate. As was the case with Joseph Antrim's and Edmund Meeks's wages, all his payments to the various workmen during this visit were made either by drawing on the account he held with Archibald Robertson in Lynchburg, or on the one he held with Patrick Gibson in Richmond. On occasion, the complicated notations in his Memorandum Book indicate that he resorted to robbing Peter to pay Paul — or at least borrowed from Patrick to pay Archibald. Though he didn't know it at the time he wrote his son-in-law, a letter was then on its way to Poplar Forest that would make Jefferson's existing financial difficulties pale in comparison with the news it brought.

Fig. 82 Campeachy Chair. At one time Monticello may have contained six or seven of these popular "siesta chairs." Poplar Forest at one time had two, though one was there only temporarily, waiting for its owner, a friend of Jefferson's, to pick it up. *(Monticello, Thomas Jefferson Memorial Foundation, Inc.)*

Wilson Cary Nicholas wrote it on August 5, and Jefferson answered it on August 11:

Your letter of the 5th finds me under the severest attack of rheumatism I have ever experienced. My limbs all swelled, their strength prostrate, and pain constant. But it fills me with affliction of another kind, very much on your account, and not small on my own. A call on me to the amount of my endorsements for you would indeed close my course by a catastrophe I had never contemplated. But the comfort which supports me is the entire confidence I repose in your friendship to find some means of warding off this desperate calamity.[21]

Nicholas had just alerted him to the fact that he had been forced to place his estate "in the hands of trustees to be sold for the payments of his debts." Even so, he assured his friend that there would be a surplus, and that Jefferson would not be affected.[22] Jefferson's response to Nicholas was a model of restraint, but he was a bit more shaken in his letter of the same day to Patrick Gibson, asking for advice. Again he resorted to the analogy he had used a year ago when he thought things were then as bad as they could get: "A letter of the 5th inst. from Col. W. C. Nicholas falls on me like a clap of thunder. In April was twelve month he requested me to endorse 2 notes for him of 10,000 each, with an assurance that he would ask a continuation but for a year." Nicholas continued to assure his guarantor that he had sufficient means to cover the debts, "if my property sells for anything like its value 6 years ago," but as Jefferson told Gibson, that was unlikely. In the Poplar Forest neighborhood, "examples of forced sales . . . have been from 1/5 to 1/30th of what the same articles sold for a year ago." The always prescient Ellen, who wrote her mother on the same day, remarked: "God grant, *we* may be enabled to weather the storm, for ours is but a shattered bark to breast the waves which have overwhelmed so many goodly ships in our view."[23]

Everyone at Poplar Forest was at his writing desk on August 11, 1819. In their letters, Ellen and Cornelia offered their comments on their grandfather's bouts of rheumatism. Cornelia told Virginia that he was "suffering under a violent attack . . . but he has got flannel & is going to apply it to every part that is affected which I hope will carry it away, & I must make haste & finish my letter, that I may make a pair of sleeves for him. His hands & feet are very much swelled indeed." Ellen added that "his knees are very much disabled." In his meticulous way, Jefferson noted in his Memorandum Book that he had "pd. for 1 yd. flannel at N. London .75" on August 10, and had then bought another yard for the same amount on the eleventh. By August 24, Jefferson reported to Martha:

I am much recovered from my rheumatism, altho' the swellings are not entirely abated, nor the pains quite ceased. It has been the most serious attack of that disease I ever had. While too weak to set up the whole day, and afraid to increase the weakness by lying down, I longed for a Siesta chair which would have admitted the medium position. I must therefore pray you to send by Henry the one made by Johnny Hemings. If it is the one Mrs. Trist would chuse, it will be so far on its way if not, the waggon may bring hers when it comes at Christmas. John or Wormley should wrap it well with a straw rope, and then bound up in a blanket.[24]

Jefferson's "siesta chair" was a campeachy chair, a reclining chair covered in leather (fig. 82). Its frame was made of a type of mahogany peculiar to the state of Campeche, Mexico, and had Jefferson had one at Poplar Forest several years earlier, he would undoubtedly have had to pay the tax imposed on mahogany furniture by the commonwealth in 1815. Actually he had ordered several in 1808, but the ship carrying them was apparently lost at sea. Campeachy chairs were all the rage among a small group of Virginia cognoscenti of the day. James Madison's was reported to be his "favorite seat," John Hartwell Cocke had them at Bremo, and Jefferson not only imported them, but had John Hemings copy the originals.[25]

Jefferson closed his letter to Martha by saying that "we have nothing new here but comfortable rains which it is thought will make us half a crop of corn, sufficient for bread and perhaps for fattening some hogs." He obviously didn't want to tell her just how serious his obligations on the Nicholas note had become. The bank, aware of Jefferson's own unpaid notes, had demanded that he provide security on the Nicholas note, and he consequently decided to deed a certain portion of Poplar Forest in trust to Thomas Jefferson Randolph for that purpose, to be sold if necessary. On the same day he wrote Martha, he informed Nicholas of his plan, adding that "we shall probably ask a breakfast of Mrs. Nicholas and yourself on the morning of the 14th or 15th of Sept., on one of which days, weather and rheumatism permitting, I have appointed to be at Monticello." The same day he also wrote Joseph Marx in Richmond that he would send "the bond and a copy of the deed immediately after my return to Monticello," and assured him "on my honor that not a dollar's worth of [the property] is under incumbrance to any mortal or for any purpose." It remained for the ever-sensitive Ellen to offer her knowing and feeling comments on the situation. She told her mother that her grandfather had mentioned the situation with Colonel Nicholas "to Cornelia & myself, probably in confidence, and not for worlds would I breathe a syllable to anyone but you." She concluded: "At present all my thoughts center in my dear grandfather; let his old age be secured from the storms which threaten us all, and I would willingly agree to abide their peltings. I am almost ready to fix my ideas of right and wrong on this single point; to believe every thing honorable which can save him — every thing base, vile & dishonorable, that tends to obscure the evening of such a life."[26]

Ellen and Cornelia escaped the dust and confusion brought on by the construction during their visit — and perhaps sought to clear their minds of the perilous financial maelstrom they and their neighbors were being engulfed in — by continuing to make the rounds of the neighborhood. In addition to telling her sister of their grandfather's rheumatism, Cornelia reported to Virginia on August 11 that "we have spent so much of our time in visiting that I really am afraid I shall do very little with my books after all, for besides the time taken up by the act of dressing and visiting I really am so stupid and so much fatigued when I return that I find the bed the most proper place for me for hours after." Mrs. Walker, whatever her faults of etiquette, had proven to be "such an excellent kind hearted woman, that we like her better than any body else and she seems to be a general favorite. Everybody visits her, and it must be from her goodness." Miss Betsy Clark didn't fare so well in Cornelia's estimation. Tell Francis — Cornelia instructed her sister — that "she is grown up, which I suppose he knew before, and quite pretty, which he has known long ago." As for her intelligence, Cornelia resorted to telling it the way "an elegant poet most elegantly expresses it: 'All the brain that little squashy head contains, wouldn't fill a musquito's eye sir.' " Furthermore, "she not only says 'nimini pimini' before her glass every day, but in company also or what comes to the same thing, she says nothing better." Mr. Woods, who had "a singular uglyness & uncouth manners," gave convincing evidence of the latter by saying "he used to know mama & asked me if she began to look old yet."[27]

Ellen also found time to report on the visits, and began her comments with a sage observation:

I think the prospect of soon having nothing to live on, makes people the more determined to live while they can — we have never been so much interrupted by visiting and invitations as since we have been here last; for the last three days the carriage has been ordered as regularly as the breakfast; yesterday we dined out with a large party, and have two invitations on hand for this week. Our plans of industry are much disconcerted by all this — & I have never found my time pass so unpleasantly. The only compensation which could be offered me for the loss of my family society, was the uninterrupted indulgence of those pursuits most congenial to my taste, and the consciousness of time usefully, profitably employed. My studies here were but rendering me more fit for the society to which I was to return, more capable of understanding all its value. But now after the heat and trial of dressing, we leave home, at a time of day when the thermometer is perhaps at 95 degrees in a little confined carriage which has got so thoroughly heated standing a few moments before the door, that it is like entering the mouth of an oven, & after a ride of four five or six miles over a rough dusty road under a broiling sun, we arrive fatigued, flushed and dirty, sit up four or five hours in company, silent and uncomfortable, too much exhausted to enjoy society even if it were of the best kind, and return home in the evening to mourn over the weary day and wasted hours. This sort of life seems however to agree with us both — I have never seen Cornelia look better or handsomer.[28]

Cornelia didn't exactly return the compliment. She communicated to the family in Albemarle that Ellen "looks better & is fatter than I ever saw her."[29]

Came time to pay the piper. After being the recipients of so many invitations, whether they wanted to be or not, it was time for the sisters Randolph to play hostess. It was near the end of their stay, after the carpenters had gone back to Albemarle. "In spite of everything," Cornelia reported on September 8:

Grandpapa insists upon the lady dinners & we are to have three families of several persons each to day to dinner with us, and such bread for dinner as we utterly disdained this morning, no one even tried to eat it & what makes matters worse one of the ladies comes entirely against her will & I have no doubt is wishing us at this time all the bad wishes that we have wished on similar occasions, but poor thing she has received three invitations & the party been put off on her account & now she must from the fear of offending us trot 3 or four miles (for she has just parted with the horses to her carriage, which she took care to tell us) thro the hottest sun that ever shone, far hotter than any we feel in our temperate zone.[30]

What made matters worse in Cornelia's opinion was that "having once broken thro the rule of never inviting ladies to dine & which was never expected, by them, we shall be obliged to continue the practice as this neighborhood is so thickly settled, & we have made so many new acquaintances in it besides those in Lynchburg, that we shall hereafter have more trouble & vexation on account of company than we ever had at Monticello."[31] She didn't record what was served besides the bad bread, but chances are that it was chicken.

No matter what was on the menu, there was much else on their minds as they prepared to leave Poplar Forest for Monticello on September 13, 1819. Evidence of just how bad things had gotten is movingly reflected by an entry in Jefferson's Memorandum Book. As usual, he paid his "debts and vales" upon leaving Poplar Forest, but this time he was barely able to cover even those. On September 12, the day before he left, he recorded: "Pd. debts and vales at Pop For. 18.25 borrowed of Joel Yancey 10. D."

"The Coup de Grace"
AND
"A Leaky House"
(1819–20)

On their way back to Monticello, Jefferson and his party crossed the James River into Albemarle County at Warren on the morning of September 14, 1819, having spent the night before in Buckingham County. Presumably they had breakfast with the Nicholas family when they called at Mount Warren, as Jefferson had suggested they might do prior to leaving Poplar Forest. On the fifteenth, back at Monticello, he signed an indenture deeding "956 acres whereof 742 acres are parcel of the Poplar Forest patent & 214 acres adjoining the same were patented by & purchased by Daniel Robertson," in trust to Thomas Jefferson Randolph. The indenture was "to secure to the President & Directors of the U. S. Bank at Richmond the payment of the sum of 20,000.D. due to the sd. bank by W. C. Nicholas, esq. as principal and for which the sd. Thomas Jefferson acknowledges himself responsible as his endorser and security."[1] Five days later, he sent the deed and a plat of the land to Joseph Marx, taking "the liberty of pressing [them] throu' you to the bank of the U. S." The plat was certified by five "gentlemen knowing the lands, & known themselves in Richmond" who vouched that the land was "ample security for the sum of $20,000." Jefferson added in his note to Marx that "the lands conveyed comprehend my best plantation in Bedford — every foot of them is or has been tobacco lands, & still in good condition."[2]

Jefferson's contention that the land he placed in mortgage — approximately one quarter of the Poplar Forest acreage — was easily worth $20,000 is borne out, more or less, by the tax assessments of the period. A year after he secured the property to the bank, Poplar Forest was re-evaluated for tax purposes. The difference between the 1820 assessment and that made five years earlier shows clearly the phenomenal increase in property values brought about by inflation that had run rampant in the interim. In 1815, he had paid $80.03 on 4,000 acres assessed at $9,41140. Now, thankfully, the *tax* had not increased greatly, being only $95.28. But, in 1820, his Bedford holdings of 3,808 acres were *assessed* at $61,958.90.[3]

On the day that Jefferson and his grandson signed the indenture, Elizabeth Trist, then staying at Monticello, gave her grandson Nicholas Trist her version of the latest news: "Mr. Jefferson and the two young ladies returned . . . yesterday in time for diner. He can't boast of very good health being rheumatick. The girls quite hearty. . . . Mr. Jefferson seems in pretty good spirits notwithstanding he has $20,000 in jeopardy. They cajole him with the hope that Wilson N will have property enough to pay off all the securityship but this family think otherwise. They called at Warren yesterday. Mr. Jefferson told me that Mr. Nicholas looked miserable and so does his lady." Mrs. Trist had obviously listened to all that the party just returned from Poplar Forest had reported, and passed along the information that "Lynchburg is deserted almost, not more than 4 stores left in the place and the Farmers round the country who let out their money at 12 percent have lost it all. The times are bad everywhere."[4]

In spite of continued assurances from Wilson Cary Nicholas that he could "rely with the most absolute certainty upon me to prevent your having to advance anything," Jefferson soon had to begin paying interest on the note. Nicholas was to live only a short while after his debacle, dying on October 10, 1820. That his friendship with Jefferson survived their mutual financial ordeal is attested by the fact that he was buried in the Monticello cemetery. Several years later, in fact only five months before he was laid to rest nearby, Jefferson wrote James Madison on the subject: "My own debts had become considerable but not beyond the effect of some lopping of property which would have been little felt, when our friend W. C. N. gave me the coup de grace. Ever since that I have been paying 1200 D. a year interest on his debt."[5]

On September 26, 1819, John Hemings, who had remained at work in Bedford after Jefferson returned to Monticello, reported discouraging news on another front: "Dear sir i am veary sorry to inform you that the flat roof over the hall Lakes vary bad. Wensday 22 we had a raine for 24 oures cleared off on Thursday at son rise and naver stop driping untill 10 oclock in the day." While Hemings felt he had located the source of the problem, and suggested a solution, he concluded that "all had better stand till you come."[6] Jefferson already had the solution in mind. A week later he wrote Bernard Peyton, his commission agent in Richmond, telling him that he would be in Bedford in two or three weeks, and asked him to forward, in care of Archibald Robertson: "50 feet, running measure, of sheet iron, that is to say as many sheets placed *endwise* together as will measure 50 ft. in length, no matter how narrow they are." In addition to the sheet iron, Jefferson asked Peyton to send a "good cheese, that is to say, rich & sweet," and "a barrel of ship biscuit, what is called, I believe, Pilot bread." In short order, Peyton responded on October 7, saying that he would send the sheet iron the next day, and that he had "employed the best baker in the city to make a barrel [of ship biscuit] especially for you of his best." Unfortunately, he had not been able to find "a first rate English cheese," but had sent a part of one of three that had been sent to Richmond that year.[7] Thus began what might be called the short saga of the cheese.

As it turned out, not only was Jefferson unable to return to Poplar Forest within the two or three weeks he had hoped to, it would be a year later, in September 1820, before he would be able to get back to Bedford. Fortunately, a number of letters passed between him and John Hemings that tell of the work then going on. On October 20, 1819, Hemings reported that he had finished "the ballustrading and the hanging of the partition doors and bed room. I am now about the shutters. I have pine enough for stiles and rails of 6 windows. I have got them all ready to put together that is the motising and tenionton I am now giting the insid stuff ready." The exterior shutters, a new embellishment to the house, were an obvious attempt to prevent future storms from repeating the havoc wrought by the June hailstorm. The roof had continued to leak, but not as badly as the first time he reported the problem.[8]

On November 2 Hemings furnished another progress report. He had finished additional blinds and had put away the "sheet iron cheese and cracers" that had arrived from Peyton in Richmond. He also asked about "the locks and hinges for these stairway doors," and concluded by saying he had "spent a great deal of disatisfaction by you not being able to return but I hope you will soon gett the better of it." On November 14 Jefferson reported to Hemings that his "letter of the 2nd got to Charlottesville last night only." He advised his workman that the locks and bolts for the stairway doors were at Poplar Forest, but "cannot be got at in my absense," suggested which rooms needed to be supplied with the blinds, and asked Hemings to say when he would be finished so that he could send the cart for him. Meanwhile, he told Hemings that the cart "carries a map which must have the straw taken off and the map put into one of the closed rooms where the rats cannot get at it." Lastly, Jefferson told Hemings to return the cart, which "must stay but one day there," back to Monticello with "the dried fruit, one firkin of butter, and the cheese which went there from Richmond, which would not keep to the spring."[9]

Jefferson also wrote Joel Yancey that same day, and both men soon responded; Hemings on November 18, Yancey a day later. Hemings hoped that he could finish "inside of ten days." Meanwhile, he reported, another rain had again caused the roof to leak, but he had discov-

ered the problem and had made temporary repairs with "some remnants of sheet iron that we have here without cutting the new at all." On the nineteenth, Yancey reported that he would send the cart back with a number of supplies, including the cheese. Unfortunately, he had observed that it "has a small hole in it, about the middle, made by the rats, while at Mr. Robertsons." Given the recent letter in which Jefferson had warned Hemings to put the map into a room "where the rats cannot get at it," one wonders if it was the Robertson rats or their Poplar Forest cousins who had attacked the cheese. Yancey also advised Jefferson that, if he wanted them, he could send back by John Hemings "two pots of nice preserved peaches" which Hanah had made. Lastly, he gave the sad news that "your old friend, Mr. Clay, I fear will not stand the winter."[10]

As usual, Hemings misjudged the time he would need to complete his work, and on November 27 Jefferson wrote him again, asking him to hang the seven sets of blinds that he had completed, and to finish and hang the remaining five that he "had put together." To these twelve, he then suggested: "If . . . you should have a little time to spare" after all else was completed, "employ yourself on the 2 blinds of the North portico. These will need only half blinds, to wit, over the lower sash to prevent people seeing into the rooms."[11] These half blinds were for the two windows flanking the front door and lighting the two small bedrooms on either side of the hall. As they were sheltered by the portico, they did not need blinds for protection from the elements, only from curious eyes peering inside from the easily accessible vantage point of the porch floor. Having only the lower sashes protected by blinds would still allow light to enter the rooms through the upper sashes (fig. 83).

Jefferson instructed Hemings to write him every Wednesday, and tried not to appear too piqued in telling him to "endeavor to guess at a day by which you think it may all be finished, that I may be ready to send for you by that day." He again wrote Yancey, thanking him for all the articles he had sent by the cart, which had arrived safely, and enclosed a list of blankets and beds to be given to the slaves that year. Whether or not Hanah's preserved peaches had anything to do with it, Jefferson advised Yancey that, even though she had been given a bed the preceding year, "to bring the annual number as even as we can, I give her one this year also"[12] (fig. 84).

By early December, John Hemings was definitely thinking of home and advised Jefferson: "Ef possible i expect to get Don on the 11th. Sunday which is 12th i should be putting evrything away & pacting up my things. I should be ready for starting on monday at Daylight." This time his guess was correct, and on the twelfth, Yancey wrote, giving a fine sense of how anxious he was to leave: "Johnny Hemings is expecting to day, every hour, that a messenger will arrive for him, and I write to day as he may not be a moment detained when you send for him as he appears so anxious to get off."[13] As far as is known, John Hemings, who had been at Poplar Forest since July, was able to have his Christmas dinner at Monticello with his beloved Priscilla.

While John Hemings was still hard at work at Poplar Forest, Jefferson received a letter from Joseph Cabell on *another* Poplar Forest — or at least on what might have become a copy of Poplar Forest that he had contemplated building in Albemarle. At the time, Cabell was visiting Bremo, the home of their fellow member of the Board of Visitors at the university, John Hartwell Cocke:

Being now at this place on my way to the Lower country I avail myself of the opportunity by Mr. Neilson to return the plan of your house in Bedford for the use of which I beg you to accept my sincere thanks. I admire it very much. But the want of suitable instruments and continued indisposition almost ever since I left Monticello have prevented me from taking a copy. It is not however important at this time that I should have the plan in my possession to study or to imitate. The wish which I felt so ardently to move into your neighbourhood and that of the University cannot now be indulged.

As with Jefferson, Cabell was in no position financially to build anew and decided instead to "make such additions to my establishment . . . as will not materially affect its sale in future and are demanded by present convenience."[14] As far as is known, this is the only time Jefferson ever lent the plans of Poplar Forest to a friend for the purpose of copying the house. Poplar Forest, like Monticello, would be copied, but not during its builder's lifetime. It may well be that the plan that Mr. Neilson returned was the same that he had drawn, and that is herein reproduced as an endpaper.

Early in the new year 1820, Jefferson wrote to Yancey, enclosing yet another "bill of sawing which I must get you to have done by Captain Martin; and the earlier it is presented the better, because water may fail, and it ought to be seasoned for the Fall's use." Obviously Jefferson had specific plans in mind for the work to be accomplished that fall, but in light of any other documentation, it is unknown just what his order was for. At the time, he was once again planning to build his own mill at Poplar

Forest, primarily for "grinding plaster as the thing which is to produce crops and improve our lands."[15] Area millers were reluctant to grind plaster, as it clogged their machinery, and it may be that this order of lumber was for Jefferson's proposed mill. Along with the mill, Jefferson was also having a canal dug.

On February 27, Yancey reported that he would send the list "to Capt. Martin in good time and if likely to be disappointed there, will endeavor to send a few to Thomson Mill, which is not much farther off." Well aware of Jefferson's precarious financial state, he was almost reluctant to ask his employer for money owed him, but decided to give it a try. If Jefferson could send him "1 or 200 dollars," it would relieve him from "several pressing claims," but "if it should be inconvenient, I must try and weather it, for it is of late not unfashionable for the most monied men to put off payment with us." He added a postscript informing Jefferson that "Mr. Clay and Mrs. Clark are both dead."[16]

As Yancey had undoubtedly surmised, Jefferson was unable to pay him. In responding on March 16, 1820, he told Yancey that his flour from Monticello had sold at a pittance: "This happening to me now a second year, has reduced me to all but bankruptcy: & disables from paying the most urgent calls upon me. . . . I am mortified therefore to say I cannot pay you even 100 Dollars." He

further promised that "until this hurricane is over I am determined not to engage for another dollar's worth that I can exist without," and asked Yancey to "do no more of the canal than barely to enable you to estimate what time it may take us hereafter."[17]

Jefferson's letter to Yancey was delivered by William Coffee, "who going on to Columbia in S. C. passes by Lynchburg, and proposes to call at Poplar Forest." As Coffee might make Poplar Forest "a short resting place, I should be glad that Hanah should accommodate him there the best she can." Yancey reported on March 28 that Mr. Coffee had arrived on the twenty-fourth and was staying at Poplar Forest, though "he has declined

Fig. 83 Poplar Forest, north elevation. As shown in this restoration drawing, the windows flanking the front door were equipped only with half blinds, or shutters. When closed, they afforded privacy from the porch. This drawing reveals how the restored north facade will appear (compare with fig. 1). *(Courtesy Mesick-Cohen-Waite, Architects, 1992)*

Distribution of blankets at Poplar Forest.

1819.	1820.	1821.

Jarry 5.) Hanah's
Phill. 8.)
	Jane Hubard.
	  a.) Edmund 9.) Hana'
	  George Welsh 12.)
		Cate.

Nisy.
  James Washington 15.)
  Harry–Anne 19.)
	Cate. Rachael's,
	  Johnny 2.) Maria's
	  Isaac. 9.)
		Hanah.
		Sally. Hannah's,

Sal. Will's.
  Abby. 4.)
  Edy. 6.)
  mary–ann 12.)
  Harriet. 15.)
  Alfred. 18.)
	Lucinda. Hanah's,
	Reuben. Hanah's,
	  a.)
	Billy. Hanah's,
	Betty. Sal's
		Armstead.
		Maria. Cate's
		  melinda 9.) Lucin-
		  Rebecca 12.) da's
		  Nelly 16.)

Sal. Cate's,
  Billy 8.)
  Anderson 10.)
  Henry. 12.)
  Nancy 18.)
	Martin 9.)
	  Moses 11.) Sal's,
	  Bill⬚as 8.) Flo-
	  Wakston 16) ra's
	  Francis 18.)
		Gawen.
		Austin

Nace	Zacharias. 13.) Fan- Martha ann 16) ny's	Flora. Will's,

Will.	Amy. Will's,	Fanny. Will's,
		  anne 15.)
		  Mehala 16.) Amy's
		  Madison. 18.)

Abby.
  Gawen 4.) Flora's
  Aleck. 6.)
  Rachael 7.) Fanny's
  Rody 11.)
	Manuel.
	Evans.
	  Jarry 2.) Dinah's,
	  Briley 5.)
		Edy. Will's.
		  Nancy 12.)
		  Thimston 19.)

Aggy	Cate Suck's	Dick.
Hanah. Dinah's,	Daniel. Suck's,	Dinah.
Lucy. Dinah's,	Stephen. Suck's,	Betty

Prince.
  Davy 6.)
  John 11.) Suck's (Cate's)
  Solomon 14.)
  Elvisly 17.)
	Mary. Betty's	Cate. Betty's,
		  Joe. 6.)
		  Shepherd. 9.)

	Hercules. Betty's	Jesse

	Nanny.	Maria. Nanny's,
		  milly 6.) Nanny's
		  George Dennis 8.)

Janetta 12.) Nanny's Ellen 14.)		
21	21	21

The Men require

Women.			
	88	112	
Young under 17.	125	175	
	129	153⅔	
	342	440⅔	
On hand	200	100	
to be brought	142	340	

Distribution of beds at P.F.

1819	1820.	1821.
Hanah.	Sal. Cate's	Cate.
Abby.	Fanny	Lucinda
Maria. Cate's	Cate. Suck's	Edy.
Sal. Will's	Hanah Dinah's	Dinah.
Flora	Amy. Will's	Betty
Nanny	Nisy.	Aggy
Mary. Betty's		Maria. Nan

Hogs. 1819. P.F.

People.   20.

This. at P.F.   12.

Overseers $900. 8.

Monticello   35
             75

going to the South this Spring."[18] Coffee had just been to Monticello, where he had modeled more busts of members of the family, and once again the indomitable Mrs. Trist gave her opinion on his work: "Mrs. Randolph says she looks like a virago. . . . Mr. Jefferson has a chin given him unmercifully long." She also reported that Jefferson planned a trip to Poplar Forest, but had postponed it because of the weather, and added that "he looks remarkably well."[19]

If William Coffee didn't go to Columbia that spring, someone close to Jefferson's heart would soon set out for the capital of South Carolina. After his second try at New London had been aborted by the headmaster's abrupt departure, Francis Eppes and his cousin Wayles Baker enrolled in a school in Charlottesville conducted by Gerard Stack, which Jefferson had helped establish and which he planned as something of a preparatory school for the university.[20] Stack's school lasted only a year, and on June 12, 1820, the distraught father, John Wayles Eppes, asked Jefferson what he thought they should do next. Jefferson, responding on June 30, unhesitatingly recommended the University of South Carolina, primarily because Thomas Cooper, who he said "has more science in his single head than all the colleges of New England, New Jersey, and I may add Virginia put together" was now a professor there. Jefferson had hoped to lure Cooper to the University of Virginia as its first professor, but continual delays in its opening, along with the dissension caused by Cooper's supposed atheistic views, made the professor decide to take the South Carolina post. Jefferson added that Columbia, the seat of the university, was in "a hilly and healthy country; and the state of society and morals there very much as our own, and much indeed of the society is of our own emigrated countrymen." Francis went, but not until October 1820. On June 30, 1821, a year to the day after Jefferson had praised Cooper to Francis's father, the professor wrote his grandfather a most gratifying letter, telling Jefferson that Mr. Eppes "passes his examination with credit to himself, and satisfaction to the faculty. . . . I have no doubt that his next year will be spent profitably, as I clearly perceive a spirit of literary emulation among the young men here of all classes." Had Cooper but known of Francis's previous academic history, he might not have been so optimistic.[21]

The June 12, 1820, letter from John Wayles Eppes to Jefferson dealt not only with Francis's education. In it Eppes made his father-in-law an extremely generous offer:

I have heard whether correctly or not that you have been unfortunate with Colo. Nicholas and will probably have to dispose of Negroes for the purpose of meeting his debt — It has occurred to me if such should be the fact that it would probably be in my power to propose to you an arrangement which might be acceptable to yourself & at the same time an accommodation to me — I have at this place a very large body of woodland to open and it would suit me very well to exchange United States bank stock for Negroe men. . . . I would employ them here a couple of years and afterwards send them to Bedford to Francis's land there. . . . The Negroes if drawn from Bedford would in fact only be in the same situation as if hired to me for a couple of years after which they would be returned to their connections in Bedford together with such as I can add to them.[22]

Jefferson was little short of ecstatic at this turn of events. He admitted to Eppes that, to settle his debts, he had thought of "selling some lands, having scruples about selling negroes but for delinquency or on their own request, but your proposition gets me over these scruples as it is in fact to keep them in the family." He noted that his Monticello slaves were engaged for three or four years, so the transfer would have to come solely from the Bedford work force. He was also reluctant to break up families by sending only men, and thus proposed to Eppes that he could part with twenty slaves, "men women and children in the usual proportions," and that this would be "more advantageous for Francis than all men."[23]

Jefferson was so pleased with the proposal that he even brought up a subject that had lain dormant for many years:

With respect to the lands in Bedford, those designated on a former occasion to you, at the South end of the tract, are not of a quality I expected. I had never at that time seen them, and was guided in their allotment by information from others, and the consideration that I had given to Mr. Randolph being in the north, it would be better to have in the middle of the tract

Fig. 84 Distribution of blankets and beds at Poplar Forest, 1819–21. Jefferson was careful to keep his slave work force supplied with blankets and beds. These notations, covering a three-year period, are in his Farm Book. *(Coolidge Collection, Massachusetts Historical Society)*

those reserved for future appropriation. But having repeated opportunities afterwards of examining the lands I found their quality not what I had supposed.

Now, he advised Eppes, he had decided to substitute "a better portion; and on that I have built a house exactly on the plan once thought of for Pantops, and intended from the beginning for Francis: and I have always proposed, as soon as he should come of age, to put him into possession of the house and a portion of land including it. . . . The beauty and healthiness of that country, his familiarity with it and its society will I am sure make it an agreeable residence to him."[24]

On July 8, 1820, Eppes wrote that he would rather take only a small force of slaves, and let the others stay in Bedford. Needless to say, Jefferson was in accord. Eppes's suggestion was "so exactly suited to my situation and feelings on the subject of the negroes for Francis, that I cannot hesitate a moment to accede to it. . . . In this way they will continue undisturbed where they always have been, without separation from their families, and pass with the ground they stand on, without being sensible of the transition from one master to another. . . . Your answer therefore may close this agreement finally on your part, as this letter is meant to do on mine." For his part, Eppes closed the deal on August 19, 1820, by agreeing to lend his father-in-law $4,000, and "receiving the interest annually, & the principal in Negroes at the end of two years."[25] In early October 1820, Eppes wrote Jefferson that the money was available, and Jefferson, after realizing that his planned trip to Bedford had to be postponed, sent to Millbrook "a sober and trusty servant by whom I must request you to send the check proposed in your letter." To assure that the papers did not go astray, Jefferson had instructed the bearer "not to trust it to any pocket, but to sew it inside of his waist coat, & not to put that off at night."[26]

It was welcome news and relief at the time that Jefferson most needed it. The arrangement with Eppes, along with the sale of a tract of land in Albemarle, from which he eventually realized $5,000, enabled him to meet his most pressing obligations and to pay the interest on his many notes. At least for the time being, Jefferson's financial plight was assuaged.

The several letters that passed between Jefferson and John Wayles Eppes regarding the proposed exchange of bank stock and slaves contain information on another gift as well, one that Ellen, who had complained on her last visit about the lack of a piano, would applaud. Francis had introduced the subject in a letter written

from Millbrook three days after Christmas 1819: "We have a harpsichord here which formerly belonged to my mother. I believe that with new strings it will be as good as ever, as none of our family play, and you have no instrument at Poplar Forest, papa told me to offer it to you, thinking it might afford some amusement to the young Ladies, as your cart passes, you might send for it without much inconvenience." Francis's father followed up on the offer in a letter of February 6, 1820: "I have thought that as you pass some time in Bedford occasionally and the young ladies with you the harpsichord might afford amusement to you and them. The box which belongs to it is here in which it could be packed. If you think it worth sending by one of your teams while passing to Bedford I shall feel great pleasure in your accepting it. It wants nothing but some new strings and is of no use here, as Mrs. Eppes does not play."[27]

In his letter of June 30, accepting Eppes's offer of the bank stock, Jefferson took up the subject of the harpsichord, and also gave an encouraging progress report on the development of the university:

In your letter of Feb. 6 you were so kind as to propose that we should remove to Poplar Forest the harpsichord of Millbrook, where you observed it was not in use. It would certainly be a relief to the heavy hours of that place to Martha and the girls. This offer therefore is thankfully accepted on the supposition it is not used where it is and on the condition that we hold and leave it in its new position in the hands of Francis & subject to your orders. On this ground I will take some occasion of sending a waggon for its transportation. In the mean time is it impossible that Mrs. Eppes yourself and family should pay a visit to Monticello where we could not be made happier than by seeing you. . . . And our university is now so far advanced as to be worth seeing. It exhibits already the appearance of a beautiful academical village, of the finest models of building and of classical architecture.[28]

Jefferson had planned to take both a spring and a summer trip to Poplar Forest, but it was not until September 7 that he was finally able to set off. He, Ellen, and Mary Jefferson Randolph, Martha's seventh child, who was then almost seventeen years old, arrived at Millbrook the next day and stayed there until the eleventh.[29] Soon after their arrival at Poplar Forest, Ellen wrote her mother about the visit to Millbrook and the state of her aunt's harpsichord. As was her habit, she used that subject only as a springboard to reflect on much else. Now, after the passage of over a century-and-a-half, the poignancy of her reflections is still touching:

I found the harpsichord in a very bad state, the sound board split for 12 or 18 inches, the strings almost all gone, many of the keys swelled so that when pressed down they do not rise again, and the steel part of the different stops so much rusted that several of them refuse to obey the hand. The music is mouldy, and some of it dropping to pieces. The instrument itself & books lay in a cellar, I think Mrs. Eppes told me six or seven years. Francis and myself turned over the books together; we found the name of Maria Jefferson & the initials of M. E. written in Aunt Maria's own hand in a great many different places; some of the songs, too, were evidently copied by herself. I have almost entirely forgotten her, but there were so many musty memories. I do not know how Francis felt, but when I looked round that comfortable establishment, and saw all those becoming children, I could not help feeling as if a stranger had usurped her right, and as if none other should have been mistress or mother there. There was no doubt a little selfishness in this for had she lived, I should have been at home at this sweet place and in this charming family and in my mother's sister and her children, I should have found another mother and other brothers and sisters.[30]

Soon after his arrival at Poplar Forest — in fact all too soon — Jefferson found out that John Hemings's roof repairs had been in vain. With what must have been some sense of exasperation, he wrote Bernard Peyton: "I am here in a leaky house which cannot be remedied but by sheet iron and tin. . . .Will you then be so good as to procure me a box of tin, and 24 sheets of iron not less than 5 feet long but as much longer as can be had. The breadth to be anywhere from 12 to 18 inches."[31] It would not be until his next visit, later in the fall, that yet another attempt would be made to fix the continuing leak.

On September 21, the day before Jefferson left Poplar Forest, he wrote Francis Eppes: "I leave at Flood's with this letter a packet containing 3 small volumes of my petit format library containing several tragedies of Euripides, some of Sophocles, and one of Aeschylus. The 1st you will find easy, the 2nd tolerably so; the last incomprehensible in his flights among the clouds. His text has come to us so mutilated and defective and has been so much plaistered with amendments by his commentators that it can scarcely be called his."[32] This is one of the few actual references from Jefferson's own hand concerning his petit format library at Poplar Forest. More than likely, Jefferson intended for Francis to take them with him to his new school in South Carolina.

As was all too often the case, Jefferson's next visit to Poplar Forest had to be postponed, this time due to "the circumstance of 3 of my carriage horses being recently taken with the disease called the sore tongue." On October 5, 1820, while Jefferson was still at Monticello, Bernard Peyton informed him that he "had the good fortune to engage the services of Mr. Stoddart, the celebrated Piano maker late from Europe, now in this city, thro' the agency of Miss. Gibbon, in selecting the strings for your harpsichord, which I send herewith, and altho this city does not afford a complete set for any instrument, yet Mr. S. hopes those sent will be made to answer. They are the best to be had here." By October 22, Jefferson's trip to Poplar Forest was still on hold, and he sent the cart to Millbrook "to bring the harpsichord [to Monticello] where my daughter with John Hemings can put it into order and string it at their leisure, and have it ready to go to Bedford by waggon at Christmas when she goes there empty."[33]

On October 28, Jefferson advised Joel Yancey that he should be able "to take the road in 12 or 14 days," but added that "the advance of the cold weather will prevent my daughter from going." He also noted that "John Hemings and his gang will go about the same time. As the season will be getting cold so fast as to require us to do everything we can to hasten repairing the roof of the house," he requested Yancey to "have 500 or 1000 chesnut shingles got and ready drawn for it. These must be of the length of those we used before, and are not to be rounded. I presume you can get some workman there to do *it immediately*."[34] At last, on November 10, Jefferson was again on his way to Poplar Forest, accompanied this time by Ellen and Virginia. During the visit, John Hemings and his gang worked on the roof, and the girls, Jefferson recounted to their father, were "both well and pursuing their studies with undisturbed industry." For his part, Jefferson took the occasion to relax, after his fashion. On November 25 he made a "List of Mountains in order in which they are seen from Poplar Forest, beginning in the S. W. and proceeding N. Eastwardly." At the age of seventy-seven, he had apparently climbed to the top of the house to tabulate the mountains (and probably to check on the roof repairs), as he added the fact that "the flat Peak of Otter bears from the top of the house N. 67 W."[35]

On December 7 Jefferson asked Archibald Robertson if he could "come and take a dinner with two or three neighbors on Sunday? It is long since you have done us that favor." In his note to Robertson, Jefferson enclosed "a 30 D. bill with a request to send me smaller bills in exchange."[36] At least, when Jefferson left Poplar Forest a week later, it appears he didn't have to borrow money from Joel Yancey, as he had the year before.

"THE MOST TEDIOUS JOURNEY"
AND
"A TRANQUILITY AND RETIREMENT MUCH ADAPTED TO MY AGE AND INDOLENCE"
(1821)

Jefferson had already put his Albemarle fields and crops in the capable hands of his grandson and namesake, Thomas Jefferson Randolph (fig. 85). Now he decided to do the same in Bedford. What he had in mind was simply to transfer his overall supervision to Randolph, from whom Joel Yancey would now take his orders. He informed Yancey of his plan on Jan. 4, 1821, in language plain and simple:

I have for sometime been becoming sensible that age was rendering me incompetent to the management of my plantations. Failure of memory, decay of attention and a loss of energy in body and mind convince me of this; as well as the vast change for the better since my plantations have been put under the direction of my grandson T. J. Randolph. His skill, his industry and discretion satisfy me that it will be best for me to place all my plantations in Bedford as well as here,

Fig. 85 Thomas Jefferson Randolph. Jefferson's eldest grandson, and a mainstay in his old age, is shown here in an oil-on-paper portrait by Charles Willson Peale, ca. 1808. Randolph was put in charge of plantation operations at Poplar Forest in 1821. *(Monticello, Thomas Jefferson Memorial Foundation, Inc.)*

under his general care instead of my own. As myself therefore he will consult and plan with you on the course of our crops and plantation proceedings generally, and in all things you may consider him as myself, and I am sure you will have more satisfaction in consultation with him who will understand the subject than with myself who did not.[1]

Yancey didn't get it. Thinking his employer meant to replace him, he tendered his resignation to Randolph, who had hand-delivered Jefferson's letter. In his letter of January 14, 1821, to Jefferson, telling him of his decision, he added: "I can assure you that no man in Virginia will be more pleased should he [Randolph] succeed here as well as he has done in your estimation in Albemarle. I have done the best I could, and I know I could do no better under the direction of Mr. Randolph or any other person." He had, at least, "promised Mr. Randolph upon his insisting, and saying that the business, and consequently you, would be injured, by my withdrawing immediately, as he was not provided with a manager, to continue to do what I can for your interests & happiness, till you procure one which I hope will be with as little delay as possible."[2]

Randolph took that letter back to Monticello, and in his reply of January 27 Jefferson told Yancey that he could not recall ever having "received anything which has given me more pain. Nothing on earth was farther from my intention than that it should be considered as intended to give you an opportunity to withdraw. It was sincerely meant, as it was expressed, to be a withdrawal of myself from a superintendence to which age has rendered me incompetent and transferring it to a younger member of my family." He stated his intentions even more succinctly and clearly in a letter he wrote to Bernard Peyton later that spring: "Age and ill health, and still more the loss of plantation skill and management by an absence of 50 years from such attentions, had for some time rendered me unequal to the proper management of my possessions so much that those in Bedford had been entirely unproductive and those here not so productive as they should have been and as Jefferson's management has lately made them." He had consequently "committed the whole of my estate here and in Bedford to Jefferson to direct as he thinks best, without any interference on my part; and I am satisfied he will double its produce at once, which even at present prices, will double present income." Even so, he told Peyton, he realized that he would have to sell some land to pay his debts, "as soon as a fair price can be got."[3]

As it turned out, Randolph would hire new overseers for the plantations, and at the end of the year Yancey would resign, this time for good. For the moment, things went along as before, and on March 12 Yancey wrote Jefferson that Nace would leave Poplar Forest that morning "for Monticello with 2 beeves and six muttons."[4] He also provided Nace with a note to be given to various innkeepers and providers along the way (fig. 86). March 1821 was the month that Jefferson had his portrait done by Thomas Sully, and a month later Elizabeth Trist, still continuing her round of visits in the Charlottesville neighborhood, and still giving the news to her grandson, declared "Mr. Jefferson I never saw look better." She continued her narrative in a somewhat more garbled fashion: "[He] will pay his Spring visit to Bedford this month. Cornelia is going certainly but they had not decided which of the remaining three will accompany him, as each puts in her claim, she should not be surprised if her Mama was to go up, indeed if her Aunt Eppes Harpsichord is sent she will be obliged to go to put it in tune." Two weeks later she wrote to Jefferson: "I hope you dont mean to risk your health by seting out on your journey to Poplar Forest while the wind is so furious and the weather so cold."[5] He obviously ignored that advice, for two days later the party set out. Ellen had won out over her other siblings and was once again selected to accompany Cornelia and their grandfather. This, the first of four trips Jefferson took in 1821, began on April 21.

In his early visits to Poplar Forest, Jefferson seems to have experimented with several possible ways to get from Albemarle to Bedford. By 1821 — actually long before — his habitual route had become well established.

Fig. 86 When Joel Yancey sent Nace, one of Jefferson's trusted slaves, from Poplar Forest to Monticello, he provided him with this note, explaining his mission and promising payment to innkeepers along the way for services rendered him. *(Coolidge Collection, Massachusetts Historical Society)*

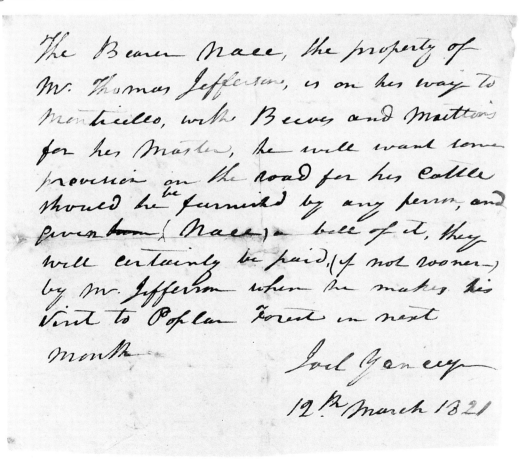

In the early nineteenth century, the shortest distance between two points in central Virginia was seldom a straight line. Certainly the route between Monticello and Poplar Forest was not. In 1801, as he was about to begin a journey to Monticello, Jefferson had written a friend from Washington about locating and building new roads, and advised him that the most important thing was to have them "as direct as can be had tolerably level; for levelness is a still more important consideration than distance. It is become more interesting now to me to find such a course, as I am setting out tomorrow for my own house, and shall be on horseback."[6] Things hadn't changed in the ensuing twenty years. Though Jefferson's route to Poplar Forest appears on a map as a thoroughly roundabout way (fig. 87), it has been de-

scribed more recently as "the levellest, driest route from here to there. . . . Indeed, one can go from Poplar Forest to Richmond and hardly 'get his feet wet' if he chooses. All along ridges."[7]

Leaving Monticello, Jefferson and his entourage probably took the Secretary's Road, skirting the eastern flanks of Carter's Mountain, though they could just as well have gone along the mountain's western foot. After crossing the Hardware River at Carter's Bridge, some ten-and-a-half miles from home, he and his party almost invariably stopped at Enniscorthy, the Coles family plantation, for a visit. Leaving Enniscorthy, the party continued through the fertile Green Mountain section of southern Albemarle County to the village of Warren on the James River, some twelve miles beyond Carter's

Poplar Forest   Hunter's   Flood's   Warren   Monticello

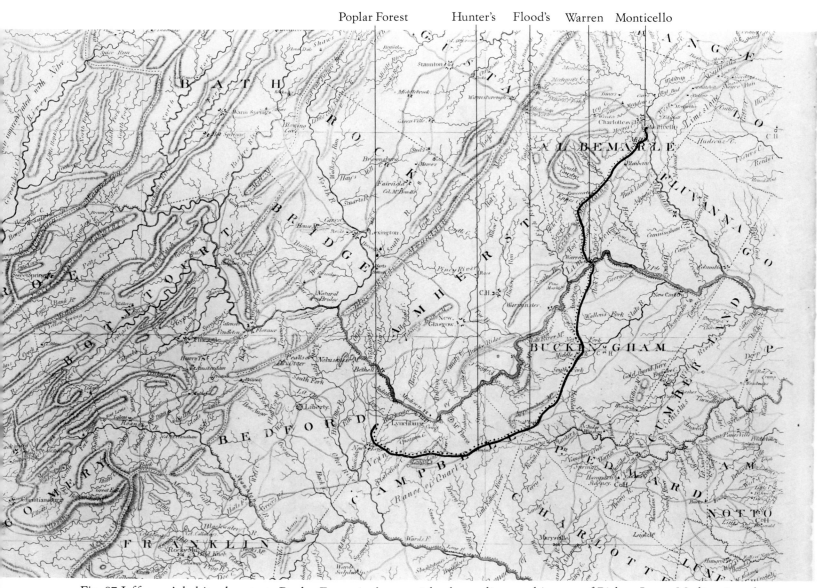

Fig. 87 Jefferson's habitual route to Poplar Forest is shown with a heavy line on this copy of Bishop James Madison's early-nineteenth-century map of Virginia. Flood's and Hunter's taverns, where Jefferson often stayed, are labeled on the map, indicating that they were well-known stops at the time. *(Geography and Map Division, Library of Congress)*

Bridge. Wilson Cary Nicholas's impressive house, Mount Warren (fig. 88), stood on a hill overlooking the town, which the Virginia General Assembly had established on thirty acres of his property, and at his instigation, in December 1795.[8] When Jefferson and his family spent the night in Warren, as they frequently did, they stayed at Mount Warren during Nicholas's lifetime. Their servants stayed at Brown's, a stone tavern nearby. The next day, the group crossed the James River on the Warren Ferry, which had been established in 1789, several years before the town.[9] Then as now, Buckingham County, on the south side of the James, was a seemingly endless stretch of farmland and woodland. Jefferson and his granddaughters seldomed mentioned anything of note in traversing Buckingham, but on a trip

taken in 1821, Cornelia conveyed this somewhat disheartening — if not callous — bit of information to her sister Virginia: "We heard as usual of a murder just committed in Buckingham."[10]

Buckingham had a number of taverns that the family and servants frequented. In order from Warren, they were Gibson's, the Raleigh, Noah Flood's (later Mrs. Flood's), and Henry Flood's. Gibson's, where they occasionally stayed when not stopping overnight at Warren, was only nine miles beyond the Warren Ferry, and the Raleigh, seven miles beyond Gibson's, was just west of the village of Buckingham Court House (fig. 89). At or near Gibson's, their route joined the main road to Richmond for a brief time, then veered southwestward. The two taverns Jefferson mentioned most frequently in his

Fig. 88 Mount Warren, Warren, Virginia. Jefferson and his entourage often stopped at the handsome home of Wilson Cary Nicholas on their trips to and from Poplar Forest, if not for the night, at least for a meal. *(photograph courtesy of Page Tapscott Massie and K. Edward Lay)*

notes and letters were located along this stretch of highway: the two Flood's taverns. That kept by Noah Flood (whose name must have caused him constant grief), was approximately five-and-a-half miles southwest of Gibson's, while Maj. Henry Flood's was eleven-and-a-half miles beyond Noah Flood's. On most of his journeys, whether coming or going, Jefferson stopped for the second night at one of the Flood's. Sometimes — probably to break up the long trip — he would stay the night at one of the two taverns and have a meal at the other. On one occasion in 1813, Jefferson had sent a note to Henry Flood: "According to present appearances I think I can get away on Saturday morning, ask a dinner of you, and a bed at Mr. Noah Flood's." As was noted above, on one of her first trips to Poplar Forest, Cornelia had written to her sister Virginia that the party "had stopt at Noah Floods to breakfast. I found that to be the best house on the road to stop at meals."[11]

After leaving Flood's, the party then journeyed ten-and-a-half miles to Hunter's, which, according to most accounts, was the pick of the lot. Owned by Robert Hunter, it was located on what was then the Buckingham-Campbell county line (as Appomattox County had

not yet been created), near present-day Spout Spring and Concord. On that same trip in which she lauded the breakfast at Noah Flood's, Cornelia reported that "at night we were better accommodated at Hunters than anywhere else." From Hunter's, rather than going down the hill into Lynchburg, and then back up again, the route continued along the flank of Long Mountain to Rustburg, or Campbell Court House, almost twelve miles from Hunter's. It then went westward, south of Candler's Mountain, along Waterlick Road, to Poplar Forest (fig. 90). Although Lynchburg was well equipped with taverns during the period of Jefferson's visits to Poplar Forest, as far as is known, he never stayed in any of them on the way between Bedford and Albemarle.[12]

In spite of the general levelness of the way he went, it seems that as often as not Jefferson did get his feet wet, but this was due more to inclement weather and the red-clay roads of central Virginia than to any streams he may have had to ford. In 1813 he had informed his granddaughter Ellen that he "had a terrible journey up, thro two days of rain, which tho' light, was nearly constant; but the roads dirtier and heavier than I have ever found them on this route. The 2nd day I was able to get but 25

Fig. 89 Buckingham Courthouse, just to the east of the route to Poplar Forest, was designed by Jefferson and rebuilt, more or less as it was originally, after a fire in 1869. It was one of several of Virginia's "county capitols" that Jefferson designed, and in many respects may be regarded as a reduced, simplified version of his earlier Virginia State Capitol (cf. fig. 10) (*Virginia Department of Historic Resources, 1969*).

miles, and on the 3rd which brought me here I was from day-light to dark getting 34 miles." As that letter states, the trip had taken three full days, and even though that particular trip was more difficult than most, Jefferson rarely made the journey, which totaled about ninety-three miles, in less than two-and-a-half days.

With all this as background, let Cornelia, who had just arrived in Bedford, tell the story of the trip taken in April 1821, which followed the standard route and which, if nothing else, proves indisputably that getting from Monticello to Poplar Forest was seldom half the fun:

We are arrived here fatigued to death as usual my dear Virginia, after the most tedious journey that ever was made. I am sure I almost died on the road from impatience. We got to Warren in the height of the rain that fell the day we left you, & were detained there all night, in consequence of which & the roads being in the most detestable order, we could not get to Hunters the next day as we intended, and spent the night at horrid Old Floods, between the sheets that Dr. Flood had been sleeping in for a month I am sure, but not between *them, exactly for finding the counter pane was clean we pinned the top sheet down close all round and laid upon that after roling ourselves up hand, foot, and face in our cloths so that our skins*

at least should not be defiled by touching pitch & covered with the counterpane next us. Strange to tell, every thing else in the house had the appearance of having been also bot more than a week before, and we did not feel ourselves poluted by breathing the air of the den usually of filth, we had very comfortable breakfasts both days, first at Warren where Kent, who the servant maid told us was mighty fond of Mr. Jefferson, gave us breakfast while we were waiting for Gill and Israel to trifle away a few hours which was in part the cause of our being obliged to spend the night at Floods, and then at Hunters whose tavern keeping seems to have improved since the death of his wife. The roads for the greater part of the way were so bad that Gill once stopped and said he thought if he ventured any farther we should certainly be upset, & once Burwell was obliged to dismount & hold up the carriage to prevent its going over. When we arrived here we found Mr. Yancey gone to Liberty Court (16 miles off) and the keys of the house could not be obtained untill his return; Burwell had shaken open the front door so that we could enter & get into several of the rooms of the house but our chamber door in which room all the bedding was locked. Besides that, nothing either to eat or drink could be obtained, & to make the matter worse, the hard winter had killed almost everything in the garden. We satisfied

Fig. 90 End of the journey. After a bend, the last stretch of the road to Poplar Forest led up the hill, on axis with the house in the distance. *(Jack E. Boucher, 1986, for the Historic American Buildings Survey, Prints and Photographs Division, Library of Congress)*

our hunger with the wrecks of our travelling provisions, &
whatever old Hannah & Burwell could find, after diligently
searching house & garden for several hours to collect the little
that had been overlooked when the house was shut up last
year, on the one hand & on the other, what the cold had
spared. We were more hungry and tired than nice though, you
may suppose, & at night were very contentedly about to
stretch off upon the outside of the beds which had a single
blanket tossed over the mattress, when the keys arrived, & in a
moment we had tea & wine & comfortable beds. I have been
writing you, I won't say entertaining you with, an account of
our journey & arrival here which I suppose was all you
expected to hear unless in addition to it the scraps of neighbor-
hood news the servants have given us, & the account of the
health of our party, this is as good as usual, grandpapa says he
is very well, sister Ellen that she is tired to death & so am I,
but we hope to recover soon & make the most of our time
while we are here.[13]

Jefferson and Joel Yancey obviously conversed about finances during the April 1821 visit, for on May 11, after his return to Monticello, Jefferson reminded him: "You mentioned that the bank of Lynchburg would accommodate me with some money should I need it. . . . I will request you to inform what is their rule as to endorsement." Yancey assured him that though each bank had different terms, "there will be no sort of difficulty of your being accommodated by either [the Farmers or the Virginia bank] upon as liberal terms, as they are able."[14]

Jefferson had planned a return visit to Poplar Forest by the first of July, but was prevented from going then by a number of factors. On August 15 he informed Yancey that he expected to start for Bedford in two days. Meanwhile, "the waggon starts this morning with a harpsichord and some necessaries and baggage. . . . The harpsichord may be laid down in the center room till we arrive." Unfortunately, on the morning they were to have left, Cornelia became ill, and the trip was postponed again. The group, probably the largest that ever went during a single visit in Jefferson's lifetime, finally left Monticello on August 21. James Madison Randolph went along, as it was now his turn to begin studying at New London Academy. As Jefferson advised Thomas Mann Randolph, Jr., then in Richmond where he was serving as governor of Virginia, "Martha will be of the party, and proposes it to Cornelia for her health. Mrs. Trist goes also."[15] Thomas Jefferson Randolph was also part of the group, which was so large that they had to stay at two different places the first night. Several stayed at Gibson's, where the next day Jefferson paid a bill of $2.00. Others were housed at Mount Pleasant, the nearby home of Maj. David Patteson, where Jefferson recorded giving

$.25 in vales.[16] Breakfast was taken at Mrs. Flood's, and cost Jefferson another $2.00. According to Cornelia the trip was little better than her last, and was accompanied by both rain and hail.[17] Soon after their arrival at Poplar Forest, Martha and Cornelia took Mrs. Trist to Liberty, leaving her there with her niece and her niece's husband, Mr. and Mrs. Peachy Gilmer. Though Cornelia reported that Mrs. Trist was by no means satisfied with the Gilmers' house, perhaps she was at least able to enjoy reclining in the campeachy chair that had arrived there from Monticello, via Poplar Forest, by this time. From her new lodgings in Liberty, Mrs. Trist would continue to report on the comings and goings of Jefferson and his family to Poplar Forest — sometimes getting things straight, more often not.

Jefferson made two fall trips to Poplar Forest in 1821, and on the latter, paid what would prove to be his last visit to Natural Bridge. Just before his return to Monticello, he wrote to Francis Eppes, in response to a letter he had received from him: "I learnt with real affliction that it was doubtful whether you would be permitted at Columbia to pursue those studies only which will be analogous to the views & purposes of your future." As Francis was obviously not happy at the University of South Carolina, he had asked his grandfather what he knew of the University of North Carolina. Jefferson responded that he knew nothing of the curriculum there, and finished with what came close to being a benediction: "The thankfulness you express for my cares of you bespeak a feeling and good heart: but the tender recollections which bind my affection to you, are such as will for ever call for everything I can do for you, and the comfort of my life is in the belief that you will deserve it. To my prayers that your life may be distinguished by it's worth I add the assurance of my constant & affectionate love."[18]

Once again, John Hemings was back at Poplar Forest, this time engaged in finishing the trim around the skylight. After Jefferson had returned to Monticello, Hemings continued in his habit of sending reports on the status of his work. On at least one occasion, he had news of another sort: "I am sorry to complain to you so near the close of my worck. Above all things on earth I hate Complants but I am bliged." His complaint was against Nace, who, he reported, "the very moment your back is turned from thee place . . . takes every thing out of the garden and carries them to his cabin and burys them in the ground and says that they are for the use of the house. I dont set up Myself for the things thats made for your table," but Nace was in the habit of burying "as common a thing is greens which we are suffering for." Apparently Nace's chicanery was well known to the Poplar Forest slaves. Hemings reported that "the people tells me that he makes market of them at the first oppentunity." Other than that, all was going well, and he reported that he was "at worck in the morning by the time I can see and the very same at night. I have got the cornice nearly don. I am bout the tow [two] last members dentils and quarter round. I should put an architrave on the skie light frame befour I take the Scaffold down. It will be 16 inchs leving the first face on the frame and planting on the twelve inches. This is 1/2 Inch thick and the ogee planted on it."[19] Hemings had just finished the full entablature of the dining room, and was preparing to complete the trim around the skylight before the scaffolding was removed. His extensive knowledge of classical moldings and profiles shines through the haze of his spelling and grammar. Two weeks later, on December 11, he proudly asserted: "Putting the architrave on the skey light has made all the improvement imaginable." He had almost finished the inside work, which would take him two more days, and "the boys is dressing the shingles and the other jobs be four me." All in all, he "should be ready to leave Poplar Forest on the 18th," and asked that the mules be sent to arrive the day before so that he could get an early start. Jefferson's response on December 18 announced that rain had prevented the mules being sent earlier, but promised they would leave that morning. He also reminded Hemings that he had "desired Jefferson [Randolph] to tell you to make out a bill of scantling for exactly such another barn as that at Poplar Forest that the stuff might be carried immediately to Capt. Martin's to be sawed. The carpenters will go up in the spring to build it."[20] In spite of claiming to have given up the entire management of his Bedford affairs to his grandson, Thomas Jefferson was obviously still very much involved, if not still in charge, at Poplar Forest.

In addition to Hemings's letters, Jefferson received at least two others in December 1821 relating to Poplar Forest. That declaring Joel Yancey's resignation was not unexpected. On the twenty-second Yancey announced: "On Sunday last Mr. Gough and his aid young Bagby arrived at Poplar Forest to take charge of your concern for the ensuing year agreeable to an arrangement previously made between him and Mr. Thos. J. Randolph." He had consequently turned over the keys, and "took my leave of the business, which has employed almost the whole of my attention for six years and six months. . . . In taking leave of your affairs I must beg to return you my highest acknowledgements for the friendship and politeness you have shewn towards me during the whole of my superintendance, as it will afford me the greatest satisfaction during life."[21]

The other letter was from John Wayles Eppes, back to his old habit of proposing land swaps. This time his preposterous idea was that he and Jefferson trade their Bedford and Buckingham properties. It made sense to Eppes, who argued that it would benefit Jefferson as Millbrook was so much closer to Monticello than Poplar Forest was. For himself, he wished to "settle in Lynchburg for the convenience of educating my younger children," and, of course, to be near Francis when he settled at Poplar Forest. If he really thought his former father-in-law would take the suggestion seriously, as he probably did, he was rudely awakened from his daydreams when he received Jefferson's reply: "Your proposition, dear Sir, of an exchange of territories is beyond the powers of my mind or body. It would be an enterprise too bold and gigantic for one near the entrance of his 80th year. To break up plantations, move all hands, bag and baggage, stock and all, to a new and distant settlement would be like beginning the world anew to one who is just going out of it." Another reason, were there need for any, the seventy-eight year old Jefferson reminded him, was the fact that he had "conveyed 1000 acres of my land there in trust to the bank of the US as a security for my unfortunate engagement for Col. Nicholas; and altho I have pretty well founded expectations of being cleared of that, the liability of the land must continue until the actual discharge of the debt."[22]

Nicholas Trist, having now finished at West Point and settled temporarily in Louisiana, also had a plan to assist in solving Jefferson's financial problems. Considered a member of the family ever since he and his brother had arrived at Monticello to live in 1817, he had become engaged to Virginia Randolph by the time he offered his suggestion to his future mother-in-law. On March 7, 1822, Martha responded, throwing cold water on the plan: "I mentioned to Jefferson [Thomas Jefferson Randolph] your idea of removing the negroes to a country where they would be so much more profitable, he assented at once to the advantage of such a step, but said what I knew to be the fact that his grandfather would never listen to it for a moment." She felt able to send him encouraging news, however, regarding the current state of the family's finances and her hopes for the future, especially regarding Poplar Forest: "But I am not with out hope that with Jefferson's management and some arrangements which he proposes the estate may be saved without any, or but a trifling sacrifice. . . . Poplar Forest which for years had been regularly falling behind hand will this year *contribute* to the maintenance of the family and in a few more will yield a considerable profit."[23] That, unfortunately, was never to happen.

"ORNAMENTS FOR BEDFORD"
AND
A MARRIAGE AT MONTICELLO
(1822–23)

Jefferson planned his spring trip to Poplar Forest in 1822 to coincide with the diocesan convention of the Episcopal Church of Virginia, to be held that year in Charlottesville. Mrs. Trist, still observing everything from her new perch in Bedford, thought it would prevent him from going "as early as usual." Actually, just the opposite happened; it propelled him to go to Poplar Forest earlier. Jefferson wrote the Reverend Frederick W. Hatch, rector of the church in Charlottesville, on May 12, saying that he had originally planned to attend the convention, where he would "have gladly profited of that occasion of manifesting my respect to that body." However, having learned that some "one or two thousand" would be attending it, and knowing that "my place [Monticello] is considered as among the curiosities of the neighborhood, and that it will probably be visited as such by most of the attendants," he decided instead to head for the hills of Bedford: "I have neither strength nor spirits to encounter such a stream of strangers from day to day, and must therefore avoid it by obeying the necessary call of my concerns in Bedford to which place I shall set out tomorrow morning." Perhaps a bit ashamed of himself, he "inclosed to Revd Mr. Fred. W. Hatch a gratuity of 20.D." in his letter.[1] Virginia Randolph had written a week or so earlier to her fiancé, Nicholas Trist, about the situation: "He is so much afraid of the concourse of people which it is said the Convention in Charlottesville will bring to the neighborhood that he has determined to remain in Bedford until it is all over, and to send the remaining part of the family to Tufton, that these doors may be closed against the curious and impertinent mob, whom he thinks would make it their resort." She added that "we are all uneasy at this arrangement of which, I fear, much will be said, and it is very probable that not more than half the persons expected, will come after all."[2]

Jefferson had his way, and two days after he wrote the Reverend Mr. Hatch, the party, which included Martha, Virginia and one or more of her sisters, along with the ever-present Burwell, set out. Even though he claimed by now to have given over all his plantation affairs to his grandson, Thomas Jefferson Randolph, letters and accounts remaining from the trip indicate that Jefferson was still master of the house and its farm. On May 21 he purchased twenty-one bushels of rye from Editha Clay, Charles Clay's widow, and on May 25, realizing that "my plantations here will be out of corn before harvest," bought thirty barrels of corn from another neighbor, Anne Moseley of Ashwood. Perhaps more astute than

some of those with whom he had dealings, she required "ready money," which necessitated Jefferson's once again having to ask Archibald Robertson for an advance.[3]

Late in May the party returned to Monticello. Virginia wrote to Nicholas that they were "all very much exhausted by the most fatiguing journey I ever made, and my dear Grand-father suffering also from a violent cold taken in Bedford, but as his sore throat has left him, and his hoarseness diminished a great deal I trust he will soon be well." According to Martha, who had written to Nicholas from Poplar Forest, the visit had been accompanied by almost incessant rain. Though they had two clear days, "it has been raining steadily from morning till night the other five."[4] John Hemings's work the past winter must have been satisfactory, as none of the letters surviving from this visit mentions anything about a leaky roof. It may have been the rainy weather, which perforce compelled him to remain indoors most of the time and perhaps to contemplate the interior embellishments, that was in part responsible for Jefferson's next architectural adornment to Poplar Forest. At any rate, soon after his return to Monticello he wrote William Coffee, who was at the time preparing ornaments for the pavilions at the university, giving him another commission: "When in Bedford I examined the Doric entablature for which I should want ornaments, on the model of that of The Thermae of Dioclesian, of which you took a note. My room will require 16 of the human busts, 20 oxsculls entire, and 4 other oxsculls cut in halves and mitered for the 4 corners, to be of composition. The spaces for the metopes are 15. I. high and 14. I. wide."[5] What must appear somewhat cryptic to an untrained architectural eye was equally unclear to Coffee, but for different reasons. Obviously trained to respect and reproduce classical architecture in its pure forms, he could not quite understand what he perceived to be a divergence from classical principles. He answered Jefferson on June 22, in a state of confusion: "As respects the ornaments for Bedford I shall promptly attend to them, but must beg your politeness to give me the following information for if I do understand your letter I am suspicious of some mistake in the ornaments for the Pavilion No. 1," which he had just cast. Pavilion No. 1 at the University of Virginia, known as the Doric Pavilion, has an entablature that was based on the Doric order of the Baths of Diocletian, the same order that Jefferson now proposed to employ at Poplar Forest, but Coffee protested that "in the example by Nicholson from the Baths of Diocletian no ox scull is shown or can I find it so in any other work that I have looked at." He was afraid that he had made a mistake in casting only human heads, and no ox skulls, for the pavilion's frieze, and feared that "this mistake of mine if it is one would extend to every frieze of that order and example." He added that "the way I looked at the subject was that you intended to ornament two rooms at Bedford. One as in the North side portico at Monticello the other as in your dining room"[6] (fig. 91).

Coffee's questions were well warranted, as Jefferson's July 10 reply acknowledged. Not only did he set the matter straight, he revealed perhaps more than at any other time just what Poplar Forest meant to him from an architectural standpoint: "You are right in what you have thought and done as to the metopes of our Doric pavilion. Those of the baths of Diocletian are all human faces, and so are to be those of our Doric pavilion. But in my middle room at Poplar Forest I mean to mix the faces and ox-sculls, a fancy which I can indulge in my own case, altho in a public work I feel bound to follow authority strictly. The mitred ox-sculls for my room are for its inner angles."[7]

Although Coffee had assumed that Jefferson meant to embellish two rooms at Poplar Forest, and showed his familiarity with Monticello in describing what he thought Jefferson had intended, Jefferson's letter of June 14 had only mentioned one room — the "middle room." Whether it was Coffee's misinterpretation that inspired him or not, he now decided to order ornaments for the friezes in both the dining room (the middle room) and the parlor: "The other room in that house of which

Au Termes de Diocletien à Rome

Fig. 91 The Doric order of the Baths of Diocletian, from Fréart de Chambray's *Parallel de l'architecture antique avec la moderne*, 1766. As William Coffee, who cast the plaster ornaments for Poplar Forest and the University of Virginia, correctly noted, this Doric order did not contain ox sculls, which Jefferson specified for his "middle room at Poplar Forest." Chambray's book was a favorite source of classical models for Jefferson. *(Rare Books Division, Special Collections, University of Virginia Library, Charlottesville)*

I meant to ornament the frieze, is the Ionic of the temple of Fortuna virilis. My frieze is 5 I wide, very nearly, I believe, of the breadth of those of the Ionics you have to do for some of the rooms of the Pavilions. I will request you to make for me 80 feet, running measure of that, of composition." This Ionic frieze for the parlor, more delicate than the Doric used in the dining room, consisted of small putti alternating with ox skulls, between which were swags of foliage (fig. 92). Jefferson told Coffee that he would "be glad to receive the ornaments for my rooms early in September when my workman will go to Poplar Forest." The ornaments for Bedford, along with those for the University, should "be forwarded by water thro' Col. Peyton."[8]

At least in the dining room, Coffee's commission was for embellishments to an already existing entablature.

John Hemings had just finished it the previous November, and in his June 14 letter to Coffee, Jefferson noted that he had "examined the Doric entablature," which he had apparently found too plain. Although he also stated to Coffee that the frieze in "the other room" was five inches wide, later correspondence suggests that the parlor entablature was not then actually in place. At any rate, Jefferson would have known the proper dimensions that he wanted.

On September 8, 1822, Coffee wrote: "About the middle of this month it was your request to have the ornaments for Bedford House, as well as the ornaments for the University. They are all in great forwardness, and will be ready for shipment on the last of this month, no time has been lost since I have been at home or have I applied a single hour to any other employment. So very

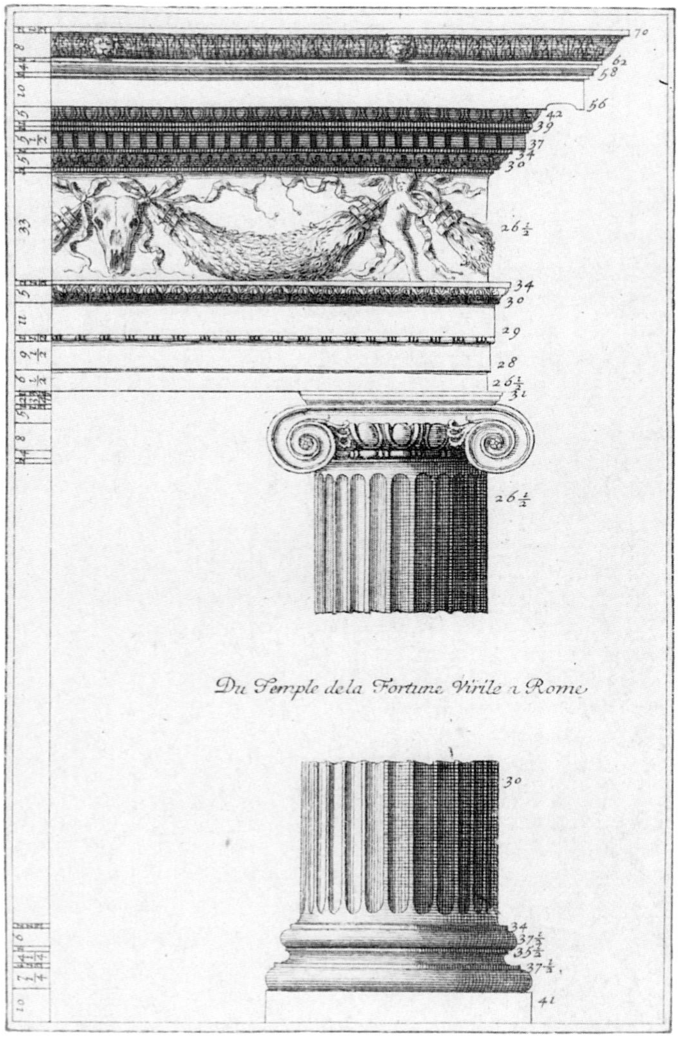

Fig. 92 The Ionic order of the temple of Fortuna Virilis, from Fréart de Chambray's *Parallel de l'architecture antique avec la moderne*, 1766. For the frieze of the parlor at Poplar Forest, Jefferson ordered ornaments from William Coffee based on this classical model. (*Rare Books Division, Special Collections, University of Virginia Library, Charlottesville*)

laborious and difficult has been this undertaking." Part of his delay was due to his having left New York, which he described as "this stinking pestilential city," for "this little town" of Newark, New Jersey. As soon as he had the casts completed, he promised "if it is at all prudent I shall go on to New York, pack them up and send them by the first ship to Richmond."[9] In his response to Coffee, Jefferson advised that his "occupations here rendering it impossible for me to go to Bedford till December you need run no yellow fever risks to hasten the shipment of mine. If they are here by December it will suffice. Let my package, if you please, be separate from that to the University because Col. Peyton will have to forward it from Richmond direct to Lynchburg." With this approval, Coffee took his time, and it wasn't until January 3, 1823, that he was able to announce enthusiastically: "I now have the pleasure of informing you that on the 16th of last month I shiped in good order and in double cases the whole of your ornaments for Bedford House, and from the great care taken in the packing I do not doubt but that they will arrive safe. They are directed to Yan[cey] at Bedford House, Linchburgh To the care of Col. Peyton in Richmond. But, of course you will give the Coln. a more particular order as may refer to his careful attention. This I think is necessary." Along with his announcement, Coffee also sent instructions for their installation, directed to John Hemings.[10] Not until over a month later, on February 15, would Coffee follow up his letter with his bill (fig. 93). Apparently Jefferson did not give Colonel Peyton "a more particular order," which turned out to be a mistake.

Meanwhile, during the half year that had transpired

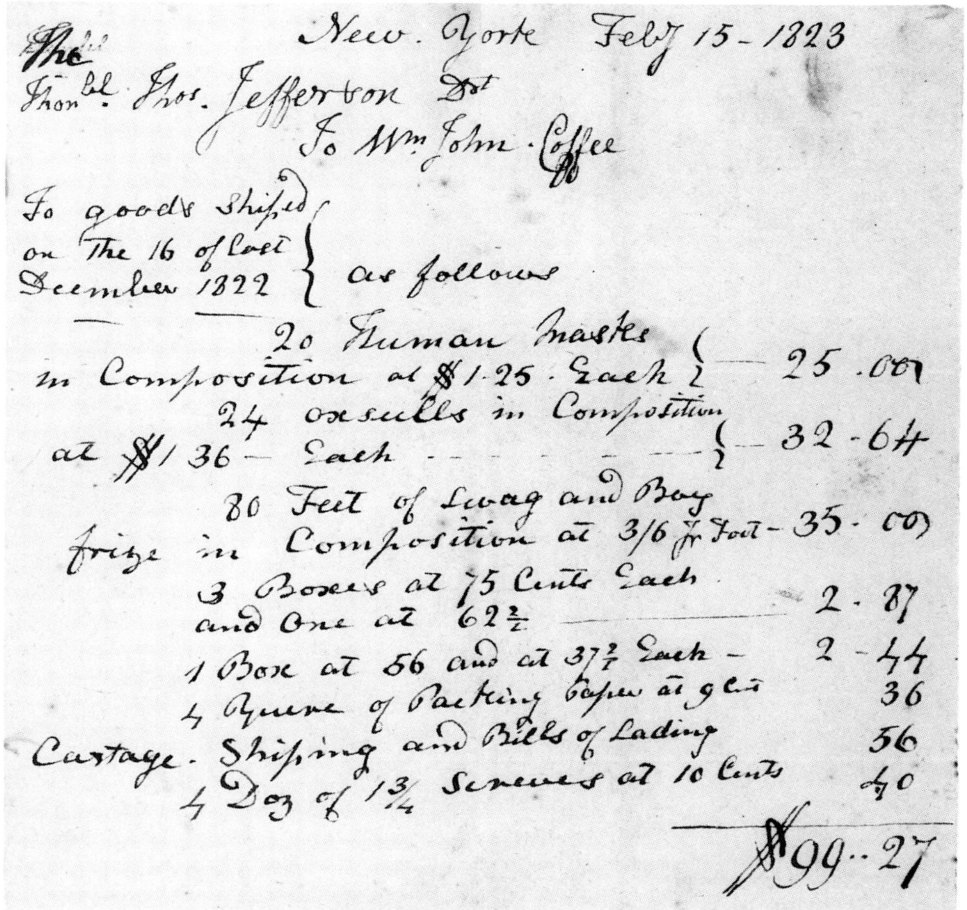
New. York Feby 15 - 1823
The Honble. Thos. Jefferson Dr
To Wm John Coffee
To goods Shiped on The 16 of last December 1822 as follows
20 Human Maskes in Composition at $1.25 Each — 25.00
24 oxsculls in Composition at $1 36 Each — 32.64
80 Feet of Swag and Bay frize in Composition at 3/6 pr Foot — 35.00
3 Boxes at 75 Cents Each and One at 62½ — 2.87
1 Box at 56 and at 37½ Each — 2.44
4 Quire of Packing paper at 9 Cts — 36
Cartage. Shiping and Bills of Lading — 56
4 Doz of 1¾ Screwes at 10 Cents — 40
$99..27

Fig. 93 On February 15, 1823, William Coffee sent this bill to Jefferson for the plaster ornaments he had prepared for Poplar Forest. *(Thomas Jefferson Papers, Special Collections, University of Virginia Library, Charlottesville)* while Jefferson and Coffee were trying to get their architectural act together, a number of other scenes that would have their effect on Poplar Forest were being played out, some in the wings, some center stage. Top billing goes to that peripatetic student, Francis Eppes. He had remained in Columbia after his letter of complaint to Jefferson in November 1821, having been able neither to change his courses there nor to transfer to Chapel Hill. In March 1822 he informed his grandfather that he was "about to return home." His father, who had "during my stay in college allowed me a certain sum to defray my expences" had informed him that "he was pressed for money and could not possibly forward any more until the sale of his crops, and as I foresaw that this would place me not only in a disagreable but distressing situation I determined to make the best use of that in my possession and return as soon as it was expended." Consequently, he wrote his grandfather, "tomorrow I set off and in 10 days expect to reach Millbrook, when I hope to find your answer as I shall feel dissatisfied until I know that you are not displeased with me for acting in the way I have done. If you approve my intention I will turn in immediately to the Study of Law and divide my time between it and other studies." In his response, written on April 9, 1822, Jefferson agreed "that you had now better turn in to the study of the law." He then proceeded to give his grandson both a schedule of how to spend his day and a list of books that he would need, chief among them "Coke's Littleton, a most valuable work . . . now, beyond question the first elementary book to be read, as agreeable as Blackstone, and more profound."[11] Upon his return, according to a report given by Virginia Randolph to her intended, Nicholas Trist, young Eppes was "reading law at Millbrook," armed with "a copy of Blackstone and a very good Law Dictionary." There was only enough money in his father's till for him to purchase two books: "Bacon's Abridgement, and Thomas's Coke Littleton," which he asked his grandfather to order for him.[12]

There was lots more on Francis's mind that any independent reading of the law, as his garbled rendition of "Coke's Littleton" might indicate. In the same letter in which Virginia Randolph announced to Nicholas Trist that Francis was studying, she added "in September he will come to be married, as he has had the good fortune to be favorably received by Elizabeth." For his part, Jefferson wrote Trist two months after that, with a more jaded observation: "His proposed marriage in Sep. with our neighbor Eliz. R. will probably be some interruption to his studies."[13]

Indeed it would be, as Francis's father even more sternly speculated in a letter to Jefferson: "I should feel much greater pleasure in furnishing Francis with the books necessary for his profession if I could induce myself to believe that he would ever practice law. I think however like most other young men who have something

he will find home after marriage too comfortable to encounter the drudgery of practice. . . . To reason however with a man or boy in love is hopeless." Realizing that Francis would "soon be of age after which I can exercise no control over him except so far as his respect for my opinions may induce a voluntary acquiescence on his part," the senior Eppes did insist on one point: "There is only one circumstance in which I shall be pointed. He must not marry until he gets possession of his property which cannot be until the end of the year. Every man who marries should in my opinion have a home whether he inhabits or not." Going on, he protested:

I confess however as a parent I cannot but consider this premature marriage as death to his future prospects. To see him settle down as a mere farmer and planter with perhaps less skill and industry than his neighbours is so different from the course my partiality as a parent perhaps had marked out for him, that I cannot look forward to his marriage before he has completed his law reading with any feelings but those of heartfelt sorrow and regret.

To the young lady of his choice there can be from what I have heard no possible objection. But I should feel the same repugnance to the most angelic woman upon earth if his marriage was either to drive or charm him from the profession for which he is destined.

I presume that Francis has communicated to you his prospects and perhaps your views on the subject may differ from mine.[14]

Eppes's insistence on his son's having possession of his property prior to his marriage was not his decision to make, but Francis's grandfather had no objections on that score. He was also of the same mind regarding Francis's early marriage: "I think with you that it has been unlucky that Francis so early adopted views of marriage. The European period of full age at 28 years is certainly more conformable with the natural maturity of the body and mind of man than ours of 21. The interruption of studies and filling our houses with children are the consequences of our habits of early marriage. Yet, being a case not under the jurisdiction of reason, we must acquiesce and make the best of it." He agreed with Eppes that Francis could not have chosen "a more amicable companion" and tried to assuage his father (and perhaps himself) by saying that Francis "gives me strong assurances that it shall occasion but little interruption to his studies." He added that "he will be accommodated, whenever he pleases, with the house at Poplar Forest and a plantation around it sufficient for the force he may have; stating to him at the same time that I must make no deed of any part of my property, while my commitment for Mr. Nicholas is hanging over my head: as the indulgence of the bank would probably be withdrawn were their security in the extent of my possession to be brought into suspicion."[15]

Francis's "amicable companion" was Mary Elizabeth Cleland Randolph, the daughter of Thomas Eston Randolph, who was in turn a brother-in-law of Thomas Mann Randolph, Jr., Martha's husband. Known in most circles as Elizabeth, she generally signed her letters MER, and came to be called Bett by her husband. She had grown up at Ashton, near Monticello, and her father had long held the lease on Jefferson's mill on the Rivanna River, as well as the lease on Pantops. She was obviously on intimate terms with the Monticello family, and when she moved to Poplar Forest, Virginia Randolph was to report that "the loss of Elizabeth will leave a chasm in our society that can never be filled up."[16]

On November 28, 1822, she and Francis, who had turned twenty-one two months earlier, were married at Monticello. A week before, Martha Randolph wrote Nicholas Trist about the upcoming event, and added that "my father will give him immediate possession of the house at Poplar Forest with 1000 acres of land." She also thanked Nicholas for warning her not to tell his grandmother in advance, though she added that his caution "was needless to us all but particularly to me who have known her 40 years. I would trust every thing to her honor but a secret." Thus forced to write her grandson after the event, Mrs. Trist got the month wrong in reporting the wedding in her letter of December 23, 1822, but proved to be more or less correct with the rest of her story: "Eppes and Elizabeth were united this month. He took her to see his friends in Buckingham, I understand that early in the Spring they take up their abode at Poplar Forest."[17]

A few days before the wedding, Jefferson received a letter from his Bedford County neighbor William Radford, who, along with Joel Yancey, had jointly purchased the land given to the Bankheads so long ago. Radford had a question "respecting the title to the land conveyed." Since the property he purchased had been part of the original Poplar Forest tract, Radford was correct in his understanding "that the land originally belonged to Mr. Wales, and that the title came to you by marriage with his daughter." He then wondered if the title was held by Jefferson alone, or whether "your daughter Mrs. Randolph and your grandson Mr. Eppes," had any claims. Radford had no worry that this would cloud his title, knowing that "releases could be obtained if necessary," and closed by telling Jefferson he "was much concerned to hear by Mr. Randolph the accident that has befallen you and hope that you may speedily recover from it." The accident was a broken left arm. As Virginia had reported to Nicholas on Nov. 12: "This morning he got a fall down one of the flights leading from the terrace, and broke his arm very near the wrist; besides cutting it badly, and getting a slight wound on his head."[18]

Jefferson answered Radford's letter on November 30, 1822, assuring him that the title to Poplar Forest was short and clear, and added: "The accident of a fractured arm is to confine me till Xmas day as my physician tells me. It will then be too cold for me to go to Bedford until the spring. In April I shall go to settle my grandson Fr. Eppes at the Pop. For. He will then be in place to become the channel of correcting any default of form not observed [with the land title]. He was married two days ago and his newly aquired spouse will add to your neighborhood a most amiable and valued member." In subsequent correspondence on the subject, Radford, a lawyer and banker as well as property owner, found a flaw in the title, which Jefferson corrected. Radford apologized for imposing "on you so much trouble in this business, but as it may be the means of preventing much greater to those who may come after us, I hope I shall be excused by you."[19] That was certainly language that Jefferson could understand and appreciate, and once the legalities were finally worked out, he wrote his Bedford friend: "I really rejoice that the defect has been discovered while it was in my power to rectify it."[20]

At the time these property transfers were being straightened out, an unfortunate event happened at Poplar Forest, one that was reported on both by Mrs. Trist, writing to her grandson, and by Radford, in his letter of December 26, 1822, to Jefferson. Jefferson had also undoubtedly heard of it from Thomas Jefferson Randolph, who went to Poplar Forest that November because of it. As Mrs. Trist reported:

We had the pleasure of seeing Jefferson Randolph last Sunday week his visit to this place [Liberty, the Bedford County seat] was in consequence of an event which took place at Poplar Forest a mulatto attacked the overseer — knocked him down and wounded him in several places with a knife. He would have bled to death but with the assistance of one of the Negroes and Hannah a Black woman who has the care of the House staunched the bleeding by holding the wounds together till they sent for a Doctor. He had eleven or twelve wounds and tho his face was horribly mutillated they entertain hopes of his recovery. They say that he was by no means a hard task master. I understand that there are 3 or 4 of them in the jail here and in the course of a month their fate will be decided.

William Radford reported in more detail on the trial, in which he had participated to a degree by hiring the lawyer for the defendants: "The trial of Billy, Hercules, and Gavin took place at Bedford court on Monday last. Billy was found guilty of stabbing & was sentenced to be burnt in the hand and whipped. The other two were acquitted, there being no positive proof of a conspiracy. They were defended by Mr. Clark who was employed by me to defend them at the request of your grandson."[21]

The overseer who had been attacked was William Gough, the first of the Poplar Forest overseers whom Thomas Jefferson Randolph had selected after Joel Yancey's resignation. At the time of the incident, he had been at his post only a year. Billy, who was found guilty, was Hannah's son.

On March 22, 1823, Jefferson wrote William Coffee, announcing that he had received the bill for the Poplar Forest ornaments, and that he had sent a request to Bernard Peyton to remit $100 to Coffee for them. He also informed Coffee that some of the ornaments for the University had arrived, and "as mine were to come with them I presume Col. Peyton has rec. and forwarded them to Bedford." Unfortunately, Peyton had done nothing of the sort, and on March 24 he informed Jefferson that "the boxes from Mr. Coffee have been fwd'd . . . to *Monticello*, altho they were directed to *Bedford*, because I thot' Mr. Coffee had certainly made a mistake in the direction. I find now however that his direction was correct, and am extremely sorry for the mistake. How can I rectify it?" On April 30 an exasperated Jefferson wrote Coffee from Monticello: "Notwithstanding your particular request to Col. Peyton to send my boxes of ornaments to Bedford, he persuaded himself it was a mistake & sent them here. As soon as it was observed at the Univ. that some of theirs were missing, we suspected they might be my boxes. I opened one, found at once it contained oxsculls for Bedford & so well packed that I could not resolve to open any more, as Col. Peyton's mistake now makes it necessary for me to send them in a waggon by land 90 miles." Still, some of the blame had to be laid at Coffee's feet, as he had mislabelled several of the boxes as to which of the projects (Poplar Forest or the University) their contents were for. After requesting Arthur Brockenbrough at the university to remit payment to Coffee, Jefferson concluded by expressing the hope that all "is finally brought to right except the delay which errors have produced."[22] Unfortunately, the comedy of errors ultimately prevented Jefferson from ever seeing just how the indulgence of his architectural fancy of mixing ornaments from different classical sources would have appeared at Poplar Forest (fig. 94).

By the time all was "brought to right" on Coffee's plaster ox sculls, the newlyweds had moved to Bedford. On March 23, 1823, Ellen Randolph, rather than her sister Virginia, wrote to Nicholas Trist, then in Louisiana: "Francis & Elizabeth are preparing to try the strength of their pinions not in a voyage across the Atlantic, but to their own snug nest at Poplar Forest, alighting awhile at Millbrook. They leave Ashton tomorrow — it will be a painful parting on all sides, but they carry with them youth and hope and love. Their prospects are as fair as their warmest friends could wish." Jefferson had "intended to have gone to Poplar Forest with my grandson . . . in order to fix him in the house there and see with what accommodations we could aid him in the beginning as beginnings are always difficult with young H-

keepers, but indispensable business" had prevented him from doing so. Instead, he asked the new overseer, William Gough, "to attend to his wants, to let him have the use of our dairy particularly as I should myself use it were I there, lambs for his table as his flock is small." He added that these and "any other accommodations or services you can render him will be approved by me and considered as obliges to myself." He enclosed the letter to Gough in a similar one he wrote the same day, April 21, 1823, to Francis. To his grandson's, he added: "I think I shall be with you about the 10th. or 12th. of May. My crippled wrist and hand are still in an useless situation and not likely soon to be otherwise."[23]

An embarrassing comment on his state of finances at the time is revealed in the letter he wrote two days later to Bernard Peyton: "I shall set out in 3 or 4 days for Bedford, and not having money for the road, & having also some petty neighborhood debts I have drawn on you this day for 140 D."[24] Finally, on May 14, Jefferson wrote in his Memorandum Book that he "set out to Bedford." Judging from the few surviving accounts of this trip it was again something of a house party. Martha went along once more, as did Cornelia and Virginia. Jefferson saw his grandson with his new bride situated, if not settled, in their new house, and when the young ladies of the family decided to go into town on a shopping spree, he sent a

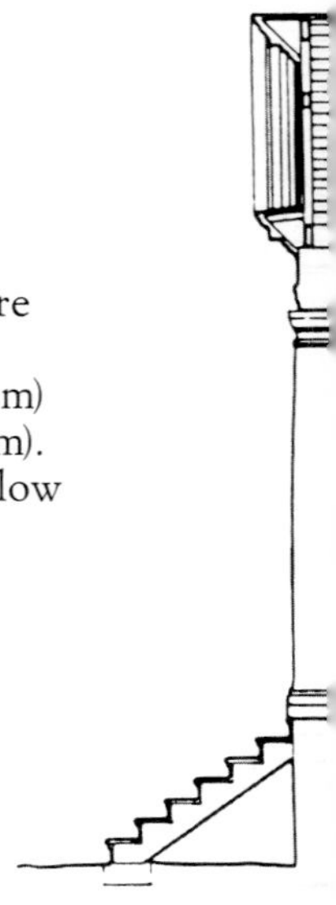

Fig. 94 Poplar Forest, sectional drawing, looking East. William Coffee's entablature ornaments are shown as they would have appeared in the dining room (central room) and parlor (to the right of the dining room). Note the floor level of the wine cellar, below the dining room. *(Courtesy Mesick-Cohen-Waite, Architects, 1992)*

note to his old Lynchburg friend and merchant, Archibald Robertson: "Two of my grandaughters are on a visit to Lynchburg with their relation Mrs. Eppes. Should anything strike their fancy in your assortment be so good as to let them have it on my account." His note also informed Robertson how he could expect to be reimbursed for anything the young ladies might purchase. In effect, he passed the buck to his grandson, Thomas Jefferson Randolph, into whose hands he had "delivered all my concerns. . . . I leave to him to communicate with you on their subject, only observing that our resources authorize us to count on making a respectable diminution of my present balance to you which altho it cannot be of the first monies received, will not fail to be done in the course of the summer or early autumn." It was a story the long-suffering Robertson had heard many times before.[25]

Upon their return to Monticello, Virginia wrote Nicholas on May 13 about "what a pleasant visit we have had to Bedford, and that Grand Papa bore the fatigue of the journey as well as usual." Mrs. Trist knew of the visit and, writing from nearby Liberty, wished she could have been part of it: "I should have gone down to New London in the stage and have got them to send for me tho one of their horses I heard was sick but I was too unwell to undertake the journey. I pleased myself with the hopse of seeing them but I fear I shall never have the pleasure to see Mr. Jefferson again. A Gentleman last evening informed me that he was in bad health and that Mrs. Randolph look'd very much depressed."[26]

Mrs. Trist's prediction about never seeing Jefferson again would come true. She herself was then elderly and —by her own admission—in feeble health. Unless she could make the longer trip to Albemarle, her only chance of seeing Jefferson again would be while he was at Poplar Forest, a short journey from her quarters in Liberty.[27] But, when he left Poplar Forest on May 25, 1823, Thomas Jefferson was never to return. He was then eighty years old, and though he contemplated visits during the next two years, none of them materialized. He may, in fact, have sensed that this trip would be his last. On his way to Bedford from Albemarle, in addition to paying his current bills at Brown's, Mrs. Flood's, and Hunter's, he had settled all his past accounts, or, as he termed them, "arrearages." Even when crossing the James River at Warren, he had written "ferrge. & arrearages 2.95."[28] Though he would still have occasion to deal with the crops its fields produced, would try to attend to the installation of Mr. Coffee's ornaments, and would send assistance to Francis to repair the damage done to the house by a fire, he would never see his beloved Bedford retreat again.

"NEXT SUMMER PERHAPS"
(1823–25)

When Francis and Elizabeth Eppes moved to Poplar Forest in the spring of 1823, Jefferson "accommodated" them, as he had said he would in his July 28, 1822, letter to John Wayles Eppes, with "the house at Poplar Forest and a plantation around it sufficient for the force he may have." As a later survey recorded, the "plantation around it" consisted of 1,074 3/4 acres, but at the time Francis moved in, no deed was drawn, as much of the land was still held as security for the W. C. Nicholas loan. The remainder of Jefferson's Poplar Forest lands in Bedford and Campbell counties remained under the overall supervision of Thomas Jefferson Randolph, though of course Thomas Jefferson himself continued to be actively involved.

Upon his return to Monticello from Poplar Forest on May 27, 1823, Jefferson tried again to straighten out his complex and disheartening financial affairs. Actually, he had begun earlier that spring to calculate just what his debts were. According to a tabulation he made in April, he then owed more than $73,000 to various creditors. The Nicholas debt alone now amounted to $21,200, as he had not yet paid off the annual $1,200 interest payment. Among his other creditors, he reckoned that he owed Archibald Robertson $1,918.85. He also owed Joel Yancey and Hugh Chisolm.[1] Perhaps it was because he made the calculations on April Fool's Day that he was able to conclude that, with annual interest payments and a proposed sale of slaves, he could pay off his other debts by 1827 and the Nicholas loan three years later, all without having to resort to selling any of his land. It was, as an authority on the subject notes, "an extraordinary exercise in wishful thinking."[2]

Reality soon dampened those hopes. Jefferson apologized to one of his creditors that he couldn't yet pay what he owed as the shipment of his tobacco to Richmond was "tardier this year than ever"—an apology that failed to satisfy the particular creditor to whom it was offered as an excuse. In fact, Jefferson was informed that if he needed more time, he would have to pay interest, to which he answered: "My grandson [Thomas Jefferson Randolph] is now on a journey to my estate in Bedford to expedite" the matter.[3] Later in 1823, in response to another similar demand, Jefferson answered that he and "T. J. Randolph . . . had before determined on a large sale of property in Bedford about Christmas," and that the funds realized from it would then be used to pay off that particular debt.[4] In referring to "property" he wasn't

thinking of land this time, but again he was to be disappointed in his expectations, as were his creditors. On January 5, 1824, he informed Bernard Peyton that "Jefferson returned last night from a sale of some negroes in Bedford. He could make no hand of selling for any portion of ready money. He sold therefore at one and two years credit." He promised Peyton some of the proceeds from this sale, and also promised that he would soon receive "a considerable surplus" from another. Jefferson Randolph, he wrote, "expects every day to recieve also from N. Orleans authority to draw for about 2500 D. for the sale and year's hire of some mutinous negroes sent thither a year ago, which we shall lodge in your hands."[5] As it turned out, he vastly overestimated the sum that sale would realize.

In March, 1824, Joel Yancey once again added his voice to the chorus of Jefferson's creditors, though, to be sure, he was as polite in this request as he had ever been: "I wrote you some time last fall, that I was very much in want of money, and that I would be very much oblig'd to you to pay me one thousand dollars as soon as you could make it convenient, which letter I am informed thro Mr. Randolph you did not recieve. I am still in great need of that sum, and would be very much obliged to you to let me have it some time this spring." Jefferson responded on April 1, having delayed his response until he could "have a consultation" with Randolph, who assured him "that the whole of the produce of the last year is so disposed of or engaged as to put it out of his power to furnish you the 1000 D. which you wished to receive this spring." Randolph, he promised, would confer with Yancey on his next trip to Bedford. He added that, if he thought the sale of any property could help relieve his debts, he would willingly sell land, but "the general outcry of the scarcity of money renders it impossible to sell but at a half or third value."[6]

In addition to consulting with his grandfather about money owed to Joel Yancey, Thomas Jefferson Randolph had other financial matters to concern him that same April 1. That was the day he assumed responsibility for his own father's debts, which were also considerable.[7] In December 1822 Thomas Mann Randolph, Jr., had returned to Albemarle after his term as governor of Virginia had ended. That spring he had been elected as one of the county's two delegates to the General Assembly, and he was reelected to the same position in the spring of 1824. But if his public life was as positive as ever, his private affairs were just the opposite. In addition to his financial problems, his relations with his wife and family, including his father-in-law, had become increasingly strained.

Meanwhile, Francis, who needed funds to establish himself on his new property, was having no better luck in Bedford. A few days after he moved to Poplar Forest he had written his first cousin, Thomas Jefferson Randolph: "The jig is up with the banks my dr. fellow—they will not take a draught on me—they will not renew the note with me as principal—they will take the cash; they will take a draught on *Richmond* at 60 days! This is the sovereign will and pleasure, of the honorable, the board of directors; which after a two weeks dangling and dancing I had the honour to learn this morning." What added insult to injury was that the bank in question was the Farmers Bank of Lynchburg, William Radford president. Probably as well as anyone, Radford knew the precarious financial situation of Jefferson and his family. Credit was so tight, and crops and land were selling for such low premiums in the early 1820s, that a number of Virginians resorted to leaving the state. From her vantage point in Liberty Mrs. Trist observed:

The times are dreadful if we may judge from the numbers that are migrating to different parts of the continent. Scarce a day passes that families are not going to the Alabama Missoura or some of those places. They carry a number of slaves with them. I dare say there has gone through this place this day two or three hundred their master and family in close carriages waggons with provisions and clothing and beding all seem to be comfortably provided with the comforts of life but I fancy they will go further and fare worse, the times are becoming disturbing.[8]

During these hard times, the rounds of visits between Monticello and Poplar Forest continued, although now by a younger generation. Even before the Eppeses moved to Poplar Forest, Ellen and Virginia had anticipated the new order, in a sentiment that one almost wishes they had never expressed. At least they were honest in declaring their feelings. Writing Nicholas Trist on January 2, 1823, Virginia revealed "how much more agreable our visits to Poplar Forest will be *then*, than they have hitherto been; Sister Ellen says she expects hers will not be so frequent, for she has been *packed off* hitherto every time that Grand Papa went, and in future we shall all put in our claims." Virginia had joined her brother Jefferson

for a visit in the fall of 1823, and received a verbal reprimand from Nicholas for not finding time to write him while she was there: "Had your visit been to Mrs. Madisons, instead of to Poplar Forest, or to any house where you could not have written perfectly at your ease, your silence might have lasted twice as long without my thinking myself authorized to complain of it."[9]

The timing of that particular visit may have been in part to console Francis, whose father, John Wayles Eppes, had died on September 15, 1823. Once Nicholas recovered from his feigned indignation toward his fiancée for neglecting him, he told her that he had learned of the senior Eppes's death from the *Enquirer*: "This is I presume the first trial of the kind that Francis has ever experienced; and from my knowledge of his character, I fear its effect will be violent as well as lasting. However, he has many to share in his grief; and that greatest of all blessings in affliction as in happiness, a wife."[10] Among other things, the effect of his father's death was to call into question some of the provisions of his will, which had been written on May 5, 1823, and was proved at Buckingham Court House on October 13. Francis was one of the executors, and the will, which called for an equal division of John Wayles Eppes's property upon the death of his widow (who was given a life interest), specified that "no advancement I have heretofore made to my eldest son Francis Eppes is to prevent his inheriting an equal portion of the property of which I may die seized and possessed on the same terms and conditions with my other children."[11] The other executors, one of whom was Francis's stepmother, contested the will. Reporting to his grandfather that "the executors seem disposed to wring from my grasp all that the law will allow," Francis had to ask Jefferson's assistance on a number of points. Jefferson's prompt and thorough answer, given after he had "diligently gone over your father's correspondence with me, which is very voluminous," apparently satisfied everyone.[12]

Francis and Elizabeth's first child, Jane Cary Eppes, had been born at her parents' house, Ashton, on November 9, 1823, and two months later, on January 9, 1824, Virginia Randolph wrote Nicholas Trist from Monticello: "Elizabeth will come to introduce little Jane to her Great Grand-father, and stay some days with us previous to her return to Bedford, which will be the first of next month when Francis proposes to come for her." She added a note that, in light of future events, was both ominous and prophetic: "He [Francis] is now there [at Poplar Forest] and apparently heartily sick of: 'solitude and the screech owl.' "[13]

In his letter to his grandfather concerning his father's will, Francis reported good news on the Bedford crops in the spring of 1824, assuring Jefferson that his wheat looked "uncommonly fine." He also urged a visit: "The neighbors are all well, and make frequent enquiries about you. They hope that your visit will not be much longer protracted, and that you will give us a larger share of your time. I need not add how much it would gratify me." He was so sure that his grandfather would come that he added a postscript: "If it will not be too troublesome I wish you to bring me a little bit of Pyracantha with the root to it." In his answer of May 1, Jefferson told Francis that he was "engaged in a piece of work here which will probably detain me till the next month, when I hope I may be able to pay you a short visit." He had also written William Short earlier that spring: "I shall visit Bedford in the months of May and June, and if you do not set out on your Journey till July you will assuredly find me here, and happy to receive you."[14] In spite of his plans, Jefferson was not able to go to Poplar Forest in 1824.

On July 3, 1824, Jefferson drew again on his account with Bernard Peyton, even though he had received from Peyton a letter that same day telling him just how much in arrears his accounts were. On July 4, a day that should have been spent otherwise, Jefferson wrote down the "state of my notes in bank" in his Memorandum Book. The picture was as bleak as ever, and all he could add after listing the various notes was "sent renewals." As the summer wore on into fall, Jefferson continued his correspondence with Peyton, and on August 19, his Richmond agent reported that, although the sales of his tobacco had started off well, eight of the twenty hogsheads from Poplar Forest had been damaged in transit. This prompted one of the most discouraging missives Jefferson ever composed, one that contained a veritable litany of his troubles:

My misfortunes of the past year have been considerable & shall be briefly stated. Four prime young men, guilty of an attack on their overseer were sent, as an example, to N. Orleans to be sold about 2 years ago. I had a right to expect with certainty 2000 D. for them. As yet I have received 400 D. only and have but uncertain expectations what more & when will be received. . . . Add to this the burning a tob. house in Bedford with all its tob. and much else in it estimated at 1000

D. makes a whole of 5000 D. short received of what I considered as certain, and would have enabled me with punctuality to meet every engagement. Deprived of this I am truly distressed.[15]

So distressed was he, in fact, that he now had to seek yet another loan from the bank, which he asked Peyton to arrange.

Elizabeth Eppes, Francis's wife, wrote frequently and at length from Poplar Forest to both Virginia Randolph and Jane Nicholas Randolph during this period, though her interests lay almost entirely in family and friends rather than in the house. On occasion, though, she portrayed vividly the life that now went on within its walls. On June 10, 1824, she wrote Jane Randolph to carp about a dinner that she had hosted for what she considered self-invited guests, although she, "the last comer to the neighborhood, have never dined with them, and moreover did not then, and never did, or shall, intimate the slightest expectation or even *hope* of so great an honour at their hands. . . . They are all utterly odious to me, . . . and yet I am forced to . . . deck my face with smiles of welcome, while in my heart I would sooner see them on their way to Jericho, or in the sailor's phrase, to the S. E. corner of h___l than to my drawing-room."[16] No gracious Virginia hostess, she. Nor was she any more courteous about an impromptu dinner later that summer, of which she gave a graphic account:

Mrs. W, self-invited, is coming over to spend the day, & will bring with her, her fair daughter, & a Miss Mitchell from Lynchburg who is at present on a visit to her — if I am not better I shall keep my room, & take no trouble about the dinner, as I cannot bear to send H to the damp cellars & wet offices, & my being sick would be excuse sufficient for every thing amiss. We had an awkward visit from these young ladies last Sunday — dinner was later than common, in consequence of Wayles Baker, Jeff Harrison, George Tucker coming in unexpectedly, & just as we had set down, Mrs. W's carriage drove up & Miss W. & Miss Mitchell alighted from it. I carried them in the drawing room, & sat there until H finished her dinner, & then I returned to the table. Francis brought out some of your grandfather's wine. It is only the 3rd time he has ever done so & when the ladies past through the dining room on their way out, the bottles were all empty, & the gentlemen's heads somewhat exalted, & they all behaved so badly, that we have done nothing but make excuses for them since to the ladies. Wayles & Mr. Harrison were each striving to shuffle

Miss [?] off, and the result was that one helped her down the steps & the other shoved her by main force into the carriage. Wayles got a dreadful wound in the service, & they all three set up such a roar of laughter the instant the carriage drove off, as to give desperate offence to the fair ones within[17] *(fig. 95).*

Elizabeth visited Albemarle soon after that, and upon her return wrote a note to Virginia that proved Francis was not the only one at Poplar Forest "heartily sick of: 'solitude and the screech owl:' "

I left home as usual with a heavy heart, & could not forbear contrasting your happy lot, in the bosom of your own family & with the prospect of never being far removed from it, with the dreariness & desolation of mine, cut off as I am from friends so kind, so affectionate, so deservedly dear to me, and placed here among strangers, upon whom I have no claim, who have no share in my joys or sorrows, & who, however friendly in their intercourse as common acquaintances, are, after all mere acquaintances, *& shew no wish ever to step beyond the limits proscribed to such.*[18]

Undoubtedly her visit to Albemarle in the late summer of 1824 had been timed in part so that she might attend another wedding at Monticello. On September 11 her correspondent, Virginia Randolph, and Nicholas Philip Trist were married there. They had been engaged for some time, but Virginia had been reluctant to move to Louisiana, where Nicholas had lived after his graduation

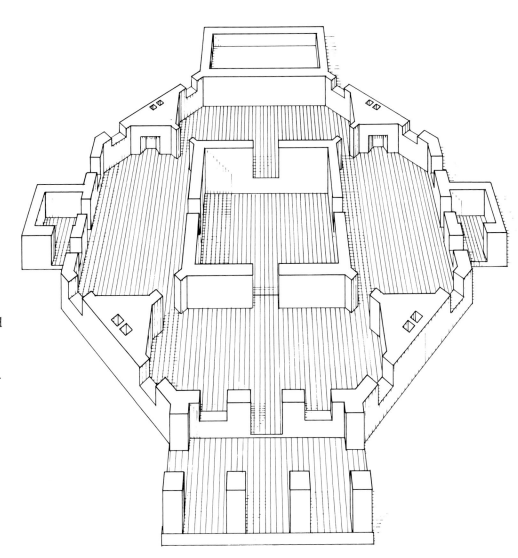

Fig. 95 "The damp cellars," as Elizabeth Eppes called them, are delineated in this perspective drawing. The central room, under the dining room on the first floor, served as the wine cellar; its floor level was several feet lower than the surrounding rooms (cf. fig. 94). The basement of Poplar Forest was largely unfinished during the Eppeses' tenure, as it had been during Jefferson's. *(Tim Buehner, delineator, 1991)*

from West Point. After their marriage, they resided at Monticello, where Nicholas read law under Jefferson's tutelage.

One of Elizabeth's few letters that reveals anything about the house at Poplar Forest during the Eppeses' tenure was written early in the new year, 1825, to Jane Randolph. A fierce, cold wind had shaken "the windows & bed curtains so violently, of any chamber in which I was a resident," she complained, that "I often wish that I could exchange those large windows (altho in the summer, nothing can be more agreeable) for the little closely chincked windows at Ashton"[19] All too soon, another fierce wind would have far more serious consequences. Even so, it was Jefferson who had to initiate the correspondence concerning the disaster it occasioned. On February 17, 1825, he wrote Francis:

We heard some time ago indirectly & indistinctly thro your friends at Ashton of the injury sustained by your house at P. F. and I have waited in hopes you would inform me of the particulars that I might know how far I could help you. I will spare J. Hem. to you & his two aids and he can repair everything of wood as well or perhaps better than any body there. I understand that the roofs of the 2 N. W. rooms and Din. room are burnt. Are the Portico & stairway burnt? The joists of the S. rooms? The cornice of the Din. room? The doors & windows destroyed? Let me know this and every particular. If the joists are burnt you will have to get others sawed at Capt. Martin's, while his mill has water to spare. I used to cut & haul him stocks, and he sawed one half for the [?]. Those for the D. Room had better not be sawed till J. H. comes up which will be as soon as I hear from you & he has finished a necessary job here.[20]

Jefferson's staccato listing of questions he wanted answered, so unlike the measured cadences in his usual writings, indicates just how concerned he was and, as he said, just how indistinct were the reports he had received from Elizabeth's family. Fortunately, as he soon learned, the damage was not as great as he had feared. A chagrined Francis wrote back on February 25, making excuses for not having written first:

I should have written to you sooner, my dr. grandfather, and given all the particulars of our late accident, had I not supposed them already detailed by Elizabeth, who writes every mail to some one of your family. It occurred during the last snow, which by its depth induced me to burn the chimnies

become very foul from long neglect. The wind it seems had blown the snow off in several places, and in two of these the fire caught: one under the balustrade and the other at the bottom of the platform, which supports the top railing. The first notice given us of the fire was the houses's filling with smoke. I ran up to the top immediately & thought all over, for the fire was burning rapidly under the balustrade and platform, and except the hostler my hands a mile off shut up in a tobacco house: it was nearly an hour before we had any help, and in that time we had scarcely got the railing down and floor off to come at the fire, but it was soon extinguished on the arrival of sufficient force. And now to the damages which I am glad to say are not as serious as you apprehend. 2000 shingles with some of the sheeting were burnt and torn off the n. w. corner. The balustrade in the same quarter burnt and cut down. The entire railing at top nearly destroyed. The platform and shingles under it in the same quarter burnt and pulled off. The cornice of the dining room was saved by the thickness of the plaistering, tho a large hole over the fire place is burnt in the ceiling. This I believe is the total damage sustained at present.

Having assumed that Jefferson's carpenters were engaged, Francis had seen to having the roof repaired "in a temporary manner with slabs, and had intended to make my carpenter tho' a rough hand, reshingle the whole if you think it desirable, but the balustrade and railing are I am afraid beyond his art." Though he did not say as much, Francis must have thought that, as long as Jefferson had offered the help of John Hemings and his two assistants, he would report on other matters that needed attention; ones that had no connection at all with the fire, which had centered on the opposite side of the house. Consequently, he added that "the terrace too is entirely gone. The joists and floor are rotted completely, and nothing but an entire renewal can render the offices again habitable." No wonder his wife had reported the previous summer that she could not bear to send her sister Harriet to the wet offices. In closing, Francis, having apparently finished reading at least the first of his law books, asked Jefferson if he would "take my Coke and give me the value in other books?"[21]

Jefferson did not reply to Francis's letter until April 6, but had good reason for waiting so long: "The difficulty with which I write, my aversion to it, and the satiating dose which is forced upon me by an overwhelming correspondence," were part of the reason. So was the fact that "John Hemings and his two aids have been engaged in covering this house [Monticello] with tin which is not yet finished." Although he didn't mention it in his letter, another reason for his delay was the fact that he had been busy seeing to affairs at the university, which had opened, at long last, on March 7, 1825. At any rate, Jefferson reported that he was "glad to learn the damage to your house by the fire was less considerable than I had supposed," and promised to send John Hemings and his aides "as soon as I can accompany them, which shall be as soon as the roads become practicable." He suggested that Francis do nothing yet to repair the terrace, as "we can make the gutters in a different way which will for ever protect the joists from decay." He also promised to ask "Colo. Peyton to send up tin for covering the dwelling house." As for the law books, after offering several suggestions, he concluded that Francis should do "as best suits you. It would be indiff't to me."[22] His indifference may have been due to his realization that Francis was obviously not terribly serious about continuing his law studies.

A month after he wrote Francis, Jefferson addressed Bernard Peyton on the subject of repairing Poplar Forest: "I must pray you to send to Lynchburg 15 boxes of tin addressed to F. Eppes by the first boats. I shall hope to find them there the 3rd or 4th week of this month [May] when I expect to be there, and I also request you to procure and send to me here by the 1st waggon a quarter cask of the best Sicily Madeira." Ten days later, Peyton announced that he had just received the tin, and had sent it off to Lynchburg, "marked for 'Francis Eppes' & consigned it to Mr. Archibald Robertson." Unfortunately, he reported, the price had now risen from eleven dollars, the cost of Jefferson's last order, to fourteen dollars per box[23] (fig. 96).

Jefferson's plan to go to Poplar Forest in the third or fourth week of May 1825 was contingent on yet another wedding at Monticello. On May 27, 1825, Ellen, following her younger sister Virginia's lead by some eight months, was wed to Joseph Coolidge, Jr., of Boston. Though she was soon to move to New England, she would remain in constant communication with her family. As for the effect her parting had on her grandfather, Virginia reported: "I fear he misses you sadly every evening when he takes his seat in one of the campeachy chairs, & he looks so solitary & the empty chair on the opposite side of the door is such a melancholy sight to us all, that one or the other of us, is sure to go & occupy it, though we can not possibly fill the vacancy you have left

in his society."[24] When the Coolidges left for their journey northward in June, Jefferson noted in his Memorandum Book: "Gave Ellen Coolidge for pocket money 100 D." A few weeks after Ellen's departure, Jefferson became a great-grandfather again. On July 4, John Wayles Eppes II, the second child of Francis and Elizabeth, was born at the Eppeses' ancestral home, Eppington.

By that time, Jefferson had apparently given up the idea of going to Poplar Forest. On July 11, he entered in his Memorandum Book: "J. Hemings by F. Eppes hhd. xp. 4.25." John Hemings was again on his way to Bedford, to take charge of the repairs following the fire. As in times past, the correspondence that followed between Hemings and Jefferson chronicles the progress and extent of the work. Hemings wrote first, on July 23, 1825, announcing: "We begin to tin the west side of the house and we have used 5 1/2 boxis We shal in a few days finish that side except the Potcos the rouft is so ruff that I am fost to imploy both of the boys." By August, Hemings was in need of more tin: "Dere Sir I hop you ar well We have got through the 15 boxis of tin and it will take 4 boxis more to finish the house I hope you have got information of before by Mr. F. Eppes."[25] Apparently he had, as Jefferson had already placed an order with Bernard Peyton for four more boxes, which were shipped to Lynchburg on August 7.

Hemings's letter of August 11 provides an extraordinarily valuable bit of information—in a single misspelled word—about the original aspect of the house at Poplar Forest: "We should go about perparing the chines railing & puting up the ornaments of the hall." The well-known drawing by John Neilson (see endpapers) shows no railing on the flat platform at the top of the roof. Francis Eppes had spoken of a top railing in his letter to Jefferson regarding the damage caused by the fire, but Hemings's letter is the only reference known to identify it as Chinese, or at least "chines." The pattern, which Jefferson termed "Chinese railing," was one he used extensively at both Monticello and the university. After telling Jefferson of the railing that he was "about perparing," Hemings reported that "Marster F. Epps was saying something about tining the flat rouff over the hall [dining room] you and him can descide it between you how it shol be don Sir plese to send the tin as soon as you can the flat rouft will take 3 boxes. That is 7 in all. Theirs tin in Linchburg at 15 1/2 Dollars which is much nearer if it could be got."[26]

Jefferson summarily dismissed Francis's suggestion

about tinning the flat roof in his response to Hemings: "The covering the rooflets of the flat top with tin would be a very useless expense, because shingles will turn the water as well, and it would be no guard against fire as a plank floor is to be laid over them." Even though John Hemings was prepared to put up "the ornaments of the hall," after "perparing the chines railing," the more realistic Jefferson probably realized that the exterior work would take all the time he had allotted for Hemings's labor that fall. He consequently advised him:

You will have to make up your mind to go once more to Bedford, to put up the entablature of the parlour. You know that the carved members are done, and the ornaments of the frieze ready. Before you come away examine the plank on hand of what we got for that cornice, and give Mr. Eppes a bill of what will be wanting to finish it, that it may be got at once and seasoned. Considering how dear and distant heart pine is, you had better lay the floor of the office terras with oak, which is as good and can be had at home. I believe you have the drawings. We may be able to do this work next summer perhaps. Your friends here are well and I wish you well.[27]

Hemings's next letter was not addressed to Jefferson, but to another member of the family, Septimia Randolph, who was then eleven years old. She had just written Hemings, who replied:

Your letter came to me on the 23rd. inst. Happy was I to embrez it to see you take it upon your self to writ to me and let me know how you Grandpapa was. I am very fearsome to hear that he is no worst. I hope you is well and all the family. Give my love to all your brothers. Georg with Randolph specially. I should gite don the house on Tuesday that is tining it. We have all the teeraste to do yet wich is one hundred feet Long and 22 feet 8 inches wide. Yesterday we just had one lode of the stuff brought home for the gutters and that is 25 miles off where it came from. I am in hope I shall be ale to com home by the 25 of November. If life last.[28]

Why Hemings thought his young correspondent would want to know the exact dimensions of the "teeraste" on which he was working must remain a mystery. Later investigation at the site has proved his dimensions to have been extremely accurate. In fact, he was more accurate than Jefferson, who on one occasion had mistakenly given the length of his wing of offices (which the terrace covered) as one hundred and ten feet long.[29] Hemings's notation that the terrace was "22 feet 8 inches wide" is the only known documentation of that fact, and again it accords well with later archeological investigation.

On September 18 Hemings answered Jefferson's letter of August 17. His work had been "thrown back 10 days" by the delay of the tin and other supplies, primarily the "gutter stuff," but he had accomplished a great deal nonetheless. Unfortunately, the terrace, which he had told Septimia he still had to do, would "have to stand until sumother time" as there was no plank remaining for it. Hemings concluded his report by telling Jefferson that he hoped "by the next to be able to let you no when I shall finich and when to send for me." Ten days later, he did just that, and he was as anxious to return as he ever had been: "Sir I hope this may find you well with all my hart for it is my wish I shall be don my work on saturday the 7th of October.... Therefore I must beg you to send for me Mr. Epps has convinced me that he cant git the plank for the floors. I should pack up on Sunday 8th of October and be ready to set out for Monticello on Monday by daylight. Sir please to order the mules and gear and the old one off. You please for me to ride."[30] Though no further correspondence seems to exist on the subject, one can be sure that Jefferson sent the mule and cart from Monticello for John Hemings to ride home in, after another job well done.

Fig. 96 Among Jefferson's papers is this series of sketches, accompanying an identification sheet labeled "Instructions for covering buildings with the tinned copper & leaded iron sheets by Charles Wyatt." Problems with the leaking roof at Poplar Forest continually plagued him — as well as later owners. *(Coolidge Collection, Massachusetts Historical Society)*

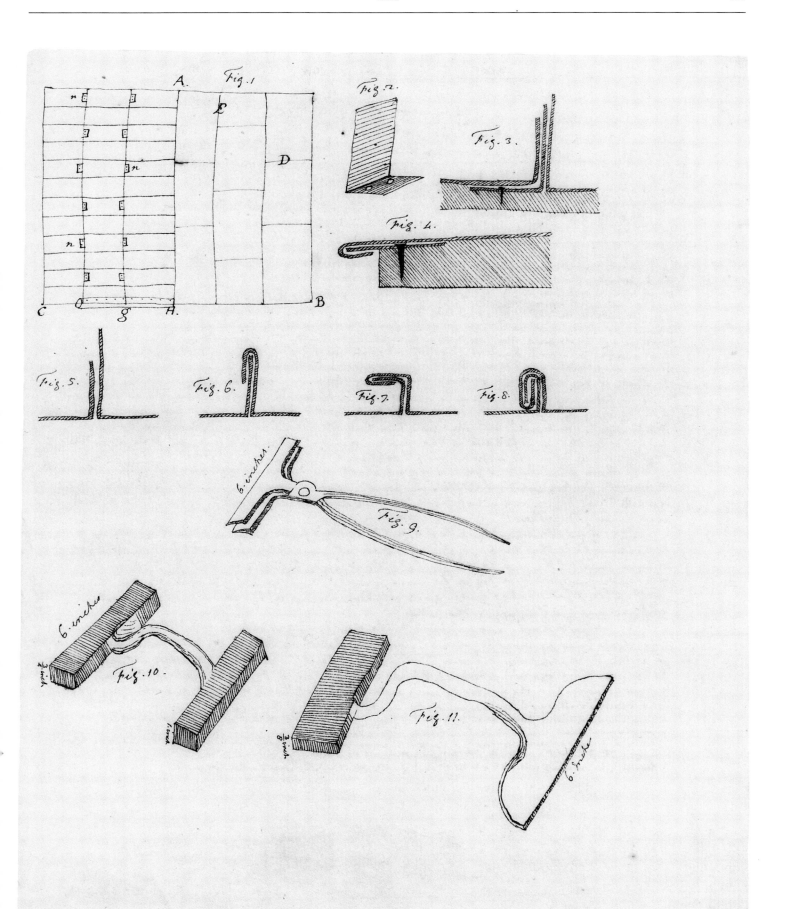

Fig. 1.

Fig. 2.

Fig. 3.

Fig. 4.

Fig. 5.

Fig. 6.

Fig. 7.

Fig. 8.

Fig. 9.

Fig. 10.

Fig. 11.

"NOT EVEN A LOG HUT TO PUT MY HEAD INTO"

(1826)

In January 1826 Jefferson wrote Joseph Cabell, then serving as a senator in the Virginia General Assembly, advising him that his grandson Thomas J. Randolph "attends the Legislature on a subject of ultimate importance to my future happiness. My own debts were considerable, and a loss was added to them of $20,000 by indorsement for a friend. My application to the legislature is to dispose of property for payment in a way which, bringing a fair price for it, may pay my debts, and leave a living for myself in my old age, and leave something for my family." For particulars, he referred the senator to his grandson, and added that he hoped Cabell would give his application "the attention which you may think the case will justify. To me it is almost a question of life and death."[1]

By now, even the eternally optimistic Jefferson realized that a dependence on the occasional sale of lands or slaves, much less the annual income from his crops, would never free him from his increasing debt. Things had come to a terrible pass, as Martha reported to Ellen, now in Boston:

The property in Bedford upon trial it was ascertained could not be sold without a sacrifice so great as to defeat the object intended. It became necessary to sell the only property that would probably command a price and Monticello was devoted. Francis was so much dissatisfied with the house at Poplar Forest that he offered it to Jefferson [Randolph] for $5,000 to be paid in land or money; the arrangement made by him and fully acquiesced in by me was that we should go to Bedford, retaining only the necessary furniture for that house, and a small but effective household of servants and sell the whole property here and as many negroes as would pay the debts.[2]

Her father's reaction to the plan, Martha continued, "was as we foresaw dreadful. He said he had lived too long, that his death would be an advantage to the family. But Jefferson [Randolph] easily convinced him that under existing circumstances it would, independent of our love for him, be a calamity of frightful magnitude, that his life was as necessary to the interests of his grandchildren and myself as it was precious to our hearts." It was then, at the depth of despair, that "the idea of the lottery came like an inspiration from the realms of bliss to my father." A portion of Jefferson's property would be offered as the grand prize, and with the sale of tickets

throughout the country, enough money would be realized to provide payment of "his debts, a maintenance for the family, the means of educating the boys, and a home for myself and children that might be unprovided for and last tho not least, the undisturbed possession of Monticello during his precious life."[3]

As her desiderata might indicate, Martha had little or nothing of her own to fall back on. By now, Thomas Mann Randolph, Jr., was virtually bankrupt and virtually estranged from his family. On January 2, 1826, Edgehill, where the Randolphs had lived in happier times, was sold at public auction, along with the slaves. The property was bought by none other than their son, Thomas Jefferson Randolph, who had to sell some of his own land and slaves to purchase it. It also fell on his strong shoulders to carry the burden of attending to the necessary details of the lottery, the first task being for the Virginia General Assembly to make it legal. That was the subject that drew him to Richmond in January 1826.

On February 3, 1826, John V. Mason, a legislator writing from Richmond, commented on what he saw as a "most astounding development.... Mr. Th. J. Randolph has been in town for some 10 or 12 days, and brings intelligence, that Mr. Jefferson's affairs are in a most ruinous condition.... The request which Mr. Jefferson makes, is by no means new. Similar benefits have been frequently extended by the Legislature — and I think the project, while I deplore its necessity, is not so objectionable." He predicted that the bill would "afford opportunity for much rancorous invection, and will, no doubt, meet no small opposition."[4] He was right, and the Monticello family spent agonizing days waiting as the assembly debated the proposal. For his part, Jefferson spent a portion of the time writing letters that are among the most personal and poignant he ever penned. On February 7, he again wrote Joseph Cabell:

I had hoped the length and character of my services might have prevented the fear in the legislature of the indulgence asked being quoted as a precedent in future cases, but I find no fault with their strict adherence to a rule generally useful, altho' relaxable in some cases under their discretion, of which they are the proper judges. If it can be yielded in my case I can save the house of Monticello and a farm adjoining to end my days in and bury my bones. If not, I must sell house and all here, and carry my family to Bedford, where I have not even a log hut to put my head into.[5]

The next day, he wrote Jefferson Randolph, still in Richmond trying to curry votes: "You kindly encourage me to keep up my spirits but oppressed with disease, debility, age and embarrassed affairs, this is difficult." Whatever the result would be, though, he thanked his grandson for his efforts: "Yourself particularly, dear Jefferson, I consider as the greatest of the Godsends which heaven has granted me. Without you what could I do under the difficulties now environing me.... And should this my last request be granted, I may yet close with a cloudless sun a long and serene day of life. Be assured, my dear Jefferson, that I have a just sense of the part you have contributed to this, and that I bear you unmeasured affection."[6]

On February 17 Jefferson wrote James Madison: "You will have seen in the newspapers some proceedings in the legislature, which have cost me much mortification. My own debts had become considerable but not beyond the effect of some lopping of property which would have been little felt, when our friend W. C. N. gave me the coup de grace. Ever since that I have been paying 1200 D. a year interest on his debt, which, with my own, was absorbing so much of my annual income, as that the maintenance of my family was making deep and rapid inroads on my capital, and had already done it." As he had told Cabell, Jefferson expressed to Madison the possibility that, if the bill failed to pass, "I must sell everything here, perhaps considerably in Bedford, move thither with my family, where I have not even a log-hut to put my head into, and whether ground for burial will depend on the depredations which, under the form of sales, shall have been committed on my property." He then apologized for burdening Madison with these details, but noted:

Pains are lessened by communication with a friend. The friendship which has subsisted between us, now half a century, and the harmony of our political principles and pursuits, have been sources of constant happiness to me thro' that long period. And if I remove beyond the reach of attentions to the University, or beyond the bourne of life itself, as I soon must, it is a comfort to leave that institution under your care, and an assurance that it will not be wanting ... To myself you have been a pillar of support thro' life. Take care of me when dead, and be assured that I shall leave with you my last affections.[7]

At last, on February 20, the legislature approved the bill. It carried the House by more than a two-to-one majority, and in the Senate, where Cabell served, the vote was a gratifying "ayes thirteen, nays four."[8] Thus, Jefferson, Martha, and the children were absolved from having to sell Monticello and move to Poplar Forest.

Three days after the lottery bill passed, but apparently before he knew it had been approved, Francis Eppes wrote his grandfather the most effusive letter he ever composed:

It was with infinite pain My Dr. Grandfather, that I saw your application to the legislature; the first information which reached me, of the immediate pressure of your difficulties: and I write as well to express, My unfeigned grief, and to assure you, that I return to your funds with the utmost good will, the portion of property which you designed for me; and which I should always have considered as yours, even had it been, legally secured to me. As long as, I was able to consider, the gift, of no evil consequence to yourself, and as the equivalent of the land intended for my mother, the possession was grateful both to my feelings, and to My sense of propriety: but now, when I learn that after the payment of your debts, but little of your property will be left, I hope that under such, or even better circumstances, you cannot do me the injustice to suppose, that I could even consent to retain the smallest portion. You have been to me ever, an affectionate, and tender Father, and you shall find me ever, a loving, and devoted son, what that son would do, I will, under all circumstances; and I now with the greatest alacrity relinquish, that competence which you so kindly gave and I do assure you, if there be sincerity in human nature, that it is with greatest satisfaction, and that I shall remain ever, as deeply indebted, as though your kind intentions had been completely fulfilled.

In addition to offering to return Poplar Forest to Jefferson, Francis also announced that "in a few months more, with the knowledge already acquired, I feel confident of obtaining admittance to the bar." He closed his letter with this sentiment: "May God bless and long preserve you My dearest Grandfather, my best friend, with most sincere love your grandson, Frans. Eppes." Francis added a postscript to his long letter: "Elizabeth is well and joins me in love to yourself and the family. May I ask, what your scheme is, for the lottery?"[9]

Somehow his concern might ring truer if one didn't know that he wanted to sell Poplar Forest to Jefferson Randolph because he was "so much dissatisfied with the house." Jefferson responded on March 9: "The sacrifice you offer to my comfort is such as few would be capable of making and is the more deeply felt in proportion as it is more rare." He quickly added that Francis, along with "the public generally," had been led into error "by a first and incorrect annunciation of the bill I asked. It was called a bill for the sale *of my property* for the payment of my debts instead of a bill for the sale of *a portion* of my property for that purpose. The very object of the bill was to protect me from the necessity of selling the whole, which might have been sacrificed by sales under the hammer." With the lottery, he could select what he wished to sell, and would be assured a fair price. While the lottery would in no way lessen the tender feelings he had for Francis's offer, "it relieves me completely from any necessity of availing myself of it. . . . All now depends on the sale of the tickets, if that results fav'bly as the newspapers would give us to hope, I shall not be left in want." He closed by suggesting that Francis might combine the vocation of farmer and lawyer, though the latter "need be of no consequence of the state of my affairs." Jefferson advised that it would be good to have "within himself a resource against the losses of property. . . . Nobody more than the farmer feels the convenience of some little supplement for current calls and contingencies."[10] How well he knew.

After learning of the successful passage of the lottery bill, Jefferson Randolph made plans to embark on a trip along the east coast to sell tickets, while Thomas Jefferson, "being of sound mind and in my ordinary state of health," wrote his last will and testament. Its first item gave "to my grandson Francis Eppes, son of my dear deceased daughter Mary Eppes, in fee simple, all that part of my lands at Poplar Forest" that were then described in the text. In addition, he once again wrote of the land promised so long ago to John Wayles Eppes, but made it clear that this was not the property being willed to Francis:

And having, in a former correspondence with my deceased son in law John W. Eppes contemplated laying off for him with remainder to my grandson Francis, a certain portion in the Southern part of my lands in Bedford and Campbell, which I afterwards found to be generally more indifferent than I had

supposed, & therefore determined to change its location for the better; now to remove all doubt, if any could arise on a purpose merely voluntary & unexecuted, I hereby declare that what I have herein given to my sd. grandson Francis is instead of, and not additional to what I had formerly contemplated.

Then, and only then, did he add the sentence: "I subject all my other property to the payment of my debts in the first place."[11]

Whether Jefferson suspected then that the lottery would not prove successful is, of course, a matter only for speculation. What is known is that his will made certain that the only surviving son of his "dear deceased daughter Mary Eppes" would be provided for. Poplar Forest could not now be claimed and sold to help settle any debts that might still be outstanding at his death.

The next day, in a codicil to his will, Jefferson bequeathed a gold watch to each of his grandchildren, and freed two of the men who had played such an important part over the years in the Poplar Forest story:

I give to my good, affectionate and faithful servant Burwell his freedom, and the sum of three hundred Dollars to buy necessaries to commence his trade of painter and glazier, or to use otherwise as he pleases. I give also to my good servants John Hemings and Joe Fossett, their freedom at the end of one year after my death: and to each of them respectively all the tools of their respective shops or callings: and it is my will that a comfortable log-house be built for each of the three servants so emancipated on some part of my lands convenient to them with respect to the residence of their wives, and to Charlottesville and the University, where they will be mostly employed and reasonably convenient also to the interests of the proprietor of the lands; of which houses I give the use of one, with a curtilage of an acre to each, during his life or personal occupation thereof.[12]

Jefferson also bequeathed his papers in this codicil, and wisely designated Thomas Jefferson Randolph as their recipient: "My papers of business going of course to him as my executor, all others of a literary or other character I give to him as of his own property."[13]

Jefferson Randolph left on his trip in early April, and on the twenty-fifth of the month reported from New York on his efforts. Though he tried to be optimistic, he could give neither good nor bad news: "I have returned thus far on my way home and can yet report nothing definitely. Some feeble attempts have been made here and in

Boston to raise money by subscription. They have neither succeeded or failed. . . . The prospectus of the lottery will be published in the course of next week, and tickets offered every where at once for sale. I am told by everybody they will sell rapidly. . . . I will write from Philadelphia by the 5 or 6 of next month when I hope to report progress." Five days later, earlier than he had predicted, he reported from Philadelphia with much the same news. Years later, Randolph's daughter Sarah recalled that her father's efforts had met with more success than he perhaps had realized at the time: "Without effort, Philip Hone, the Mayor of New York, raised $8,500, which he transmitted to Mr Jefferson on behalf of the citizens of New York; from Philadelphia he received $5000, and from Baltimore $3000."[14] By the time any such news arrived at Monticello, it was too late to be of much use.

On June 23, 1826, Francis wrote what would prove to be his last letter to his grandfather. With none of the niceties he had shown in his previous letter offering the return of Poplar Forest, he began immediately with the subject at hand:

Knowing that all your pavilions at the University have tin coverings, I write to learn whether they have ever leaked, and if so what method of prevention has been used. Our roof here was perfectly close until about mid winter. It then began to leak not in one but a hundred places, and from that time I have endeavored to determine the cause without effect. . . . The plaistering of the parlour is so entirely wet every rain, that I begin to fear it will fall in. . . . Your room is nearly as bad and the others leak more and more in every rain. The hall is in fact, the only dry room in the house.

He then took the occasion to inform Jefferson about other damage caused by "three of the most destructive rains ever known in this neighborhood. The tobacco hills on flat land were entirely swept off. Mine were hilled over twice, and the third swept off soil and all. I count my loss equal to a good hogshead. Your loss would more than double that in first rate tobacco; for the land was heavily manured, and nothing but the clay is left behind. The wheat is fairly buried in the mud every where. My love to all, my dearest love to you my dear grandfather."[15]

Given the long time it then took letters to travel

between Bedford and Albemarle, Jefferson may never have seen this one. Or, if it arrived at Monticello in time for him to have seen it, his family may never have shown it to him. One can only hope that this was the case. It was written on June 23, only eleven days before Jefferson died, and the day before he first summoned his doctor, Robley Dunglison, to attend him in what would prove to be his final illness. The subject of leaky roofs, though a familiar one, was not one that would concern Jefferson anymore.

The day he called Dr. Dunglison to come to Monticello, Jefferson wrote a letter to Roger Weightman, mayor of the nation's capital. Weightman had written Jefferson earlier, inviting him, as he had the other surviving signers of the Declaration of Independence, to "honor the city with your presence" on the occasion of the "fiftieth anniversary of American Independence." Should he be able to attend, Weightman promised that "a special deputation will be sent to accompany you from your residence to this city and back again to your home."[16]

In responding, Jefferson regretted that his illness would prevent him from attending, and then added a benediction to the celebration of the Fourth of July, 1826, or, for that matter, for all years to come:

I should indeed, with particular delight, have met and exchanged there, congratulations personally, with the small band, the remnant of that host of worthies, who joined with us, on that day, in the bold and doubtful election we were to make, for our country, between submission, or the sword; and to have enjoyed with them the consolatory fact that our fellow citizens, after half a century of experience and prosperity, continue to approve the choice we made. May it be to the world what I believe it will be, (to some parts sooner, to others later, but finally to all) the signal of arousing men to burst the chains, under which monkish ignorance and superstition had persuaded them to bind themselves, and to assume the blessings & security of self government. The form which we have substituted restores the free right to the unbounded exercise of reason and freedom of opinion. All eyes are opened, or opening, to the rights of man.[17]

His own eyes, of course, had been open to the rights of man throughout his life. They closed at Monticello at 12:50 P.M. on July 4, 1826, fifty years to the day from the adoption of the Declaration of Independence.

Fig. 97 Jefferson's bedroom at Monticello. Here, shortly after noon on July 4, 1826, Thomas Jefferson died. Jefferson's two alcove beds at Poplar Forest were similar to the one shown here. *(Robert C. Lautman, 1992, for Monticello, The Thomas Jefferson Memorial Foundation, Inc.)*

"WHAT SAY YOU TO FLORIDA"
OR
"GOOD NIGHT OLD VIRGINIA"
(1826–29)

When Jefferson's will was probated, Francis Eppes became the legal owner of Poplar Forest. His Poplar Forest, however, was a much-reduced tract from the one that Thomas Jefferson had first known. Jefferson's will specifically devised a certain portion of the acreage to him, which, according to a survey Eppes undertook a year later, amounted to 1,074 3/4 acres.[1] Jefferson had transferred other portions of his Bedford and Campbell property to Thomas Jefferson Randolph as part of a complex arrangement involving the renegotiation of the still-outstanding Nicholas loan.[2] Any remaining property would also go to Randolph to be sold to settle the remaining debts from Jefferson's estate. Complicating the situation further, both the Eppes and the Randolph tracts continued under the rubric of Poplar Forest, and were so identified in the numerous sales that followed Jefferson's death.

In addition to the lands, Thomas Jefferson Randolph, as executor, also had to tend to the personal property left in Bedford and Campbell. On August 1, 1826, three gentlemen were sworn in to appraise the Campbell County effects: Archibald Robertson, Jefferson's former Lynchburg factor; William Gough, the last of his many overseers at Poplar Forest; and Henry Langhorne, whose wife was the daughter of Jefferson's old friend James Steptoe. Their report, submitted on December 13, was recorded by the Albemarle County Court on New Year's Day, 1827. First on the list were twenty-eight slaves — twelve men, eleven women, and five boys — whose total value was given as $7,090. Following was a tremendously detailed and varied list of items, including, among other things, six work horses, three ploughs, sixty head of hogs, six crocks, and one tin pan. Including the value of the slaves, the total value of the Campbell personal property was given as $9,229.25.[3] Although no similar appraisal seems to have survived for the equivalent personal property in Bedford County, one was made, as Francis noted in a letter to his cousin the same December day that the Campbell commissioners made their report: "The value of the perishable 'stuff' on the Bedford side amounts to $10,259, some cents: that on the Campbell side not yet valued but is supposed to be greater."[4] Unfor-

Fig. 98 Attempting to obtain some of his grandfather's effects after his death, Francis Eppes was especially anxious to secure a bracket, or brackets. This elegant mahogany bracket, which descended through the family who purchased Poplar Forest from him, is now at Monticello, and may well be the one that Eppes acquired. *(Monticello, The Thomas Jefferson Memorial Foundation, Inc.)*

tunately, it wasn't, but together the value of Jefferson's personal property in the portions of Poplar Forest under Randolph's control came to over $19,000, almost a fifth of the $107,273.63 debt owed by his estate at the time of his death.[5]

Even before the appraisers submitted their reports, Jefferson Randolph had arranged to sell the Poplar Forest lands he held, along with the personal property, to help settle his grandfather's estate. In November 1826, local newspapers carried notices: "Will be sold on the premises, on the first day of January, 1827, that well known and valuable estate called Poplar Forest, lying in the counties of Bedford and Campbell, the property of Thomas Jefferson, dec. within eight miles of Lynchburg, and three from New London; also about 70 likely and valuable negroes, with stock, crops, etc. The terms of sale will be accommodating and made known previous to the day." The advertisement, which also announced a similar sale to be held at Monticello on January 15, was signed: "Thomas J. Randolph, Executor of Th. Jefferson, Dec." On Jan. 25, 1827, writing from Monticello, Nicholas Trist told James Madison: "The sales both in Bedford and here, have been *very good*."[6]

Even though Francis Eppes was by then also planning to sell *his* Poplar Forest, he continued to supplement the utensils and furnishings that he had inherited with the house. On November 26, 1826, he purchased a number of items from one William Smithson. Included in his bill of $11.75 were a frying pan costing 65 cents and a dining table that cost $5.25. He also obtained several of his grandfather's effects when they were sold at Monticello in January 1827. In a letter written that month to Nicholas Trist, he asked: "Will you direct the bearer where to find the clock, lamps, *brackets*, etc. The map if Cornelia does not want it, may be sent also. Repeat to her that I did not mean to interfere, but Jeff [Thomas Jefferson Randolph] was so pressing you know!" The brackets, or bracket, were apparently especially important to Francis, and in the first of two postscripts to his letter, he reminded Trist: "Don't forget the *Bracket*"[7] (fig. 98).

By this time the lottery was virtually moribund. After Jefferson's death, few Americans were willing to sub-

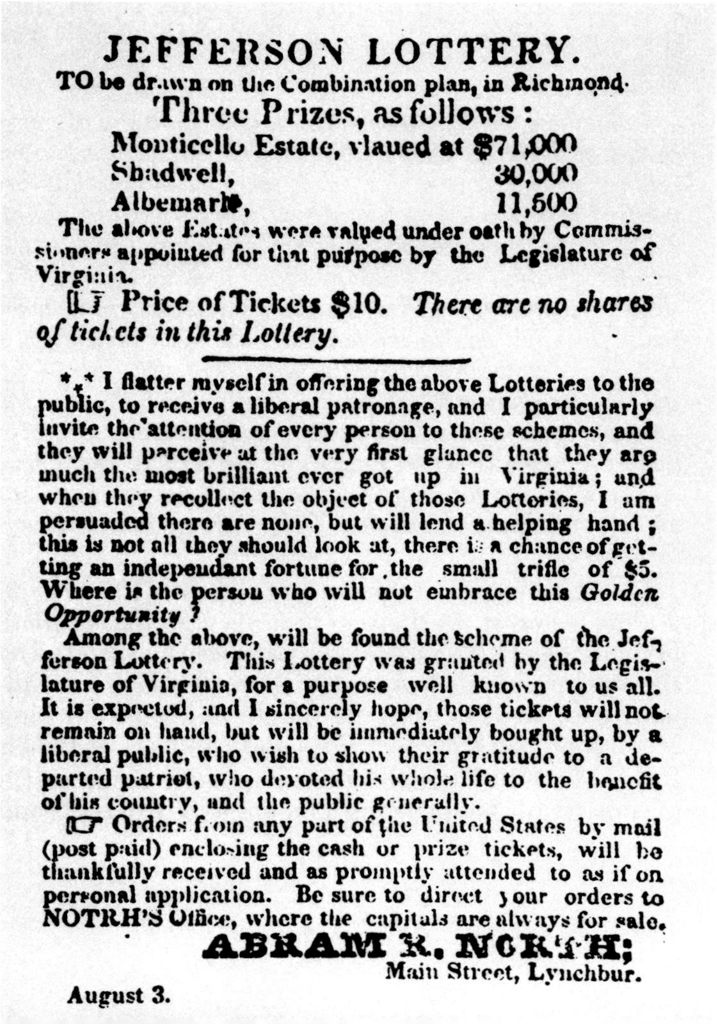

JEFFERSON LOTTERY.

TO be drawn on the Combination plan, in Richmond.

Three Prizes, as follows:

Monticello Estate, vlaued at	$71,000
Shadwell,	30,000
Albemarle,	11,500

The above Estates were valued under oath by Commissioners appointed for that purpose by the Legislature of Virginia.

☞ Price of Tickets $10. *There are no shares of tickets in this Lottery.*

⁂ I flatter myself in offering the above Lotteries to the public, to receive a liberal patronage, and I particularly invite the attention of every person to these schemes, and they will perceive at the very first glance that they are much the most brilliant ever got up in Virginia; and when they recollect the object of those Lotteries, I am persuaded there are none, but will lend a helping hand; this is not all they should look at, there is a chance of getting an independant fortune for the small trifle of $5. Where is the person who will not embrace this *Golden Opportunity?*

Among the above, will be found the scheme of the Jefferson Lottery. This Lottery was granted by the Legislature of Virginia, for a purpose well known to us all. It is expected, and I sincerely hope, those tickets will not remain on hand, but will be immediately bought up, by a liberal public, who wish to show their gratitude to a departed patriot, who devoted his whole life to the benefit of his country, and the public generally.

☞ Orders from any part of the United States by mail (post paid) enclosing the cash or prize tickets, will be thankfully received and as promptly attended to as if on personal application. Be sure to direct your orders to NOTRH'S Office, where the capitals are always for sale.

ABRAM R. NORTH;
Main Street, Lynchbur.

August 3.

Fig. 99 Jefferson Lottery advertisement. The November 9, 1826, issue of the *Lynchburg Virginian* carried this announcement, which urged purchasers to buy tickets "to show their gratitude to a departed patriot." The advertisement had apparently been placed on August 3. *(Courtesy Jones Memorial Library, Lynchburg, Va.; photograph by Tom Graves, Jr., 1991)* scribe to a scheme whose primary purpose, that of eradicating his debt and ensuring him the tranquil old age he had so long desired, was no longer valid. In September 1826, Martha Randolph wrote Ellen that, although Jefferson "died tranquil under [the] belief" that the lottery would "leave his family independent," such would not be the case: "If they sell 1/2 the tickets the lottery will be drawn in December the 15th," but even if that many were sold, there would still be a debt.[8] On November 7, 1826, Francis wrote Nicholas Trist, having "received a letter from Jefferson [Randolph] a few days ago in which I learn the small chance of success to the lottery scheme. It was not unexpected."[9] Even so, an advertisement for the lottery ran in the *Lynchburg Virginian* two days later (fig. 99).

In his letter to Nicholas Trist acknowledging that he had learned the lottery would probably not succeed, Francis launched into a diatribe that soon became almost an obsession with him:

Many circumstances of late, have induced me to believe, that the liberality and generosity, and patriotism of the old Dominion, is on the wane.... Yankee notions, and Yankee practices, have wrought a thorough change in the public mind.... You may depend, that the settling of this hardhearted, copper souled race of tin pedlars, amongst us, has had a great effect in poisoning the public minds; and that added to the continued emigration of the old settlers from the state, and the more equal distribution of property, has smothered the flame which once burnt in our bosoms.

Francis invited the young Trists to come for a visit to Poplar Forest, echoing all too loudly Virginia's observation almost three years earlier about solitude and the screech owl: "I can offer you what you have so long desired—solitude and books—uninterrupted solitude, if you wish it. We are not much pestered with company I can assure you. There is not enough even for me, for I like that degree of sociability, which does not interfere with more important duties."[10] Obviously, Jefferson's extensive library at Poplar Forest was still in place, but one wonders how much use it was getting.

Had the Trists visited at this time, one topic of conversation would certainly have centered on a plan that was beginning to materialize in Francis's mind. Following his diatribe on the current situation in Virginia in his letter to Nicholas, he launched into a proposal that he hoped his cousins might entertain: "What say you to a *general* move to a more southern latitude. I want to go where I can make more money.... What say you to Florida, or Kentucki, or Tenessee, or Missouri? I will go anywhere so that we may all settle together: but from accounts lately received should greatly prefer E. Florida. I am told that money and health, are the spontaneous productions of that soil.... Here lies the road to wealth!

Bundle up, and let us leave our gullies to the Yankee pedlars, who covet them so much."[11]

Virginia and Nicholas didn't take Francis up on either of his offers: to visit them or to move to Florida. Instead, Cornelia did the family honors by coming for a visit in November 1826, and her letter to Ellen announcing the trip reveals the heavy hearts that burdened the entire family as they faced an unknown future: "I am about to make a visit which I have long had in contemplation, but now that I have an opportunity to do so, leave home with a very, very heavy heart; any time but this I would have gone willingly; it is to Poplar Forest." Later that month, Nicholas reported to James Madison: "We are still at the mountain [Monticello], having been detained by the repairs at Tufton. These being nearly completed, we shall move down early next week. Cornelia set out this morning to spend a month in Bedford—Mr. Randolph having made his journey down on a hard trotting horse for the purpose of taking her back with him in a gig." Near the end of the month, Mary J. Randolph wrote her sister Ellen Coolidge: "At last we have quitted Monticello.... Cornelia safely arrived at New London."[12]

Actually, Monticello was not yet entirely quitted, as Virginia and Nicholas would return, albeit only temporarily, to finish arrangements before its final sale. Perhaps surprisingly—because her letters were usually so much more prosaic than poetic—it was Elizabeth Eppes, Francis's wife, writing from Poplar Forest, who spoke most eloquently of the changes the family was facing:

I shudder sometimes when I contrast the dark and troubled period of the last 3 years with the uninterrupted peace, tranquility, and pleasure which dwelt there [at Monticello] formerly. Prosperous as to worldly affairs they could not be called, and there were some most trying circumstances in the whole course of their lives; but they neither saw nor felt these....sometimes ruffled, sometimes depressed, but never really unhappy, and to the farthest back I can remember, I have ever felt cheered and enlivened by my visits there—by the God-like benevolence and tranquility which shone in Mr. Jefferson's countenance and voice and manner; and the hope-inspiring presence—that mixture of tenderness, gentleness, and sprightliness for which my aunt was so remarkable. But alas that happiness is now fled. Those days are gone forever.[13]

During this time of trauma for the family, life went on at Poplar Forest. In the year that his grandfather died, Francis began his own Memoranda, perhaps inspired by the Memorandum Book that Jefferson had kept so assiduously for so long. In it, he sought to keep a running account of his farm operations and expenses at Poplar Forest (fig. 100). Though he was ultimately unsuccessful in consistently maintaining it for any length of time, and

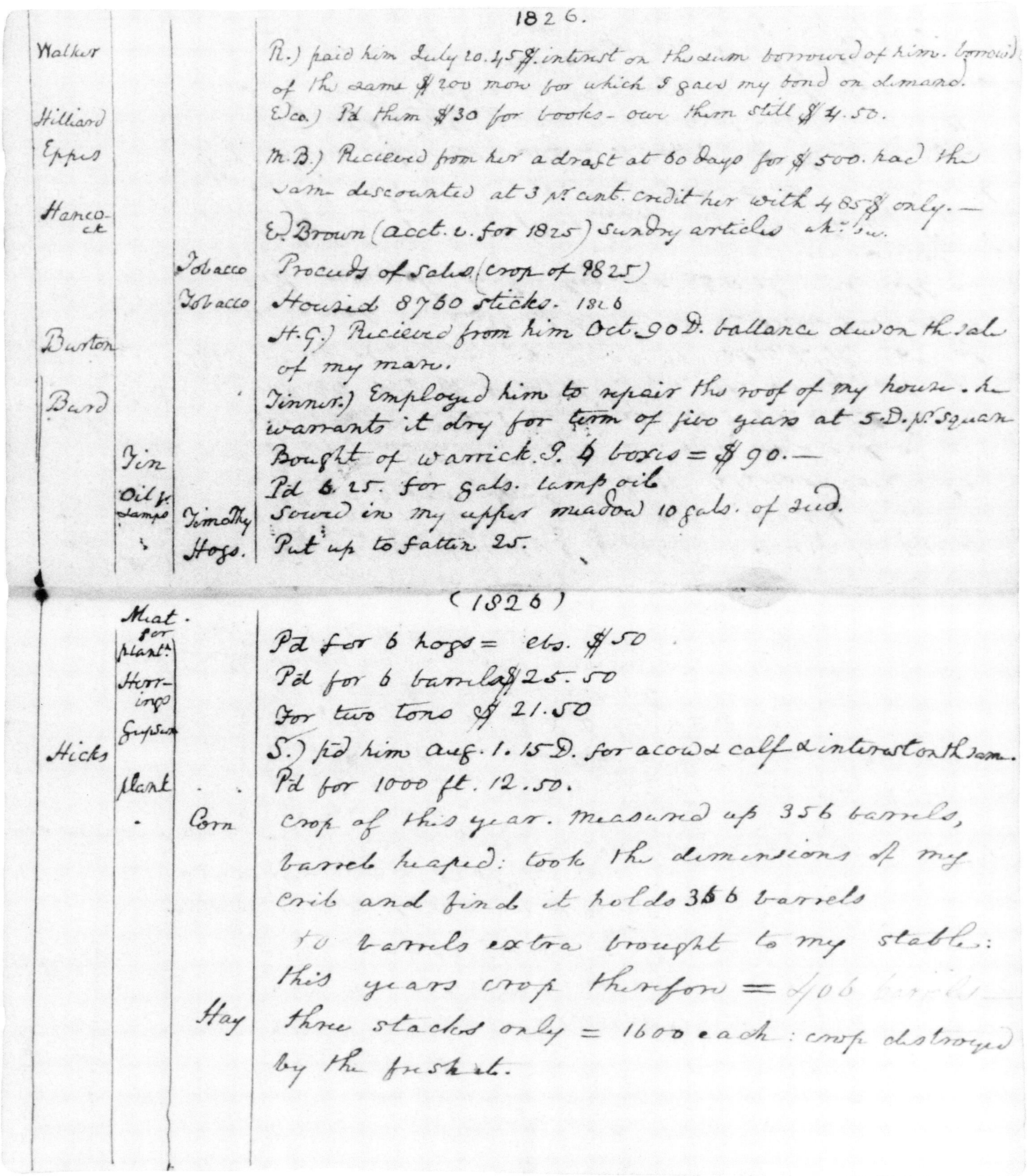

1826.

Walker		R.) paid him July 20. 45 $. interest on the sum borrowed of him. borrow'd of the same $ 200 more for which I gave my bond on demand.
Hilliard		Wca.) Pd them $30 for books- owe them still $ 4.50.
Eppes		M.B.) Recieved from her a draft at 60 days for $ 500. had the same discounted at 3 p. cent. credit her with 485$ only. —
Hancock		E. Brown (acct. v. for 1825) sundry articles ch'd. $w.
	Tobacco	Proceeds of sales (crop of 1825)
	Tobacco	Housed 8760 sticks. 1826
Burton		H.G.) Recieved from him Oct. 9 D. ballance due on the sale of my man.
Bard		Tinner.) Employed him to repair the roof of my house. he warrants it dry for term of five years at 5 D. p. square
Tin		Bought of warrick. I. 4 boxes = $ 90. —
Oil f. lamps		Pd 6.25. for gals. lamp oil
	Timothy	Sowed in my upper meadow 10 gals. of seed.
	Hogs.	Put up to fatten 25.

(1826)

Meat for plant.		Pd for 6 hogs = lbs. $50 .
Herrings		Pd for 6 barrels $ 25. 50
Gypsum		For two tons $ 21.50
plant		S.) pd him Aug. 1. 15 D. for a cow & calf & interest on th. sam.
Hicks		Pd for 1000 ft. 12.50.
	Corn	crop of this year. measured up 356 barrels, barrels heaped: took the dimensions of my crib and find it holds 356 barrels
		to barrels extra brought to my stable: this years crop therefore = 406 barrels
	Hay	three stacks only = 1600 each : crop destroyed by the freshet.

Fig. 100 A page from Francis Eppes's Memoranda. During the years he lived at Poplar Forest, Eppes kept this record of some of his activities and expenses. (*The Corporation for Jefferson's Poplar Forest*)

though he seldom gave exact dates, the entries that he did make are invaluable in documenting his efforts and activities during his brief tenure at Poplar Forest. One of his earliest notations, made in January 1826, recorded an agreement he made with one R. Tonny "to dig my ice house at $20 pr. month. He left me after 12 days work. due to him 8. D."[14] At least the young Eppeses would no longer have to depend, as Jefferson and his granddaughters had, on the neighbors to provide ice during the hot summer months, nor on "refrigerators" that failed to do their job.

As far as his farming efforts were concerned, Francis had no better luck than Jefferson had habitually experienced, especially with his tobacco crops and sales. The weather was responsible for the poor showing in 1826, as he noted in his Memoranda: "The early part of this season was extremely wet. between the 20th of May and the 20th of June we had six freshets, the last immensely destructive. from that time till our tobacco was cut the season proved unusually dry. We had a few light showers but not enough for tobacco; as in many places it lost its colour and never reached any size." He was more candid in a letter he wrote to his cousin Thomas Jefferson Ran dolph on June 8, 1827, in which he used the failure of his tobacco crop to launch into his favorite tirade: "Quality of the tobacco thin, short, and yellow. Rich tobacco such as I have seen Papa sell at $15, selling at $6 because it is dark brown! Damn the crop say I, and the State to boot. Our staple is worth nothing certain, is always fluctuating, and the population, with the exception of ourselves,

in all honour and reverence be it spoken, is totally changed. . . . I want much to see you. to have a little chate on the subject of emigration."[15]

The subject was one that was also on the minds of others in the extended family. In April, Francis's wife had written Jefferson Randolph's wife: "Your letter has thrown us all into a *ferment* my dearest Jane, and 'emigration' has been the sole topic of conversation, the one engrossing subject of our sleeping and waking thoughts, since the moment it was received." She almost predicted what her husband soon said about the crops, and echoed his feelings about the house:

These gullied worn out fields, and this unfinished leaking hull of a house, have become more than ever distasteful to both Francis and myself, and we needed little before to render them altogether odious. Tobacco is the only thing which can be made here, and after vast labour and expense, in raising and manufacturing the vile weed, and aquiring both skill and judgement in the business, to find still that no profit must be expected, is disheartening indeed, and Francis who began with sanguine hopes on the subject is now as much wearied and sickened with a planters life, as I who from the first abhored it.[16]

There was more to her revelation that the house was an "unfinished leaking hull" than might at first be supposed. Francis's letter to his grandfather on the subject of leaky roofs, written only days before Jefferson's death, had obviously gone unanswered, and with Jefferson's death, the ever-faithful John Hemings, who had been

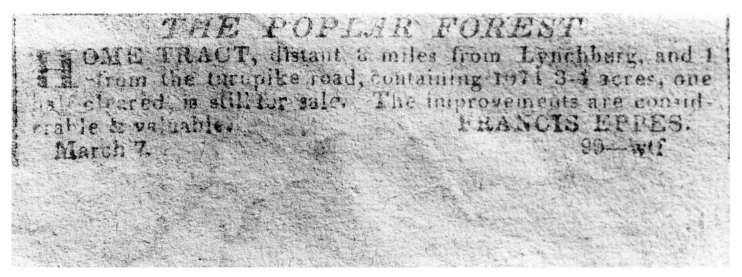

Fig. 101 In the spring of 1828, Francis Eppes placed an advertisement to run in the *Richmond Enquirer*, announcing that the Poplar Forest "home tract" was "still for sale." *(Courtesy Jones Memorial Library, Lynchburg, Va., photograph by Tom Graves, Jr., 1991)*

called so often to go to Poplar Forest upon such emergencies, was soon to be a free man. Consequently Francis had to attend to the repair himself. A short notation in his Memoranda records that he employed Burd, a tinner, "to repair the roof of my house. He warrants it dry for term of five years at 5. D. pr. square." The tin was "bought of Warrick," and Francis paid a total of ninety dollars for the material. Francis didn't date his Memoranda entry, but that it was done in the early fall is evidenced by his letter of September 21, 1826, to Jefferson Randolph: "I have just had a workman here examining the roof of the house. There appears to be a radical fault in the putting on of the tin which can be remedied only, by removing and recutting it. He made an estimate of the expence, . . . and I have engaged him thereupon to recover the house." Thomas Jefferson's design for the roof obviously proved just as immune to Burd's efforts to make it watertight as it had to John Hemings's attempts less than ten years earlier. It was just over six months from the time that Burd had given his estimate that Elizabeth could still call Poplar Forest an "unfinished leaking hull of a house." Her reference to the house also being unfinished, of course, could have referred to any number of things. Ellen later recalled that the house "was still unfinished when the property passed to my cousin Francis Eppes."[17] In all likelihood, Francis had never tended to installing William Coffee's ornaments for embellishing the entablature of the dining room, and may never have installed the parlor entablature, much less its ornaments.

At least the Poplar Forest peach trees continued to produce. In a letter written on August 26, 1827, Elizabeth informed Jane: "How I wish you could have some of our superabundance. I never saw such a profusion of peaches, and they certainly make the most wholesome as well as the *cheapest* diet that can be. We have lived upon them for the last three weeks."[18] Peaches were hardly reason enough to stay, however, and plans for the move were already well under way.

In her April 1827 letter, Elizabeth had informed Jane that they would more than likely move to the Tallahassee area of Florida, where "Francis and myself will settle in a log house in the woods, he to begin life anew as a sugar planter and I as _____ what? for I know not what my particular avocations will be there, or how I shall employ myself beyond the customary occupation of our unlucky sin in 'making children' as the old Dutch woman expressed it."[19] Customary occupation or not, three

months later, on June 29, 1827, Elizabeth gave birth to their third child. Named Thomas Jefferson Eppes, he was, appropriately, their only child to be born at Poplar Forest, but was destined to spend only a short time there.

Elizabeth also revealed in her letter to Jane Randolph that not only were she and Francis and their young children planning to move to Florida, her parents and her siblings would eventually join them there. In 1826, the Thomas Eston Randolphs had moved from Ashton, their Albemarle home, to New London, where they established a school. They soon moved again, into Lynchburg, where Elizabeth's sisters, Harriet, Lucy, and Mary Page "immediately established a boarding-school of the very first order."[20] It may have been of the very first order, but although "their reputation as teachers [was] deservedly high, even among the Goths and Vandals of [Lynchburg]," Elizabeth reported that for the fall session of 1828 "only eight scholars arrived and two or three more talked of."[21]

Although he had made plans for an earlier exploratory trip before arranging for a permanent move, it was not until early March 1828 that Francis finally embarked. His timing may have been influenced by a letter from Nicholas Trist, which he answered on March 2: "You are mistaken if you think that I have ever for a moment swerved, from my purpose of emigration. So far from it — your letter found me, in the act of apprising Jefferson of my final determination to sell without reserve to the highest bidder. This however cannot be done to advantage before the fall." Trist had asked Francis if he might consider taking a look at Louisiana, where he and Virginia were thinking of settling, and although Francis was still unsure of his final destination, he noted that "the girls [his sisters-in-law] prefer F. [Florida] and have heard that there is a fine opening in Tallahassee. The neighboring people are rich, and anxious to educate their children, but have no schools." Once again Francis sought to justify his proposed move: "I see no ties which should bind any descendants of our grandfather to this state. The people are cold to his memory, the soil is exhausted, the staple reduced almost to the prime cost of the materials — a level to which it is fast progressing. What inducement is there to remain! Our children may grow rich under a different system, but *we* will never witness better times — here."[22] For Francis, the die was obviously cast. The day before he wrote Trist, he had sent an advertisement to be placed in the *Richmond Enquirer* (fig. 101).

While Francis was looking for property in Florida, Elizabeth and their children moved into Lynchburg with her parents and siblings. On April 20 she wrote Jane Randolph: "I am separated for the first time in my life (my wedded life, of course, I mean) from Francis, & have just made the discovery that his presence is as essential to my happiness as the breath of life is to my existence."[23] She also reported that he had written several times, and that he hoped to be back by the first of May. That he was back at least by early June is proved by a letter he wrote Nicholas Trist on the second of that month. He had not looked at Louisiana, as he was "entirely satisfied with the part of Florida that I visited:"

The character of the surface, elevated undulating approaching in many places the broken appearance of the S. W. Moun-

tain lands almost perfectly resembling ours of the Forest; the water cool and pure, none stagnant, and a perpetual current of fresh air from the Gulf is constantly sweeping the country and carrying off all impurities from the atmosphere. . . . What is left to desire? You will say Society. And here Florida possesses a decided advantage over every other country new, or old. Unlike that of other new countries, the society is composed of men, young, enterprising, enlightened; of capital and of family;— of the best that the Carolinas, Virginia, and Georgia can afford. Such society I had never expected to see removed from the vicinity of a large city. For the mass of intelligence, fine feeling and enterprise assembled here, no other portion of the U. S. can compare to it.[24]

On July 9, 1828, Elizabeth wrote Jane Randolph that "our removal is still uncertain, but Francis is making

Fig. 102 The November 24, 1828, issue of the *Lynchburg Virginian* carried this advertisement placed by T. J. Randolph for an auction sale to be held the next month at Poplar Forest. *(Courtesy Jones Memorial Library, Lynchburg, Va.; photograph by Tom Graves, Jr., 1991).*

strenuous efforts to sell, and by October the affair will be decided, I suppose."[25]

Jefferson Randolph was also still making strenuous efforts to sell the remaining portions of his share of Poplar Forest. Days after Elizabeth wrote his wife, he placed advertisements in at least two Virginia newspapers: "The lands of the Estate of THOMAS JEFFERSON, dec'd, lying in the counties of Campbell and Bedford, will be offered on the premises, if not previously sold privately, on Monday the 22nd of September next." In addition, Randolph announced that Monticello, "will be offered on the premises, if not previously sold privately, on Monday, the 29th of September next. The whole of the property will be divided to suit purchasers. The sale being made for the payment of the testator's debts, the desire to sell is sincere."[26] Randolph's efforts in Albemarle were unsuccessful, and it was not until 1831 that Monticello was finally sold. Only later in the same decade was he able to dispose of all of the Poplar Forest lands for which he was responsible.

Perhaps thinking that a larger tract than the acreage he owned would make a quicker and more profitable sale, Francis seriously considered purchasing some of the original Poplar Forest land back from his cousin. By late September 1828, however, he no longer held out any hope that he could afford such a purchase and asked Randolph "to forget if you can my precipetate and inconsistent conduct." Finding himself "utterly unable from want of funds to comply with your terms," he took back his offer to buy, and excused himself on the grounds that he had not "in any way prevented your selling to another."[27] Indeed, he had not prevented the sale, though Jefferson Randolph probably wished that he had. Nicholas Trist, writing from Monticello, informed James Madison in October that "the sales both in Bedford & here were failures. There, a few hundred acres of land were disposed of at a very low price, (I *believe* $6.00) & very long terms."[28]

Francis's efforts to sell his portion of Poplar Forest had also met with little success, and in August 1828 his wife had written their cousin Mary H. Eppes that "the chances for selling seem daily to grow worse, & I sometimes almost despair of our doing so atall." At last, in November, a buyer appeared. On November 6, Francis wrote Jefferson Randolph, giving him the news coupled with a very perceptive observation: "You will learn from Lewis, that I have sacrificed the home tract, whether for better or worse, the events must decide and by that event I must be judged. If I am fortunate and make money I shall be esteemed bold and judicious; if the reverse injudicious and rash. And it may be that I am. But let me squeeze through this scrape and damn me if you ever find me in another. Tho I was as bold as a lion before the contract, I have felt like a whipped puppy ever since!" He then advised his cousin: "I shall leave this for Tallahassee early next month. . . . In the spring shall take Bett a flying trip to see you and then good night Old Virginia!"[29]

He wrote the same day to Nicholas Trist, advising him that "among other perishables I shall be obliged to sell the clock which I purchased at Monticello. My reasons are simply a want of money, the impossibility of taking it with me, and the impossibility of having it repaired in the savage wilderness to which I shall go. As it is a family piece, I did not like to dispose of it otherwise without informing you of the intention; nor shall it be sold until I again hear from you. I would sell it for what I gave, and I believe I can easily dispose of it here, if none of you want it."[30]

In July 1814, Thomas Jefferson had advised Francis Eppes's father that the whole of Poplar Forest "as it now stands, could not be valued at less that 10,000 D. and I am going on." Fourteen years later, in 1828, the Bedford County appraisers valued the property at $25,704 for tax purposes. Admittedly, fewer acres were now included in the property, but even so, and even considering the difficulties in finding a purchaser, it is almost painful to record what he received. The deed of sale that Francis made, dated November 28, 1828, reveals that he sold his inheritance for a grand total of $4,925.[31]

Now that the sale of his real estate was sure, Francis could attend to the sale of the personal property from Poplar Forest. On November 6, 1828, the same day he wrote Jefferson Randolph that he had a buyer for the house and land, the *Lynchburg Virginian* carried his advertisement for practically everything else:

PUBLIC SALE. Will be sold to the highest bidder at Poplar Forest on Monday the 24th day of November, if fair, if not the next fair day, all the crop of corn, oats, and fodder made on the premises the present year, together with a large quantity of hay and straw: also 20 head of cattle, including 3 yoke of oxen, 70 head of sheep, 40 head of hogs, 5 work horses and two colts, together with the plantation utensils and household and kitchen furniture. A liberal credit for all [items] exceeding twenty dollars will be given, under that, cash will be required.

On the day of that sale, readers of the *Lynchburg Virginian* were informed that there would be still another similar sale in less than a month, this one authorized by Thomas Jefferson Randolph (fig. 102).

In December 1828, after having sold "the home tract" of Poplar Forest, Francis set off again for Florida to make final arrangements for the move before taking his family with him. Returning in the spring of 1829, he stayed only briefly in Lynchburg, where his wife and children had again been living with Mrs. Eppes's parents, and made the flying trip to Albemarle to see the Randolphs, as he had promised. Back in Lynchburg, on May 15, Elizabeth copied the words of a hymn on a sheet of paper, noting that it "was sung at Papa's in Lynchburg at prayer meeting the Friday before we left. It was selected and altered for the occasion by the rev. Smith." The hymn was "Blest Be the Tie That Binds." Three days later, the Reverend Franklin Smith noted in the Register of St. Paul's Episcopal Church in Lynchburg: "18 May 1829 at res. of Tho Eston Randolph, Esq. Lynchburg I baptised Thomas Jefferson, an infant son of Francis Eppes, Esq."[32] Two days later, on May 20, 1829, Francis and his family left on their odyssey.

Fortunately, the move was probably the best thing Francis Eppes could have done under the circumstances, and while he disappeared from the Poplar Forest story, it would be unfair to leave him on the trail to Florida, and not to tell of his subsequent life far to the south. On June 6, 1829, Elizabeth wrote Jane Randolph from Augusta, "one of the unhealthy capitals of deadly Georgia, about to enter on its untried wildernesses under a sun which *we* should consider burning in the heart of summer. How we shall stand it, Heaven only knows, & Harriet has the most gloomy forebodings of 'sickness, suffering, & death.'" They did stand it, and on July 18, 1829, Cornelia Randolph wrote her sister Virginia Trist that "they have got letters from Florida; the party there were 30 days making the journey. Harriet & Mary were made sick by bad water on the road, Elizabeth bore the journey better than any of them. They were well pleased to get to their journey's end." Harriet's forebodings on sickness, suffering, and death were unwarranted, but she hated the journey so much that she wrote her mother the day they reached their destination: "*Bonaparte's Russian campaign* could not have been harder upon a soldier, than this journey to a delicate woman."[33] For their part, the senior Randolphs, along with two other children, sailed from Norfolk to Florida later in the year.

Francis spent a portion of Independence Day 1829 telling Nicholas Trist just how pleased he was with his move: "Well here we are, once more at home, and quietly vegetating in the monotonous style of plants of our tribe. Our crops are laid by, and the woods sending forth the music of my axes. The sound is a pleasant one." The only fly in the ointment was his sister-in-law Mary, who was "sadly out of humour with my log palace. Looks, looks, looks; woman cares for little else! I will tack to this complement my love to cousin Jane, and my sincere belief that she is *one* of the exceptions." A descendant later described the family's first house in Florida as "a rude house of logs [that] took the place of the tent in which [they] had slept for many long weeks." Francis was far more content with his rude "log palace" than he had ever been with Poplar Forest, and far more enthusiastic about the crops the sandy loam of Florida produced than those he had labored with in the thick red clay of Piedmont Virginia. Later in July he wrote Nicholas Trist again: "So far I am more pleased with Florida than ever. No one who has seen with his own eyes the richness of the soil and the quality and quantity of the sugar and Sea Island cotton which it produced to the acre, can doubt of the permanent success of the crops."[34]

Francis grew up in Florida—figuratively if not literally. There he came out of the shadows of both his father, a distinguished United States congressman, and his illustrious grandfather, and began to stand tall on his own. He first purchased property in Leon County, named for Ponce de Leon, some fifteen miles north of Tallahassee. Before the Civil War, Leon was the most populous and prosperous county in the state, having grown rich on the slave-supported cotton economy that Francis participated in. Francis named his new home "L'Eau Noir," or as he might have called it had he stayed in central Virginia, Blackwater. In 1835, he left this property, as Indian raids that were to prove harbingers of the Seminole War were beginning to occur in the hinterlands. Mary Elizabeth Eppes died that same year, a month after giving birth to their sixth child, and was buried in the cemetery of St. John's Episcopal Church in Tallahassee, which Francis had helped establish. After selling his first property, Francis bought an entire city block in Tallahassee, where he built a town house, and was prosperous enough to also buy another cotton plantation closer to the Florida capital. He remarried in 1837 and would have seven more children. In 1841 he was elected mayor, or as the office was called then, intendent, of Tallahassee, and was subsequently elected to three more consecutive terms. He was, according to one account, "a human dynamo reform mayor" during a time when Tallahassee was in desperate need of law and order.[35]

Francis's relations with his Virginia kin seem to have tapered off as the years went on, though that supposition is based more on a dearth of remaining correspondence than on anything else. It seems most fitting that, of all his children, Thomas Jefferson Eppes, born at Poplar Forest and christened at St. Paul's Church in Lynchburg, would attend the University of Virginia; something his father, through a variety of circumstances, had never been able to do.[36] In the 1850s Francis was asked by Henry S. Randall, one of Jefferson's biographers, to provide a description of Eppington, his family's ancestral home in Chesterfield County, Virginia. He furnished a remarkably complete and accurate account of a place that, in all probability, he had not seen in years.[37]

Just before the Civil War ended, Francis sold his Florida plantation for Confederate money. That, along with the forced freeing of his slaves at the war's end, ruined him financially. In 1868, at the age of sixty-seven, he moved to Orange County, Florida, where he appropriately planted an orange grove. Again, his first house there has been described as "a little log cabin in the wilds," but he soon replaced it with a more substantial dwelling.[38] Once again, Francis took the religion of his youth with him. The first Episcopal services held in central Florida were conducted at his new home, and a church was soon founded.

In 1873, Francis sold a portion of his grandfather's inheritance that he had kept longer than might have been expected. His library was sold by the New York auction house of George A. Leavitt & Co., whose catalog identified it as "a portion of the late Thomas Jefferson's Library, offered by his grandson, Francis Eppes, of Poplar Forest, Va.,"[39] Whether he had taken the books with him to Florida or had kept them in storage in Virginia is unknown. Probably the sellers, in listing Francis as "of Poplar Forest, Va.," assumed the books would bring higher prices if he were still identified with Virginia. Fortunately, many of the other family items remained in the family. Years later, the obituary of his son John Wayles Eppes noted that he "left, among many priceless family treasures, a rare collection of letters written by Jeffer-

son and old china and silver and furniture used by Jefferson."[40]

Francis Eppes died at his Orange County estate, called Pine Hill, on May 30, 1881, only several months short of his eightieth birthday, and was buried in Greenwood Cemetery in Orlando. His daughter-in-law recalled that he read scripture in Latin and Greek every day, and "never allowed himself to become rusty in French, Spanish, Italian, or German."[41] Those French and Spanish lessons that his grandfather had insisted on during his youth, and that he and Francis's cousin Ellen Randolph had largely tutored, stood him in good stead, and he apparently learned Italian and German on his own in later years. After his death, he was lauded as one of the founders of the Episcopal Diocese of Florida, and the Reverend Charles R. Ward, who conducted his funeral service, had this to say about him: "His career was not distinguished by prominence — he was not a noted man — but it was 'distinguished by its worth.' " The clergyman noted that the phrase "distinguished by its worth" had come from a letter that Jefferson had written to him in his youth.[42] It was the letter written on November 17, 1821, shortly after Francis had turned twenty (see chap. XVIII, n. 18). While it would be nice to think that Francis had kept that letter all this time, the good Mr. Ward instead credited it and others that he used in his memorial to Henry Randall's *Life of Thomas Jefferson*, which had been published in 1858 and which contained the letter.

But if he might not have kept that letter, Francis did keep another item that has a far more intimate association with Poplar Forest. The Memoranda that he began at Poplar Forest in 1826 was in a carriage for thirty days on the long journey south, in two log houses, and who knows where else. Later generations of the Eppes family, who also treasured it, placed various newspaper items such as obituary notices and testimonials in it, and it became something of a family album. Now, thanks to a descendant who cherished it, this small reminder of a person whose relationship and friendship with Thomas Jefferson is such an essential part of the Poplar Forest story, has come back home.[43] No one can know whether Francis had occasion to examine it from time to time in Florida to bring back memories of his Virginia past. One hopes that he did.

"FIRE IN BEDFORD"
(1828–77)

When Francis Eppes sold Poplar Forest in November 1828, its purchaser was William Cobbs, born in 1792, presumably in Campbell County, Virginia.[1] A second cousin to the William Cobbs whose land had infringed on Jefferson's (see chap. XV), he remains a relatively obscure figure. His grandson recalled years later that his "health was greatly impaired from a blow on the head having been thrown from his horse in a military parade on the streets of Lynchburg."[2] A more immediate indication of some sort of impairment, or at least a description that indicates he may have borne a passing resemblance to Don Quixote, was furnished by his son-in-law, Edward Sixtus Hutter, who wrote his wife on one occasion that "your father [was] cutting quite a figure urging Rosa on at her best speed with his umbrella turned inside out all in tatters."[3] In light of his purchase of Poplar Forest, one of the few other known facts about Cobbs is — to say the least — ironic. He was married to Marian Stannard Scott, the daughter of none other than Maj. Samuel Scott, whom Jefferson — in a fit of pique during their dispute over property boundaries — had dubbed "the old drunkard Scott" (see chap. VIII). Though perhaps not as outspoken as her father, Marian Scott Cobbs inherited some of his irascibility. Judging from her surviving correspondence, she also had a delightful personality and a well-tuned sense of humor. And, from all accounts, there seems little doubt as to who wore the pants in her immediate family. She and William Cobbs had been married on November 1, 1821, and they probably moved into Poplar Forest soon after Francis Eppes left for Florida in December 1828, the month after their purchase of the 1,074 3/4 acre tract was recorded.

Their daughter, Emily Williams Cobbs, had been born on October 5, 1822. From all descriptions, she was lovely, popular, and, as an only child, perhaps somewhat spoiled. Her mother once confessed: "I am afraid I have ever made Emily too much an idol and think without much watchfulness I may make one of you." She made that observation to a young man in love. In August 1840, two months before Mrs. Cobbs's letter to him, and on the eve of his marriage, Edward Hutter had described Emily in a letter to his sister, Amalia Reeder:

I wish you could know Emma as I know her. . . . Imagine her extremely beautiful — accomplished — artless & innocent — with every virtue that adorns the sex. . . . Educated as she has been always accustomed to have every wish gratified and every wayward, girlish whim — it would almost seem impossible that she is what she is. . . . You will not be surprised to learn that she is deficient in many accomplishments which would be indispensable in a wife North of Maryland. She can neither bake, now brew, nor cook and can do but little with a

needle beyond embroidering an apron or something of the sort. . . . She is (a great pity) obliged to use a glass, & notwithstanding the beauty of her eye is a little nearsighted — her teeth are regular but somewhat decayed — were they otherwise she would be perfection.[4]

Edward Hutter, born in Bethlehem, Pennsylvania, was the son of Christian Jacob Hutter, a prominent newspaper publisher in nearby Easton. His courtship with Emily Cobbs and subsequent marriage to her were practically preordained. The couple met in 1838 while Edward was in Lynchburg visiting his half-brother, George Christian Hutter, who, with his wife, Harriet, then owned Sandusky, the former home of Jefferson's friend Charles Johnston (see fig. 45). Prior to the visit, George had written Edward:

Mrs. Cobbs, an intimate friend of ours made us promise to bring you out to see her and she would have some company at her house for you — she has an only daughter, about 15 years of age — whom I wish you very much to see — Mr. Cobbs lives about 10 miles from town — at the old summer residence of the great and good Thomas Jefferson — The young lady is handsome, amiable, intelligent (she goes to school yet) and is withal wealthy — the whole family have taken a great partiality to me — they frequently speak of a connection between you and Miss Emily (the name of the young lady).

George Hutter perhaps protested too much in adding, "although I might desire to see you well married — I would not wish to influence you in any way."[5] In addition to showing the age at which family and friends then thought proper to begin marrying off young Virginia girls, his letter is also interesting for identifying Poplar Forest as "the old summer residence" of Thomas Jefferson. Although it was far from true, the notion that Poplar Forest was Jefferson's summer residence had gained currency only a dozen or so years after his death.

After his return to Pennsylvania, Edward Hutter received a letter from friends he had met in Lynchburg, urging his return that fall: "Miss Cobbs is just returned from the Springs. Her health is very much improved. She is called very beautiful. Bye the bye I have a message for you from Mrs. Cobbs. She requests me to say to you she has set her heart upon a visit from *yourself* and Harriet with them. I think she must have some *design* upon you." Hutter, a man of no faint heart, soon won his fair lady. After a trip to Lynchburg late in 1839, he reported: "During my first visit to the Forest, my most formidable rival Mr. Howard made his appearance there. He was expected as he had sent a letter two days ahead of him from Richmond as an avant courier — I knew his fate — and left him on the field. He took his last farewell an hour after I left, and the next day was on his return to Richmond." Hutter also reported that "Lynchburg promises to be very gay this winter. I was at four parties during my visit there. Tomorrow night Miss Cobbs gives her first party — her 'turning out' party as they call it in the Old Dominion. I wished very much to stay to it. It would have been something new to me. The company at those country parties remain together all night."[6] Poplar Forest was beginning to witness a life-style far different from the one that had prevailed during its builder's time.

At the time of his marriage to Emily, Hutter was in the navy, but he had already considered tendering his resignation, a decision that met with wholehearted approval from his future in-laws. On April 11, 1840, his sister-in-law, Harriet, reported a conversation she had recently had with Mrs. Cobbs: "She said you must not resign before you were married but she did not care how soon after.... You must come on looking your very best now let me beg you to cut off or have cut some of that beautiful hair (tho I shall regret it) but Mrs. Cobbs and many others say it disfigures you so exceedingly."[7]

The marriage took place at Poplar Forest on October 7, 1840, two days after the bride's eighteenth birthday. Hutter reported that "there will be no party in consequence of the illness of Mr. Cobbs and no one will be present but our nearest friends." He also observed that "her mother with whom she is a perfect idol sometimes acts as if she was preparing for her daughter's funeral instead of her bridal."[8]

Less than a month after the wedding, while the young couple were still on their honeymoon, Mrs. Cobbs wrote her new son-in-law from Poplar Forest: "Mr. Cobbs and myself have frequent conversations on the subject of your resigning, it is his wish as much as mine. He thinks if you could get a furlough for twelve months in that time you could better know how you would like the life of a farmer. *I would* say *you must like it.*" Mrs. Cobbs also reported on the news of the day, especially on the recent excitement caused by a political convention. Ellen and Cornelia Randolph could hardly have done better in their heyday:

The town [Lynchburg] has been in a perfect state of excitement, with the whig convention, Mr. Comb from Kentucky has done much for there cause he has brought over some staunch democrats, the ladies are all warm polititions. One lady remarked she felt as if she was newly converted. As an instance of my brother's wife's feelings, when the Bedford company of about 200 passed her gate, they stopped to cheer the flag which was hoisted on the house. She was in the porch with a broom in her hand, she becaim so animated that she whearled the broom with such vilance and cheered so loud, Roy had to take fast holt of her and beg her to be still, she

declared she was quite unconscious of what she did. Mr. Pannell (Emily's acquaintance) traveled 40 mils in a log cabben drawn by splended horses, the cabben was decorated with coon skins redpaper brooms a live coon live chickens in a coop which was attached to the back of the cabben, when ever the cheering for Harrison the hero of Tippacanoe commenced the chickens would all commence a loud crowing. What well trained whigs, you may think, though a whig I think it very ridiculous. The orators were all very complimentary in their speeches to the ladies. As we love flattery that was quite suffienct to make us whigs.[9]

The newlyweds returned to Poplar Forest in December 1840, and on Christmas Day Edward informed his sister in Easton: "I have as yet not learned much at farming but have qualified myself for a purser and if every thing else fails me I can ship for that." He also told her to tell their father "that his portrait is very much admired and I find it was a very poor policy in me to bring it here for all the ladies say he is a better looking man than either of his sons."[10]

In 1841, while on assignment with the Navy in Washington, Hutter received letters from his wife and mother-in-law again urging him to resign and take up the full-time life of a Virginia planter. In a joint letter that the two wrote on September 14, Mrs. Cobbs implored: "I most sincerely wish you were at home to exercise some good management. It is what's wanting here very much I think more than ever. Mr. Cobbs bad health more and more incapacitates him every day I am more convinced his mind should be kept quiet.... I do wish you would get back as soon as possible we cannot get on without you."[11]

Fortunately for all concerned, Edward Hutter did decide to become a farmer, and indeed did like it, as Mrs. Cobbs had said he must. Although he had no previous experience along such lines, he became an adept agriculturist, and like Jefferson before him, kept a detailed farm journal, though his entries are notoriously brief. Hutter began his systematic "Journal of Events for every Day" in 1844, and maintained it through 1854. Beginning each year with a list of slaves and their duties, he followed with a list of livestock, and then noted what work had been accomplished each month. His first entry, dated January 1, 1844, recorded that there were "42 Negroes 7 horses 40 head of cattle — 59 sheep 50 swine" at Poplar Forest.[12] During February 1844 he noted planting both peach and pear trees, and on May 9 "took out stalls and put benches in coocoonery." The peach trees were perhaps to replace some of the earlier trees, or at least to ensure a continuous supply in future years, for those that Jefferson had planted and that the Eppeses had enjoyed were, by all accounts, still flourishing. In 1841, Emma had reported on their quality and quantity several times, and eventually peaches were to become a cash crop for the Hutters. The work in the cocoonery was done to assist Mrs. Cobbs in a project that she, along with many others at the time, was engaged in: the domestic manufacture of silk.

On "Washington's Birthday 1843," George C. Hutter sent a note to Edward from Sandusky reporting that his wife was "sending a cart to Poplar Forest for Raspberries" and noted that "she thinks Mrs. Cobbs has also promised her some Box, which she would be now happy to get." As far as is known, this is the first reference to boxwood at Poplar Forest. Now an important feature of the landscape there, as it is at almost every other Virginia house of its vintage, boxwood were notably absent from Jefferson's own properties and are not listed in his recorded plantings at Poplar Forest. Interestingly, both Hutter properties, Sandusky and Poplar Forest, have similar groupings of boxwood in their front yards.[13]

Two letters from members of the family written while Edward was on a trip to St. Louis in June 1844 tell of activities undertaken at Poplar Forest during his absence. One, from his father, who was then on an extended visit to Virginia, informed him of the state of his crops: "Your corn throughout, not withstanding the cool weather, looks remarkably well and healthy. I wish I could say so much about your wheat — but — rust is playing the mischief with it: particularly where the grain is the strongest — for instance between the cornhouse and the old Barn — and wherever there is a rich spot it seems to me the havoc is the greatest. I think the sooner it can be cut, the better it will be." He also reported on the family: "Mr. Cobbs has been well (in his way) since you left and Mrs. Cobbs is so busy with reeling her silk — which turns out very fine this year — that she has hardly time left for her meals — however she is now also writing to you which is a sure sign how much she thinks of you!" Judging from the date, it took Mrs. Cobbs two days to finish her letter, which, among other things, reported on his wife: "Emily has had more fortitude than I expected. She keeps her spirits up by constant employment. She looks very well, her saddest hours are at night, after a tear steals its way it affords relief, she gets to sleep with all her cares and troubles, not to awake until the morning not then untill a half dozen summons to breakfast. Miss Emma breakfast is waiting. Miss Emma breakfast is waiting. You must make her a better farmers wife." Christian Hutter, then almost seventy-three years old, had lived up to the promises inherent in his portrait, and Mrs. Cobbs happily noted that she was "kept stimulated with the complements I get from your Father. If he was not a Hutter I would not prize them but the name carries

Fig. 103 Poplar Forest, southeast elevation, before 1910. This early-twentieth-century view shows the complete elimination of fenestration by the Hutters on the southeast wall following the 1845 fire, and the small porch that they later added to shelter the door of the east stair pavilion (cf. fig. 113). *(The Corporation for Jefferson's Poplar Forest).*

with it every thing to be relied on." She added: "You my dear son is every thing I could wish, though I sometimes get a little out of humor, it is not the want of confidence, but feel a little momentary vexation. Upon mature reflection, it would be of little importance and soon forgotten."[14]

After his return to Easton, Hutter's father wrote his daughter-in-law: "Every thing respecting Poplar Forest is interesting to me. Give my best respects to your parents, your own Hub, Mrs. Page and Mr. Lewis Cobbs. Give your little William Christian (alias Sugar pie) many kisses from me." Later, after receiving a missive from his son accusing him of preferring his Pennsylvania to his Virginia family, the senior Hutter replied: "You wrong me very much indeed," and proceeded to assure him how mistaken he was:

Not a day passes that I am not spiritually in Poplar Forest, see your industry and improvements — talk with Emma about her mossroses, tuberoses, Jacobean Lillies, etc., hear sweet William Christian say "here I stand as big as a man — Hurrah for Polk" — see Mrs. Cobbs in her indefatigable zeal to raise silk — produce all kind of home manufactures, etc. or walk to my favorite — by you neglected — Springs — and then I walk along the Turnpike to Sandusky, find fault with the Captain for working too hard — rejoice with Harriett over the birth of a dear and much desired daughter — look at the sports of the boys in their yard and look at the neighbor's boys taking their grists to the mill. Not a spot on either of the plantations with which I became acquainted while in Virginia exists which I have not repeatedly visited again since I am returned to the old hearthstone.[15]

The day before his father's letter was written, Edward's nephew William H. Hutter also sent a letter, apparently in response to an invitation that he come for a visit. Asking his uncle "how far are you from Washington City," as he thought he might "attend Mr. Polk's inauguration," he contemplated venturing "as far down as Poplar Forest. To stand upon ground once occupied by the great apostle of Democracy — to look upon Furniture used by him and perhaps seize some ancient Relic of his own would indeed be to me a sincere pleasure."[16] Whether he made the visit or not, the wording of his letter adds credence to the long-held belief that the Cobbs family had purchased some of the Poplar Forest furniture that Francis Eppes sold upon his departure.

Life was obviously going well at Poplar Forest. Edward Hutter was making a success of farming in a way that Jefferson only sometimes had, and that Francis Eppes had never been able to do, at least not in Virginia. The family was increasing; after the death in 1842 of their first child, who had lived only three months, William Christian (a.k.a. Sugar pie) had been born in March 1843, and was followed by Imogene, born in May 1845.

Then, in November 1845, tragedy struck. Unfortunately, though they cared for and obviously appreciated the house and property that had been Mr. Jefferson's, this first Hutter generation at Poplar Forest is remembered all too much for something over which they had absolutely no control. Edward Hutter's entries in his Journal are notoriously laconic, never more frustratingly so than the one he penned on November 21: "High S. W. wind — *Dwelling house destroyed by fire.*" Three days later the *Lynchburg Virginian* reported the event in more detail:

FIRE IN BEDFORD

We regret to hear that the dwelling-house of Wm. Cobbs Esq. of "Poplar Forest," in Bedford, about seven miles from Lynchburg, (extensively known as the former residence of Ex. President Jefferson, by whom the building was erected,) was burnt to the ground on Friday last. The disaster was occasioned by sparks falling onto the roof from the chimney, which had taken fire. This should serve as a warning to others, to use the proper precautions to guard against a similar misfortune from the same cause. We are glad to hear that Mr. Cobbs saved nearly the whole of his furniture.[17]

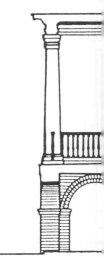

Fig. 104 Although this sectional drawing shows the house as it was in 1985, major elements had not been changed since the 1845 fire. Note the reduced ceiling height of the center room, the attic, and the basement floor installed above the original floor level of the wine cellar (cf. fig. 94). (*Historic American Buildings Survey, Prints and Photographs Division, Library of Congress*)

In Easton, Christian J. Hutter's daughter, Amalia, showed the newspaper article to her father:

When on Saturday the 29th of November, after getting shaved at Finley's shop, I stopped in at Reeders, think of my terror when Ida accosted me with the news that Poplar Forest had been burnt down; it bewildered me in a manner that I could scarcely put any belief in the Story! — but presently Amalia entered the room and handed me the Virginian mentioning the dreadful calamity. — I concluded that You had forwarded the paper in order to prepare my mind somewhat for the most shocking account, but that you certainly would not keep me in a horrid suspense for weeks before Ida would inform me of the extent of your misfortunes? You however held me in anxious expectation of the worst until the 9th Instant when your letter of the first Instant arrived and gave me the soothing Tidings that Emma bore the horrid accident with heroic force and suffered not the least injury in her health![18]

Unfortunately, the letter written *from* Poplar Forest, to which he referred, and on which his observations were based, has not been found. Even so, in the remainder of his letter, Christian J. Hutter provided a very lucid account of what had occurred:

If you rebuild your house upon the same plan as it was before which I would infer from your letter to be your intention, I hope you will take special care not to leave a sufficient space between the shingles of the roof and the balustrade around the same, for sparks of fire from the chimney to lay concealed a sufficient time therein to kindle in such a manner that it becomes unconquerable before you can discover it. You knew the dangerous situation of your roof already when I was with you — which is sufficiently proven by the ladder which you kept constantly on the one gable end of the house.[19]

The similarities between his account and the report that Francis Eppes had given Jefferson in February 1825 after a less-disastrous conflagration are eerily alike: "The wind it seems had blown the snow off in several places, and in two of these the fire caught: one under the balustrade and the other at the bottom of the platform, which supports the top railing."[20]

As far as is known, there was never any suspicion that the 1825 fire during Francis Eppes's ownership was caused by anything other than an accident. While no proof exists that the situation was any different in 1845, there was at least a feeling that it might have been due to

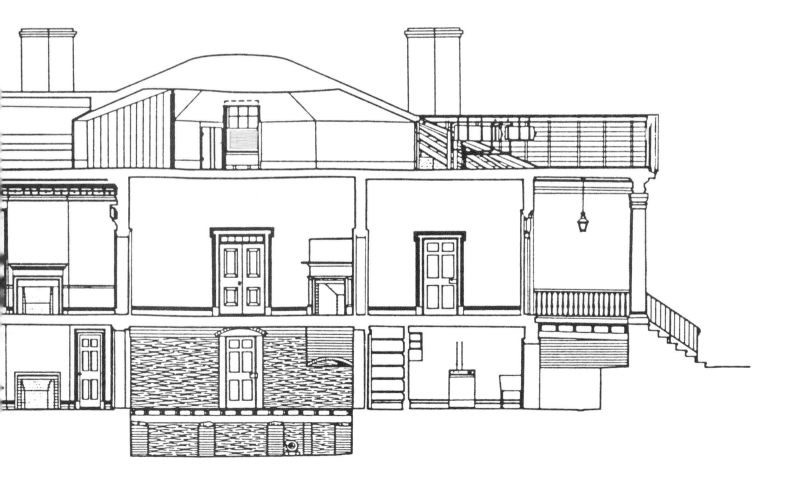

the hands of an incendiary, presumably one of the slaves. Christian J. Hutter brought up the subject in his letter to his son:

Query, Might it not possibly be that crazy Harry ascended that ladder in the night before the fire, in order to make his prophesy good and then died a voluntary death out of fear to be discovered after all? This idea I have not uttered to anybody — but the story as you relate it, is so highly romantic that the mind is naturally drawn to the contemplation of some natural cause that is possible and plausible. Are the large Columns in the front and rear of the building left standing? I should suppose that as the destruction was so thorough that even the weaving room and wine cellar would not be saved, those Columns would of necessity also have perished, because they lost a principal part of their support.[21]

What crazy Harry's prophesy was is not known. Entries in Edward's Journal bolster the suspicion that Harry may have been involved, but are so brief that, other than the coincidence of timing, they can hardly be taken as proof of anything. Hutter's entries from November 20 through November 26 are here given in full:

Nov. 20   Harry came back.
Nov. 21   High S. W. wind — Dwelling house destroyed by fire — Davy came home sick.
Nov. 23   Stowing away furniture, etc., etc.
Nov. 24   Moving furniture to Maj. Smith's house. Harry fell dead in his path.
Nov. 26   Buried Harry.

In his reporting of the earlier 1825 fire, Francis Eppes had fortunately been able to tell Jefferson that the damages, largely confined to the roof and balustrade, were "not as serious as you apprehend." The 1845 fire was obviously far more serious, but in spite of Edward Hutter's notation in his Journal that the house was "destroyed," the *Virginian's* report that it "burnt to the ground," and Christian Jacob Hutter's secondhand opinion that it "had been burnt down," the fire was not as cataclysmic as any of those accounts would indicate. Paul Wilstach, in an article written in 1928, gave credit to Cobbs rather than Hutter for the rebuilding, but noted: "Mr. Cobbs at once restored the house, completing it in 1846, but there are changes which distinguish the new details from the originals, the walls, chimneys, and columns however, survived unaltered and unharmed." He had obviously obtained that information from the Hutters. A member of a later generation of the Hutter family, Christian S. Hutter, Jr., recalled much the same thing: "The brick work including the columns North and South were not hurt"[22] (fig. 103). These several accounts have been bolstered by recent architectural investiga-

tions, which have found far more evidence of Jefferson's fabric behind later accretions than the accounts contemporary with the fire itself would have suggested as possible.

As Edward's Journal entries and the newspaper article stated, much of the furniture was saved as well. Edward's son, Christian S. Hutter, not yet born at the time of the fire, wrote in 1909 that "most of the household goods were saved," and in 1943 his son, Christian S. Hutter, Jr., claimed that "the house burnt so slowly that I think all the furniture etc. was removed, even the doors on the main floor, and window blinds, but the house was gutted."[23]

In the November 24, 1845, entry to his Journal, Edward Hutter had noted that he was "moving furniture to Maj. Smith's house." Smith was John Smith, Jr., a neighbor who had purchased 500 acres of the Yancey tract, Rothsay, in 1834.[24] The Hutters themselves moved there temporarily, and in February 1846 Edward's father wrote his son: "The family pictures you have drawn in both your last letters have been highly interesting to me as I felt as if I actually was in your Circle — altho in Poplar Forest still — not knowing Major Smith's."[25]

Almost immediately after the fire Edward made plans to repair the damage. On December 4, Lynchburg builder George Curle provided a detailed "Estimate for work to be done at Poplar Forest:"

To repairs to brick work	*$250.00*
800 yards plastering	*320.00*
bill of painting complete	*150.00*
Tin Roof & gutters	*525.00*
	$1,245.00
2 porches 22 1/2 ft. by 10	
including materials	*320.00*
3,000 ft. flooring plnk	*115.00*
5,000 " inch do	*75.00*
18 windows & doors including	
all materials locks hinges	
and glass timber inside & out	
side finish complete	*375.000*
18 window & door frames only	*54.00*
184 ft. cornis complete 2	*230.00*
400 " bace & sub bace	*120.00*
5000 framing timbers	*150.00*
6000 ft framing work	*60.00*
4000 ft sheting	*40.00*
2200 ft. floor loges	*88.00*
8 chimney pieces Materials	*50.00*
3 starcacies complete	
including materials	*90.00*
	2,962.00
	say 2800

He added: "The above is what I am willing to do your work for as far as I understand you to say you would have it finished you will please let me hear from you as soon as possible as it is important that I shuld know your determination in order that I may begin to make sum preperations if you should conclude to get me to do your work which I have very little doubt you will as I will be expeditious of you. Respct Geo. G. Curle"[26]

Whether Curle, who was one of Lynchburg's leading antebellum builders, actually did the work is unknown. From the scant records remaining, it would seem that Hutter himself had as great a part in the rebuilding — or at least in furnishing lumber for the work — as anyone else. Although Curle submitted his estimate early in December, Edward apparently waited until the next spring before rebuilding, as it was not until April 20, 1846, that he wrote "commenced house" in his Journal. Earlier that month his father had written: "I presume you are at present over head and ears in work, busy with rebuilding what that dreadful element Fire destroyed. I was however a good deal surprised to see that in the middle of March you only finished cutting timber for your house! How in the world can you season it? We would think all timber quite unfit to go into a building, unless it was *at least* one year previously cut!"[27]

On April 27 Hutter recorded that he "moved to overseer's house," perhaps so he could supervise the work more closely than from Mr. Smith's. He certainly didn't move there for comfort! In the same letter in which he had criticised his son's use of green lumber, Christian J. Hutter, having been told of the move and obviously familiar with the overseer's house in some detail, observed: "I really should like to see you parked up helter skelter in a room 16 by 18 in the Overseer's house of course your bed must stand in that room too, for how could Emma climb up the ladder to the floor above? I was in the house when Mrs. Cobbs had her silk reeled therein — and can form no idea how you can be accommodated therein during the time you are building."[28] He needn't have worried. A letter from Edward to "Emily at Lynchburg" shows that she was spending the interim with friends, or family, there: "The workmen come on but slowly being prevented by the bad weather. We are all as 'comfortable as might be expected' in our new domicil — but it is no place for you and although it is at a sacrifice of my own wishes and feelings, to be separated from you — I should regret to see you here and hope you will stay away till the house is completed if your friends will tolerate you that long."[29] Emily's parents were apparently staying with Mrs. Cobbs's family, the Scotts, at Locust Thicket, where some of the furniture had eventually been taken.

From August 24 through August 26, 1846, Hutter recorded in his Journal that he was "cleaning up about the house," and on August 27 he noted that he "moved back to the mansion house." On September 1 he "set after furniture from S. Scotts," but it was not until December 1848 that Edward noted in his Journal: "Finished basement and attic of mansion house."

The family had been out of the house from November 21, 1845, to August 27, 1846, a total of 9 months. The actual period of reconstruction lasted a far shorter time, from April 20 to August 27, only four months. Those brief periods help support the contention that the fire, though extensive, certainly could not have destroyed the house. In September 1846, having learned that the family had moved back, Christian J. Hutter congratu-

Fig. 105 The post-fire front door was trimmed with Greek Revival moldings and incorporated both sidelights and a glazed transom. This 1985 drawing shows the exterior moldings on the left, and the interior on the right. *(Historic American Buildings Survey, Prints and Photographs Division, Library of Congress)*

lated his son "from the bottom of my heart that kind Providence has smiled upon your exertions, and enabled you to restore the ruins to an habitable dwelling and gathered your family again under its roof . . . Phoenix like, out of its ashes." He also, perhaps inadvertently, gave another clue as to how extensive the damage had — or had not — been in telling his son to take care of his health, "which you know by experience is more difficult to restore than a half burnt house!" He added: "I have no doubt that you have been able to make some valuable improvements in the rebuilding of your mansion, and that in some instances it is now more commodious than it was before the unfortunate fire occurred. It would certainly give me infinite pleasure to see you all in your improved house altho I should not agree with Dr. Nelson that you have been the gainers by the fire."[30]

Few architectural historians would agree with either Christian J. Hutter's assessment or with whatever Dr. Nelson said. Changes were indeed made to the house; improvements, at least from a strictly architectural point of view, were not. As far as convenience was concerned, however, the changes certainly made sense for the Hutters and the Cobbses. Both architecturally and sociologically, the cumulative effect of the changes was the completion of something that had already been started: the conversion of Poplar Forest from a villa to a farmhouse.

In his 1943 letter commenting on the extent of the fire, Edward's grandson, Christian S. Hutter, Jr., listed a few of the alterations: "Many windows and doors were closed by brick, and the monitor top with glass was not put back, and the pitch of the center room was lowered"[31] (fig. 104).

There were far more changes than that, though the elimination of Jefferson's balustraded platform and skylight ("the monitor top with glass") was certainly among the major ones. Indeed, the decision not to replace the skylight was responsible for additional alterations. To "borrow" light for the center room, now without a natural, direct source of exterior light, Jefferson's narrow front entry hall was widened just enough to accommodate sidelights flanking the front door. A glazed transom topped the door, and the whole frontispiece was trimmed with Greek Revival moldings (fig. 105). Between the hall and the center room, a half-glazed double door was installed (fig. 106). Presumably, its twin stood opposite it, leading to the parlor. These features were doubtless somewhat similar to Jefferson's originals at these locations, which had also provided additional light, though Jefferson's doors were likely fully glazed. More light was borrowed from the bedrooms to either side of the center room by transoms over solid double

Fig. 106 Center room, showing the Hutter alterations after the 1845 fire. Notice the Greek Revival trim on the door surrounds and on the mantel. (*G. O. Green, photographer, July 11, 1940, for the Historic American Buildings Survey, Prints and Photographs Division, Library of Congress*)

doors leading into them, though these lights were so shallow that they could hardly have afforded much additional illumination, even on the sunniest of days.

In addition to closing the skylight, other windows were bricked up, as Christian S. Hutter, Jr. reported. Comparisons between figures 49 and fig. 117, and between figures 103 and 113 clearly show the effect of these closings on the exterior. On the southeastern and southwestern angular walls, all fenestration was removed and bricked up except for one small basement window in the latter. On the corresponding northeastern and northwestern angular walls, first-floor windows nearest the north front were maintained, but those farthest from the door were taken out, and the openings then bricked up. The parlor, or drawing room, was perhaps most affected by these fenestration changes. Where there had formerly been four windows, there were now only two, the pair flanking the door leading to the south portico. And where Neilson's drawing had shown triple-hung windows extending to the floor in this room, the Hutter windows were only double-hung, with paneled, solid wooden gib doors taking the place of the bottom sash. Jefferson's light-filled room, where he had been in the habit of reading and writing, was darkened and became a formal Victorian parlor (fig. 107). Blocking of other windows made the bedrooms far darker than before, but at least provided more usable wall space. Perhaps needless to add, Jefferson's favorite alcove beds were not rebuilt. Indeed, his own west bedroom was now partitioned into two rooms, the smaller of which had only one window (fig. 108). The two doorways that Jefferson had instructed Hugh Chisolm to add between the several bedrooms on the main floor were also bricked up (see chap. VI).

With all these changes, new trim had to be installed, and the builder utilized woodwork with extremely simple, flat, Greek Revival profiles, absolutely typical of their time and place. Door and window frames were given crossettes, or "dog ears," where the side and top members met, and, at least in the parlor, these were echoed in the mantels. Other rooms were given far simpler mantels with no such architectural niceties. The center room in Jefferson's and Francis Eppes's time had been the dining room, and albeit inconvenient from a practical standpoint, it was architecturally the most important space in the house, with its perfect cubical proportions and elegant Doric cornice (whether Mr. Coffee's decorations had ever been installed or not). The parlor had been accorded only slightly less importance in this original architectural hierarchy. Now, in the Hutters' Poplar Forest, the parlor became the major room in the house, at least from an architectural viewpoint,

Fig. 107 Parlor. A window in the angular wall to the left of the mantel was closed by the Hutters after the fire, and the mantel shows the Greek Revival influence in the woodwork installed then. (cf. fig. 118, showing the same view after a later, partial restoration). *(G. O. Green, photographer, July 11, 1940, for the Historic American Buildings Survey, Prints and Photographs Division, Library of Congress)*

while the former dining room lost its former pivotal role, both in its decorative treatment and in its use.

It now became known simply as the center room, and was used more as a circulation hall than anything else. The replacement mantel in this room was far simpler than that in the parlor, and diagonally opposite it a closed, boxed stairway with winders, was installed. Leading upward to a newly created attic and downward to a remodeled ground floor, it made the former dining room not only the convergence of horizontal circulation but of vertical as well. The stairs in the east and west pavilions were either rebuilt or repaired (that the former, a more extensive treatment, was needed is perhaps indicated by George Curle's wording in his estimate: "3 starcacies complete including materials"), but were probably relegated to the position of secondary stairs once the new, more centrally located one that bypassed the bedrooms was installed.

Though the new stairway in the center room led downward to the ground level, there was no opening there into the room directly below—the space that had been Jefferson's wine cellar. Instead, a solid frame wall enclosed that space at the foot of the stairway, preventing entry into it at this location, and directing passage instead to the room under the east bedroom. This—the eastern, elongated octagonal space on the ground floor—now became the dining room, if, in fact, it had not already begun to be used as such by the Hutters before the fire.

The new stairway rested at its base level, not on the brick floor of Jefferson's wine cellar, but on a new wooden floor that was installed several feet above it, on the same level as the other ground-floor rooms (see fig. 104). As late as 1928, this arrangement was noted by Paul Wilstach, who wrote, perhaps a bit dramatically: "The square space on the lower level below the central room is a dark hole indifferently practical for either cellar or storage. But underneath it there is a second dungeon, identical in size, where Jefferson kept his fine wines, of which he was so fond."[32]

The new attic was divided into several storage areas, with one large space in the center of the house. This center room was lit by two dormer windows, one facing east, one west. A lower dormer, equipped with a door

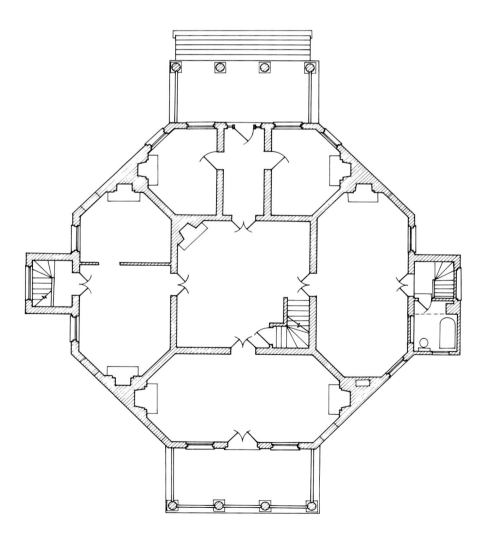

Fig. 108 Reconstructed first floor plan, showing changes made by the Hutters after the 1845 fire. The front hall was widened, a stairway was placed in a corner of the central room, and the west bedroom was divided into two spaces. The bath shown, added to the eastern stair pavilion, was a still later alteration. (*Tim Buehner, delineator, 1991*)

rather than a window, extended south from the attic stair hall and opened onto the flat deck above the south portico, where the original pediment shown in the Nielson drawing (see endpapers) was not replaced This "dormer door," which afforded easy and convenient access to the roof for the first time, may well have been prompted by an effort to ensure that any fires in the future could be extinguished more easily than had heretofore been possible.

In April 1854, while her son-in-law and daughter were on a trip, Mrs. Cobbs wrote two letters to "my dear children," proudly telling them of the good work she was accomplishing during their absence. In the first she announced: "I have been much engaged [turning?] the house up. I have papered the dining-room, it makes a great improvement. This weather will enable Mr. R. to put up the porch I hope. Your aunt thinks I will leave you nothing to do. You know I can accomplish a great deal, when left with out opposition." In the second, written a week and a day later, she reported on further work: "I have had your rume whitewashed. Indeed every part of the lower part of the house done, the dining rume you

will think very much improved. I have every thing very much in order, and hope you will keep it thus when you get home, which I sincerely hope will be very soon."[33]

From Mrs. Cobbs's comments, it would seem that the Hutters habitually slept on the lower floor instead of on the main one, and that the Cobbses, still masters of the house, maintained their quarters on the floor above. Mr. R. was apparently Richard Roberts, an overseer whom Hutter had hired on September 21, 1853, according to his Journal. The porch he was to put up may well have been the small, shed-roofed cover protecting the ground-level doorway of the eastern stair pavilion (see fig. 103). However, it may not have been constructed as soon as Mrs. Cobbs had hoped. On November 20, 1856, more than two years after she wrote, Edward Hutter recorded in his Journal paying: "timber for porch 2.57." That this payment had nothing to do with either of the main porticoes would seem to be indicated by the small price involved; in his bid for work following the fire, George Curle had estimated that work on those two porches would cost a total of $320.

Except for the minor addition of the porch attached to

Fig. 109 At some point during the Cobbs-Hutter ownership, likely before the 1845 fire, these two structures were built in place of Jefferson's office wing. The nearer building housed a kitchen; the farther one, nestled against the east mound, a smokehouse. This photograph dates from the early twentieth century, before the two were connected and converted into guest quarters. *(The Corporation for Jefferson's Poplar Forest)*

the eastern stair pavilion, nothing was done to alter the original exterior configuration of Poplar Forest during the nineteenth century. Beyond the main house, though, dramatic changes were made. In his 1943 letter to Norma Cuthbert, C. S. Hutter, Jr., noted: "His office wing is missing also, but for the Smoke House, next the mound, and the kitchen next to it with a open space between them and a different roof. Jefferson had a flat roof over the wing, which was one building. I think the change was made, that is I think office and weaving wing was torn down to get brick for the plugging of door and windows."[34]

On the surface, C.S. Hutter, Jr.'s assumptions seem feasible enough, but no contemporary documentation exists to prove that Jefferson's office wing was demolished following the fire. Though Edward Hutter's notations are brief, it would seem logical that he would have at least mentioned such work had it occurred during the years when he was keeping his Journal, from 1844 to 1854. In fact, archeological evidence suggests that the wing disappeared, at least in part, before the fire and that the present outside kitchen was built before it

occurred. Apparently at about that same time, the western portions of the original office wing were taken down, and it may well be that bricks stacked from that undertaking were reused "for the plugging of door and windows" when the fire struck the main house several years later. Archeological excavations have also shown that the kitchen and smokehouse were built *above* the foundations and walls of Jefferson's former office wing, and that, except for the stone north wall and the lower courses of one or two brick walls, they are not part of the original 1814 construction. Nor are the two buildings contemporaneous with each other. The smokehouse, which has walls constructed in part of machine-made bricks, postdates the kitchen (fig. 109).

The kitchen and smokehouse were capped with steeply sloping roofs (gable on the kitchen, pyramidal on the smokehouse), an arrangement that certainly precluded evening exercises on a flat terrace among the owls and bats. But if Jefferson's arrangement had encompassed poetic as well as practical overtones, the Hutters' new arrangement had none of the former and lacked a very important component of the latter. There was now

Fig. 110 North (left) and south quarters. These substantial brick houses were built sometime during the Hutter ownership of Poplar Forest and are located just to the east of the east mound (see fig. 112). The northern building traditionally housed the Hutter and Watts farm overseers; the southern housed black workers. (*Jack E. Boucher, 1986, for the Historic American Buildings Survey, Prints and Photographs Division, Library of Congress*)

no covered walkway from the kitchen to the house. Under the old arrangement, servants had been able to carry their dishes under cover from the kitchen to the dining room, but they now had to walk uncovered the same distance. More than likely, the porch that Mrs. Cobbs mentioned in her 1854 letter was constructed to provide at least a modicum of shelter just outside the small vestibule that led into the new dining room.

In addition to their work on the main house and its service buildings, the Hutters also added a number of farm buildings during their long ownership. In Jefferson's time, the slaves that he brought with him on so many occasions (especially Burwell and John Hemings) were quartered in the house itself, more than likely on the ground floor. It is also known that on some occasions Jefferson's overseers also occupied the ground floor. After the Hutters adapted this part of the house to their own use, there was hardly any room left there for the servants. In addition, social customs in mid-nineteenth-century Virginia dictated a far more stratified role between servant and master than had prevailed in earlier times. At some time in the mid-to-late nineteenth

century, two substantial brick houses were built east of the eastern mound to house members of the work force (figs. 110 and 112). These two buildings are far more commodious and permanent than any of the houses that Jefferson had provided for his Poplar Forest slaves, who lived for the most part in log cabins. While the original occupants for whom these quarters were built are not known, traditionally the one to the north was occupied by a white overseer and his family; that to the south by a black family or families. At least, it is known that this was the pattern of occupancy in later years of the Hutter ownership.[35] The northernmost of the two is slightly more distinguished architecturally, with its two chimneys, rather than one, and with its slightly more elaborate interior trim. Archeological investigations in the southern building have located a three-foot-deep, brick-lined "root cellar," measuring four feet square. This feature, typical of slave housing, contained objects that indicated it had been used by the occupants both for food storage and to keep personal items of value.[36]

In June 1851, according to notes in his Journal, Edward Hutter built a new carriage house. Two years later he

Fig. 111 Barn, or granary. Built in part of reused materials, and having a datestone of 1857, this simple building is the only nineteenth-century farm building remaining at Poplar Forest. *(Jack E. Boucher, 1986, for the Historic American Buildings Survey, Prints and Photographs Division, Library of Congress)*

recorded "barn & shed built." Whether this referred to the barn still standing to the northwest of the main group of farmyard buildings, which has the date 1857 inscribed on a stone in its foundation, is not known (fig. 111). Later generations of the Hutter family called it the granary, and Edward's grandson remembered that as many as 4,000 bushels of wheat or oats had been stored in it on occasion. Members of the family who succeeded the Hutters at Poplar Forest knew it as the sheep barn. While the structure appears at first glance to be all of a piece, closer examination reveals that many of its supporting timbers are reused, indicating they had originally been part of an earlier structure.

Ironically, the very year that Poplar Forest burned was the year that it was mentioned, perhaps for the first time, in a widely read book. *Historical Collections of Virginia* was one of several state-histories-cum-travelogues published by Henry Howe. While his account definitely lacked historical accuracy — among other things, Poplar Forest was discussed in the chapter on Campbell County rather than Bedford County — it nevertheless was an important first step in bringing the house to general public attention: " 'Poplar Forest,' 3 miles NE. of New London, is the name of the seat of William Cobbs, Esq., which was originally the property of Jefferson and occasionally his residence in the summer months. It is an octagonal brick edifice built by him, on the same plan with Monticello, although much smaller. Its situation is commanding, within sight of the Blue Ridge, and the grounds around are beautifully laid out, and adorned with shrubbery"[37]

Once again, the "summer house" reference reared its head, though that inaccuracy pales in comparison to Howe's assertion that Poplar Forest was built "on the same plan with Monticello." Howe's account remained the only one until 1858, when the publication of Henry Randall's monumental three-volume *Life of Thomas Jefferson* brought a far more accurate account of Poplar Forest to the public. Randall's description was provided primarily by Ellen R. Coolidge, in letters written to him in 1856. As they are so detailed, and remain the best account of the house and the life that Jefferson and his family enjoyed there, they are included herein as an appendix. Ellen was almost sixty years old when she corresponded with Randall, and had not seen Poplar Forest since her last trip there in the 1820s. Some of her remembrances seem colored with a more romantic tinge than her contemporary accounts had been. Her recalling that the innkeepers along the road to Poplar Forest "set out for [Jefferson] the best they had, gave him the nicest room, and seemed to hail his passage as an event most interesting to themselves," for example, contrasts sharply with her earlier recollections and observations of Flood's and Greenlee's taverns quoted above.[38]

When Ellen wrote her letters in 1856, the Hutters were still living at Poplar Forest, but a number of changes had occurred in the decade since the fire. By the mid-nineteenth century, a new mode of transportation had replaced (or at least supplemented) travel over the roads that had always brought family and friends to Poplar Forest. In 1848 the Lynchburg and Tennessee Railroad, rechristened the next year as the Virginia and Tennessee, was chartered by the Virginia legislature. Soon tracks were laid from Lynchburg westward to Bristol, on the Tennessee border. Although through service to Tennessee was not available until 1856, trains ran through the original Poplar Forest tract, which the line bisected, several years earlier. Members of the Hutter family and their guests arrived and departed at Forest Depot, named for their property. Located on what had been part of the estate, the depot was close to the old Lynchburg Road, soon to be known as the Forest Road. One of the earliest notices of the railroad's arrival was on March 5, 1853, when Edward Hutter wrote in his Journal: "2 hogs killed on railroad." To give an idea of the scale of farm operations at the time, at the beginning of 1853 Hutter listed "46 hogs, along with 7 horses, 2 mules, 76 sheep, and 40 cattle" as belonging to Poplar Forest. He also reported a work force of thirty-eight slaves.

A year before the unfortunate incident between the iron horse and the hogs occurred, Poplar Forest received a most unusual honor, as announced in a letter from Amalia Hutter Reeder, in Easton, Pennsylvania, to her sister-in-law Emma Hutter:

I am very busy now preparing Ida to leave home for Norristown. . . . She has had some of her music published, and the publisher made a mistake, and she was so much vexed and mortified that she cried about an hour. The one was the Poplar Forest Polka dedicated to Mrs. E C Hutter and he has it to Miss E C Hutter and the Sandusky Polka instead of dedicating to Mrs. G C Hutter, he has it to Mrs. E C Hutter so you see my dear Emma you have them both, that is, if you are willing to be the Miss.[39]

Ida, who had first announced the news of the fire at Poplar Forest to her grandfather, was Amalia Hutter Reeder's eldest child, and was only fourteen years old in 1852. Whether the "Poplar Forest Polka" was ever danced at Poplar Forest is not known, but given the Hutters' penchant for good times and family loyalty, it probably was. By 1858 it could have been played on a new piano. On November 29 of that year, Hutter recorded in a ledger entitled Income and Expenses (which had by this time replaced his Journal), that he had paid $360 for "piano forte and cover." That was more expensive than the $220 he had paid on June 15 of the same year "for iron steps at Front of House." The iron steps, which lasted well into the twentieth century, and can be seen in early photographs, may not have been as happy a purchase as the piano. Two of the Hutter children are said to have died from falls on them, though no documentation exists to prove that such tragedies actually occurred.[40]

When William Cobbs died on September 5, 1852, he left Poplar Forest to his daughter, Emily, rather than to her and her husband. Edward was appointed executor, and was given the task of ensuring that Mrs. Cobbs would receive an annuity of $400. By the time of Cobbs's death, the Hutters had six children, not counting their first, who had died in infancy. Two more were to die in 1853, one in January, one in February, both of scarlet fever. Four more children were born after 1853, the last, Christian Sixtus, in 1862. He was soon to have a starring role in a Civil War incident at Poplar Forest.

Physically, the Civil War touched Poplar Forest only briefly, although — depending on who told the story — somewhat dramatically. In June 1864, Federal troops under the command of Maj. Gen. David Hunter passed through the area, coming from the Peaks of Otter eastward along the Forest Road. Gen. Ulysses S. Grant had given Hunter orders to destroy the railroad and canal facilities in Lynchburg and to try and capture the city. On June 17 Hunter's troops burned the depot at Forest, and, looking for spoils, searched Poplar Forest. That afternoon they commandeered the other Hutter home, Sandusky, closer to the city, as their headquarters. The battle that ensued the next day was a complete Confederate victory, and on the eighteenth, before dawn, the Union troops retreated along the same route they had come. At some time during the turmoil, a Union soldier who had typhoid fever is said to have been buried at Poplar Forest, in the still-extant poplar grove northeast of the house.

Later Hutter family accounts speak vividly of the atrocities purportedly committed by the "Yankees" at Poplar Forest. In his Memoir, written in 1909, Christian S. Hutter, the youngest of Edward and Emily's children, wrote that "General Hunter with his troops . . . carried off everything with life except of about 10 faithful negroes out of 48 slaves. Not a horse cows hogs or sheep was left by the raiders who were low enough to invade the personal belonging of the ladies of the house." At the time of the raid, he was not quite two years old, and one of the Union soldiers who invaded the house is said to have kissed him, an act of horror that he duly told to his grandmother, the indomitable Mrs. Cobbs. Although by then unable to walk, she figuratively, if not literally, rose

to the occasion by responding: "In that case, don't ever kiss me again."[41]

Physically, the war may have touched Poplar Forest only briefly. Emotionally and economically, its effect was far more serious, and it had far more lasting consequences. William Christian Hutter was mortally wounded during the battle between the Monitor and the Merrimac at Hampton Roads in March 1862. His body was brought back to Bedford and interred at St. Stephen's Episcopal Church, alongside three siblings who had predeceased him. St. Stephen's, where the Hutters, and the Eppeses before them, were communicants, had been built on part of the original Poplar Forest tract, on land given for that purpose by Anne Moseley of Ashwood.[42]

Edward Hutter's resources were "swept away" by the "fortunes of war," and by 1866 he was unable to pay the regular $400 annuity to Mrs. Cobbs that her late husband's will had mandated. A comparison of personal property lists from 1861 and 1867 shows a decrease in both value and number of livestock and indicates that Christian Hutter was not exaggerating much in his enumeration of the losses his father had experienced when the Union troops departed. Finally, in 1871, an arrangement was made whereby Hutter, still unable to provide his mother-in-law with her annual payment of $400, began to serve as her farm manager. Also attesting to the evaporation of his estate during these postwar years were a number of suits that his associates (including the family doctor) initiated against him for nonpayment of debts.[43] It was as if the financial history of Poplar Forest's most famous owner were repeating itself. Down in Florida, it might be recalled, Francis Eppes was having his own postwar financial difficulties. The year that Edward Hutter was sued by his doctor, 1868, was the same year that Francis left Tallahassee to start life anew, at the age of sixty-seven, in Orange County.

On July 9, 1870, Emily Cobbs Hutter died, and five years later, on November 7, 1875, her husband, Edward Sixtus Hutter, followed her. They were buried in the churchyard at St. Stephen's, where by this time so many of their children lay. Marian Cobbs, who had outlived her husband, her daughter, and her son-in-law, died on May 30, 1877, at the age of seventy-six, and was eulogized by the *Lynchburg Virginian*: "For twenty years she has been wracked by pain. For twenty years she has been unable to walk. For five years she has been unable to see. And yet her bright and cheerful soul continued to linger in its tenement of clay long after the latter was in ruins. . . . How grateful must be that perfect rest which is the reward of so much patient suffering and Christian fortitude!"[44] When she was laid to rest with her family at St. Stephen's, yet another era had ended at Poplar Forest.

"SOMEONE WHO WOULD... PRESERVE IT"
(1877–Present)

Christian Sixtus Hutter, the youngest of Edward and Emily Hutter's children, was to become the next important figure in the Poplar Forest story after his parents and grandmother's death. Born on October 19, 1862, he was seven years old when his mother died, thirteen when his father passed away, and fourteen when his grandmother, Marian Cobbs, followed them in May 1877. At that time five of his siblings were alive, and he was one of three still living at Poplar Forest. He and his sister Emily remained there after the third, Charlotte, married her cousin James Risque Hutter, of the Sandusky branch of the family. The Hutter wedding was celebrated at Poplar Forest on October 30, 1877, and was one of the last family events held at the house for more than a decade. In 1881, at the age of nineteen, Christian moved to Lynchburg to seek his fortune, and after Emily married the next year, the house was subsequently rented to tenants.[1] In January 1885, Christian Hutter was married to Ernestine Booker, and the couple began housekeeping in Lynchburg. A year before his marriage, Christian and his siblings had attempted to sell Poplar Forest, and had advertised it in the *Lynchburg Virginian* on September 20, 1884:

POPLAR FOREST PLANTATION FOR SALE. . . . containing one thousand twenty-one and three-fourths acres of Valuable Land. . . . The tract has been divided, and will be sold in parcels, or as a whole, to suit purchasers. This plantation was owned and improved by Thos. Jefferson, who gave it the name of Poplar Forest. The dwelling house was built by him in the most substantial manner — of thick walls and convenient arrangement. It contains 11 rooms and 12 closets, with a deep cellar underneath. Near by are two good brick houses for tenants, each containing 4 rooms: also barn, stables and cabins.

While some of the personal property and a few small parcels were sold following the advertisement, the main body of the estate was not. Instead, the Hutters decided to divide the property among themselves. Four years after the attempted sale, according to Christian Hutter's Memoir, three gentlemen viewed "the farm and divided the lands in 5 equal parts the house with 150 acres was to pay $500 to equalize with the other parts."[2] This division was made to give each of the five siblings an equal share in the estate, and it was agreed that whoever drew the house in the lot would reimburse the others for its greater value. Although the division was made in 1888, deeds recording the new arrangements were not recorded until two years later. By that time, Christian

had already started acquiring the interests of his brothers and sisters. In March 1889 he obtained the "home tract" of 149 acres from the James Risque Hutters, and "the place was first used as a summer house" by his family that year.[3] By this time, Hutter's business in Lynchburg as a "wood, coal and lumber dealer" was burgeoning, and he would prosper in the next several years with the phenomenal growth and building boom that the city was to experience. By 1894, according to his letterhead, he had added to his three main products "lime, cement, plaster, laths, plastering hair, etc."[4] By the turn of the present century, Christian Hutter and his wife had six children (a seventh had died in infancy); and four more were to follow, the last born in 1910.

At the time of his purchase of the home tract, Christian Hutter embarked on a series of improvements to the house at Poplar Forest. The first of these was a new water system, which was begun in 1889. It was a gravity system, and was installed in part to replace the old lead pipe that had been "dug up in 64 & used for bullets to repel the invaders of our state." The new arrangement had to be replaced in 1909, due to corrosion in the pipes. The second system used as its source a spring "southwest from house 3200 ft.," from which water was piped to the cistern, located just south of the tenant houses.[5] From there, the water was pumped to a holding tank, raised on metal stilts on the eastern mound (fig. 112). This water supply, according to Christian's son Beverly, was used solely for toilets and bathing, not for drinking. Drinking water came from a well to the southeast of the house, and there was always a full bucket on a table within the brick arcade under the south portico.[6]

The new water system supplied two bathrooms that the Hutters added to the house. One, easily visible in early twentieth-century photographs, adjoined the eastern bedroom, which now served as the master bedroom (fig. 113). This bathroom was adjacent to the eastern stair pavilion, and was entered from it. It was directly above the small porch that had been added by the Hutters (or by Mrs. Cobbs), was supported in part by the pillars of that porch, and replaced the porch roof in protecting the ground entry below. The new bathroom was covered with stucco and was dubbed the "dirt-dauber's nest," an apt description judging from its appearance.[7] If nothing else, it was an obvious addition, and made no attempt to blend with the older construction. The addition of the "dirt-dauber's nest" necessitated closing the bedroom window immediately to the south of the stair pavilion. As that source of light to the master bedroom was now blocked, the window in the southeastern angular wall of the house — which had been bricked-in after the rebuilding following the 1845 fire — was reopened. A comparison between figures 103 and 113 shows the old and new window patterns at this location.

The second interior bathroom was located at the foot of the stairway in the western pavilion, just where an indoor privy had apparently been installed during Jefferson's time. As recalled by a later generation, this toilet was an extremely tight fit, as it was located directly under the winding stairway. Only the toilet was in the stair pavilion; the accompanying wash basin was located in the southernmost of the two basement bedrooms immediately adjacent to the stairway.[8]

Other changes in the ground floor were also made, though it is uncertain just when some of these were accomplished. Essentially, the large south room, directly beneath the parlor and identical to it in size, was divided into three spaces, replicating, in effect, the arrangement of the north front on the floor above: a narrow hallway flanked by two small, irregularly shaped rooms. A kitchen was installed in the eastern room, adjoining the Hutter dining room. As this was a very small space, and as the house was now occupied only during the summer, the outdoor kitchen to the east of the house more than likely continued as the main kitchen. A corridor led from the exterior southern door to the central room above Jefferson's wine cellar, while to the west, the third space was used as a bedroom.

During the period that the Hutter family used Poplar Forest as a summer residence, actual farm operations were the responsibility of overseers, beginning with L. B. Singleton, who "entered on his duties as manager from 89 to 1906 [and] served faithful & well." In many ways, it was a return to the same system that Jefferson had employed, and it would continue after the Hutter ownership. On November 20, 1894, the "large new barn with 22 horse stalls 32 cow stalls and sheds burned," and was rebuilt the next year.[9] The "farmyard" of the Hutter period was, as it remains today, to the west and southwest of the mansion (fig. 114).

Early in the twentieth century, Poplar Forest began to

Fig. 112 The north (left) and south quarters, immediately east of the east mound. Note the water tank on the mound in this photograph taken in 1943. (*The Corporation for Jefferson's Poplar Forest*)

be visited by scholars interested in the architecture and history of the house. Without exception, the Hutters welcomed them and generously shared the information they had gleaned over the years. Sometime before 1916, when his monumental *Thomas Jefferson, Architect* was published, Fiske Kimball came to visit. A graduate of Harvard, he had been commissioned by Ellen Randolph Coolidge's descendants to write the book as a memorial to Jefferson's great-great grandson Thomas Jefferson Coolidge, Jr., who had died in 1912. The Coolidges had inherited, "and then added by purchase, the major collection of Jefferson architectural drawings," including those related to the development of Poplar Forest, that they then donated to the Massachusetts Historical Society.[10] Though some of Kimball's interpretations are perhaps suspect in light of later research and documentation, he clearly identified Poplar Forest as a major component in Jefferson's architectural oeuvre and was the first authority to recognize its overall importance in the story of the nation's architectural patrimony as well: "The house intended, until 1804 for Jefferson's farm of

Pantops, and finally begun by him at Poplar Forest in 1806, was of a type hitherto unused in America — a single regular octagon." At the same time, Kimball did not hesitate to acknowledge the plan's shortcomings and well realized that "the use of the central, distributing room as a dining room is an instance of freedom which would not have been admissible had the life at Poplar Forest been less simple." Kimball also traced the development of the several earlier Jefferson drawings for his "house for Bedford," before he built the house "exactly on the plan once thought of for Pantops." At the end of his discussion of Poplar Forest, Kimball noted that "the present owner, Mr. Christian S. Hutter, has kindly permitted an examination of the premises, and given the benefit of his knowledge of the earlier form of many features."[11]

A decade after Fiske Kimball's visit, the Woman's Club of Lynchburg made their own pilgrimage to Poplar Forest. Their visit was oriented more to history than to architecture and encompassed far more history than Poplar Forest had ever experienced — before or since.

Fig. 113 The "dirt-dauber's nest," a bathroom installed over the basement entry to the east stair pavilion, is seen in this early twentieth-century photograph (cf. fig. 103). *(The Corporation for Jefferson's Poplar Forest)*

In May 1926 the club staged a pageant entitled "An Afternoon of Retrospection," consisting of four parts, each highlighting one aspect of American history and each presented by members of a different patriotic society. The Boy Scouts served as the cast for act one — "The Beginnings of Religion"— and were followed by the three Lynchburg chapters of the Daughters of the American Revolution, who jointly presented "The Beginnings of Education." Members of the Little Theatre of Lynchburg performed "The Beginnings of Independence," while the concluding act, "The Beginnings of Social Culture," was produced by the Lynchburg Committee of the National Society of the Colonial Dames of America.[12] A photograph of the cast, gathered on the cast-iron steps that Edward Hutter had installed in 1858, was taken. Claudine Hutter, the eldest daughter of the family, who became something of a family historian and who organized the event, is seen flanked by two kneeling pages[13] (fig. 115).

The *Norfolk and Western Magazine* took note of the "Afternoon of Retrospection" in its July 1926 issue. The author, who used the unfortunate nom-de-plume of Tag A. Long, noted that "the present owner (C. S. Hutter) has succeeded in buying the table and chairs shown in the picture [that accompanied the article], they having been a part of the original furniture at Poplar Forest." During the afternoon, Miss Hutter poured tea from "Jefferson's table."[14] That table (now at Monticello) is the one that Cornelia had drawn on one of her visits (see figs. 55 and 56). The Hutters had repurchased the table after it had been sold following Mrs. Cobbs's death in 1877. In addition to the interest in Jeffersoniana that Claudine Hutter obviously relished, both her father, Christian S. Hutter, Sr., and his son and namesake collected Jefferson letters over the years, and donated them to various institutions.[15]

After Fiske Kimball, Paul Wilstach was the next nationally recognized architectural historian to visit Poplar Forest. His article, entitled "Thomas Jefferson's Secret Home," was published in *Country Life* in April 1928. Again, he depended on Christian S. Hutter for much of his information, including the discussion of the

Fig. 114 This aerial view of Poplar Forest shows both the "dirt-dauber's nest" (see fig. 113) and the water tower on the east mound. To the left, a barn indicates the location of the farmyard to the west of the yard (cf. figs. 7 and 122). *(October 1924, Virginia State Library and Archives)*

extent of damage done by the 1845 fire, quoted above. Some of Wilstach's (and by extension, Hutter's), observations are suspect in light of subsequent research: "Across [the lawn south of the house] there is evidence that here once there was a broad graveled walk and the present owner says that this walk was once bordered with cedars whose feathers swept the ground and which, on their nearer sides, were trimmed so that Jefferson's white walk led down an arched tunnel of dark green."[16] As far as is known, no reference to such a landscape treatment dates from Jefferson's period, or from any later time.

Poplar Forest almost had a clone in the early nineteenth century, when Jefferson lent the plans to his friend and fellow member of the Board of Visitors of the University of Virginia, Joseph Cabell. Now, more than 100 years later, a replica of the house was finally built. Though not quite in the shadow of Monticello, it was placed in the shadow of another of Jefferson's architectural creations, Farmington, the Albemarle County home of his friends Mr. and Mrs. George Divers. By this

time a country club, Farmington and its golf course were ringed with handsome suburban houses, and in 1933 Lynchburg architects Stanhope S. Johnson and R. O. Brannan designed a copy of Poplar Forest that was built there for Mr. and Mrs. E. J. Perkins. Combining elements of Poplar Forest both before and after the 1845 fire, it fits well into its woodland setting. Even its name is something of a clone: Oak Forest.[17]

Norma Cuthbert never came to visit Poplar Forest, but corresponded with the Hutters in preparation for her article "Poplar Forest: Jefferson's Legacy to His Grandson," published in the May 1943 issue of the *Huntington Library Quarterly*. She also credited as one of her sources the description of the house written by Claudine Hutter that had been published in *Homes and Gardens in Old Virginia* in 1930.[18] Ms. Cuthbert's article, which quotes numerous letters from Jefferson to John Wayles Eppes, also helped inform the public of the important Jefferson holdings at the Huntington Library in California.

The first four decades of the twentieth-century, by

Fig. 115 An "Afternoon of Retrospection," highlighting events in American history, was held at Poplar Forest in 1926. The cast is seen here on the cast-iron steps installed by Edward Hutter in 1859. *(The Corporation for Jefferson's Poplar Forest)*

and large, were pleasant, idyllic years for the Hutters at Poplar Forest, and in some respects the house served them during this time much in the way it had served its builder. Depression years and two World Wars could be forgotten, if only temporarily, during the periods they were at Poplar Forest. Summers were family-oriented, and the house was crowded with brothers, sisters, children, and cousins. "We'd always go after the last day of school," Beverly Hutter recalled. Suitcases would be piled on a wagon, and the family "would follow in carriages. We always stopped for a picnic along the way." Once they arrived, there were "all the horses we wanted to ride and we'd dam up the creek and go swimming."[19] The Pennsylvania branch of the clan stayed in touch, and a letter that Christian Hutter, Sr., wrote in July 1936 to his first-cousin Frank Reeder gives a fine sense of the warmth and hospitality all could expect:

You must be sure to stop at Poplar Forest 20 minutes out in Bedford Co. You will find a house full of cousins there & I want you & yours to know my children. We summer there & it is the place we all gather during the hot months June July & August. At present we have Fontaine and others waiting for bed room, as soon as some move out. We will count on your stopping & hope you will hit a time when we can give you comfortable beds at any rate you will have a hearty welcome & delight us all. Your Father visited Poplar Forest on his 40th anniversary & found the same old cook that served us on his wedding trip. Advise me when we may expect you.[20]

Beverly S. Hutter and his wife, Frances Forward, who were married in 1929, recalled such family gatherings. For those arriving by train, a carriage would be sent to Forest Depot and would bring them through the fields, woods, and orchards to the house. On the hill sloping down from the front of the house, apples were on one side of the road, peaches on the other. Watermelons were kept cool in an icehouse to the southeast of the house, but there was also an icebox inside. Toward the end of the Hutter ownership, electricity was installed and the icehouse became a relic of the past.[21]

The only problem was the lack of bedrooms, as Christian Hutter's letter to his cousin made clear. In addition to occasionally not having enough, there was a definite order of preference. No one wanted either of the two small front rooms, which were still as unpopular as they had been in Ellen and Cornelia Randolph's time. Known as the bride-and-groom rooms, as the most recently married members of the family were usually assigned to them, they offered little privacy for their occupants,

especially when other members of the party habitually gathered on the front porch on summer evenings. Perhaps the Hutters didn't know of Jefferson's solution: to close the half-shutters that he had instructed John Hemings to fabricate so long ago.

In 1943 the family circle was broken when Mrs. Christian S. Hutter died. Her widower stopped coming to Bedford in the summer and three years later, at the age of eighty-three, he decided to sell Poplar Forest. At the time, he felt that none of his children was in a position to maintain the property, and with his great interest in its history, he "wanted it to be owned by someone who would live in it, appreciate it and be able to preserve it."[22] He had already decided who that someone would be before the intended himself knew. James Owen Watts, Jr., a friend and scion of a prominent Lynchburg family, knew Poplar Forest well, having driven out to visit on many occasions with his wife and young son. At a meeting in Lynchburg, Hutter casually asked Watts if he knew where his son, Jimmy, was at the time. Watts replied that he assumed he was in school, but Hutter countered with this observation: "I know where he ought to be." Watts then asked if Mr. Hutter meant what he thought he did, and Hutter said yes. On July 1, 1946, "C. S. Hutter, Widower, party of the first part," sold Poplar Forest to "James O. Watts, Jr. and Sarah Key Watts, husband and wife, parties of the second part." The property was listed in the deed as containing 1,002 acres, more or less, and the purchase price was $100,000.[23] The timing of his sale to the Wattses was right; a year later, at the age of eighty-four, Christian S. Hutter died. It was again the end of one period in the history of Poplar Forest and the beginning of another.

Almost immediately after purchasing Poplar Forest, the new owners embarked on a plan both to restore it and to modernize it for comfortable, year-round use. They employed New York architects W. Stuart Thompson and Phelps Barnum, whose plans and specifications give a clear picture of the scope of work. Barnum, a family friend, was in charge of the project, and as the drawings clearly show, he was well versed in classical architectural principles. They also show that he had obviously devoted a great deal of study to the house. His son later recalled that he had spent "quite a bit of time in Charlottesville at the time of the restoration researching all he could find about Poplar Forest."[24] Had all that Barnum proposed been carried out, what would have emerged would have been a very creditable restoration of the house to its original condition, including a recreation of the skylight and the office wing. Preliminary plans are dated October 1946, and working drawings were prepared in December of that year.[25] Construction, which began in 1947, was under the direction of the Lynchburg firm of C. W. Hancock.

As with previous changes to the house, the basic octagonal form was respected (fig. 116). Reopening of the windows that had been bricked in following the 1845 fire was the most visible exterior change. The specifications directed the contractor to "cut out, with great care, the blocked up windows indicated being most careful not to damage the sides, sills and heads which will remain. Rebuild where necessary using old brick out of openings as much as possible. Contractor shall assume full responsibility for not damaging adjoining brickwork."[26] The accomplished manner in which this work was performed is still evident (fig. 117). The specifications also directed the contractor to match new window and door frames to existing ones. No attempt was made to change the Hutter-era Greek Revival trim to more Jef-

fersonian profiles on the exterior, and in the interior, only in one room. Additionally, the original triple-sash windows that opened from the parlor to the south porch, as shown in John Neilson's drawing, were not reconstructed.

One of the windows reopened was the one on the eastern wall that had been closed when the Hutters' dirt-dauber" bathroom had been added early in the twentieth century. That bathroom was now removed and the door that had led into it, which opened from the south wall of the stair pavilion, was bricked up. This now-eliminated bath was replaced by a new master bathroom, created in the former northeast bedroom, with a new door installed just where Jefferson's original had been, between it and the bedroom. The opening from the entrance hall to this space was blocked up, and its door and trim were reused at the new location. Within the eastern stair pavilion, the stairway was removed altogether and a dressing area with closets and built-in chests was constructed in its stead (see fig. 116).

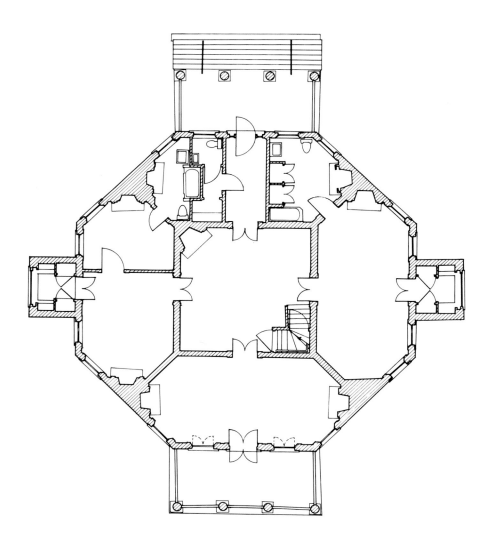

Fig. 116 Main floor plan, as remodeled by the Watts family. The two small rooms flanking the front entrance were converted into bath and closet space, and the two stair pavilions were made into closet/dressing areas (cf. figs. 21 and 108). (*Tim Buehner, delineator, 1991*)

On the opposite side of the entry hall from the new master bathroom, the former northwest bedroom was also completely eliminated, and the space divided into a guest lavatory with adjacent closet entered from the front hall. Also within the space formerly occupied as a bedroom, a full bath was added to serve the adjoining western bedroom and dressing area. A new opening was created between that dressing area and the new bath, and as with the new connection between the master bathroom and bedroom on the eastern side of the house, this door was in the same spot as the one that Jefferson had instructed Hugh Chisolm to add early in the original construction period. As was noted, both had been bricked during the rebuilding after the 1845 fire. At the time the Wattses undertook their initial restoration, the stairway in the west pavilion was left in place. It was later removed, and built-in closets and chests, similar to those in the opposite pavilion, were installed. In addition, a trapdoor with a ladder was introduced in this area as an escape hatch from the main floor to the ground

floor, to be used in case of emergency.[27]

The only main-floor room that received major decorative changes was the parlor, soon to be termed the living room. During the Hutter years, it had become the most architecturally prominent room in the house, and its primacy was now made even more manifest. The Thompson/Barnum specifications, which gave notice of its new prominence by labeling it the drawing room, summarized the work: "All doors and window trim and doors to porch shall be new also mantels, chairrail, and cornice according to Architect's drawings and full size details"[28] (fig. 118). There was more to it than that. At the time the Wattses undertook their work, they communicated with Francis Berkeley, Jr., at the University of Virginia and obtained copies of the correspondence between Jefferson and William Coffee regarding the plaster decorations that Jefferson had ordered in the 1820s. A photographer was sent to the university to photograph Coffee's work at the pavilions there, and these pictures served as the basis for the living-room entabla-

Fig. 117 Southwest view. A comparison between this view and fig. 49 shows the dramatic difference made when the Wattses reopened the windows in the southwestern wall. *(September 24, 1964, A. B. Rice, Virginia State Library and Archives)*

Fig. 118 Poplar Forest, living room, showing Watts-era trim (cf. fig. 107). *(Jack E. Boucher, 1986, for the Historic American Buildings Survey, Prints and Photographs Division, Library of Congress).*

ture.[29] The frieze was embellished by casts of "boy and swag" (as Coffee had described them) taken from the Ionic order of the Temple of Fortuna Virilis (fig. 119). In addition, a triangular pediment, similar to those Jefferson had at Monticello, was added above the door leading from the living room into the central room. The intent of all these changes was to give at least one of the rooms in the house a proper Jeffersonian flavor, and in this it succeeded.

If the drawing room, or living room, now assumed an ever greater hierarchical position in relation to the other spaces in the house, the central room descended to an even lower rung on the architectural ladder, but here the plans and specifications diverged on what was to be accomplished. Jefferson's once-elegant dining room, known as the center room by the Hutters, was listed only as "stair hall" in the new specifications, which stated simply: "No [change] except repairs if necessary and ordered by Owner."[30] The drawings, on the other hand, indicate that, although the room was not to be heightened to its original cubical proportions, a full entablature — including replicas of the frieze ornaments Jefferson had ordered from Coffee — was to be installed. According to the owner, the decision not to carry out the proposed changes in the stair hall was based on the fact that there was "no solid information as to the size, type or location of the skylight in this room."[31] The drawings, on the other hand, indicate that Barnum had a very good idea of the original nature of this feature.

The drawings also proposed removing the Hutter-era stair in this room, and replacing it with a far more elegant circular one. As it turned out, this was not done, but while the old stair continued to lead up to an unchanged attic, it now led downward to a completely altered ground floor. In order to gain height, all basement floor levels were lowered six to eight inches, and a new concrete slab replaced the termite-ridden wooden floors in several of the rooms. The center stairway now led directly into the room under the center room, or "stair hall." This "dark hole" as Paul Wilstach had termed it, was now dubbed the rock room, and was so labeled on the drawings. With its original solid rock walls, now painted white, and with its flooring of random-width pine boards taken from a Hutter-era barn that the Wattses demolished, it became as cozy a den as could be wished. A trapdoor was installed in the northwest corner of the room to give access to the crawl space beneath — the remainder of Jefferson's wine cellar and the area that Wilstach had termed a "dungeon." The spaces that the Hutters had assigned to kitchen and dining room were reversed. As the eastern stair pavilion no longer contained a stairway, a small servants' lavatory was installed there, adjacent to the outside entry. The Hutter dining room (the eastern room) was converted into a kitchen and serving pantry, while the former kitchen, as well as the narrow hall and bedroom adjoining, were made into one space corresponding to the living room directly above. With its central door leading to the arcade under the south portico, and with its above-grade windows, this room was considered the most formal and appropriate space for a dining room. The western spaces on the ground floor remained as bedrooms, and a new bath was installed directly under the bath occupying the western portion of the former northwest bedroom above. A boiler room and a storage area were incorporated in the north end of the basement. Later during the Wattses' ownership, the former crawl space under the front portico was dug out and opened to the basement, to give additional storage space and to serve as a wine cellar.

Although the Thompson & Barnum specifications noted that, in general, the plastering was to consist "mostly of patching after other trades," new ceilings were installed throughout. These were done to accom-

Fig. 119 For the frieze of the living-room entablature, architect Phelps Barnum designed for the Wattses this replica of the Ionic order from the temple of Fortuna Virilis, which Jefferson had specified for the same room over a hundred years earlier (cf. fig. 92.) *(1985, Historic American Buildings Survey, Prints and Photographs Division, Library of Congress)*

modate copper coils for radiant heat, installed by the Lynchburg engineering firm of Wiley & Wilson. The installation of this then relatively new system was a conscious and successful attempt to provide adequate heat without disfiguring the interior with "radiators or registers which . . . would be unsightly at Poplar Forest."[32]

Perhaps surprisingly, in light of all the problems it had caused over the years, the roof was given only summary attention. The specifications directed: "No work to be done at present except flashing of vents through roof and inspection of flashings, roofs, gutters and leaders with report on any repair necessary or leaks which should be fixed." Again, the specifications were directed more to the immediate situation, while the plans proposed work that could be accomplished in the future. In his drawings, Barnum proposed a restoration of the full balustrade — based on that shown in John Neilson's drawing — around the perimeter of the roof, though he was not aware of the Chinese railing that had enclosed the deck above. The Wattses also kept the cast-iron steps leading to the front entrance, at least until they collapsed under the weight of a visiting dignitary in later years. After that mishap, the iron steps were replaced with simple wooden steps, intended as a temporary

expedient until further research could determine what the configuration and design of the original stairway might have been[33] (fig. 120). Barnum's plans called for a stone stairway with iron railings which, whether anything like the original or not, would at least have been a handsome and appropriate treatment.

The extensive new kitchen and pantry facilities obviously made an outside kitchen completely redundant. Although they did not rebuild the office wing to the Jeffersonian plan, the Wattses converted the old exterior kitchen and the adjacent smokehouse into a guest suite, and added a bath and closets in a connecting hyphen that was built between them. The connection was given a flat roof, while new wooden shakes were installed on the distinctive gable and pyramidal roofs of the two outbuildings. During the summer, the guest suite was taken over by the Wattses' younger son, Stephen.

To the east of the guest suite, the Wattses had planned to convert the two brick tenants' houses into a single house to serve Mrs. Watts's mother. Thompson and Barnum prepared a plan, dated May 15, 1947, showing a hyphen joining these two structures, but this project was never undertaken. Instead, the two buildings continued as tenants' houses.

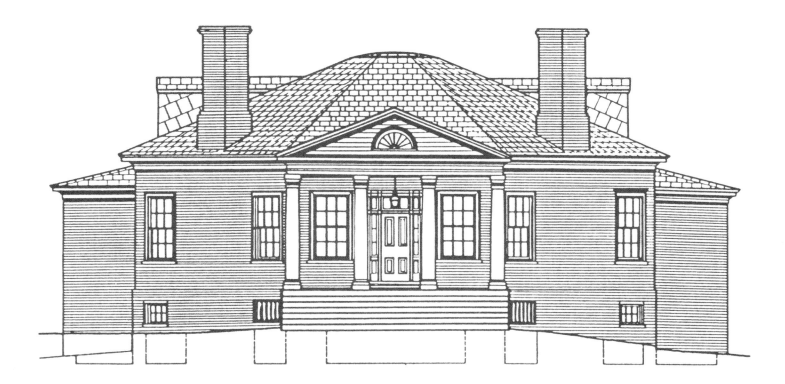

Fig. 120 North elevation, Poplar Forest, 1985. After the Watts restoration, the roof and front doorway were left unchanged from the Hutter years. A wooden stairway later replaced the cast-iron steps they had installed, and windows were reopened in the northeastern and northwestern angular walls. *(Historic American Buildings Survey, Prints and Photographs Division, Library of Congress)*

Changes were also made in the yard. The level of the sunken south lawn was lowered approximately a foot in an attempt to improve ground-floor drainage, a change deemed necessary because the ground-floor level of the house had been lowered. Although the relative slope of the original grade was kept largely intact, this work unfortunately destroyed much of the evidence that may have remained to indicate former landscaping patterns here, such as the purported gravel walk that Paul Wilstach discussed. By the time the Wattses purchased Poplar Forest, the several remaining trees of the rows formerly lining the upper edges of the swale were long past their prime, and they were subsequently removed (cf. figures 49 and 117). To the southeast of the sunken lawn, a brick-enclosed rose garden was built. In conscious imitation of Jeffersonian precedent at the University of Virginia, the western wall of the garden was built in serpentine form.

The net effect of the many modifications undertaken by the Watts family was to change the nature of Poplar Forest once again. From the farmhouse the early Hutters knew and the summer place that later generations of that family loved and enjoyed, it now became an elegant, year-round, country house, complete with guest quarters and swimming pool (built after the initial renovation work, to the south of the walled garden). Conscious efforts were made as well to restore the flavor of the Jefferson period to the house and grounds, with plans to continue the restoration if time and finances permitted (fig. 121).

As in the Hutter period, the main farmyard area continued to be to the west and southwest of the house. As mentioned above, one of the Hutter barns was demolished and its timbers used as flooring for the rock room, but the Watts family also added to the farmyard complex. A shed was attached to an existing barn (known to the Wattses as the horse barn), the largest of the farm structures. A new smokehouse was also built in this area, and sometime later, a frame garage was built adjacent to it. In more recent years, the horse barn has been converted into offices and an archeological laboratory, while the smokehouse/garage has been converted into a visitors' entrance and gift shop.

Early in their ownership, the Wattses also turned their attention to the surrounding farmland, which had been neglected in the many years that the property had served as a summer place. With the help of a land-use map provided by the U.S. Department of Agriculture Soil Conservation Service, a four-year plan was undertaken, and Elmer E. Obenchain was hired as farm manager. Lands

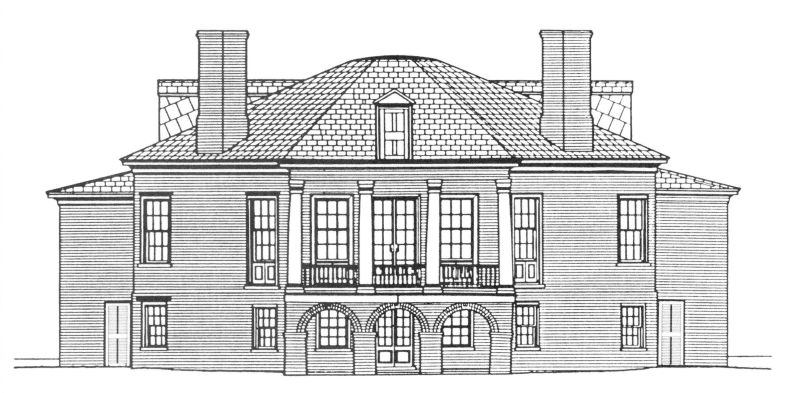

Fig. 121 South elevation, Poplar Forest, 1985. This is the condition in which the house appeared at the time it was acquired by the Corporation for Jefferson's Poplar Forest. (Compare endpapers and fig. 32). *(Historic American Buildings Survey, Prints and Photographs Division, Library of Congress)*

were cleared, fields were plowed, crops were planted, and a dairy herd was eventually added. The barn known in the Hutter period as the granary was renamed the sheep barn, as the Wattses reintroduced sheep to the Poplar Forest scene.[34] Mr. Jefferson would surely have approved (fig. 122).

Like the Hutters before them, the Wattses were always willing to show Poplar Forest to interested visitors. And, as had increasingly been the case in the Hutter years, the property continued to receive at least a modicum of scholarly attention. "Thomas Jefferson's Favorite Hideaway" was the title of an article by William H. Gaines, Jr., published in the Summer 1955 issue of *Virginia Cavalcade*, while Lynchburg historian Lucille McWane Watson called her study that was published in the April 1957 issue of *The Magazine Antiques* "Thomas Jefferson's other home."[35] As founder, and for many years editor, of the *Iron Worker*, a quarterly house organ of the Lynchburg Foundry Company, Mrs. Watson was also responsible for the coverage that journal gave Poplar Forest over the years. Frederick D. Nichols's "Jefferson's Retreat: Poplar Forest" was the lead article in its Spring 1974 issue.[36]

In her 1957 article, "Thomas Jefferson's other home," Mrs. Watson had been able to write of Poplar Forest that "more than a thousand acres of the original tract still guard its traditional privacy." That condition, unfortunately, was not to last, and by the time Professor Nichols wrote his article in 1974, it was no longer true. In late January 1972, Mr. Watts telephoned James A. Bear, Jr., then curator of Monticello, and "boldly broached the question, 'would the Foundation be interested in acquiring Poplar Forest?'" A feasibility study that was quickly prepared for the Thomas Jefferson Memorial Foundation, owners of Monticello, summarized the situation: "The owners wish to see the house and the property preserved as an historic site. As their resources will not allow them to do this, they must sell the property. Mr. Watts has offered the Foundation, as his first choice, the consideration of the responsibility of restoring Poplar Forest. If something cannot be worked out, the owners will turn to real estate interests for financial relief."[37] The study was presented to the directors of the Thomas Jefferson Memorial Foundation at their April 1972 meeting, and "after considerable discussion it was the sense of the Board that the . . . Foundation could not pursue the acquisition, maintenance and operation of Poplar Forest single handed, but that the Foundation would provide any possible leadership and moral persuasion in an effort toward such preservation in cooperation with residents of Lynchburg and the National Trust for Historic Preservation."[38]

According to the feasibility study, "preliminary and

ensuing discussions yielded nothing in the form of an asking price that was seriously considered." The Wattses next made a similar offer to sell Poplar Forest to the Lynchburg Historical Foundation for $1,250,000, along with the condition that they be given life tenancy. In a December 1, 1972, letter to Mrs. Watson, Monticello Board member Francis L. Berkeley, Jr., correctly gauged that the life-tenancy stipulation would prove a problem and urged that a shorter-term lease be arranged.[39]

In a report she gave to the Lynchburg Historical Foundation, Mrs. Watson concluded: "The benefits to be derived from the restoration of this beloved 'other home' of the great Thomas Jefferson are too obvious to need enumeration. A rare opportunity has been offered us to perform a national service. What will we do about it?" On March 13, 1973, George C. Palmer II, vice-president and treasurer of the Thomas Jefferson Memorial Foundation, offered the "enthusiastic cooperation of all of us at Monticello" to Mrs. Watson and her associates in the Lynchburg Historical Foundation and the Lynchburg Bicentennial Commission who were then attempting to take advantage of the Watts offer and to put together a plan to purchase and restore Poplar Forest.[40] Julian P. Boyd, then editor of *The Papers of Thomas Jefferson* at Princeton, offered "to help in any way that I can," but also saw that the owners' stipulation of life tenancy as a precondition to the sale might prove an insurmountable difficulty.[41] Ultimately it was.

At the time the Watts offer was made to the Thomas Jefferson Memorial Foundation, there were still 872 acres in the Poplar Forest tract. As no satisfactory arrangements could be made to sell to a historical foundation, the Wattses began the process of selling off the land in parcels for residential development, reserving 50 acres surrounding the house for themselves.[42] By this time, the suburbs of Lynchburg were already encroaching on the property, and lots sold well. As the former farmland was being sold, the farm equipment was no longer needed. On March 30, 1973, before any final decision had been made regarding the possible purchase of the property by a historical group, the Lynchburg *News* carried an advertisement for a sale to be held on April 7. Four diesel tractors, a Ford dump truck, two bush hogs, and many other items were listed, giving an idea of the extent of the farm operations that were now ceasing. Except for the mechanical nature of the equipment, the advertisement could be regarded as something of a repeat performance of the sales that Francis Eppes and Thomas Jefferson Randolph had conducted when they were disposing of their respective portions of Poplar Forest almost a hundred and fifty years earlier.

Soon the house and its remaining acreage were put on

the market. The Charlottesville, Virginia, realty firm of Stevens & Company was given the commission to sell the house, and soon prepared a handsome brochure promoting it. The price for the house and adjoining fifty acres was listed as $600,000, and the hope that a buyer could be found who would maintain the house as a private country estate was implied in the language of the brochure: "Views northward to the Blue Ridge are unobstructed. Besides the pleasant and quaint dependencies, there are old barns and granary for conversion to stables. A fitting part of the Jefferson plantation heritage. A brook meanders across the north edge of the estate."[43] In addition to the brochure, advertisements were placed in appropriate magazines, and the one in *The Magazine Antiques* caught Dr. James A. Johnson's eye. A physician in High Point, North Carolina, and an enthusiastic admirer of Jefferson for many years, Johnson called William T. Stevens, principal in the realty firm, to ascertain that it actually was *the* Poplar Forest that was being offered. Stevens not only assured him that it was, but revealed that a contract was already being prepared to sell the property to a prospective purchaser who planned to convert the house into a restaurant. Acting immediately, Johnson wired $50,000 as a down payment, and his purchase was recorded on November 6, 1980. Johnson's stated plan was to hold Poplar Forest until an appropriate organizational structure could be set up by a historical foundation to acquire it, preserve and restore it, and open it to the public.[44]

Poplar Forest was not yet secured, however. In April 1981, while local groups continued to discuss its purchase, Dr. Johnson had the Stevens firm send letters to potential buyers with a new proposal. Two options were now given. The house could still be acquired with the fifty acres immediately surrounding it, or it could be purchased with an additional 333 acres that were then being developed as a sports complex. The price for the first option, half a year after Dr. Johnson had bought it for $600,000, had virtually doubled, to $1,150,000. For the second option, the price was set at $2,656,000. The Stevens Company's brochures were sent out again, with the new prices pasted over the old. While the brochure continued to address the historical and aesthetic attributes of the property, a letter that accompanied it was more blatant in its approach: "Combined shrewdness and good taste can make an enjoyable money-machine out of the property, at the same time, teaching history to millions of Americans and foreigners, young and old."[45]

Realizing that the threat was now real and imminent, local historical organizations mobilized. The Bedford Historical Society and the Lynchburg Historical Foundation agreed to share start-up costs, and sponsored the

formation of the Poplar Forest Foundation.[46] This group —whose board consisted of representatives from the two lead organizations as well as from the Thomas Jefferson Memorial Foundation and the Association for the Preservation of Virginia Antiquities—was incorporated in December 1982.[47] Poplar Forest was again taken off the market while negotiations between the owner, Dr. Johnson, and the new foundation began. Ultimately, the two parties were unable to agree on a price, a condition that had been hinted at when a representative of the foundation stated: "We're trying to solve the problem of what we have, which is zero, and what he wants, which is a lot."[48] Negotiations were finally discontinued in September 1983, and a new group began its plans to purchase the property. On December 19, 1983, the Lynchburg *News* announced: "Group agrees to buy Poplar Forest." The day before, Sunday, December 18, "nearly 200 people crowded into Jefferson's Poplar Forest to witness the new committee cap several months of negotiations begun by an informal group and sign a contract to purchase the house and its 49.5 acres for about $927,000." Gerald A. Baliles, soon to be Virginia's governor, was among those present to sign as a witness to the agreement. The committee, "officially called the Corporation for Jefferson's Poplar Forest," had been formally organized only a few hours before the ceremony. Four days later, the Lynchburg *News* editorialized that "it was the best Christmas present Central Virginia could have received, and we have a small group of dedicated citizens to thank for it."[49] In January 1984 the deed recording the transfer of title was recorded at the Bedford County Courthouse. Later in 1984, an additional 255 acres of land were purchased, and in 1987, 109 more acres were acquired, ensuring that as much as possible of the still pastoral landscape surrounding Poplar Forest would remain inviolate to development.

The story of the work accomplished by the non-profit Corporation for Jefferson's Poplar Forest since its formation and purchase of the property continues to be exciting and rewarding to all concerned. It is, however, a story that must be reserved for another time and place. Suffice it to say that, at long last, Poplar Forest is in good hands, and its future preservation is secured. Thanks to the discoveries that have been made, and that are continuing to be made regarding its original condition, the decision has already been reached that a restoration to the way Thomas Jefferson knew Poplar Forest is not only feasible, it can be achieved with as high a degree of accuracy as current state-of-the-art expertise can provide. Once that is accomplished, Poplar Forest will contribute enormously to the better understanding and appreciation of one of the most important individuals in history.

Fig. 122 Poplar Forest, aerial view. Taken in April 1955, this view shows contour plowing — Jefferson would have called it horizontal ploughing — in the huge field to the upper left of the photograph. (*Virginia State Library and Archives*)

Henry S. Randall, in his *Life of Thomas Jefferson* (New York, 1858), pp. 342–44, published the following letter that Jefferson's granddaughter Mrs. Joseph Coolidge (née Ellen Wayles Randolph) had written him in 1856. Presumably in answer to his inquiry for a description of Poplar Forest as it was in Jefferson's time, her letter gives not only that, but also discusses the life he led there, what the property meant to him, and his relations with his family and his neighbors. Excerpts have been used from this source throughout my text. Inasmuch as this letter remains the most detailed and eloquent description yet known of Poplar Forest by one who knew it in Jefferson's lifetime (although the author wrote of it some thirty years after her last known visit there), it is herein reproduced from Randall's volume verbatim:

_____ _____, 1856

My Dear Mr. Randall:

The house at Poplar Forest was very pretty and pleasant. It was of brick, one story in front, and, owing to the falling of the ground, two in the rear. It was an exact octagon, with a centre-hall twenty feet square, lighted from above. This was a beautiful room, and served as a dining-room. Round it were grouped a bright drawing-room looking south, my grandfather's own chamber, three other bedrooms, and a pantry. A terrace extended from one side of the house; there was a portico in front connected by a vestibule with the centre room, and in the rear a verandah, on which the drawing-room opened, with its windows to the floor.

Mr. Jefferson, from the time of his return home in 1809, was in the habit of visiting this Bedford plantation, but it was some years before the house was ready for the reception of his family. It was furnished in the simplest manner, but had a very tasty air; there was nothing common or second-rate about any part of the establishment, though there was no appearance of expense. As soon as the house was habitable, my grandfather began to take the ladies of his family, generally two at a time, with him, whenever he went. His first visit of a fortnight or three weeks was in the spring — the second, of about six weeks, in early or late autumn. We have staid as much as two months at a time. My mother went occasionally — not very often — for she had too much to do at home. I . . . generally accompanied him with one of my younger sisters. Mr. Jefferson greatly enjoyed these visits. The crowd at Monticello of friends and strangers, of stationary or ever-varying guests, the coming and going, the incessant calls upon his own time and attention, the want of leisure that such a state of things entailed as a necessary consequence, the bustle and hurry of an almost perpetual round of company, wearied and harassed him in the end, whatever pleasure he may have taken, and it was sometimes great, in the society and conversation of his guests. At Poplar Forest he found in a pleasant home, rest, leisure, power to carry on his favorite pursuits — to think, to study, to read — whilst the presence of part of his family took away all character of solitude from his retreat. His young grand-daughters were there to enliven it for him, to make his tea, preside over his dinner table, accompany him in his walks, in his occasional drives, and be with him at the time he most enjoyed society, from tea till bed time. The weather was generally fine (the autumn climate of this part of Virginia is delightful, and even the spring is pleasant), the neighbors, who were to a man exceedingly attached to him, were very friendly, without being oppressive in their attentions. There were some excellent people among those Bedford neighbors of ours, and something touching in their affection for their old friend, whose arrival they watched for with pleasant anticipation, and hailed with a sort of loyal satisfaction. It was no sooner known in the neighborhood that Mr. Jefferson had arrived, than our neighbors hastened to help our housekeeping with all kinds of fruit; vegetables, poultry, game (I remember once a quarter of a bear's cub), the product of rich farms and an abundant country.

By and by the gentlemen came dropping in — the ladies soon followed — we were invited out to dine, and the neighbors came to dine with us — but not often enough to consume much time, or interrupt our home occupations. I remember among these neighbors a certain "Parson" Clay, as he was called, who must have been an Episcopal clergyman before the Revolution, to whose four sons my grandfather used to lend books, and who astonished me with their names of Cyrus, Odin, Julius and Paul.

My grandfather was very happy during these sojourns in a comparatively simple and secluded district — far from noise and news — of both of which he got too much at Monticello; and we, his grand-daughters, were very happy too. It was a pleasant change for us, a variety in life and manners. We saw, too, more of our dear grandfather at those times than at any other. He was most desirous that we should find congenial occupations, and we had books, drawing materials, embroidery, and never felt time heavy on our hands. He interested himself in all we did, thought, or read. He would talk to us about his own youth and early friends, and tell us stories of former days. He seemed really to take as much pleasure in these conversations with us, as if we had been older and wiser people. Such was the influence of his affectionate, cheerful temper, that his grandchildren were as much at their ease with him, as if they had not loved and honored and revered him more than any other earthly being. I… not only listened with intense interest to all he said, but answered with perfect freedom, told my own opinions and impressions, gave him my own views of things, asked questions, made remarks, and, in short, felt as free and as happy as if I had been with companions of my own age. My grandfather missed my mother of course. Her company had become very necessary to him, but her absence seemed the only drawback on his unalloyed satisfaction during these short and highly prized intervals of rest and leisure.

Our days at Poplar Forest were cheerful and uneventful. We met in the morning for an early breakfast, which, like all his other meals, he took leisurely. Whilst sipping his coffee or tea he talked with us, and if there was anything unusual to be done, arranged our plans for the day. The forenoon, whilst we followed our own desires, he passed in the drawing room with his books. With the exception of an occasional visitor, he was seldom interrupted until the hour of his ride. We dined about three, and as he liked to sit over his wine (he never took more than three glasses, and these after, and not during dinner), I always remained at table till he rose. His conversation was at this time particularly pleasant — easy, flowing, and full of anecdote. After dinner he again retired for some hours, and later in the afternoon walked with us on the terrace, conversing in the same delightful manner, being sometimes animated, and sometimes earnest. We did not leave him again til bed-time, but gave him his tea, and brought out our books or work. He would take his book from which he would occasionally look up to make a remark, to question us about what we were reading, or perhaps to read aloud to us from his own book, some passage which had struck him, and of which he wished to give us the benefit. About ten o'clock he rose to go, when we kissed him with warm, loving, grateful hearts, and went to our rest blessing God for such a friend.

Mr. Jefferson had decidedly one of the evenest and most cheerful tempers I ever knew. He enjoyed a jest, provided it were to give pain to no one, and we were always glad to have any pleasant little anecdote for him — when he would laugh as cheerily as we could do ourselves, and enter into the spirit of the thing with as much gaiety.

It was pleasant to see him in company with the country gentlemen of the neighborhood, they treated him with so much affectionate and respectful frankness — were so much at their ease with him, whilst they held him in such high honor. Their wives too were as happy as queens to receive him, and when he called or dined with them, were brimful of satisfaction and hospitable devotion. This frank and free homage, paid by independent people, who had nothing to gain, to one whose public character had merited their approbation, and whose private virtues they loved and revered, was equally honorable to those who rendered and him who received it.

Our journeys to and from Bedford, were almost always pleasant. The weather at the season of our visit was good of course, though we were once or twice caught by an early winter. The roads were not bad for country roads. My grandfather travelled in his own carriage, with his own horses, his faithful Burwell on horseback by his side. It took us nearly three days to make the hundred miles. We always stopped at the same simple country inns, where the country-people were as much pleased to see the "Squire," as they always called Mr. Jefferson, as they could have been to meet their own best friends. They set out for him the best they had, gave him the nicest room, and seemed to hail his passage as an event most interesting to themselves. These were pleasant times, but I have dwelt on them long enough. . . .

With great regard, my dear Mr. Randall,
Very truly yours.

Thomas Jefferson's letters, as well as other documents cited in these notes, are held by a number of repositories throughout the country. Acronyms of these repositories following the citations are those used by the National Union Catalog:

CSmH   Henry E. Huntington Library, San Marino, Calif.
DLC   Library of Congress, Washington
MHi   Massachusetts Historical Society, Boston
MoSHi   Missouri Historical Society, St. Louis
NcD   Duke University, Durham, N.C.
NcU   University of North Carolina, Chapel Hill
NNPM   J. P. Morgan Library, New York
PPAMP   American Philosophical Society, Philadelphia
PPRF   Rosenbach Foundation, Philadelphia
Vi   Virginia State Library and Archives, Richmond
ViW   Swem Library, William and Mary University, Williamsburg, Va.
ViHi   Virginia Historical Society, Richmond
ViU   University of Virginia, Charlottesville

The great majority of letters cited will be either to or from Thomas Jefferson, whose name will be abbreviated throughout as TJ.

INTRODUCTION

1. TJ to John Adams, July 5, 1814, DLC.

2. TJ to William Short, Nov. 24, 1821, MHi; [Ellen Randolph Coolidge] to Henry S. Randall, 1856, published in Henry S. Randall, *Life of Thomas Jefferson* 3:342. The complete text from which this quotation is taken is reproduced herein as the Appendix.

3. Dumas Malone, *Jefferson and the Ordeal of Liberty*, vol. 3 of *Jefferson and His Time*, p. 222, n. 4 (quoting B. L. Rayner, *Sketches of the Life, Writings, and Opinions of Thomas Jefferson*). The statement was first credited to Jefferson by Margaret Bayard Smith in her *A Winter in Washington* (New York, 1824) 2:261.

4. Frederick D. Nichols, "Jefferson's Retreat: Poplar Forest," *Iron Worker* 38, no. 2 (Spring 1974): 13; TJ to John Wayles Eppes, Sept. 18, 1812, CSmH.

5. TJ to Elizabeth Trist, April 27, 1806, MoSHi; Elizabeth Trist to TJ, May 19, 1806, Nicholas P. Trist Papers, NcU.

6. TJ to Gideon Granger, Sept. 20, 1810, DLC.

7. TJ to A. F. deLaage, Aug. 17, 1817, DLC.

8. Henry Howe, *Historical Collections of Virginia* (Charleston, S.C., 1845), p. 214; Alf J. Mapp, Jr., *Thomas Jefferson, Passionate Pilgrim* (Madison, N.C., 1991), p. 192.

9. Nathan Schachner, *Thomas Jefferson: A Biography* 2:1038. The reference is found in n. 6 to chap. 65.; Mary Denham Ackerly and Lula Eastman Jeter Parker, *"Our Kin,"* (Lynchburg, 1930), p. 13.

10. TJ to Martha J. Randolph, Feb. 24, 1811, MHi.

11. TJ to Robert Walsh, April 5, 1823, ViU.

CHAPTER I

1. TJ to Madame de Tessé, Oct. 26, 1805, MoSHi, cited in Edwin Morris Betts, ed., *Thomas Jefferson's Garden Book*, pp. 305, 306. Jefferson's Garden Book, begun in 1766 and ending in 1824, contains a variety of entries that will be cited throughout this work. The original Garden Book is in the Coolidge Collection, Massachusetts Historical Society, Boston. All citations to the *Garden Book* that follow will be to the Betts edition.

Jefferson had met Madame de Tessé, who was Lafayette's aunt, during his years in France. Both were ardent botanists, and this letter accompanied seeds of the tulip poplar, along with those for other plants, that he sent to her. In the letter Jefferson stated that the Quercus alba (white oak) was "the only tree with us which disputes for pre-eminence with the Liriodendron. It may be called the Jupiter while the latter is the Juno of our groves."

2. *Executive Journals of the Council of Colonial Virginia* (Richmond, 1945), vol. 5 (November 1, 1739–May 7, 1754), pp. 182, 217, 309. These journals were published by the Virginia State Library "from photographic copies of the original manuscripts which were sent . . . to the home authorities in England and are now preserved among the Colonial Office papers in the Public Record Office of Great Britain, London" (5: vii).

3. Bedford County was formed in November 1753 by "An Act for dividing the county of Lunenburg," to take effect May 10, 1754 (William Waller Hening, *The Statutes at Large*, [Richmond, 1819], 6:381). In October 1754 "all that part of the county of Albemarle, on the south side of James River" was added to the new county of Bedford (Ibid., 6:441). In 1781 Campbell County was formed from the eastern portion of Bedford, and part of the Poplar Forest tract was thereafter included in it (Ibid., 10:447). Thomas Jefferson used the terms *Bedford* and *Poplar Forest* interchangeably.

4. Lee Marmon, *Poplar Forest Research Report* 1:5. See also Land Patent Books cited therein.

5. See entry for William Stith in *Dictionary of American Biography* (New York, 1936) 18:34–35.

6. Thomas Jefferson, *Notes on the State of Virginia*. This important work, discussed more fully in chapter II, was first printed in Paris in 1785, followed by an English edition published in London in 1787. An easily available volume that contains *Notes* in its entirety is Merrill D. Peterson, ed., *The Portable Thomas Jefferson*, pp. 23–232. The quote concerning Stith's *History* is on Page 230 of the Peterson edition. All citations to *Notes* that follow will also be from this edition. Information on Jefferson's purchase of Stith's *History* is from Silvio A. Bedini, *Thomas Jefferson, Statesman of Science*, p. 92.

7. According to the Julian calendar then in use, Jefferson's birthday was April 2, 1743. The Gregorian calendar, adopted during his youth, changed the date to April 13, which has ever since been celebrated as his birthday.

8. *Executive Journals*, 5:182; Marmon, *Poplar Forest*, 1:1.

9. Martha Jefferson Randolph to Ellen Randolph Coolidge, undated letter (ca. 1826), ViHi. Ironically, in light of the importance that Poplar Forest (which he inherited through his wife) would assume in his land holdings, by 1776 Jefferson had sold all the Bedford County property he inherited from his own father (Marmon, *Poplar Forest*, 1:2).

10. TJ to William Radford, Nov. 30, 1822, MHi. For further information regarding Radford's inquiry and his correspondence with Jefferson, see Chap. XIX.

11. Edgehill-Randolph Papers, box 1, no. 1397, ViU.; Marmon, *Poplar Forest*, 1:6–8.

12. TJ to William Radford, Nov. 30, 1822, MHi. Wayles's land books were then in Jefferson's possession, but have since disappeared.

13. Ibid. A transcript of John Wayles's will may be found in *Tyler's Quarterly Historical and Genealogical Magazine* (Richmond, 1925) 6:268–70. Mrs. E. was Elizabeth (Mrs. Francis) Eppes, and Mrs. S. was Anne (Mrs. Henry) Skipwith. Elizabeth was the mother of John Wayles Eppes (born a month before John Wayles died), who would later marry Jefferson's daughter Maria. Martha Jefferson was a half sister of both Elizabeth and Anne.

14. Thomas Jefferson, Memorandum Book, Dec. 3, 1773. This and other Memorandum Book references are from: James A. Bear, Jr., and Lucia C. Stanton, eds., *Jefferson's Memorandum Books: Accounts, with Legal Records and Miscellany, 1767–1826*, forthcoming from Princeton University Press as part of *The Papers of Thomas Jefferson*, Second Series. Jefferson's thirteen Memorandum Books, covering the years 1767 to 1826, are in a number of different repositories (see Library of Congress, *Index to the Thomas Jefferson Papers*, p. xvi, n. 66). Unless additional explanation is needed, future quotations from the *Memorandum Book* in this text will be cited only to date of entry and will not be footnoted.

15. Dumas Malone, *Jefferson the Virginian*, vol. 1 of *Jefferson and His Time*, app. 2, pp. 441–45: "The Wayles Inheritance."

16. It is unclear who (or what) Smith was, but it is more than likely that Jefferson referred here to a blacksmith rather than to someone whose last name was Smith. In 1774, Jefferson noted in his Farm Book (p. 7) that one of the slaves at Poplar Forest was "Billy boy. Smith." (See n. 17 below for information on Farm Book). Jefferson had been to Bedford County on earlier occasions, but the September 8, 1773, entry is the first in his Memorandum Book in which the name Poplar Forest appears. Lynch's was the ferry operated by John Lynch at the future site of Lynchburg.

17. Edwin Morris Betts, ed., *Thomas Jefferson's Farm Book*, p. 7. This is a facsimile edition, with commentary, of Jefferson's original Farm Book, which is in the Coolidge Collection, Massachusetts Historical Society. All citations to the *Farm Book* that follow will be to the Betts edition.

18. *Farm Book*, pp. 16, 17. Although Judith's Creek, or Dun lora, had less acreage than Poplar Forest, judging from the relative numbers of slaves at each place, it must have been the larger plantation operation at the time.

19. Ibid., p. 19. In this listing Jefferson made no distinction between Wingo's and Poplar Forest. Wingo's comprised the acreage that Jefferson would devise to his daughter Martha upon her marriage in 1790 (see chap. III).

20. *Notes on Virginia*, pp. 218, 219.

21. *Farm Book*, pp. 255–310. Betts's commentary provides good information on tobacco culture on Jefferson's properties. In the decade following Jefferson's comment that tobacco was "a culture productive of infinite wretchedness," he was shipping hogsheads from both Albemarle and Bedford counties to Richmond, then to Philadelphia, for export and sale in England, France, and Germany.

22. *Notes on Virginia*, p. 219.

23. In *Farm Book*, pp. 201–26, Betts discusses the production of wheat and flour at Monticello and Poplar Forest.

CHAPTER II

1. Jefferson did not remain in Philadelphia continuously after his arrival in June 1775. He was in Virginia from August through September 1775 and from January until May 1776. He then remained in Philadelphia from May 14 until September 3, 1776.

2. Fiske Kimball, quoting Jefferson's bill to remove the seat of government, in "Jefferson and the Public Buildings of Virginia, II. Richmond, 1779–780," *Huntington Library Quarterly* 12, no. 3 (May 1949):303.

3. TJ to William Phillips, June 25, 1779, DLC.

4. On page 72 of his edition of Jefferson's *Garden Book*, Edwin Morris Betts notes a trip Jefferson took to Bedford in 1777, but gives no evidence for it. No reference to such a trip appears in Jefferson's Memorandum Book for that year. If, indeed, the trip was taken, which is doubtful, it was of short duration and of little importance.

5. June 12, 1781, entry in the House of Delegates Journal, cited in Malone, *Jefferson the Virginian*, p. 361.

6. TJ, *Memorandum Book*, entries for July 18 and 22, 1781; TJ to John Trumbull, June 1, 1789, DLC.

7. Isaac, "Memoirs of a Monticello Slave," in James A. Bear, Jr., ed., *Jefferson at Monticello* (Charlottesville, Va., 1967), p. 11. Years afterward, Jefferson recorded the barest of essential facts about the trip: "Tarleton had retired after 18 hours stay in Charlottesville. Mr. Jefferson then rejoined his family, and proceeded with them to an estate he had in Bedford, about 80 miles S. W. where, riding in his farm sometime after, he was thrown from his horse, & disabled from riding on horseback for a considerable time" (Thomas Jefferson Papers, DLC, quoted in Julian P. Boyd, ed., *The Papers of Thomas Jefferson* 5:268). Pages 256–78 of Boyd discuss Tarleton's raid and Jefferson's records of it.

8. TJ, "Autobiography" (begun Jan. 6, 1821), quoted in Paul Leicester Ford, ed., *The Writings of Thomas Jefferson* 1:85.

9. TJ to Chevalier d'Anmours, Nov. 30, 1780, DLC; See also Malone, *Jefferson the Virginian*, p. 374.

10. TJ to Marquis de Barbè-Marbois, March 4, 1781, cited in Ford, *Writings* 3:314.

11. TJ, *Notes on the State of Virginia*, advertisement to the 1787 edition, cited in Merrill D. Peterson, ed., *The Portable Thomas Jefferson*, p. 25; Charles Thomson to TJ, March 6, 1785, DLC. The amount of work done on Notes at Poplar Forest has long been the source of some speculation. Apparently, Jefferson took much of the material he had gathered with him when he left Monticello, edited it, "completed the greater part of the work in several weeks during the summer," and, while still at Poplar Forest, made notes of additional questions he needed to have answered (Bedini, *Thomas Jefferson, Statesman of Science*, pp. 89–93). In his advertisement to the 1787 edition, Jefferson wrote: "The following Notes were written in Virginia in the year 1781 and somewhat corrected and enlarged in the winter of 1782."

12. *Notes on Virginia*, p. 203.

13. Kimball, pp. 308–10.

14. *Notes on Virginia*, p. 49.

15. Ibid. p. 54.

16. In his land roll of 1794, found on page 32 of his *Farm Book*, Jefferson noted that he had patented his 157-acre Natural Bridge tract on July 5, 1774 (see fig. 12). Later trips Jefferson took to the bridge are discussed in chaps. XII and XIV.

17. *Notes on Virginia*, pp. 216, 217.

18. Pliny the Elder, *Naturalis Historia*, XVIII. iii, 13, cited in James S. Ackerman, *The Villa*, p. 39.

19. *Notes on Virginia*, pp. 127, 128. Jefferson used population figures for 1782 in his Notes, an indication that this portion of his work was finished after his 1781 visit to Poplar Forest (see n. 11, above).

20. Bedford County, Virginia, Court Order Book no. 6 (Bedford Co. Courthouse, Bedford, Va.), pp. 333, 334.

21. Henry S. Randall, *Life of Thomas Jefferson* 3:341.

22. A slight possibility exists that a plan drawn by Jefferson in August 1782 may represent an early house at Poplar Forest. The drawing is numbered 263a and labeled "Plan of buildings for Forrest Plantation" in Frederick D. Nichols, *Thomas Jefferson's Architectural Drawings*. The plan shows a rectangular house (forty-six feet by eighteen feet) containing a central passage with a room on each side, and a single-room rear ell, measuring eighteen feet by sixteen feet. Nichols groups the drawings with others for Poplar Forest, but it is more likely that it was a plan of John Wayles's house at his plantation, The Forest, in Charles City County.

23. TJ to Jeremiah Goodman, Oct. 10, 1812, PPAmP.

24. TJ to Edmund Randolph, Sept. 16, 1781, DLC.

25. Hening, *The Statutes at Large* 10:568.

26. *Garden Book*, p. 94.

27. Campbell County, Virginia, Court Order Book no. 1 (Campbell Co. Courthouse, Rustburg, Va.), p. 12 (entry for April 1782), cited in Marmon, *Poplar Forest* 1:60.

28. Malone, *Jefferson the Virginian*, p. 399.

29. TJ, "Autobiography," quoted in Ford, *Writings* 1:84.

30. *Memorandum Book*, entry for July 5, 1784.

31. John Tyler to TJ, May 20, 1784, DLC.

CHAPTER III

1. TJ, "Autobiography," in Ford, *Writings* 1:88; Howard C. Rice, Jr., *Thomas Jefferson's Paris*, p. 51.

2. TJ to James Madison, Sept. 20, 1785, DLC; Clérisseau had illustrated the building in his *Monumens de Nimes*, a copy of which Jefferson owned.

3. TJ to Dr. James Currie, Jan. 28, 1786, DLC.

4. TJ, "Autobiography," in Ford, *Writings* 1:63–65. TJ also arranged to have the French sculptor Houdon carve the statue of George Washington that stands in the rotunda of the Virginia State Capitol.

7. Fiske Kimball, *Thomas Jefferson, Architect*, pp. 40–43, 142–48.

6. TJ to Madame de Tessé, March 20, 1787, DLC.

7. *Garden Book*, p. 103.

8. Francis Eppes to TJ, Sept. 16, 1784, MHi.

9. TJ to Nicholas Lewis, July 29, 1787, DLC; TJ to Lewis, July 11, 1788, DLC.

10. TJ, "Autobiography," in Ford, *Writings* 1:88.

11. TJ to Thomas Mann Randolph, Sr., Feb. 4, 1790, MHi.

12. Ibid.; Deed, TJ to Martha Jefferson, Feb. 21, 1790, ViU. Jefferson's "Land Roll in 1794" (fig. 12) noted that 1,000 acres of Poplar Forest were "conveyed to TM. & M. Randolph." In his "Land Roll, 1810" (fig. 46), Jefferson noted "1,441 1/2 acres . . . with 8 1/2 acres adjoining . . . having been conveyed to T. M. Randolph & Martha."

13. Deed, TJ to Martha Jefferson, Feb. 21, 1790, ViU. The deed names the slaves, many of whom had been included in the Farm Book list of slaves that Jefferson made in 1774. Jefferson also listed and named the slaves given Martha in his Farm Book (p. 25), and noted that he gave the Randolphs eight more on November 6, 1790. (Pages 25 and 26 were missing when the Betts annotated version of the Farm Book was published in 1987. The pages have since been located and John Catanzariti, editor of *The Papers of Thomas Jefferson*, furnished copies to me.)

14. Martha Jefferson Randolph to Ellen Randolph Coolidge, undated letter (ca. 1826), ViHi.

15. Mary Lewis to TJ, April 14, 1790, ViU; Marmon, *Poplar Forest* 1:33–37. Perhaps Mrs. Lewis can be forgiven her spelling of Lynchburg. It had then been in existence only four years, having been established in 1786.

16. TJ to Nicholas Lewis, July 4, 1790, DLC.

17. TJ to Maria Jefferson, July 4, 1790, ViU.

18. TJ to Thomas Mann Randolph, Jr., May 1, 1791, cited in Ford, *Writings* 6:250–51, and in *Garden Book*, p. 163; TJ to Philip Mazzei, Aug. 2, 1791, ViU. For more information on the interesting Philip Mazzei, see *Garden Book*, p. 63.

19. Hamilton quotes are from Dumas Malone, *Jefferson and the Rights of Man*, vol. 2 of *Jefferson and His Time*, pp. 291, 287.

20. *Farm Book*, p. 25 (This is one of the "missing pages" of the *Farm Book*; see n. 13 above); Marmon, *Poplar Forest* 3:18; TJ to Francis Eppes, March 11, 1792, DLC.

21. TJ to T. M. Randolph, Jr., Oct. 12, 1792, ViU.

22. TJ to Bowling Clark, Sept. 21, 1792, DLC; *Farm Book*, p. 25 (This is one of the "missing pages" of the *Farm Book*; see n. 13, above).

23. "Roll of the negroes Nov. 1794 and where to be settled for the year 1795," *Farm Book*, p. 30. This list names forty-eight slaves in Bedford. Old Will and Old Judy are the last two names on the roll.

24. TJ to Martha J. Randolph, Jan. 15, 1792, ViU; TJ to Martha J. Randolph, March 22, 1792, quoted in James A. Bear, Jr., and Edwin Morris Betts, *The Family Letters of Thomas Jefferson*, p. 96.

25. James Madison to TJ, May 27, 1793, quoted in Dumas Malone, *Jefferson and the Ordeal of Liberty*, vol. 3 of *Jefferson and His Time*, p. 87.

26. TJ to Angelica Church, Nov. 27, 1793, DLC.

CHAPTER IV

1. Sarah N. Randolph, *The Domestic Life of Thomas Jefferson*, pp. 228, 229.

2. TJ to George Washington, April 25, 1794, cited in *Garden Book*, p. 217.

3. TJ to Henry Knox, June 1, 1795, DLC.

4. Betts in *Farm Book*, pp. 426–53, has a comprehensive discussion of the Monticello nailery. See also James A. Bear, Jr., "Thomas Jefferson—Manufacturer," *Iron Worker* 25, no. 4 (Autumn 1961), pp. 1–11.

5. TJ to James Steptoe, Aug. 16, 1794, DLC; TJ to Francis Eppes, Aug. 28, 1794, ViU; TJ to James Madison, April 27, 1795, DLC; TJ to James Steptoe, May 17, 1795, DLC.

6. TJ to Thomas Mann Randolph, Jr., Aug. 18, 1795, DLC; *Farm Book*, p. 48.

7. TJ to Martha J. Randolph, June 8, 1797, NNPM; TJ, "Land Roll in 1794," in *Farm Book*, p. 32.

8. TJ to Thomas Mann Randolph, Jr., Nov. 28, 1796, DLC.

9. See Appendix.

10. Albemarle County Deed Book 12, pp. 363, 364, cited in Bear and Betts, *Family Letters*, p. 147; *Farm Book*, p. 25, names the thirty-one slaves given as a "marriage settlement to J. W. Eppes, Oct. 97" (See n. 13 to Chap. III regarding this page in the *Farm Book*).

11. TJ to Thomas Mann Randolph, Jr., March 22, 1798, DLC.

12. Martha J. Randolph to TJ, May 12, 1798, MHi.

13. Maria J. Eppes to TJ, May 27, 1798, inquiring if the harpsichord had arrived at Monticello. TJ had written her on May 18, 1798, that it had arrived, but their letters apparently crossed in the mails (Bear and Betts, *Family Letters*, p. 163). See also Maria to TJ, Feb. 2, 1801, asking for time to choose between the harpsichord and a piano (ibid., p. 194).

14. TJ to Maria J. Eppes, June 14, 1797, cited in Bear and Betts, *Family Letters*, p. 148; TJ to Maria J. Eppes, Dec. 2, 1797, cited ibid., p. 149.

15. *Memorandum Book*, Oct. 27 through Nov. 3, 1800.

16. Randall, *Life of Thomas Jefferson* 3:341. Randall depended a great deal on Ellen's recollections in his treatment of Poplar Forest. Her well-known description of the house follows this description of the 1800 trip (see Appendix).

CHAPTER V

1. See Saul K. Padover, ed., *Thomas Jefferson and the National Capital* (Washington, 1946), for information on Jefferson's connections with the development of the Federal City.

2. Thomas Jefferson, "First Inaugural Address," March 4, 1801, in Peterson, ed., *The Portable Thomas Jefferson*, pp. 290–95. Dumas Malone, *Jefferson and the Ordeal of Liberty*, vol. 3 of *Jefferson and His Time*, pp. 491–505 discusses the politics of the election and the voting sequence that finally resulted in Jefferson's election as president.

3. Contrary to popular opinion, the President's House was painted, or at least whitewashed, as early as 1798, long before its burning by the British in the War of 1812 necessitated its being painted afterwards to hide the smoke stains. See William Seale, *The White House: The History of an American Idea* (Washington, 1992), p. 23. During Jefferson's tenure, the building was generally referred to as the President's House.

4. William Seale, *The President's House: a History* (Washington, 1986) 1:91; Padover, *Thomas Jefferson*, p. 338.

5. Seale, *President's House* 1:112.

6. C. Allan Brown, *Thomas Jefferson's Poplar Forest: the mathematics of an ideal villa*, pp. 121–123, also n. 61, p. 136.

7. Frederick L. Kramer, *The White House Gardens* (New York, 1973), pp. 13, 14.

8. Brown, *Thomas Jefferson's Poplar Forest*, pp. 123, 127. Brown's essay is the first to my knowledge to have demonstrated the "striking similarities" between the landscaping at the President's House and Poplar Forest.

9. TJ to Albert Gallatin, Sept. 18, 1801, DLC.

10. Bedford County Land Tax Record, 1800, Microfilm roll 32, Vi; *Memorandum Book*, entry for Aug. 17, 1801; Wilson Cary Nicholas to TJ, Aug. 12, 1801, DLC.

11. TJ to Thomas Mann Randolph, Jr., Oct. 8, 1801, CSmH; TJ to John Wayles Eppes, Oct. 9, 1801, CSmH. Both letters are

reproduced in Norma B. Cuthbert, "Poplar Forest: Jefferson's Legacy to His Grandson," *Huntington Library Quarterly* 6, no. 3 (May 1943), pp. 334–36.

12. John Wayles Eppes to TJ, May 6, 1803, MHi.

13. TJ to John Wayles Eppes, Oct. 9, 1801, CSmH; TJ to Maria J. Eppes, Oct. 26, 1801, cited in Bear and Betts, *Family Letters*, p. 210.

14. Four of the plans are in the Massachusetts Historical Society's collection of Jefferson papers and are numbered 185–188 by Fiske Kimball in his *Thomas Jefferson, Architect*. In that work, Kimball also considered nos. 189 and 190 to be preliminary plans for Poplar Forest, but later decided these were for Farmington, a Jefferson-designed house in Kentucky — not to be confused with the Farmington in Albemarle County, Va., which he also designed (See Fiske Kimball, "Jefferson's Designs for Two Kentucky Houses," in *Journal of the Society of Architectural Historians* 9 [1950]: 14–16). In addition to these drawings, there is another related drawing in the Nicholas P. Trist papers at the Southern Historical Collection at the University of North Carolina, of which Kimball did not know. See also Nichols, *Thomas Jefferson's Architectural Drawings*, with his comments on nos. 19, 20, and 256–59.

15. TJ to James Madison, May 19, 1793, DLC, cited in Conover Hunt-Jones, *Dolley and the "great little Madison"*, p. 63. See also Fiske Kimball, *Domestic Architecture of the American Colonies and of the Early Republic* (New York, 1922), p. 155.

16. Jefferson's plans for these outbuildings at Bedford may be related to another unrealized plan that he had drawn earlier for another house. Thought to be a plan for the Governor's House in Richmond, and presumably dating from the time Virginia's capital was moved there in 1780, it shows twin dependencies on either side of a square house, connected to it by open colonnades. The fenestration patterns of the wings are identical to those in the plans for Bedford, and the room arrangements are not dissimilar (see Kimball, "Jefferson and the Public Buildings of Virginia," fig. 6). Kimball mistakenly identified the drawing as being in the Coolidge Collection at the Massachusetts Historical Society in Boston. It is in the Thomas Jefferson Papers at the University of Virginia (see Thurlow and Berkeley, *The Jefferson Papers*, p. 275).

17. Dumas Malone, *Jefferson the President, First Term*, vol. 5 of *Jefferson and His Time*, p. 275.

18. Meriwether Lewis to his mother, July 3, 1803, quoted in Seale, *The President's House* 1:96.

19. TJ to Madame de Tessé, Jan. 30, 1803, DLC.

20. TJ to Maria J. Eppes, Jan. 18, 1803, quoted in Randall, *Life of Thomas Jefferson* 3:44–45. Thomas Mann Randolph, Jr., served in Congress from 1803 to 1807, while John Wayles Eppes served from 1803 to 1811. Eppes was then defeated by John Randolph, but in 1813 he won the seat back from him, and served until Randolph once again defeated him in the next election. In 1816, Eppes was elected to the United States Sen-

ate, where he served from March 1817 until he resigned because of ill health in April 1819. Thomas Mann Randolph, Jr., served in the War of 1812 and in 1819 was elected to the Virginia House of Delegates. He was elected governor of Virginia the same year, and served in that capacity until 1822. He was again a member of the state legislature from 1823 to 1825.

Jefferson's relations with both his sons-in-law were cordial at the outset of their marriages to his daughters, or at least Jefferson did his best to make them so. Numerous strains and misunderstandings from time to time, along with supposed slights by their father-in-law perceived by Randolph and Eppes, prevented a completely harmonious association. Of the two, Eppes maintained the closer relationship to Jefferson, strengthened by Jefferson's devotion to Francis Eppes, the only child of John Wayles Eppes and Maria's to reach maturity. Although (or perhaps because) Randolph was almost always in closer proximity, his relationship, not only to his father-in-law, but to his whole family, deteriorated. By the end of Jefferson's life, Randolph had become estranged from his family.

21. Maria J. Eppes to TJ, Jan. 24, 1802, cited in Betts and Bear, *Family Letters*, pp. 216, 217.

22. TJ to Maria J. Eppes, Jan. 29, 1804, quoted in Randolph, *Domestic Life of Thomas Jefferson*, p. 296.

23. TJ to John Wayles Eppes, March 15, 1804, ViU; TJ to James Madison, April 9, 1804, DLC; Thomas Mann Randolph, Jr., to C. A. Rodney, April 16, 1804, MoSHi.

24. TJ to John Wayles Eppes, June 4, 1804, quoted in Randall, *Life of Thomas Jefferson* 3:99.

25. John Wayles Eppes to TJ, June 14, 1804, MHi.

26. Alfred L. Bush, *The Life Portraits of Thomas Jefferson* (Charlottesville, Va., 1962), p. 69.

27. TJ to William Short, Oct. 17, 1812, ViW. At the time, Short was considering buying property near Monticello, and Jefferson offered to give bond for a portion of the price. He told Short: "My portion of Mr. Wayles's great debt was finally discharged about 8. years ago."

28. In his letter to Martha J. Randolph of January 5, 1808 (cited in Bear and Betts, *Family Letters*, p. 319), Jefferson stated that he would leave his office "loaded with serious debts." In his letters to Thomas Mann Randolph, Jr., Jan. 17, 1809, DLC, and to Martha J. Randolph, Feb. 27, 1809, MHi, he gave the actual dollar amount of $10,000.

29. TJ to Martha J. Randolph, Feb. 27, 1809, MHi. See also Dumas Malone, *The Sage of Monticello*, vol. 6 of *Jefferson and His Time*, p. 36.

CHAPTER VI

1. TJ to John Wayles Eppes, March 25, 1805, CSmH; TJ to John Wayles Eppes, May 27, 1805, DLC.

2. Both in 1805 and in 1810, Jefferson paid the same five-year tax on the same number of acres in Bedford as he had in 1800, giving evidence that no land transfers were recorded during

those years. His 4,000 acres were assessed at $9,840, and the tax paid was $47.25 in 1800, 1805, and 1810 (Bedford County Land Tax Record, Microfilm roll 32, Vi). According to his Memorandum Book, he "set out for Poplar Forest" on July 26, 1805, and spent the first night of his return trip (July 31) at Hunter's, a tavern on the Campbell-Buckingham county line.

3. Betts, *Farm Book*, p. 516; TJ to James Madison, Sept. 5, 1808, DLC.

4. TJ to Elizabeth Trist, April 27, 1806, MoSHi. Mrs. Trist, the daughter of his Philadelphia landlady, Mrs. House, would become the grandmother-in-law of Virginia Randolph, Jefferson's granddaughter. Late in life, she moved to Virginia, and continued to visit and correspond with Jefferson and members of his family. Another reference to the completion of work at Monticello had been given in a note Jefferson had received the previous October from John Jordan, one of his master builders there. In it Jordan announced: "I have finished the building of your house and would thank you to let me know when it will be convenient for you to settle with me for it" (John Jordan to TJ, Oct. 26, 1805, MHi). Of course, Monticello, like most of Jefferson's architectural projects, was never completely finished, but the fact that the beginning of construction at Poplar Forest coincided with an expected cessation of work at Monticello is certainly not accidental. It was time for Jefferson to turn his attention once again to one of his favorite pursuits, "putting up and pulling down," which he had already begun to do by the time he wrote Mrs. Trist.

5. TJ to John Wayles Eppes, May 24, 1806, CSmH. As it turned out, Eppes did not remarry at this time, but did so three years later (see chap. VIII).

6. TJ to John Wayles Eppes, June 30, 1820, ViU.

7. In the checklist in Nichols, *Thomas Jefferson's Architectural Drawings*, the Monticello example is no. 57, the chapel is no. 419, and the log building is no. 469. Nichols also shows the Monticello plan with the octagonal pavilions as plate 3 in his work.

8. Brown, *Thomas Jefferson's Poplar Forest: the mathematics of an ideal villa*, pp. 120, 121.

9. Isaac Coles to Gen. John Hartwell Cocke, Feb. 23, 1816, Cocke Family papers, ViU.

10. Brown, pp. 130 (fig. 11), 131.

11. TJ to Martha J. Randolph, June 16, 1806, MHi.

12. TJ to George Jefferson, August 17, 1806, MHi. George Jefferson, a cousin, was Jefferson's Richmond factor and agent in many of his commercial dealings.

13. TJ to Hugh Chisolm, Sept. 7, 1806, MHi. The Mr. Perry mentioned in the letter was either John or Reuben Perry (see chaps. VIII and IX).

14. Kimball, *Thomas Jefferson, Architect*, p. 71; James S. Ackerman, *The Villa*, p. 209.

15. Ackerman, The Villa, p. 9.

16. TJ to Edmund Bacon, Sept. 29, 1806, quoted in James A.

Bear, Jr., ed., *Jefferson at Monticello*, pp. 62, 63.

17. TJ to Martha J. Randolph, Oct. 20, 1806, NNPM.

18. Malone, *Jefferson the President, Second Term*, vol. 5 of *Jefferson and His Time*, pp. 199, 203.

19. TJ to James Dinsmore, Dec. 28, 1806, Vi.

20. *Memorandum Book*, entry for June 13, 1798. See also n. 63 with that entry in Bear and Stanton, eds., *Jefferson's Memorandum Books: Accounts, with Legal Records and Miscellany, 1767–1826*, forthcoming from Princeton University Press as part of *The Papers of Thomas Jefferson*, Second Series; K. Edward Lay, "Jefferson's Master Builders," *University of Virginia Alumni News* 80, no. 1 (Oct. 1991): 17.

21. TJ to Charles Clay, Jan. 11, 1807, DLC.

22. Ibid.

23. Malone, *Jefferson the President, Second Term*, contains a complete account of the Burr conspiracy and its attendant trial in chaps. 8–20.

24. Hugh Chisolm to TJ, June 1, 1807, MHi.

25. Ibid; See also *Memorandum Book*, entry for April 15, 1807, documenting Jerry's return to Poplar Forest.

26. Hugh Chisolm to TJ, June 1, 1807, MHi.

27. TJ to Hugh Chisolm, June 5, 1807, MHi.

28. Ibid.

29. Brown, pp. 123, 126. Jefferson's mention of the width as ninety feet in the postscript of his letter to Hugh Chisolm referred to the "floor" of the sunken lawn, but did not include the sloping sides.

30. Hugh Chisolm to TJ, June 15, 1807, MHi.

31. TJ to Chisolm, August 5, 1807, MHi.

32. TJ to James Steptoe, June 8, 1807, MHi; Zebulon Pike quoted in Seale, *The President's House* 1:97.

33. John Wayles Eppes to TJ, Aug. 9, 1807, MHi; John Wayles Eppes to TJ, Nov. 1, 1810, ViU.

34. TJ to William Couch, Sept. 26, 1807, MHi.

35. James Dinsmore to TJ, Oct. 16, 1807, MHi; TJ to Dinsmore, Oct. 25, 1807, MHi.

36. TJ to George Jefferson, Nov. 7, 1807, MHi.

37. John Perry to TJ, Dec. 11, 1807, MHi; TJ to Hugh Chisolm, Dec. 15, 1807, MHi.

38. TJ, "Memorandum," quoted in *Garden Book*, pp. 356–58. This list of instructions to Bacon, Jefferson's Monticello overseer, is undated except for the year (1807). Jefferson's memoranda to his overseers were generally given in December, and the wording (eg. "when the wagon goes up at Christmas") hints that such was the case in this instance. Jefferson habitually referred to going up to Poplar Forest from Monticello.

39. TJ to Elizabeth Trist, Dec. 27, 1807, MoSHi.

CHAPTER VII

1. TJ to Martha J. Randolph, Jan. 5, 1808, cited in Bear and Betts, *Family Letters*, p. 319.

2. Martha J. Randolph to TJ, Jan. 16, 1808, cited in ibid., pp. 322, 323.

3. TJ to James Dinsmore, Dec. 29, 1807, MHi; Dinsmore to TJ, Jan. 1 and Jan. 28, 1808, MHi.

4. *Memorandum Book*, March 28, 1805. See also n. 57 for this entry in the forthcoming Bear and Stanton edition of this work.

5. TJ to Dinsmore, Feb. 6, 1808, MHi; TJ to Dinsmore, March 20, 1808, MHi.

6. Hugh Chisolm to TJ, Feb. 1808, MHi.

7. TJ to Chisolm, Feb. 23, 1808, MHi; Note of Hugh Chisolm, Feb. 1808, MHi.

8. Edmund Bacon to TJ, March 19, 1808, MHi.

9. TJ to Bacon, March 22, 1808, MHi. See chap. VIII for more information on Mr. Brown.

10. TJ to John Perry, March 29, 1808, MHi.

11. Dinsmore to TJ, April 21, 1808; Bacon to TJ, April 23, 1808; MHi.

12. TJ to Bacon, June 7, 1808, quoted in Bear, *Jefferson at Monticello*, pp. 67, 68; TJ to Dinsmore, June 12, 1808, MHi; Dinsmore to TJ, June 24, 1808, MHi.

13. Bacon to TJ, June 30, 1808, ViU.

14. TJ to Dinsmore, June 27, 1808, MHi; Dinsmore to TJ, July 1, 1808, MHi.

15. Note of Hugh Chisolm, Feb. 1808, MHi. (Although the note also contains dates later than February 1808, that is the first date given, and the note is filed chronologically in MHi under that date.)

16. Chisolm to TJ, July 22, 1808, MHi.

17. TJ to Benjamin Henry Latrobe, Feb. 28, 1804, DLC.

18. Mesick-Cohen-Waite, Architects, *Jefferson's Poplar Forest*, Report on Phase II-A Investigations, 1991, pp. 9–15, contains an impressive discussion on the proper proportions of classical orders.

19. Isaac Coles to John Hartwell Cocke, Feb. 23, 1816, Cocke Family papers, ViU.

20. Mesick-Cohen-Waite, Architects, *Jefferson's Poplar Forest*, p. 9.

21. Hunt-Jones, *Dolley and the "great little Madison"*, pp. 62, 63; TJ to James Oldham, Dec. 24, 1804, quoted ibid., p. 131, n. 11.

22. Chisolm to TJ, Sept. 4, 1808, MHi.

23. Chisolm to TJ, June 1, 1807, MHi.

24. Edwin Betts, on page 377 of his edition of Jefferson's *Garden Book*, quotes a segment of this letter and translates as *nursery* the word I have rendered as *necessary*. While much of Chisolm's handwriting is virtually undecipherable, I am of the opinion that he definitely meant *necessary* in this instance. His statement that he had done "one" of them and would soon complete "the other" would indicate that there would be two —which there are. In addition, Chisolm would likely have had

nothing to do with any aspect of planting or gardening, although he did, of course, have a great deal to do with building.

25. The existence of this privy was discovered during the architectural excavations undertaken in 1990–91. See William M. Kelso, M. Drake Patten, and Michael A. Strutt, Poplar Forest Archaeology Research Report, pp. 17, 18.

26. TJ to Chisolm, Sept. 8, 1808, MHi.

27. TJ to James Madison, Sept. 5, 1808, DLC.

28. Articles of Agreement between Thomas Mann and Martha Randolph and Charles Lewis Bankhead and Anne Cary Randolph, Sept. 17, 1808, ViU.

29. TJ to Martha J. Randolph, Nov. 29, 1808, quoted in Bear and Betts, *Family Letters*, p. 366.

30. TJ to Madison, Sept. 23, 1808, DLC.

31. Chisolm to TJ, Oct. 20, 1808, MHi.

32. Hugh Chisolm's note, February 1808, MHi (See n. 15 above concerning the dating of this note). Provisions for spirits as partial compensation in building operations were not unusual at the time. Workers building the President's House in Washington had been given their choice of a pint of whiskey or rum each day, and during the heat of August and September they had been given an extra half-pint per day (Seale, *The President's House: a History* 1:67). Jefferson also provided whiskey to his slaves during harvest season, according to records kept in his Farm Book. Jefferson apparently did not settle this bill completely with Chisolm until November 1810 (see chap. IX).

33. Hunt-Jones, *Dolley and the "great little Madison"*, pp. 66–72, discusses Chisolm's work at Montpelier.

34. TJ to Martha J. Randolph, Feb. 27, 1809, MHi.

35. TJ to Madame de Corny, March 2, 1809, DLC; TJ to Pierre Samuel duPont de Nemours, March 2, 1809, DLC.

CHAPTER VIII

1. Edmund Bacon to TJ, Dec. 29, 1808, ViU; TJ to Bacon, Jan. 3, 1809, CSmH.

2. More than any other individual, John Perry was responsible for the actual construction of the University of Virginia, which was built on land purchased from him. After his work there, he built Frascati (1821–23) in Orange County and Castle Hill (1823–24) in Albemarle County. See K. Edward Lay, "Jefferson's Master Builders," *University of Virginia Alumni News* 80, no. 1 (Oct. 1991): 16–19; Calder Loth, ed., *The Virginia Landmarks Register*, 3d. ed. (Charlottesville, Va., 1986), pp. 10, 311.

3. Reuben Perry, "Account with Jefferson," Dec. 10, 1813, ViW; TJ to Robert Richardson, Dec. 10, 1812, MHi; TJ to Reuben Perry, May 10, 1811, ViW.

4. TJ to Thomas Mann Randolph, Jr., Jan. 17, 1809, DLC; TJ to Martha J. Randolph, Feb. 27, 1809, MHi.

5. Elizabeth Trist to "my dear friend" [Nicholas P. Trist], April 3, 1809, Nicholas P. Trist Papers, NcU; TJ to John Barnes, April 27, 1809, DLC. At the time of her letter, Mrs. Trist was

visiting Mr. and Mrs. George Divers, mutual friends of hers and Jefferson's, at Farmington, their home near Charlottesville, which Jefferson had designed. Nicholas Philip Trist and his younger brother, Hore Browse Trist, came to live at Monticello late in 1817 and were reared there. Nicholas would later marry Virginia Randolph, Jefferson's granddaughter (see chap. XX).

6. TJ to George Jefferson, June 12, 1809, MHi.

7. TJ to Gideon Granger, Sept. 20, 1810, DLC.

8. Ellen Randolph Coolidge, from a letter of 1856, published in Henry S. Randall, *Life of Thomas Jefferson*, 3:342–43. See Appendix.

9. Virginia Department of Historic Resources, "Federal Hill," (Nomination form, National Register of Historic Places, 1982); "Invitation from Jefferson," in Works Progress Administration of Virginia, Historical Inventory, Nov. 25, 1939 (copy at Poplar Forest).

10. TJ, Note of agreement with James Martin, Nov. 14, 1809, MHi; TJ to Martin, Nov. 17, 1809, MHi; TJ, notes on sale of tobacco, Nov. 18, 1809, MHi; TJ to James Steptoe, Nov. 17, 1809, MHi.

11. Reuben Perry to TJ, Dec. 23, 1809, ViW.

12. TJ to Charles Clay, Dec. 15, 1809, DLC; TJ to James Steptoe, Dec. 15, 1809, ViHi; TJ, authorization to Thomas Mann Randolph, Jr., Dec. 15, 1809, MHi.

13. Burgess Griffin to TJ, Dec. 27, 1809, ViU; James Martin to TJ, Jan. 15, 1810, MHi; TJ to Bowling Clark[e], May 14, 1812, ViU.

14. *Memorandum Book*, April 11, 1810. See also nn. 66 and 68 for the year 1810 in the forthcoming Bear and Stanton edition of this work.

15. Peggy J. Spinks, Scott v. Burton Lawsuit (Copy in Jones Memorial Library, Lynchburg).

16. Burgess Griffin to TJ, Dec. 27, 1809, ViU.

17. John Richardson to TJ, Jan. 16, 1810, MHi.

18. *Memorandum Book*, April 11, 1810.

19. John Wayles Eppes to TJ, July 10, 1809, MHi.

20. TJ to John Wayles Eppes, Dec. 25, 1809, CSmH; TJ to Eppes, Jan. 24, 1811, DLC.

21. TJ to Francis Eppes, Sept. 6 1811, Hubard Family Papers, NcU.

22. Deed, Thomas Mann Randolph and Martha to Anne Moseley, Feb. 19, 1810, Gray Family Papers, ViHi. The acreage had been reduced when the Randolphs had given a portion of their land to their daughter Anne as her dowry in 1808.

23. TJ to Archibald Robertson, May 25, 1822, MHi.

24. Marmon, *Poplar Forest* 1:83–85, discusses the claims that have been made for an earlier date for Ashwood.

25. TJ to Charles Johnston, Feb. 18, 1810, MHi; *Memorandum Book*, April 14, 1810 (recording Johnston's payments for the tobacco). See Janet Shaffer, "Sandusky, 'By the Still Waters,'" *Lynch's Ferry* 4: no. 1 (Spring/Summer 1991), pp. 31–36, for

information on Johnston and Sandusky, which would again have a connection with Poplar Forest in later years (see chap. XXIII); TJ to Martha J. Randolph, February 27, 1809, MHi.

26. "Roll of Negroes in Bedford, April 1810," in *Farm Book*, p. 129. In this roll (see fig. 47), Jefferson termed his two plantation operations Poplar Forest and Bear Creek. He more often used the term Poplar Forest to encompass *both* of his subsidiary operations, and then labeled the two individually as Tomahawk and Bear Creek. The house was in the center of the Tomahawk tract; the Bear Creek plantation was to the north of Tomahawk.

27. TJ to Joseph Darmsdatt, May 27, 1810, MHi.

28. W. Asbury Christian, *Lynchburg and Its People* (Lynchburg, 1900), pp. 46, 47.

29. TJ to Wm. A. Burwell, Sept. 5, 1810, MHi.

30. *Memorandum Book*, entries for Sept. 6 and Sept. 9, 1809; TJ to Gideon Granger, September 20, 1810, DCL.

31. TJ to James Dinsmore, Sept. 26, 1810, MHi.

32. See Malone, *The Sage of Monticello*, vol. 6 of *Jefferson and His Time*, app. 3, pp. 513, 514, for a succinct discussion of the Hemings family; see also Bear, *Jefferson at Monticello*, opposite p. 24, for their family tree. Jefferson used both "Johnny" and "John" in referring to Hemings, and traditionally spelled his last name with one m. Hemmings spelled his last name with two m's.

33. *Memorandum Book*, April 11, 1811. See also n. 84 accompanying this entry in the forthcoming Bear and Stanton edition of this work.

34. William Burwell to TJ, Oct. 12, 1810; MHi; TJ to Hugh Chisolm, Sept. 10, 1810, MHi.

35. TJ to Hugh Chisolm, Nov. 17, 1810, MHi; *Memorandum Book*, Sept. 17 and Nov. 17, 1810. The final payment made to Chisolm for his work at Poplar Forest work was $136.61.

36. TJ to John Barnes, Jan. 10, 1811, DLC.

37. TJ to Martha J. Randolph, Feb. 24, 1811, MHi. A portion of this letter is quoted in the Introduction (above) as evidence that Jefferson's journeys to Poplar Forest were not limited solely to summer visits.

38. TJ, "Planting Memorandum for Poplar Forest 1811," cited in *Garden Book*, pp. 464, 465. Originally Jefferson had intended to plant the Athenian poplars instead of willows on top of the mounds, and willows instead of aspens at the bases. He lined through the first suggestion, and wrote the new instructions above (see also C. Allan Brown, *Poplar Forest: the mathematics of an ideal villa*, pp. 136, 137, n. 82).

39. Charles Bankhead to TJ, June 29, 1811, ViU. In addition to his financial problems, which may have prompted the sale, Charles Bankhead later became an alcoholic and an embarrassment to the Monticello family. See Malone, *Sage*, pp. 159, 160.

40. Deed between Thomas Jefferson and Reuben Perry, Feb.

1811. ViW; Marmon, *Poplar Forest* 3:111.

41. *Richmond Enquirer*, April–May 1811, cited in Marmon, *Poplar Forest*, 3:111.

42. TJ to Reuben Perry, May 10, 1811, ViW.

43. TJ to Wilson J. Cary, July 28, 1811, ViU; *Memorandum Book*, Aug. 4, 1811.

44. Marmon, *Poplar Forest* 1:42. See n. 26, above, for information on the two plantation operations at Poplar Forest.

45. TJ to William Burwell, Aug. 9, 1811, DLC.

46. TJ to Benjamin Rush, Aug. 17, 1811, DLC.

47. TJ to Charles Willson Peale, Aug. 20, 1811, DLC.

48. TJ to Rev. Charles Clay, Aug. 20, 1811, DLC.

49. TJ to John Wayles Eppes, Sept. 6, 1811, DLC; TJ to Francis Eppes, Sept. 6, 1811, Hubard Family Papers, NcU (both letters noted TJ would visit in November); *Memorandum Book*, Nov. 20–22, 1811.

50. TJ to Jeremiah Goodman, Dec. 1811, quoted in *Garden Book*, pp. 465–67; TJ to Edmund Bacon, Dec. 5, 1811, DLC.

51. Charles Bankhead to TJ, June 29, 1811, ViU; Deed, TJ to William Radford and Joel Yancey, December 7, 1811, ViU. Radford and Yancey paid $12,800 for the property (see also Wm. Radford to TJ, Nov. 19, 1822, MHi [in chap. XIX], and Marmon, *Poplar Forest* 1:45).

52. TJ to Benjamin Rush, Dec. 5, 1811, DLC.

53. Ibid. The complete story of the reconciliation is told in Lester J. Cappon, ed., *The Adams-Jefferson Letters* 2:283–87.

CHAPTER IX

1. TJ to Jeremiah Goodman, May 12, 1812, PPRF. This letter is also reproduced in *Garden Book*, pp. 487, 488. The original is badly torn, necessitating the bracketed insertions.

2. Betts, commenting in his edition of *Farm Book*, p. 112.

3. TJ to Joseph Dougherty, May 24, 1810, DLC; TJ to William Caruthers, March 12, 1813, DLC.

4. TJ to John Wayles Eppes, June 3, 1812, ViU.

5. TJ to John Wayles Eppes, June 25, 1812, DLC.

6. TJ to Reuben Perry, August 9, 1812, ViW.

7. Addendum to Agreement of Feb. 1811, dated Sept. 3, 1812, ViW; TJ to Reuben Perry, Sept. 12, 1812, ViW.

8. TJ to John Wayles Eppes, Sept. 18, 1812, CSmH.

9. Ibid.

10. TJ to Goodman, Oct. 10, 1812, PPAmP.

11. TJ to Goodman, Oct. 18, 1812, CSmH.

12. TJ to Charles Johnston, Nov. 15, 1812, MHi (Jefferson misspelled his neighbor's last name as Johnson).

13. *Memorandum Book*, Nov. 17, 1812; Charles Clay to TJ, Nov. 21, 1812, MHi.

14. TJ, "Planting Memorandum for Poplar Forest, 1812," cited in *Garden Book*, p. 494.

15. Ibid.; TJ to Charles Clay, Nov. 18, 1815, ViU.

16. TJ, "Planting Memorandum for Poplar Forest, 1812."

17. TJ to John Wayles Eppes, Sept. 18, 1812, CSmH. Brown, *Thomas Jefferson's Poplar Forest: the mathematics of an ideal villa*, treats these and other aspects of the landscape at Poplar Forest.

18. TJ to Robert Richardson, Dec. 10, 1812, MHi.

19. TJ to Reuben Perry, Dec. 10, 1812, ViW.

20. TJ to Jeremiah Goodman, Dec. 13, 1812, ViW; TJ to Reuben Perry, Dec. 26, 1812, ViW; TJ to David Ross, Aug. 1, 1813, MHi.

21. TJ to Jeremiah Goodman, Dec. 13, 1812, PPRF.

22. TJ to Charles Clay, Dec. 14, 1812, DLC; Charles Clay to TJ, May 1, 1813, MHi; TJ to Charles Clay, May 6, 1813, ViU.

23. TJ to Jeremiah Goodman, Memorandum, Dec. 1811, PPRF.

24. TJ to Jeremiah Goodman, Feb. 21, 1812, MHi; TJ to Goodman, Dec. 13, 1812, PPRF; TJ to Goodman, March 5, 1813, DLC.

25. TJ to Martha J. Randolph, May 6, 1813, MHi; TJ to Randolph Jefferson, May 25, 1813, ViU; TJ to Goodman, March 5, 1813, DLC.

26. TJ to Martha J. Randolph, May 6, 1813, MHi.

27. Reuben Perry, "Bill of work," July 1, 1813, ViW.

28. Reuben Perry, "Account with Jefferson," Dec. 10, 1813, ViW.

CHAPTER X

1. TJ to John Wayles Eppes, April 18, 1813, CSmH. The note to which Jefferson referred as "your last letter" has not been found.

2. Ibid.

3. Francis Eppes to TJ, April 11, 1813, quoted in Bear and Betts, *Family Letters*, p. 482; John Wayles Baker to TJ, April 11, 1813, MHi.

4. John Wayles Eppes to TJ, May 25, 1813, ViU.

5. TJ to John Wayles Eppes, June 24, 1813, ViU.

6. TJ to Francis Eppes, Aug. 28, 1813, CSmH; TJ to Thomas A. Holcombe, Aug. 28, 1813, MHi (Jefferson misspelled his name as Holcomb).

7. [Margaret Anthony Cabell], *Sketches and Recollections of Lynchburg by the Oldest Inhabitant*, p. 249.

8. TJ to John Wayles Eppes, July 16, 1814, CSmH.

9. TJ to Jeremiah Goodman, July 17, 1813, DLC.

10. TJ to William Shirman, April 16, 1814, MHi. Jefferson addressed his correspondent as Mr. Sherwin, but the response (Wm. Shirman to TJ, April 20, 1814, MHi) indicates his mistake.

11. TJ to William Shirman, April 16, 1814, MHi; Hugh Chisolm to TJ, May 22, 1814, MHi.

12. Kelso, Patten, and Strutt, Poplar Forest Archaeology Research Report, pp. 21–35, discusses the wing excavations and includes the illustration shown here as fig. 50.

13. TJ to Martha J. Randolph, June 6, 1814, MHi.

14. *Memorandum Book*, June 23 and July 5, 1814; TJ to John Adams, July 5, 1814, DLC.

15. TJ to John Wayles Eppes, July 16, 1814, CSmH. Jefferson was slightly mistaken in describing the office wing at Poplar Forest as "110 feet long," which is the length of the Monticello wing. As archeological investigations determined, the Poplar Forest wing was only a hundred feet long (See Chap. XX).

16. TJ to Jeremiah Goodman, Oct. 4, 1814, DLC.

17. Ellen Randolph Coolidge to Henry S. Randall, in Randall, *Life of Thomas Jefferson* 3:343; TJ to Martha J. Randolph, Aug. 31, 1817, MHi.

18. Kelso, Patten, and Strutt, Poplar Forest Archaeology Research Report, p. 26.

CHAPTER XI

1. TJ to Jeremiah Goodman, Dec. 10, 1814, MoSHi.

2. *Memorandum Book*, April 29, 1815.

3. TJ, note on taxes, Feb. 11, 1815, MoSHi; see also Bedford County (Northern District) Personal Property Tax Books, 1815, Vi. At Montpelier, James Madison also had to pay the tax; see Hunt-Jones, *Dolley and the "great little Madison"*, p. 56, n. 118.

4. Bedford County (Northern District) Personal Property Tax Books, 1815, Vi; TJ to James Oldham, Dec. 15, 1807, DLC.

5. Randall, *Life of Thomas Jefferson* 3:344–45. Randall depended heavily on information he requested and received from Jefferson's grandchildren in preparing his biography. While Randall does not identify the source of the information concerning the petit-format library, it may well have been Francis Eppes, who owned the books at the time, and who later sold them. Eppes is known to have furnished other information for Randall's Life (see also n. 6, following).

6. Geo. A. Leavitt & Co., Auctioneers, *Catalogue of a portion of the late Thomas Jefferson's Library*, pp. 36–40. This catalog was prepared for the sale of Jefferson's library, then owned by his grandson Francis Eppes, in 1873.

7. I am indebted to Susanne M. Olson, assistant curator at Monticello, and to "Duffy" (Mrs. Edwin C.) Hutter, of Princeton, New Jersey, for providing information on the Poplar Forest furnishings.

8. TJ to Edmund Bacon, Dec. 5, 1811, DLC.

9. TJ to George Jefferson, March 10, 1809, MHi. The chairs were ready to be shipped by June (see George Jefferson to TJ, June 19, 1809, MHi). Thomas Jefferson had ordered the same number of chairs for Poplar Forest a year and a half earlier, but that order had apparently never been filled (see TJ to William Couch, Sept. 26, 1807, MHi., noted in chap. VI).

10. [Ellen Randolph Coolidge] to Henry S. Randall, 1856, in Randall, *Life of Thomas Jefferson* 3:342. See Appendix for the full letter.

11. TJ to James Bowdoin, July 10, 1806, DLC, cited in Silvio A. Bedini, *Thomas Jefferson and His Copying Machines*, p. 147. This excellent work discusses the polygraph as well as other copying machines that Jefferson used throughout his lifetime. See

also pp. 39–41 for information on Hawkins, inventor of the polygraph.

12. TJ to Charles Willson Peale, Aug. 7, 1819, MHi; TJ to Benjamin Rush, Dec. 5, 1811, DLC and ViU.

13. Bedini, *Copying Machines*, pp. 181, 182.

14. TJ to Jeremiah Goodman, Jan. 6, 1815, PPRF.

15. TJ to William P. Newby, Jan. 20, 1815, DLC.

16. TJ to Elizabeth Trist, June 1, 1815, MHi. The friends were Mr. and Mrs. George Divers of Farmington, with whom Jefferson had an annual contest to see who could bring the first plate of peas to table (see *Garden Book*, pp. 538, 539).

17. TJ to William Newby, June 21, 1815, DLC. Newby had decided that he would accept Jefferson's offer if was still open, and Jefferson was explaining here why he had already hired someone else to manage his affairs.

18. Charles Clay to TJ, May 23, 1815, DLC.

19. TJ to Charles Clay, May 25, 1815, ViU; TJ to Archibald Robertson, June 1, 1815, ViU; Robertson to TJ, June 1, 1815, ViU. Jeremiah Goodman had not expected to be fired, and wrote his former employer: "I never knew what it was to have my feelings hurt. . . . My daily study has bein for your interest but Mr. Yancey will judge of this and I prauy [sic] to God he will give me justice" (Goodman to TJ, June 16, 1815, ViU).

20. TJ to Newby, June 21, 1815, DLC.

CHAPTER XII

1. TJ to Joel Yancey, July 25, 1815, MHi.

2. Mesick-Cohen-Waite, Architects, *Jefferson's Poplar Forest*, Report on Phase II-A Investigations, pp. 11, 12, discusses the balustrades, especially in relation to the classical orders.

3. TJ to Charles Clay, Aug. 25, 1815, ViU; TJ to Martha J. Randolph, Aug. 31, 1815, MHi.

4. TJ to John Rhea, Sept. 22, 1815, ViW.

5. Francis W. Gilmer to Peachy R. Gilmer, Nov. 3, 1814, cited in Richard Beale Davis, *Francis Walker Gilmer: Life and Learning in Jefferson's Virginia*, p. 77; Francis W. Gilmer to Peter Minor, Aug. 28, 1815, cited in ibid., p. 89.

6. TJ to Dr. William Steptoe, Sept. 13, 1815, Jones Memorial Library, Lynchburg, Va.

7. Christopher Clark to TJ, Aug. 31, 1815, MHi; TJ to Christopher Clark[e], Sept. 14, 1815, DLC; Clark to TJ, Sept. 17, 1815, MHi. Although Clark himself spelled his name without a final *e*, Jefferson spelled it with an *e*.

8. Peachy R. Gilmer to Francis W. Gilmer, Oct. 3, 1815, cited in Davis, *Gilmer*, p. 90.

9. *Memorandum Book*, March 12, 1814. See also n. 72 accompanying this entry in the forthcoming Bear and Stanton edition of this work; *Farm Book*, p. 114.

10. Dates and places noted for the trip are from *Memorandum Book* entries during September, 1815. Gilmer's paper on Natural Bridge, given on February 16, 1816, was later published by

the society. See *Transactions of the American Philosophical Society*, new series, vol. 1, no. 13, pp. 187–92.

11. TJ to John Rhea, Sept. 22, 1815, ViW; TJ to John Milledge, Sept. 22, 1815, DLC.

12. TJ to Randolph Harrison, Sept. 28, 1815, MHi.

13. Loth, *Virginia Landmarks Register*, p. 115.

14. TJ to Patrick Gibson, Sept. 29, 1815, ViHi; TJ to Archibald Robertson, Sept. 29, 1815, MHi; Penn (for Robertson) to TJ, Sept. 29, 1815, MHi.

15. *Memorandum Book*, Oct. 1, 1815. Jefferson's first recorded use of the term *vales* is a *Memorandum Book* entry dated April 26, 1786 (see n. 13 accompanying that entry in the forthcoming Bear and Stanton edition of *Jefferson's Memorandum Books*).

16. TJ to Christopher Clark[e], Nov. 2, 1815, MHi; Christopher Clark to TJ, Nov. 2, 1815, MHi; *Garden Book*, p. 549 (entry for Nov. 2, 1815).

17. TJ to Martha J. Randolph, Nov. 4, 1815, MHi. I am indebted to Gail Pond, researcher at Poplar Forest, for finding many of the references to Andrew Jackson's visit to Poplar Forest.

18. TJ to Christopher Clark[e], Nov. 5, 1815, MHi; *Richmond Enquirer*, Nov. 15, 1815.

19. John Reid to Mrs. Sophia Reid, Oct. 15, 1815, Reid Papers, DLC. "The City" refers to Washington; Betsy was Reid's wife.

20. *Richmond Enquirer*, Nov. 15, 1815.

21. R. H. Early, *Campbell Chronicles*, p. 240. Illustrations of the wallpaper are shown throughout this volume, which was written by a Cabell descendant.

22. *Richmond Enquirer*, Nov. 15, 1815; Robert V. Remini, *Andrew Jackson and the Course of American Empire, 1767–1821* (New York, 1977), p. 320; Marquis James, *The Life of Andrew Jackson* (Indianapolis, 1938), p. 272.

23. *Richmond Enquirer*, Nov. 15, 1815.

24. Mary Pocahontas Cabell to Mrs. Susan Hubard, Dec. 23, 1815, Hubard Family Papers, Southern Historical Collection, NcU.

25. TJ to John Wyche, Nov. 10, 1818, MoSHi; TJ to Capt. Alden Partridge, Jan. 2, 1816, DLC.

26. *Notes on Virginia*, p. 49 (see also chap. II).

27. TJ to Charles Clay, Nov. 18, 1815, ViU.

28. TJ, Planting Memorandum for Poplar Forest, Nov. 2 and Nov. 25, 1815, cited in *Garden Book*, p. 549.

29. TJ to Pierre Samuel duPont de Nemours, Dec. 31, 1815, DLC; TJ to Martha J. Randolph, Nov. 4, 1815, MHi; TJ to William Short, Jan. 15, 1816, ViW.

CHAPTER XIII

1. TJ to Charles Willson Peale, May 8, 1816, DLC.

2. TJ to Gideon Granger, Sept. 20, 1810, DLC.

3. S. Allen Chambers, Jr., *Lynchburg: An Architectural History*, p. 39.

4. John Holt Rice, "An Excursion into the Country," *Virginia Evangelical and Literary Magazine* 1, no. 40, (Nov. 1818): 507–08.

5. Holcombe's house and school, somewhat remodeled, still stand at 917 Federal Street in Lynchburg.

6. Charles Yancey to TJ, July 12, 1821, DLC. In requesting a plan for the Buckingham County, Virginia, courthouse (see fig. 89), Yancey wrote Jefferson that he and his fellow county commissioners would like to be able to say that they had "built upon a plan presented by Mr. Jefferson."

7. TJ to Samuel J. Harrison, Sept. 18, 1817, ViU.

8. Peregrine Prolix (pseudonym of Philip Holbrook Nicklin), *Letters Descriptive of the Virginia Springs* (Philadelphia, 1837), p. 141. This account dates from 1834, by which time the hotel was no longer owned by Harrison.

9. TJ to Archibald Robertson, March 28, 1816, MHi; TJ to Robertson, April 25, 1817, ViU.

10. John Wayles Eppes to TJ, April 28, 1817, ViU.

11. John Wayles Eppes to TJ, Dec. 11, 1815, ViU.

12. TJ to John Wayles Eppes, March 30, 1816, DLC.

13. *Memorandum Book*, April 30, 1816.

14. TJ to Francis Eppes, May 21, 1816, DLC.

15. TJ to John Wayles Eppes, April 30, 1816, CSmH; TJ to Eppes, June 24, 1816, MHi.

16. Ellen Randolph Coolidge to Henry S. Randall, Feb. 18, 1856, in Ellen Randolph Coolidge's Letter Book, ViU.

17. Joel Yancey to TJ, July 24, 1816, MHi. In all likelihood, the Goodman referred to in the letter was Jeremiah Goodman's brother, whom Jefferson mentioned in a letter to Joel Yancey (TJ to Joel Yancey, July 1815, MHi). It is doubtful if the sawmill at Poplar Forest was ever built. As late as August 7, 1819, in referring to Poplar Forest, Jefferson wrote that he had "a gristmill and saw mill to build at this place" (TJ to Mr. Hepburn, August 7, 1819, MHi).

18. Joel Yancey to TJ, Aug. 29, 1816, MHi; TJ to Joel Yancey, Sept. 13, 1816, MHi.

19. Joel Yancey to TJ, Aug. 29, 1816, MHi; TJ to Mr. Colclaser, Aug. 8, 1817, MHi.

20. Ellen Randolph to Martha J. Randolph, Sept. 27, 1816, ViU.

21. *Memorandum Book*, Oct. 29, 1816.

22. Cornelia Randolph to Virginia Randolph, Oct. 25, 1816, Nicholas P. Trist Papers, NcU; Ellen W. Randolph to Martha Randolph, Nov. 1816, ViU.

23. "Planting Memorandum for Poplar Forest, 1816," Nov. 1, 1816, cited in *Garden Book*, p. 563.

24. TJ to Martha J. Randolph, Nov. 10, 1816, MHi; Martha J. Randolph to TJ, Nov. 20, 1816, MHi.

25. "Planting Memorandum for Poplar Forest, 1816," Nov. 22, 1816, cited in *Garden Book*, p. 563.

26. TJ to Dr. George Cabell, May 1, 1817, MHi. George Flower eventually settled in Illinois (see n. 28, below).

27. TJ to George Flower, Aug. 18, 1816, DLC.

28. George Flower, *History of the English Settlement in Edwards County, Illinois, founded in 1817 and 1818, by Morris Birkbeck and George Flower*, vol. 1 in Chicago Historical Society's Collections (Chicago, 1882), p. 43.

29. TJ to Elizabeth Trist, Nov. 23, 1816, MHi; TJ to Martha J. Randolph, Dec. 3, 1816, MHi; *Memorandum Book*, Dec. 6, 1816.

30. TJ to John Wayles Eppes, March 6, 1817, CSmH; TJ to Eppes, March 30, 1816, DLC.

31. TJ to John Wayles Eppes, June 6, 1817, MHi; John Wayles Eppes to Francis Eppes, May 17, 1817, Eppes Family Papers, NcD.

32. TJ to John Wayles Eppes, April 7, 1817, CSmH.

CHAPTER XIV

1. *Richmond Enquirer*, May 13, 1817; John Adams to TJ, May 26, 1817, DLC.

2. TJ, quoted in Philip Alexander Bruce, *History of the University of Virginia* 1:179, 180; TJ to Joseph C. Cabell, Dec. 23, 1822, DLC.

3. Peachy R. Gilmer to Nicholas Trist, April 8, 1819, Nicholas P. Trist Papers, DLC. Jefferson's plans for the University consisted of many buildings, and it may be that Gilmer was referring here solely to the Rotunda (not yet begun when he wrote) in writing *building* rather than *buildings*.

4. Indenture, May 1, 1817, in Eppes Family Papers, NcD. The indenture was recorded in the Albemarle County Courthouse in Charlottesville on August 13, 1817.

5. TJ to John Wayles Eppes, Aug. 6, 1817, CSmH.

6. TJ to Philip Thornton, Feb. 7, 1816, MHi; Cornelia Randolph to Virginia Randolph, Aug. 17, 1817, Nicholas P. Trist Papers, NcU.

7. Cornelia Randolph to Virginia Randolph, Aug 17, 1817, Nicholas P. Trist Papers, NcU.

8. Cornelia Randolph to Virginia Randolph, Aug. 30, 1817, Nicholas P. Trist Papers, NcU.

9. Ibid.; Ellen Randolph to Martha J. Randolph, Aug. 18, 1817, Ellen R. Coolidge Correspondence, ViU; Cornelia Randolph to Virginia Randolph, Aug. 30, 1817, Nicholas P. Trist Papers, NcU.

10. *Memorandum Book*, Aug. 14, 1817.

11. The 1774 deed to Natural Bridge is recorded in the Botetourt County Courthouse in Fincastle, Va. At the time Jefferson patented the grant from George III, the bridge was in that county. It is now within the bounds of Rockbridge County, formed four years later, in 1778, and named for the Natural Bridge.

12. TJ to Maximilian Godefroy, Nov. 11, 1816, DLC.

13. TJ to William Jenkins, July 1, 1809, reproduced in E. P. Tompkins and J. Lee Davis, *The Natural Bridge and its Historical Surroundings* (Natural Bridge, Va., 1939), opposite p. 5. I am indebted to Mary Denny Wray for bringing this letter to my attention.

14. Philip Thornton to TJ, Nov. 19, 1814, MHi. The Memorandum of Agreement, attached to the letter, is dated December 2, 1814. Thornton agreed to lease Jefferson's Natural Bridge property for five years at $180 per annum. At the same time, William Caruthers also offered to lease the bridge, but Thornton, whose request was made several days earlier, was given priority. See TJ to William Caruthers, Dec. 3, 1814, quoted on pp. 7, 8 of Tompkins and Davis, *The Natural Bridge and its Historical Surroundings*.

15. Pamela H. Simpson, *So Beautiful an Arch: Images of the Natural Bridge, 1787–1890* (Lexington, Va., 1982), p. 3.

16. E. A. Entwisle, *French Scenic Wallpapers*, 1800–1860 (Leigh-on-Sea, 1972); Catherine Lynn, *Wallpaper in America* (New York, 1980), p. 192.

17. Ellen Randolph to Martha J. Randolph, Aug. 18, 1817, Ellen R. Coolidge Correspondence, ViU.

18. TJ to Martha J. Randolph, Aug. 31, 1817, MHi.

19. [Ellen R. Coolidge to Henry S. Randall], 1856, in Randall, *Life of Thomas Jefferson* 3:342. See Appendix for full letter.

20. TJ to Hugh Chisolm, Aug. 31, 1817, ViU.

21. TJ to Joel Yancey, March 6, 1817, MHi. The bill that accompanied the letter is no longer with it.

22. TJ to Joel Yancey, March 19, 1817, MHi; TJ to David Higginbotham, March 16, 1817, MHi.

23. Cornelia Randolph to Virginia Randolph, Aug. 30, 1817, Nicholas P. Trist Papers, NcU.

24. Geo. A. Leavitt & Co., Auctioneers, *Catalog of a Portion of the late Thomas Jefferson's Library* (see also chap. XI).

25. [Ellen R. Coolidge to Henry S. Randall], 1856, in Randall, *Life of Thomas Jefferson* 3:343. See Appendix for full letter.

26. Ellen Wayles Randolph to Martha J. Randolph, Sept. 1817, ViU.

27. Ibid.

28. At Monticello, for example, a somewhat gruesome painting titled *Salome, Daughter of Herodias, Bearing the Head of St. John* still hangs over the parlor mantel.

29. TJ to Hugh Chisolm, Aug. 31, 1817, ViU.

30. TJ to Joseph Cabell, Sept. 9, 1817, ViU.

31. TJ to James Newhall, Sept. 18, 1817, MoSHi; [Cabell], *Sketches and Recollections of Lynchburg*, p. 265.

32. Martha J. Randolph to Virginia Randolph, Sept. 24, 1817, Nicholas P. Trist Papers, NcU.

CHAPTER XV

1. TJ to Joel Yancey, Nov. 3, 1817, MHi; TJ to Joseph Cabell, Oct. 24, 1817, ViU.

2. TJ to Martha J. Randolph, Nov. 22, 1817, NNPM; TJ to Martha J. Randolph, Nov. 29, 1817, MHi. Jefferson was referring to William A. Burwell, his former private secretary, not to his slave Burwell, in his correspondence with Martha.

3. [Cabell], *Sketches and Recollections of Lynchburg*, p. 105 quotes

Humphries's advertisement from the *Lynchburg Press*, June 27, 1817.

4. TJ to Martha J. Randolph, Nov. 29, 1817, MHi.

5. TJ to John Wayles Eppes, Sept. 18, 1812, CSmH. This William Cobbs was a cousin of the William Cobbs who would eventually purchase Poplar Forest from Francis Eppes (see chap. XXIII).

6. TJ to Joseph Cabell, Dec. 18, 1817, ViU.

7. TJ to John Wayles Eppes, Aug. 6, 1817, CSmH; John Wayles Eppes to TJ, Dec. 11, 1817, MHi.

8. Francis Eppes to TJ, Dec. 28, 1817, MHi (see also John Wayles Eppes to TJ, Feb. 14, 1818, MHi).

9. TJ to Francis Eppes, Feb. 6, 1818, CSmH.

10. Bruce, *History of the University of Virginia* 1:209.

11. TJ to Wilson Cary Nicholas, April 5, 1818, MHi; *Memorandum Book*, April 14, 1818 (Jefferson noted in this entry that he had "omitted" to list his payment to Coffee on the twelfth, the day he had actually made it).

12. Elizabeth Trist to Nicholas Trist, June 15, 1819, Nicholas P. Trist Papers, DLC.

13. Ellen W. Randolph to Martha J. Randolph, April 14, 1818, ViU; *Memorandum Book*, April 14, 1818.

14. Ellen W. Randolph to Martha J. Randolph, April 14, 1818, ViU. A year earlier, Jefferson had ordered from James Oldham "100 feet of mahogany to work up into commodes or chest of drawers, one half to be fine, the other half of second rate" (TJ to Oldham, May 1, 1817, MHi). Whether this was for the chest taken to Poplar Forest is not known.

15. TJ to Wilson Cary Nicholas, May 1, 1818, DLC. See Bear and Betts, *Family Letters*, p. 431, n. 4, for information on the circumstances of TJ's loan that Nicholas endorsed.

16. TJ to Patrick Gibson, Feb. 18, 1818, MHi.

17. Hunt-Jones, *Dolley and the "great little Madison"*, p. 102.

18. TJ to John Wayles Eppes, May 3, 1818, ViU; TJ and Reuben Perry, Account, June 29, 1818, ViW.

19. TJ to William Short, May 29, 1818, MHi.

20. Bruce, *History of the University of Virginia* 1:217. See also 1:209-21.

21. TJ to Joel Yancey, Sept. 11, 1818, MHi; TJ to Francis Eppes, Sept. 11, 1818, CSmH; John Wayles Eppes to TJ, Oct. 17, 1818, ViU.

22. TJ to Joel Yancey, Nov. 10, 1818, MHi. The bill of sawing was for: "10 joists 8 by 10 I. 24 f. long clear of bad knots, windshakes, & cracks, heart of poplar. 10 (joists) 4 by 10 I. 24 f. long heart of poplar clear of bad knots. 5 pieces 6 I. square 16 f. long heart of poplar. 500 f. sheeting plank. Poplar."

23. Hannah to TJ, Nov. 15, 1818, MHi.

24. Joel Yancey to TJ, Dec. 24, 1818, MHi; TJ to Joel Yancey, Jan. 4, 1819, MHi. (In his letter, TJ mistakenly gave the date as Jan. 4, 1818, much as anyone does at the beginning of a new year, and it is consequently filed in MHi under that date. On the reverse of the copy he kept, which is the copy at MHi, he corrected the date for his own filing system, and listed it as Jan. 4, 1819.)

25. Joel Yancey to TJ, Jan. 9, 1819, MHi; TJ to Yancey, Jan. 17, 1819, MHi.

26. TJ to John G. Jackson, Dec. 27 1818, DLC; TJ to John Adams, Dec. 31, 1818, DLC.

27. Elizabeth Trist to Nicholas P. Trist, Jan. 28, 1819, Nicholas P. Trist Papers, DLC.

28. TJ to Patrick Gibson, July 30, 1818, MHi. The situation is discussed in Malone, *The Sage of Monticello*, vol. 6 of *Jefferson and His Time*, p. 304.

29. TJ to Patrick Gibson, Feb. 22, 1819, MHi.

30. TJ to Joel Yancey, Feb. 22, 1819, MHi.

31. Elizabeth Trist to Nicholas P. Trist, March 9, 1819, Nicholas P. Trist Papers, NcU.

32. Joel Yancey to TJ, April 10, 1819, MHi; TJ to Patrick Gibson, April 22, 1819, MHi.

33. Indenture, Reubin [sic] Perry and Ann his wife with William M. Rives *et al.*, June 12, 1819, Deed Book 15, pp. 226–27, Charlotte County Courthouse, Charlotte Court House, Va. I am indebted to Gerald T. Gilliam for bringing this item to my attention. Perry's indenture is also recorded in the Lynchburg Courthouse.

34. [Cabell], *Sketches and Recollections of Lynchburg*, p. 200.

35. *Garden Book*, p. 587; Elizabeth Trist to Nicholas P. Trist, May 2, 1819, Nicholas P. Trist Papers, DLC.

36. TJ to Joel Yancey, May 25, 1819, MHi.

37. TJ to Smith and Riddle, May 6, 1819, MHi.

CHAPTER XVI

1. Joel Yancey to TJ, June 13, 1819, MHi.

2. Joel Yancey to TJ, June 20, 1819, MHi; TJ to Joel Yancey, June 25, 1819, MHi; Andrew Smith to TJ, June 18, 1819, MHi; Joel Yancey to TJ, July 1, 1819, MHi.

3. TJ to Bernard Peyton, July 17, 1819, MHi. "Sounds" were air bladders of fish, and were considered a delicacy at the time.

4. Cornelia Randolph to Virginia Randolph, July 18, 1819, Nicholas P. Trist Papers, NcU.

5. Ellen W. Randolph to Martha J. Randolph, July 18, 1819, ViU.

6. Ibid.

7. Ibid.

8. TJ to Edmund Meeks, July 19, 1819, MHi.

9. TJ to Arthur Brockenbrough, July 29, 1819, ViU; TJ to Brockenbrough, Aug. 17, 1819, ViU.

10. Lay, "Jefferson's Master Builders," p. 19.

11. Ellen Wayles Randolph to Martha J. Randolph, July 28, 1819, ViU; William Steptoe to TJ, July 24, 1819, MHi; Ellen Wayles Randolph to Virginia Randolph, Aug. 4, 1819, ViU; Ellen Wayles Randolph to Martha J. Randolph, July 28, 1819, ViU.

12. Cornelia Randolph to Virginia Randolph, [July] 28, 1819,

Nicholas P. Trist Papers, NcU.

13. Bernard Peyton to TJ, July 28, 1819, MHi.

14. Ellen Wayles Randolph to Martha Randolph, Aug. 24, 1819, ViU.

15. On July 18, 1804, Jefferson had recorded in his Memorandum Book paying "Isaac Briggs for Thos. Moore 13. D. for a refrigerator." (See also Thomas Moore to TJ, June 21, 1802, DLC; and Moore to TJ, June 1, 1805, DLC.) Moore, an engineer who was Briggs's brother-in-law, developed this simple mechanism, consisting of a wooden oval tub set inside a tin box, with holes "at which ice was put into the vacuity between the tin & wood, the butter being in the tin," to transport butter from his Maryland farm to the market in Georgetown, D.C.

16. Ellen W. Randolph to Virginia Randolph, Aug. 4, 1819, ViU; Ellen W. Randolph to Henry S. Randall, Feb. 27, 1856, Ellen Randolph Coolidge's Letter Book, ViU.

17. Ellen W. Randolph to Martha J. Randolph, Aug. 24, 1819, ViU.

18. TJ to Arthur Brockenborough, Sept. 1, 1819, ViU.

19. TJ to Joseph Antrim, Aug. 8, 1819, MHi.

20. TJ to Thomas Mann Randolph, Jr., Aug. 9, 1819, DLC.

21. TJ to Wilson Cary Nicholas, Aug. 11, 1819, MHi.

22. Ellen W. Randolph to Martha J. Randolph, Aug. 11, 1819, ViU; Wilson Cary Nicholas to TJ, August 5, 1819, DLC.

23. TJ to Patrick Gibson, Aug. 11, 1819, MHi; Ellen W. Randolph to Martha J. Randolph, Aug. 11, 1819, ViU.

24. Cornelia Randolph to Virginia Randolph, Aug. 11, 1819, Nicholas P. Trist Papers, NcU; Ellen W. Randolph to Martha J. Randolph, Aug. 11, 1819, ViU; TJ to Martha J. Randolph, August 24, 1819, DLC.

25. TJ to William Brown, Aug. 18, 1808, MHi; Martha J. Randolph to TJ, Feb. 17, 1809, quoted in Bear and Betts, *Family Letters*; TJ to Elizabeth Trist, March 24, 1809, CSmH. See also Bear and Betts, *Family Letters*, p. 382, n. 3; and Hunt-Jones, *Dolley and the "great little Madison"*, p. 87, fig. 84. Ultimately the first campeachy chair sent to Poplar Forest was delivered to Peachy Gilmer, Mrs. Trist's nephew-in-law, in Liberty (Bedford). A second chair was then sent from Monticello for Jefferson's use at Poplar Forest (see Peachy R. Gilmer to TJ, Jan. 14, 1821, MHi; TJ to Gilmer, Jan. 27, 1821, MHi; TJ to Yancey, Jan. 27, 1821, MHi.).

26. TJ to Martha J. Randolph, Aug. 24, 1819, ViU; TJ to Wilson Cary Nicholas, Aug. 24, 1819, DLC; TJ to Joseph Marx, Aug. 24, 1819, DLC; Ellen W. Randolph to Martha J. Randolph, Aug. 24, 1819, ViU.

27. Cornelia Randolph to Virginia Randolph, Aug. 11, 1819, Nicholas P. Trist Papers, NcU.

28. Ellen Wayles Randolph to Martha J. Randolph, Aug. 11, 1819, ViU.

29. Cornelia Randolph to Virginia Randolph, Aug. 11, 1819, Nicholas P. Trist Papers, NcU.

30. Cornelia Randolph to Virginia Randolph, Sept. 8, 1819, Nicholas P. Trist Papers, NcU.

31. Ibid.

CHAPTER XVII

1. Deed, Thomas Jefferson and Thomas Jefferson Randolph, Sept. 15, 1819, MHi.

2. Ibid.; TJ to Joseph Marx, Sept. 20, 1819, DLC. The statement that the value of the lands was "ample security" is on the plat of the acreage accompanying the deed, MHi.

3. Bedford County Land Tax Records, 1815, 1820, Vi.

4. Elizabeth Trist to Nicholas P. Trist, Sept. 15, 1819, Nicholas P. Trist papers, DLC.

5. Wilson Cary Nicholas to TJ, Sept. 20, 1819, MHi; TJ to James Madison, Feb. 17, 1826, DLC.

6. John Hemings to TJ, Sept. 26, 1819, MHi.

7. TJ to Bernard Peyton, Oct. 4, 1819, MHi; Peyton to TJ, Oct. 7, 1819, MHi.

8. John Hemings to TJ, Oct. 20, 1819, MHi.

9. John Hemings to TJ, Nov. 2, 1819, MHi; TJ to Hemings, Nov. 14, 1819, MHi.

10. John Hemings to TJ, Nov. 18, 1819, MHi; Joel Yancey to TJ, Nov. 19, 1819, MHi.

11. TJ to John Hemings, Nov. 27, 1819, MHi.

12. Ibid.; TJ to Joel Yancey, Nov. 27, 1819, MHi.

13. John Hemings to TJ, Dec. 2, 1819, MHi; Joel Yancey to TJ, Dec. 12, 1819, MHi.

14. Joseph Cabell to TJ, Nov. 2, 1819, ViU. I am indebted to Calder Loth for bringing this letter to my attention.

15. TJ to Joel Yancey, Dec. 25, 1819, MHi.

16. Joel Yancey to TJ, Feb. 27, 1820, MHi.

17. TJ to Joel Yancey, March 16, 1820, MHi.

18. Ibid.; Joel Yancey to TJ, March 28, 1820, MHi.

19. Elizabeth Trist to Nicholas P. Trist, April 18, 1820, Nicholas P. Trist Papers, DLC.

20. *Memorandum Book*, May 17, 1819. See also n. 17 accompanying this entry in the forthcoming Bear and Stanton edition of this work.

21. TJ to John Wayles Eppes, June 30, 1820, ViU; Thomas Cooper to TJ, June 30, 1821, MHi.

22. John Wayles Eppes to TJ, June 12, 1820, ViU.

23. Ibid.

24. TJ to John Wayles Eppes, June 30, 1820, ViU.

25. John Wayles Eppes to TJ, July 8, 1820, MHi; TJ to John Wayles Eppes, July 29, 1820, ViU; John Wayles Eppes to TJ, Aug. 19, 1820, ViU.

26. John Wayles Eppes to TJ, Oct. 7, 1820, MHi; TJ to John Wayles Eppes, Oct. 13, 1820, CSmH.

27. Francis Eppes to TJ, Dec. 28, 1819, MHi; John Wayles Eppes to TJ, Feb. 6, 1820, MHi.

28. TJ to John Wayles Eppes, June 30, 1820, ViU.

29. *Memorandum Book*, various entries for Sept. 1820; Elizabeth Trist to Nicholas P. Trist, Sept. 10, 1820, Nicholas P. Trist Papers, DLC.

30. Ellen Wayles Randolph to Martha J. Randolph, Sept. 13, 1820, Ellen R. Coolidge Correspondence, ViU.

35. TJ to Bernard Peyton, Sept. 16, 1820, MHi.

32. TJ to Francis Eppes, Sept. 21, 1820, DLC.

33. TJ to John Wayles Eppes, Oct. 13, CSmH; Bernard Peyton to TJ, Oct. 5, 1820, MHi; TJ to John Wayles Eppes, Oct. 22, 1820, MHi.

34. TJ to Joel Yancey, Oct. 28, 1820, MHi.

35. TJ to Thomas Mann Randolph, Jr., Nov. 20, 1820, MHi; "List of Mountains" Nov. 25, 1820, ViU.

36. TJ to Archibald Robertson, Dec. 7, 1820, MHi.

CHAPTER XVIII

1. TJ to Joel Yancey, Jan. 4, 1821, MHi.

2. Joel Yancey to TJ, Jan. 14, 1821, MHi. Yancey had already heard rumors that Randolph "had taken management of your Estate here for the ensuing year," and wondered if he would be kept on or let go (Yancey to TJ, Sept. 6, 1820, MHi).

3. TJ to Joel Yancey, Jan. 27, 1821, MHi; TJ to Bernard Peyton, March 4, 1821, MHi.

4. Joel Yancey to TJ, March 12, 1821, MHi.

5. Elizabeth Trist to Nicholas P. Trist, April 5, 1821, Nicholas P. Trist Papers, DLC; Elizabeth Trist to TJ, April 19, 1821, MHi. The Sully portrait of Jefferson is reproduced on the dust jacket of this volume.

6. TJ to Colonel Little, March 31, 1801, MoSHi.

7. Nathaniel Mason Pawlett, Virginia Transportation Research Council, Charlottesville, Va., to author, May 16, 1991.

8. Samuel Shepherd, *The Statutes at Large* (Richmond, 1835), 1:425.

9. William Waller Hening, *The Statutes at Large* (Philadelphia, 1823), 13:48. On Dec. 11, 1789, the General Assembly enacted that a public ferry be constantly kept: "from the lands of Wilson Cary Nicholas, in the county of Albemarle, across Fluvanna river, to the land of John Hardy, on the opposite shore, in the county of Buckingham the price for a man three pence, and for a horse the same." At the time, the James River above its confluence with the Rivanna was known as the Fluvanna. The Warren Ferry remained in existence until 1972.

10. Cornelia Randolph to Virginia Randolph, April 22, 1821, Nicholas P. Trist Papers, NcU.

11. TJ to Henry Flood, Sept. 8, 1813, MHi; Cornelia Randolph to Virginia Randolph, Oct. 25, 1816, Nicholas P. Trist Papers, NcU.

12. Much of Jefferson's route between Monticello and Poplar Forest can still be traced. The Albemarle County portion is now secondary highway 627, portions of which are unpaved now as they were then. In Buckingham, the route south from Warren is now approximated by secondary routes 627 and 602.

U. S. Route 60 takes the trail from Denton's Corner to Mount Rush, from which Jefferson's route is traced by primary highway 24 through Buckingham, Appomattox, and Campbell counties as far as Rustburg. There secondary highway 622 picks up the trail and brings it into Bedford County a mile or so from Poplar Forest. Mileage distances between the various stopping places given in my text are taken from an undated "Table of Mileages" in the Thomas Jefferson Papers, ViU.

13. Cornelia Randolph to Virginia Randolph, April 22, 1821, Nicholas P. Trist Papers, NcU. Ellen had written her mother, Martha, about similar conditions at Flood's Tavern the previous year. See Ellen W. Randolph to Martha J. Randolph, Sept. 13, 1820, Ellen R. Coolidge Correspondence, ViU.

14. TJ to Joel Yancey, May 11, 1821, MHi; Yancey to TJ, May 22, 1821, MHi.

15. TJ to Joel Yancey, Aug. 15, 1821, MHi; TJ to Thomas Mann Randolph, Jr., July 30, 1821, DLC.

16. *Memorandum Book*, Aug. 22, 1821. See also n. 17 accompanying this entry in the forthcoming Bear and Stanton edition of this work.

17. Cornelia Randolph to Virginia Randolph, Aug. 28, 1821, Nicholas P. Trist Papers, NcU.

18. TJ to Francis Eppes, Nov. 17, 1821, MHi.

19. John Hemings to TJ, Nov. 29, 1821, MHi. Nace probably buried the foodstuffs in a root cellar in his cabin.

20. John Hemings to TJ, Dec. 11, 1821, MHi; TJ to John Hemings, Dec. 18, 1821, MHi.

21. Joel Yancey to TJ, Dec. 22, 1821, MHi.

22. John Wayles Eppes to TJ, Dec. 8, 1821, ViU; TJ to John Wayles Eppes, Jan. 17, 1822, ViU.

23. Martha J. Randolph to Nicholas P. Trist, March 7, 1822, Nicholas P. Trist Papers, NcU.

CHAPTER XIX

1. TJ to Rev. Frederick W. Hatch, May 12, 1822, MHi; *Memorandum Book*, May 12, 1822.

2. Virginia Randolph to Nicholas P. Trist, April 23, 1822, Nicholas P. Trist Papers, DLC. Tufton was one of Jefferson's properties adjoining Monticello.

3. TJ to Archibald Robertson, May 25, 1822, MHi.

4. Virginia Randolph to Nicholas P. Trist, May 31, 1822, Nicholas P. Trist Papers, DLC; Martha J. Randolph to Nicholas P. Trist, May 21, 1822, Nicholas P. Trist Papers, NcU.

5. TJ to William Coffee, June 14, 1822, MHi.

6. William Coffee to TJ, June 22, 1822, DLC.

7. TJ to William Coffee, July 10, 1822, MHi.

8. Ibid.

9. William Coffee to TJ, Sept. 8, 1822, DLC. This letter is mistakenly dated in the DLC collections, and is located there in chronological sequence as Sept. 8, 1820.

10. TJ to William Coffee, Sept. 26, 1822, MHi; William Coffee

to TJ, Jan. 3, 1823, ViU.

11. Francis Eppes to TJ, March 22, 1822, ViU; TJ to Francis Eppes, April 9, 1822, DLC.

12. Virginia Randolph to Nicholas P. Trist, April 23, 1822, Nicholas P. Trist Papers, DLC; Francis Eppes to TJ, May 13, 1822, ViU.

13. Virginia Randolph to Nicholas P. Trist, April 23, 1822, Nicholas P. Trist Papers, DLC; TJ to Nicholas P. Trist, June 14, 1822, DLC.

14. John Wayles Eppes to TJ, June 22, 1822, MHi.

15. TJ to John Wayles Eppes, July 28, 1822, ViU.

16. Virginia Randolph to Nicholas P. Trist, March 7, 1823, Nicholas P. Trist Papers, DLC.

17. Martha J. Randolph to Nicholas P. Trist, Nov. 22, 1822, Nicholas P. Trist Papers, NcU; Elizabeth Trist to Nicholas P. Trist, Dec. 23, 1822, Nicholas P. Trist Papers, DLC.

18. William Radford to TJ, Nov. 19, 1822, MHi; Virginia Randolph to Nicholas P. Trist, Nov. 12, 1822, Nicholas P. Trist Papers, DLC.

19. TJ to William Radford, Nov. 30, 1822, MHi (see chap. I, for Jefferson's tracing of the title); William Radford to TJ, Dec. 26, 1822, MHi.

20. TJ to William Radford, late 1822 or early 1823, MHi (no date given, but the letter is in response to that from Radford to TJ, Dec. 26, 1822). Jefferson enclosed the "deeds for the completion of the titles for the lands held by yourself and Mr. Yancey" in a letter to Radford dated February 27, 1823, MHi.

21. Elizabeth Trist to Nicholas P. Trist, Nov. 28, 1822, Nicholas P. Trist Papers, DLC; William Radford to TJ, Dec. 26, 1822, MHi; see also Elizabeth Trist to Nicholas P. Trist, Dec. 23, 1822, Nicholas P. Trist Papers, DLC.

22. TJ to William Coffee, March 22, 1823, DLC; Bernard Peyton to TJ, March 24, 1823, MHi; TJ to William Coffee, April 30, 1823, ViU.

23. Ellen Wayles Randolph to Nicholas P. Trist, March 28, 1823, Nicholas P. Trist Papers, DLC; TJ to William Gough, April 21, 1823, MHi; TJ to Francis Eppes, April 21, 1823, CSmH.

24. TJ to Bernard Peyton, April 23, 1823, MHi.

25. TJ to Archibald Robertson, May 21, 1823, MHi. At the time of his death, on July 4, 1826, Jefferson still owed Robertson $6,164.33 (figure given in Malone, *The Sage of Monticello*, vol. 6 of *Jefferson and His Time*, p. 511, citing Edgehill-Randolph Papers, ViU).

26. Virginia Randolph to Nicholas P. Trist, May 13, 1823, Nicholas P. Trist Papers, DLC; Elizabeth Trist to "My beloved friends," May 29, [1823], Nicholas P. Trist Papers, DLC.

27. Mrs. Trist did return to Monticello after Jefferson's death, while her grandson Nicholas P. Trist and Virginia, then married, were there. On May 30, 1828, Nicholas wrote from Monticello: "We have quite a hospital here at present," and reported that his grandmother was ill: "Her *physical* health

was & promised to continue, excellent—her mind has long been leaving her & is entirely gone" (Nicholas P. Trist to James Madison, May 30, 1828, ViHi).

28. *Memorandum Book*, May 14–16, 1823.

CHAPTER XX

1. TJ, "Financial Statement," April 1, 1823, ViU. See also TJ, "March Statement of Debts," in *Memorandum Book*, March 21, 1823.

2. *Memorandum Book*, n. 17 accompanying March 21, 1823 entry in the forthcoming Bear and Stanton edition of this work.

3. TJ to Leroy & Bayard, July 8, 1823, and July 18, 1823, MoSHi; Leroy Bayard & Co. to TJ, July 10, 1823, MoSHi.

4. TJ to Samuel Garland, Aug. 4, 1823, DLC.

5. TJ to Bernard Peyton, Jan. 5, 1824, MHi.

6. Joel Yancey to TJ, March 18, 1824, MHi; TJ to Joel Yancey, April 1, 1824, MHi.

7. Dumas Malone, *The Sage of Monticello*, vol. 6 of *Jefferson and His Time*, p. 453.

8. Francis Eppes to T. J. Randolph, April 24, 1823, Edgehill-Randolph papers, ViU; Elizabeth Trist to Nicholas P. Trist, Jan. 21, 1823, Nicholas P. Trist Papers, DLC.

9. Virginia Randolph to Nicholas P. Trist, Jan. 2, 1823, Nicholas P. Trist Papers, DLC; Nicholas P. Trist to Virginia Randolph, Oct. 25, 1823, Nicholas P. Trist Papers, NcU.

10. Nicholas P. Trist to Virginia Randolph, Oct. 25, 1823, Nicholas P. Trist Papers, NcU.

11. John Wayles Eppes's Will, May 5, 1823, copy in Hubard Family Papers, Southern Historical Collection, NcU.

12. Francis Eppes to TJ, April 23, 1824, ViU; TJ to Francis Eppes, May 1, 1824, CSmH.

13. Virginia Randolph to Nicholas P. Trist, Jan. 9, 1824, Nicholas P. Trist Papers, NcU.

14. Francis Eppes to TJ, April 23, 1824, ViU; TJ to Francis Eppes, May 1, 1824, CSmH; TJ to William Short, April 10, 1824, MHi.

15. TJ to Bernard Peyton, Aug. 28, 1824, MHi.

16. Mary Elizabeth Randolph Eppes to Jane Randolph, June 10, 1824, Edgehill-Randolph Papers, ViU.

17. M. E. R. Eppes to Virginia Randolph, Aug. 18, 1824, Nicholas P. Trist Papers, NcU.

18. M. E. R. Eppes to Virginia Randolph, Nov. 14, 1824, Nicholas P. Trist Papers, NcU. Earlier, she had expressed similar sentiments in her letter of June 10, 1824, to Jane Randolph (Edgehill-Randolph Papers, ViU).

19. M. E. R. Eppes to Jane Randolph, Jan. 2 1825, ViHi.

20. TJ to Francis Eppes, Feb. 17, 1825, ViU.

21. Francis Eppes to TJ, Feb. 25, 1825, MHi.

22. TJ to Francis Eppes, April 6, 1825, CSmH.

23. TJ to Bernard Peyton, May 6, 1825, MHi; Bernard Peyton to TJ, May 10, 1825, MHi.

24. Virginia Trist to Ellen R. Coolidge, June 27, 1825, Ellen R.

Coolidge Correspondence, ViU.

25. John Hemings to TJ, July 23, 1825, MHi; John Hemings to TJ, Aug. 11, 1825, MHi.

26. John Hemings to TJ, Aug. 11, 1825, MHi.

27. TJ to John Hemings, Aug. 17, 1825, MHi.

28. John Hemings to Septimia Randolph, August 28, 1825, ViU. "George with Randolph" was John Hemings's way of spelling George Wythe Randolph, Septimia's youngest brother, who was then seven years old.

29. TJ to John Wayles Eppes, July 16, 1814, CSmH (see also chap. X).

30. John Hemings to TJ, Sept. 18, 1825, MHi; John Hemings to TJ, Sept. 28, 1825, MHi.

CHAPTER XXI

1. TJ to Joseph Cabell, Jan. 20, 1826, ViU.

2. Martha J. Randolph to Ellen R. Coolidge, April 5, 1826, Coolidge Papers, ViU.

3. Ibid.

4. John V. Mason to Gen. William Brodnax, Feb. 3, 1826, Vi.

5. TJ to Joseph Cabell, Feb. 7, 1826, ViU.

6. TJ to Thomas Jefferson Randolph, Feb. 8, 1826, DLC.

7. TJ to James Madison, Feb. 17, 1826, DLC.

8. Randolph, *The Domestic Life of Thomas Jefferson*, pp 416–18.

9. Francis Eppes To TJ, Feb. 23, 1826, MHi.

10. TJ to Francis Eppes, March 9, 1826, ViU.

11. Thomas Jefferson's Will, March 16, 1826, Albemarle County Courthouse, Charlottesville, Va.

12. Thomas Jefferson's Will, codicil, March 17, 1826, Albemarle County Courthouse, Charlottesville, Va. Joe Fossett, who had little or no association with Poplar Forest, was the Monticello blacksmith.

13. Ibid. The Library of Congress *Index to the Thomas Jefferson Papers*, pp. vii–xviii, has a good account of the history of Jefferson's papers and their dispersal after his death.

14. Thomas Jefferson Randolph to TJ, April 25, 1826, ViU; Thomas Jefferson Randolph to TJ, April 30, 1826, quoted in Bear and Betts, *Family Letters*, p. 477; Randolph, *The Domestic Life of Thomas Jefferson*, pp. 416–18.

15. Francis Eppes to TJ, June 23, 1826, MHi.

16. Roger Weightman to TJ, June 14, 1826, DLC.

17. TJ to Roger Weightman, June 24, 1826, DLC. The letter was printed in the *National Intelligencer* on July 4, 1826.

CHAPTER XXII

1. Alexander Austin, Survey of Poplar Forest for Francis Eppes, Feb. 8, 1827, Campbell County Surveyors' Record 1:183, Campbell County Courthouse, Rustburg, Va. Although the survey is located in the Campbell County records, the land is described as "lying in Bedford County."

2. Ludwell H. Johnson III, "Sharper than a Serpent's Tooth," *The Virginia Magazine of History and Biography* 99, no. 2 (April

1991): 153–55, treats this complex affair; see also chap. XVII above; Bedford County Deed Book 17, pp. 300, 301, Bedford County Courthouse, Bedford, Va.

3. Inventory and Appraisal of the Estate of Thomas Jefferson in Campbell County, Dec. 13, 1826, ViU.

4. Francis Eppes to Thomas Jefferson Randolph, Dec. 13, 1826, Edgehill-Randolph Papers, ViU.

5. Malone, *The Sage of Monticello*, vol. 6 of *Jefferson and His Time*, p. 511; Summary of debt of Thomas Jefferson and Thomas Jefferson Randolph, July 4, 1826, Edgehill-Randolph Papers, ViU.

6. *Lynchburg Virginian*, Nov. 16, 1826. An identical advertisement from an unidentified newspaper, dated Nov. 3, is in the Nicholas P. Trist Papers, NcU; Nicholas P. Trist to James Madison, Jan. 25, 1827, ViHi.

7. Francis Eppes, bill for items purchased from William Smithson, Nov. 26, 1826, Edgehill-Randolph Papers, ViU; Francis Eppes to Nicholas Trist, Jan. [?], 1827, Nicholas P. Trist Papers, NcU.

8. Martha J. Randolph to Ellen R. Coolidge, [Sept.] 1826, ViHi.

9. Francis Eppes to Nicholas P. Trist, Nov. 7, 1826, Nicholas P. Trist Papers, NcU. Trist passed on to James Madison the information that "the lottery is considered as still born—with some faint prospect of vivification" (Nicholas P. Trist to James Madison, Nov. 18, 1826, ViHi). Six months later, Trist reported to Madison that "the lottery is again prostrate, without the least hope of another revival" (Nicholas P. Trist to James Madison, May 6, 1827, ViHi).

10. Francis Eppes to Nicholas P. Trist, Nov. 7, 1826, Nicholas P. Trist Papers, NcU.

11. Ibid.

12. Cornelia Randolph to Ellen R. Coolidge, Nov. 12, 1826, Coolidge-Jefferson Correspondence, ViU; Nicholas P. Trist to James Madison, Nov. 18, 1826, Nicholas P. Trist Letterbook, ViHi; Mary J. Randolph to Ellen R. Coolidge, Nov. 26, 1826, Coolidge-Jefferson Correspondence, ViU.

13. Mary Elizabeth Randolph Eppes to Jane Randolph, July 9, 1828, Edgehill-Randolph Papers, ViU.

14. Francis Eppes, Memoranda, Jan. 1826, Corporation for Jefferson's Poplar Forest (original at Poplar Forest).

15. Ibid., undated entry for 1826; Francis Eppes to Thomas Jefferson Randolph, June 8, 1827, Edgehill-Randolph Papers, ViU.

16. M. E. R. Eppes to Jane Randolph, April 1, 1827, Edgehill-Randolph Papers, ViU.

17. Francis Eppes, Memoranda [Sept.] 1826; Francis Eppes to Thomas Jefferson Randolph, Sept. 21, 1826, Edgehill-Randolph Papers, ViU; Ellen R. Coolidge to Henry S. Randall, Feb. 18, 1856, in Ellen Randolph Coolidge's Letter Book, ViU.

18. M. E. R. Eppes to Jane Randolph, Aug. 26, 1827, Edgehill-Randolph Papers, ViU.

19. M. E. R. Eppes to Jane Randolph, April 1, 1827, Edgehill-

Randolph Papers, ViU.

20. [Cabell], *Sketches and Recollections of Lynchburg*, p. 192.

21. M. E. R. Eppes to Jane Randolph, July 9, 1828, and Oct. 26, 1828, Edgehill-Randolph Papers, ViU.

22. Francis Eppes to Nicholas P. Trist, March 2, 1828, Nicholas P. Trist Papers, NcU.

23. M. E. R. Eppes to Jane Randolph, April 20, 1828, Edgehill-Randolph Papers, ViU.

24. Francis Eppes to Nicholas P. Trist, June 2, 1828, Nicholas P. Trist Papers, NcU.

25. M. E. R. Eppes to Jane Randolph, July 9, 1828, Edgehill-Randolph Papers, ViU.

26. *Lynchburg Virginian*, advertisement, July 17, 1828. The advertisement also appeared at various dates in the *Richmond Enquirer*.

27. Francis Eppes to Thomas Jefferson Randolph, Sept. 29, 1828, Edgehill-Randolph Papers, ViU.

28. Nicholas P. Trist to James Madison, Oct. 9, 1828, Nicholas P. Trist Letterbook, ViHi.

29. M. E. R. Eppes to Mary H. Eppes, August 24, 1828, Eppes Family Papers, ViU; Francis Eppes to Thomas Jefferson Randolph, Nov. 6, 1828, Edgehill-Randolph Papers, ViU.

30. Francis Eppes to Nicholas P. Trist, Nov. 6, 1828, Nicholas P. Trist Papers, NcU.

31. TJ to John Wayles Eppes, July 16, 1814, CSmH; Marmon, *Poplar Forest* 2:19; Bedford County Deed Book 21, pp. 184, 185.

32. Note in handwriting of M. E. R. Eppes, May 5, 1829, Eppes Family Papers, ViU; Parish Register, St. Paul's Episcopal Church, Lynchburg, Va. (entry May 18, 1829, quoted in [Cabell], *Sketches and Recollections of Lynchburg*, p. 60 of supplement by Louise A. Blunt).

33. M. E. R. Eppes to Jane Randolph, June 6, 1829, courtesy of Mrs. W. B. Moss, Athens, Georgia (letter now on deposit at ViHi); Cornelia Randolph to Virginia Trist, July 18, 1829, Nicholas P. Trist Papers, NcU; Harriet Randolph to Mrs. Thomas Eston Randolph, June 19, 1829, quoted in Randolph Whitfield and Dr. John Chipman, *The Florida Randolphs* (Atlanta, 1987), p. 33.

34. Francis Eppes to Thomas Jefferson Randolph, July 4, 1829, Edgehill-Randolph Papers, ViU; Mrs. Nicholas Ware Eppes, "Francis Eppes (1801–1881), Pioneer of Florida," *Florida Historical Society Quarterly* 5, no. 2 (October 1926):96; Francis Eppes to Nicholas P. Trist, July 25, 1829, Nicholas P. Trist Papers, NcU.

35. Bertram H. Groene, *Ante-Bellum Tallahassee* (Tallahassee, 1971), p. 95.

36. Thomas Jefferson Eppes, obituary notice [August, 1869], inserted in Francis Eppes, Memoranda, Corporation for Jefferson's Poplar Forest (original at Poplar Forest).

37. The description of Eppington, written by Francis from Tallahassee, appears in Randall, *Life of Thomas Jefferson* 2:359, 360. Ellen Randolph Coolidge, Francis's first cousin, provided the description of Poplar Forest, which has been used throughout this text, for the same publication (see Appendix).

38. Mrs. Eppes, "Francis Eppes," p. 102. Mrs. Eppes, however, gives the date of his move to Orange County as 1867. His obituary (copy inserted in Francis Eppes, Memoranda) gives the date as 1868, and notes that he was in Madison County, Florida, during the year 1867.

39. Geo. A. Leavitt & Co., Auctioneers, *Catalog of a Portion of the Late Thomas Jefferson's Library*.

40. John Wayles Eppes, obituary notice [n.d.], Ashville, Florida, inserted in Francis Eppes, Memoranda, Corporation for Jefferson's Poplar Forest (original at Poplar Forest).

41. Mrs. Eppes, "Francis Eppes," p. 102.

42. "In Memory of Francis Eppes," [1881], copy in Francis Eppes, Memoranda, Corporation for Jefferson's Poplar Forest (original at Poplar Forest).

43. Francis Eppes's Memoranda was donated to the Corporation for Jefferson's Poplar Forest by William Lattimore, a direct descendant of Francis Eppes, in his own name, and in those of his siblings, Edna Eppes Lattimore Clancy, and Harry Hays Lattimore.

CHAPTER XXIII

1. Deed, Francis Eppes to William Cobbs, Nov. 28, 1828, Bedford County Deed Book 21, pp. 184–85, Bedford County Courthouse, Bedford, Va.; Marmon, *Poplar Forest* 2:54. Mr. Marmon has conducted exhaustive research on the post-Jefferson period at Poplar Forest. I am indebted to him for much of the information included in this chapter and the next.

2. Christian S. Hutter, Memoir, Nov. 10, 1909, handwritten ms. in possession of the Corporation for Jefferson's Poplar Forest. Mr. Hutter's Memoir is a six-page document dealing primarily with Poplar Forest, but contains a few sketchy details about his life as well.

3. Edward Sixtus Hutter to Emma Hutter, June 30, 1850, Hutter Family Papers, currently (1993) in possession of Mrs. Edwin Christian Hutter, Princeton, N.J. This collection, from which a number of references in this chapter will be cited, is hereafter referred to as HFP. "Emma" was her husband's name for Emily Cobbs Hutter.

4. Marion Scott Cobbs to Edward S. Hutter, Oct. 26, 1840, HFP; Edward S. Hutter to Amalia Hutter Reeder, Aug. 15, 1840, HFP.

5. George C. Hutter to Edward S. Hutter, Jan. 6, 1838, HFP.

6. Mr. and Mrs. Ward to Edward S. Hutter, Sept. 16, 1838, HFP; Edward S. Hutter to Amalia Hutter Reeder, Nov. 25, 1839, HFP.

7. Harriet Hutter to Edward S. Hutter, April 11, 1840, HFP.

8. Edward S. Hutter to Amalia Hutter Reeder, Aug. 15, Sept 14, and Oct. 3, 1840, HFP.

9. Marion Scott Cobbs to Edward S. Hutter, Oct. 26, 1840, HFP.

10. Edward S. Hutter to Amalia Hutter Reeder, Dec. 25, 1840, HFP.

11. Marion Scott Cobbs & Emma Hutter to Edward S. Hutter, Sept. 14, 1841, HFP.

12. Edward S. Hutter, "Journal of Events for every Day" (1844–54), in possession of Mrs. Edwin Christian Hutter, Princeton, N.J., as part of the Hutter Family Papers (HFP). As Hutter's journal is unpaginated, future references to it will cited only in the text, with the date of the item described.

13. George C. Hutter to Edward S. Hutter, "Washington's Birthday, 1843," HFP; Early, *Campbell Chronicles*, p. 238 states that the boxwood circle in front of the house was planted by Mrs. Sextus (Emily) Hutter. I am indebted to C. Allan Brown for calling my attention to the similarity of the boxwood plantings at the two Hutter homes.

14. Christian J. Hutter to Edward S. Hutter, June 17, 1844, HFP; Marion Scott Cobbs to Edward S. Hutter, June 19, 1844, HFP.

15. Christian J. Hutter to Emma Cobbs Hutter, Sept. 9, 1844, HFP; Christian J. Hutter to Edward S. Hutter, Dec. 31, 1844, HFP.

16. William H. Hutter to Edward S. Hutter, Dec. 30, 1844, HFP. I am indebted to Duffy (Mrs. E. C.) Hutter for bringing this letter to my attention.

17. *Lynchburg Virginian*, Nov. 24, 1845.

18. Christian J. Hutter to Edward. S. Hutter, Dec. 15, 1845, HFP.

19. Ibid.

20. Francis Eppes to TJ, Feb. 15, 1825, MHi (see also chap. XX).

21. Christian J. Hutter to Edward S. Hutter, Dec. 15, 1845, HFP.

22. Paul Wilstach, "Thomas Jefferson's Secret Home," *Country Life* (April, 1928): 43; Christian S. Hutter, Jr., to Norma Cuthbert, Oct. 1, 1943, HFP.

23. Christian S. Hutter, Memoir, Nov. 10, 1909; C. S. Hutter, Jr., to Norma Cuthbert, Oct. 1, 1943, HFP.

24. Marmon, *Poplar Forest* 2:69.

25. Christian J. Hutter to Edward S. Hutter, Feb. 20, 1846, HFP.

26. George G. Curle, "Estimate for work to be done at Poplar Forest," Dec. 4, 1845, HFP. Curle's estimate was further defined as being "for the finish of the first or middle story of house for Mr. W. Cobbs." Because Mr. Cobbs was still the owner of Poplar Forest, the estimate was addressed to him, though his son-in-law, Edward S. Hutter, seems to have been in charge of having the work done.

27. Christian J. Hutter to Edward S. Hutter, April 7, 1846, HFP.

28. Ibid. In his 1909 Memoir, Christian S. Hutter recalled that the overseer's house into which his father moved after the fire "was burned by a supposed incendiary in 1867."

29. Edward S. Hutter to "Emily at Lynchburg," April 19, 1846, HFP.

30. Christian J. Hutter to Edward S. Hutter, Sept. 30, 1846, HFP.

31. Christian S. Hutter, Jr., to Norma Cuthbert, Oct. 1, 1943, HFP.

32. Wilstach, "Thomas Jefferson's Secret Home," p. 42.

33. Marion Scott Cobbs to Edward S. and Emily Hutter, April 16, 1854, HFP; Marion Scott Cobbs to Edward S. and Emily Hutter, April 24, 1854, HFP.

34. Christian S. Hutter, Jr., to Norma Cuthbert, Oct. 1, 1943, HFP.

35. Mr. and Mrs. Beverly S. Hutter, Sr., interview with author, Sept. 19, 1987. Mr. Hutter was a grandson of Edward S. Hutter.

36. William M. Kelso, "Thomas Jefferson's Time Capsule: Archaeology at Poplar Forest," *Lynch's Ferry* 4, no. 1 (Spring/Summer 1991):26. The root cellar in the south tenant house was uncovered as the building was being repaired. Although no full investigation has yet been made below the first floor of the north tenant house, preliminary probing has indicated that there is a disturbed area there as well.

37. Henry Howe, *Historical Collections of Virginia* (Charleston, S.C., 1845), p. 214.

38. Henry S. Randall, *Life of Thomas Jefferson* 3:344 (see Appendix).

39. Amalia Hutter Reeder to Emma Hutter, April 11, 1852, HFP.

40. Edward S. Hutter, Income and Expenses: 1856–61, HFP. This register apparently continues the record-keeping Edward Hutter started in his Journal, which recorded the years 1844 to 1854 (see n. 12, above). This second record commences with entries dated July 1856 and ends in December 1861. No records are known to exist for the year 1855, nor for the first half of 1856; Hutter interview. Although the statement that the children died from falling on the stairway is often made, obituaries of the several Hutter children who died in infancy do not give this as the cause of death.

41. Christian S. Hutter, Memoir, Nov. 10, 1909; Marmon, *Poplar Forest* 2:81.

42. Helen Strange Patterson, *St. Stephen's Episcopal Church*, p. 6.

43. Marmon, *Poplar Forest* 2:82–84.

44. *Lynchburg Virginian*, June 1, 1877, p. 3, col. 3.

CHAPTER XXIV

1. The situation at Poplar Forest immediately following the death of Mrs. Cobbs is treated in detail in Marmon, *Poplar Forest* 2:93–95.

2. Christian S. Hutter, Memoir, Nov. 10, 1909, copy at Poplar Forest.

3. Marmon, *Poplar Forest* 2:95, 96; Christian S. Hutter, Memoir.

4. Marmon, *Poplar Forest* 2:98, 99.

5. Christian S. Hutter, Memoir.

6. Mr. and Mrs. Beverly S. Hutter, Sr., interview with author, Sept. 19, 1987.

7. Ibid.

8. Ibid.

9. Christian S. Hutter, Memoir.

10. Richard Guy Wilson, "Palladio Redux," *Building by the Book*, Palladian Studies in America 1, no. 3 (Charlottesvillle,

Va., 1990); pp. 65, 66.

11. Fiske Kimball, *Thomas Jefferson, Architect*, pp. 71, 72, 183.

12. Early, *Campbell Chronicles*, p. 238, describes the event and lists the organizations involved. See also Tag A. Long, "Poplar Forest," *Norfolk and Western Magazine* 4, no. 7 (July 1926).

13. Cranston Williams, Jr., a grandson of Christian S. Hutter, brought the photograph to the attention of Lynn A. Beebe, Executive Director of the Corporation for Jefferson's Poplar Forest (Cranston Williams, Jr., to Lynn A. Beebe, Oct. 1, 1990).

14. Tag A. Long, "Poplar Forest," p. 525.

15. Christian S. Hutter, Jr., donated a number of Jefferson papers to the University of Virginia. See Constance E. Thurlow & Francis L. Berkeley, Jr., *The Jefferson Papers of the University of Virginia*, index, p. 426.

16. Wilstach, "Thomas Jefferson's Secret Home," p. 43.

17. The architectural drawings for Oak Forest, dated January 1933, are in the Lynchburg Architectural Archive, Jones Memorial Library, Lynchburg, Va.

18. Cuthbert, "Poplar Forest: Jefferson's Legacy to His Grandson"; Susanne Williams Massie and Frances Archer Christian, eds., *Homes and Gardens in Old Virginia*, p. 137.

19. Beverly S. Hutter, Sr., quoted in Pat Rice, "For Generations Poplar Forest Was a Retreat," *The News & Daily Advance*, Lynchburg, Va., June 29, 1986.

20. C. S. Hutter to Frank Reeder, July 18, 1936, HFP.

21. Mr. and Mrs. Beverly S. Hutter, Sr., interview, Sept. 19, 1987.

22. James Owen Watts, Jr., interview with author, May 10, 1989.

23. Deed, July 1, 1946, copy presented by James Owen Watts, Jr., to the Corporation for Jefferson's Poplar Forest, May 10, 1989.

24. William M. Barnum to Travis C. McDonald, Jr., Sept. 17, 1990, copy at Poplar Forest. Mr. Barnum, the son of Phelps Barnum, recalled that his father had also worked in the firm of John Russell Pope and, during the time he was in partnership with Thompson, had participated in the restoration of the Stoa of Attalos in Athens.

25. W. Stuart Thompson and Phelps Barnum, Architects, Specifications for Restoration of Poplar Forest for James Owen Watts, Jr., Lynchburg, Virginia (undated); plans for same, dated October 1946 and December 1946. Other drawings bear later dates. Copies of all these materials are at Poplar Forest.

26. Thompson and Barnum, Specifications, p. 5.

27. Key Watts Giles, interview with author, May 10, 1989.

28. Thompson and Barnum, Specifications, p. 11.

29. James Owen Watts, Jr., letter to author, July 4, 1989, and interview, May 10, 1989.

30. Thompson & Barnum, Specifications, p. 11.

31. Watts, letter to author, July 4, 1989.

32. Ibid.

33. James Owen Watts, Jr., interview, May 10, 1989.

34. Ibid.; Barbara McEwan, *Thomas Jefferson's Poplar Forest*, pp. 85–87, discusses the restoration of the farm undertaken by the Wattses.

35. Publication of Mrs. Watson's article resulted in the "discovery" of George Flower's 1816 description of the house (see chap. XIII). Francis S. Ronalds, Flower's great-grandson, read the *Antiques* article and sent a copy of Flower's description, from his Journal, to Alice Winchester, the magazine's editor. (See Francis S. Ronalds to Alice Winchester, April 8, 1957, and Martha Rivers Adams, "Browsings," in *The News*, Lynchburg, Va., August 9, 1957. Copies of both items are at Poplar Forest).

36. See Bibliography for other articles on Jefferson that appeared in the *Iron Worker*.

37. Thomas Jefferson Memorial Foundation, "Feasibility Study of Poplar Forest," April 11, 1972, copy at Poplar Forest.

38. Minutes, Directors of the Thomas Jefferson Memorial Foundation, April 14, 1972, copy at Poplar Forest.

39. Francis L. Berkeley, Jr., to Lucille McWane Watson, Dec. 1, 1972, copy at Poplar Forest.

40. Report of Lucille McWane Watson [to the Lynchburg Historical Foundation, n.d.], copy at Poplar Forest; George C. Palmer II to Lucille McWane Watson, March 13, 1973, copy at Poplar Forest. James A. Bear, Jr., curator at Monticello, wrote the same day with similar expressions of assistance and encouragement.

41. Julian P. Boyd to Lucille McWane Watson, August 28, 1973, copy at Poplar Forest.

42. Poplar Forest, boundary plat, July 7, 1972; survey, 1974, showing division of the property into building lots: copies of both at Poplar Forest.

43. "Poplar Forest: Monograph of a Country House," brochure (undated) prepared by Stevens & Company, Charlottesville, Va., copy at Poplar Forest.

44. Deed between James O. Watts, Sarah K. Watts; and James A. Johnson, Nov. 6, 1980, Bedford County Deed Book 511, p. 818, Bedford County Courthouse, Bedford, Virginia; Dr. James A. Johnson, interview with author, July 20, 1989.

45. e.g. William T. Stevens to Mr. F. H. Ludington, April 24, 1981, copy at Poplar Forest.

46. Mrs. Glenn W. Tharp and Mrs. Bolling Lambeth [representing the Bedford Historical Society] to Mrs. Lydia Daniel [representing the Lynchburg Historical Foundation], May 14, 1982; also Mrs. Daniel to Dr. James A. Johnson, June 3, 1982. Copies of both items are at Poplar Forest.

47. "Groups Join to Preserve Poplar Forest," Lynchburg *News*, Dec. 16, 1982.

48. "Money to Buy Landmark Sought," Lynchburg *News*, July 23, 1983.

49. Lynchburg *News*, Dec. 19, 1983, and Dec. 22, 1983.

I. PRIMARY SOURCES

A. Jefferson manuscripts

The main source for the text has been letters written by and to Thomas Jefferson. This is especially true for the years from ca. 1805 to 1826, the years of Jefferson's greatest involvement with Poplar Forest. Jefferson's papers, of which some 40,000 survive, are housed in several major institutions throughout the United States. The three major collections are: the Thomas Jefferson papers at the Library of Congress, the Thomas Jefferson Papers at the University of Virginia, and the Thomas Jefferson Papers in the Coolidge Collection at the Massachusetts Historical Society. All three collections have been microfilmed, and the letters and other documents in each collection have been cataloged in the following publications sponsored by the individual institutions:

Library of Congress. *Index to the Thomas Jefferson Papers*. Washington, D.C., 1976. In addition to a complete listing of the Library's holdings, the *Index* contains an invaluable essay by Paul G. Sifton that describes the convoluted disposition of Jefferson's papers after his death (pp. vii–xvii).

Thurlow, Constance E., and Francis L. Berkeley, Jr. *The Jefferson Papers of the University of Virginia*. Charlottesville, Va., 1973. This second edition of a work originally published in 1950 contains, in Part 2, a supplementary calendar of Jefferson items acquired by the university between 1950 and 1970. In addition, the university has published Douglas W. Tanner, ed., *Guide to the Microfilm Edition of The Jefferson Papers of the University of Virginia*, Charlottesville, 1977. This volume contains an essay on the provenance of the university's collection, and lists eleven other institutions that contain important Jefferson holdings.

Collections of the Massachusetts Historical Society, Seventh Series, Vol. 1. Boston, 1900.

In addition to these three main collections of Jefferson documents, two other repositories hold writings that were extremely important for this work: the Thomas Jefferson Papers and the Tucker-Coleman Papers at the Earl Greg Swem Library of the College of William and Mary at Williamsburg, Virginia, and the Jefferson Papers at the Henry E. Huntington Library, San Marino, California. Original Jefferson items were also consulted at the American Philosophical Society (Jefferson Papers) and the Historical Society of Pennsylvania (Jefferson Papers), both in Philadelphia; the Missouri Historical Society (Bixby-Jefferson Collection), St. Louis; and the New-York Historical Society (Jefferson Papers), New York.

B. Jefferson's published works

In addition to correspondence, Jefferson's Garden Book, Farm Book, and Memorandum Books have all been consulted. The first two are conveniently available in annotated publications:

Betts, Edwin Morris, ed. *Thomas Jefferson's Farm Book*. Charlottesville, Va., 1987. This annotated volume contains a facsim-ile of the original Farm Book, which Jefferson maintained from 1774 to 1826. The original is in the Coolidge Collection at the Massachusetts Historical Society.

Betts, Edwin Morris, ed. *Thomas Jefferson's Garden Book*, (vol. 22 of *Memoirs of the American Philosophical Society*), Philadelphia, 1944. The original Garden Book, maintained by Jefferson from 1776 to 1824, is also in the Coolidge Collection at the Massachusetts Historical Society.

Jefferson's thirteen Memorandum Books, covering the years 1767 to 1826, are in a number of different depositories. (See Library of Congress, *Index to the Thomas Jefferson Papers*, p. xvi, n. 66.) I deem it a special favor to have been given access to a soon-to-be-published, annotated edition of these books: Bear, James A., Jr., and Lucia C. Stanton, eds., *Jefferson's Memorandum Books: Accounts, with Legal Records and Miscellany, 1767–1826*, forthcoming from Princeton University Press as part of *The Papers of Thomas Jefferson*, Second Series.

Thomas Jefferson's *Notes on Virginia*, written in part at Poplar Forest, was first published in 1785 (Paris), followed by a second edition in 1787 (London). The London version is included in its entirety in Peterson, Merrill D., ed. *The Portable Thomas Jefferson*, New York, 1985.

Boyd, Julian P., ed. *The Papers of Thomas Jefferson*. Princeton, 1950 – . Beginning in 1950 under the direction of the late Julian P. Boyd, and now under the editorship of John Catanzariti, Jefferson's papers are being edited and published by the Princeton University Press, primarily in chronological order. When completed, these volumes will comprise the most authentic published collection of Jefferson's many writings. Unfortunately, Jefferson's writings from the period of greatest interest to the study of Poplar Forest (ca. 1805 to 1826) have not yet appeared in print as part of this series.

C. Other primary records

In addition to Jefferson's correspondence and other items written by and to him, I have also relied on a number of other related original documents. For the most part, these were letters written by various family members. Among the many collections consulted are two major collections of papers related to Nicholas P. Trist, one of Jefferson's grandsons-in-law: the Nicholas P. Trist Papers at the Library of Congress and the Nicholas P. Trist Papers at the Southern Historical Collection, University of North Carolina, Chapel Hill. The Virginia Historical Society has Trist's Letterbook, as well as other Trist letters, and an extensive collection of Gilmer family documents. Collections of Eppes family papers are held at the University of Virginia (Eppes Family Papers) and Duke University (John Wayles Eppes Papers). The Coolidge and Edgehill-Randolph papers at the University of Virginia were also extremely useful.

Eppes, Francis. Memoranda. Beginning with entries dated January 1826, and concluding with 1828 (with no entries for 1827), this is the record of Francis Eppes's farming and building activities during his short tenure at Poplar Forest. In addition, the booklet (now in the possession of the Corporation for Jefferson's Poplar Forest) contains newspaper clippings related to a number of Eppes's descendants.

Hutter, Edward Sixtus. Poplar Forest Journal. This journal, beginning on January 1, 1844, and continuing through the late 1850s, records farm and building activities conducted at Poplar Forest by Edward Hutter during those years. The original is in the Hutter Family Papers, in the possession of Mrs. Edwin Christian Hutter, Princeton, New Jersey.

Hutter, Christian Sixtus. Memoir, November 10, 1909, in Hutter Family Papers, Mrs. Edwin Christian Hutter, Princeton, New Jersey. A copy of this work is also at Poplar Forest.

Hutter Family Papers. This extensive collection of Hutter family correspondence, along with the Poplar Forest Journal and the Hutter Memoir, both noted above, is in the possession of Mrs. Edwin Christian Hutter, Princeton, New Jersey.

II. SECONDARY SOURCES

A. Books

Ackerman, James S. *The Villa*. Princeton, N.J., 1990.

Bear, James A., Jr., and Edwin Morris Betts. *The Family Letters of Thomas Jefferson*. Columbia, Mo., 1966.

Bear, James A., Jr., ed. *Jefferson at Monticello*. Charlottesville, Va., 1967.

Bedini, Silvio A. *Thomas Jefferson and his Copying Machines*. Charlottesville, Va., 1984.

—. *Thomas Jefferson, Statesman of Science*. New York, 1990.

Brown, C. Allan. *Thomas Jefferson's Poplar Forest: the mathematics of an ideal villa*. Reprinted from the *Journal of Garden History* 10, no. 2 (1990): 117–39.

Bruce, Philip Alexander. *History of the University of Virginia*, vol. 1. New York, 1920.

[Cabell, Margaret Anthony]. *Sketches and Recollections of Lynchburg by the Oldest Inhabitant*. Richmond, Va., 1858; reprinted Lynchburg, Va., 1974, with notes by Louise A. Blunt.

Cappon, Lester J., ed. *The Adams-Jefferson Letters*. 2 vols. Chapel Hill, N.C., 1959.

Chambers, S. Allen, Jr. *Lynchburg: An Architectural History*. Charlottesville, Va., 1981.

Davis, Richard Beale. *Francis Walker Gilmer: Life and Learning in Jefferson's Virginia*. Richmond, Va., 1939.

Early, R. H. *Campbell Chronicles*. Lynchburg, Va., 1927.

Flower, George. *History of the English Settlement in Edwards County, Illinois, Founded in 1817 and 1818, by Morris Birkbeck and George Flower*, vol. I in Chicago Historical Society's Collections. Chicago, 1882.

Ford, Paul Leicester, ed. *The Writings of Thomas Jefferson*, 10 vols. New York, 1892–99. This work includes Jefferson's "Autobiography" (begun January 6, 1821) in volume 1.

Hunt-Jones, Conover. *Dolley and the "great little Madison"*. Washington, D.C., 1977.

Kelso, William M., M. Drake Patten, and Michael A. Strutt. *Poplar Forest Archaeology Research Report*. Prepared for National Endowment for the Humanities, 1991. Copy at Poplar Forest.

Kimball, Fiske. *Thomas Jefferson, Architect*. Boston, 1916.

Leavitt, Geo. A., & Co., Auctioneers. *Catalog of a Portion of the late Thomas Jefferson's Library*. New York, 1873.

Libscomb, Andrew A., and Albert Ellery Bergh, eds. *The Writings of Thomas Jefferson*. Washington, 1903.

McEwan, Barbara. *Thomas Jefferson's Poplar Forest*. Lynchburg, Va., 1987.

Malone, Dumas. *Jefferson and His Time*, 5 vols. Boston, 1948–77. This monumental work is the definitive biography of Jefferson and has become essential for any subsequent studies of him.

Marmon, Lee. Poplar Forest Research Report, 3 vols. Lynchburg, Va., 1991. Privately printed for the Corporation for Jefferson's Poplar Forest. Copy at Poplar Forest. This report is a revised and expanded version of one originally printed in 1990.

Massie, Susanne Williams, and Frances Archer Christian, eds. *Homes and Gardens in Old Virginia*. Richmond, Va., 1930.

Mendel-Mesick-Cohen-Waite-Hall, Architects. *Jeffersonian Precinct of the University of Virginia* (Comprehensive Historic Structures Report, Phase I). Albany, N.Y., 1987.

—. *Pavilion I, University of Virginia* (Historic Structure Report). Albany, N.Y., 1988.

Mesick-Cohen-Waite, Architects. *Jefferson's Poplar Forest*, Report on Phase II–A Investigations, June 1991; Report on Phase II–A&B Investigations, November 1991; and Report on Phase III–A Investigations, April 1992. Copies at Poplar Forest.

Nichols, Frederick D. *Thomas Jefferson's Architectural Drawings*. Charlottesville, Va., 1988.

Patterson, Helen Strange. *St. Stephen's Episcopal Church of Bedford County, Forest Virginia*. Forest, Va., 1983.

Peterson, Merrill D., ed. *The Portable Thomas Jefferson*. New York, 1985. In addition to *Notes on Virginia*, this volume contains a number of Jefferson's other papers, addresses, and letters.

—, ed. *Visitors to Monticello*. Charlottesville, Va., 1989.

Randall, Henry S. *The Life of Thomas Jefferson*, 3 vols. New York, 1858.

Randolph, Sarah N. *The Domestic Life of Thomas Jefferson*, New York, 1871. Reprint. Charlottesville, Va., 1978.

Reeder, Frank. *Record of the Family and Descendants of Colonel Christian Jacob Hutter of Easton, Penn'a*. Easton, Pa., 1903.

Rice, Howard C., Jr. *Thomas Jefferson's Paris*. Princeton, N.J., 1976.

Schachner, Nathan. *Thomas Jefferson: A Biography*. New York, 1951.

B. Articles

In addition to the following individual articles cited by author, two magazines published issues in 1991 containing several articles of interest relating to Poplar Forest. These are noted at the end of the list.

Albaugh, E. Kurt. "Thomas Jefferson's Poplar Forest." *Fine Homebuilding* 42 (October–November 1987): 74–79.

Bear, James A., Jr. "Thomas Jefferson — Manufacturer." *Iron Worker* 25, no. 4 (Autumn 1961): 1–11.

Cuthbert, Norma B. "Poplar Forest: Jefferson's Legacy to His Grandson." *Huntington Library Quarterly* 6, no. 3 (May 1943): 333–56.

Davis, Richard Beale. "The Abbé Correa in America." *Transactions of the American Philosophical Society*, n.s. 45, pt. 2 (1955).

Eppes, Mrs. Nicholas Ware. "Francis Eppes (1801–1881), Pioneer of Florida." *Florida Historical Society Quarterly* 5, no. 2 (October, 1926).

Gaines, William H., Jr. "Thomas Jefferson's Favorite Hideaway." *Virginia Cavalcade* 5, no. 1 (Summer 1955): 36–39.

Johnson, Ludwell H., III. "Sharper than a Serpent's Tooth." *Virginia Magazine of History and Biography* 99, no. 2 (April 1991): 145–62.

Kimball, Fiske. "Jefferson and the Public Buildings of Virginia, II. Richmond, 1779–1780." *The Huntington Library Quarterly* 12, no. 3 (May 1949): 303–10.

Lay, K. Edward. "Jefferson's Master Builders." *University of Virginia Alumni News* 80, no. 1 (October 1991): 16–19.

Nichols, Frederick D. "Jefferson's Retreat: Poplar Forest." *Iron Worker* 38, no. 2 (Spring 1974): 2–13.

Tag A. Long [pseudonym]. "Poplar Forest." *Norfolk and Western Magazine* 4, no. 7 (July 1926).

Watson, Lucille McWane. "Thomas Jefferson's other home." *The Magazine Antiques* 71 (April 1957): 342–46.

Wilstach, Paul. "Thomas Jefferson's Secret Home." *Country Life* (April 1928): 41–43.

Lynch's Ferry 4, no. 1 (Spring/Summer, 1991), contains articles on the documentary, architectural, and archeological investigations underway at Poplar Forest.

University of Virginia Alumni News 80, no. 1 (October 1991), contains articles on the restorations of Jefferson's buildings at the University, Monticello, and Poplar Forest, as well as an article on Jefferson's builders, cited under Lay, K. Edward, above.

C. Other

Hutter, Mr. and Mrs. Beverly S., Sr. Interview with author, September 19, 1987.

Johnson, Dr. James A. Interview with author, July 20, 1989.

Stevens & Company. "Poplar Forest, Monograph of a Country House." Undated brochure, Charlottesville, Va. Copy at Poplar Forest.

Thompson, Stuart, and Phelps Barnum, Architects. Specifications for Restoration of Poplar Forest for James Owen Watts, Jr., Lynchburg, Virginia. New York, n.d. Plans for same, dated October 1946 and December 1946. Copies at Poplar Forest.

Watts, James O., Jr., Stephen Hurt Watts, and Sarah Key Watts Giles. Interview with author, May 10, 1989.

Thomas Jefferson's willingness to share his knowledge is alive and well. At least it certainly remains with all those who are fortunate enough to be entrusted with his properties and his papers, and with those associated with him in other ways. Without exception, all of my many requests for assistance with the research leading to this volume met with the most positive and helpful responses I could have hoped for. Some of the people I asked may not know just how much they helped, and any attempt to give proper credit to all would be an impossible task.

Among the many are the talented director and staff of the Corporation for Jefferson's Poplar Forest:

Lynn A. Beebe, Executive Director, has steered the course with skill and grace, presiding over one of the most important ongoing restoration and interpretive efforts in the country.

Dorsey Bodeman, former interpretation coordinator, is the unsung heroine of this work. She has patiently waded through the manuscript in all stages of its development, has provided all sorts of information, and has prevented me from making countless errors. She has done all this and more with the utmost skill, tact, and good humor.

Special thanks go to the professionals at Poplar Forest for always being willing to share their exciting discoveries both below and above ground:

Dr. William Kelso, who served as director of archeology from 1989 to 1991, and his cohorts: former laboratory supervisor M. Drake Patten, and archeological field supervisor, Michael Strutt.

Travis C. McDonald, Jr., restoration coordinator and long-time professional associate, and Andrew Ladygo, architectural conservator. With them, the fabric of Mr. Jefferson's "other home" could not possibly be in better hands.

The consulting architects, Mesick-Cohen-Waite, of Albany, New York, who bring to the project their wealth of knowledge about Jefferson's architecture. John Mesick and Jack Waite, principals in the firm, have given generously of their time and talents, as has Jeff Baker. The drawings the firm prepared (shown in this text as figures 32, 81, 83, and 94) are among the first tangible hints of how a restored Poplar Forest will appear.

Each of the members of the board of directors of the Corporation for Jefferson's Poplar Forest has helped in many, many ways. My bare-bones listing of them gives but scant evidence of my appreciation for all their support and help: Mrs. T. Eugene Worrell, president; Mrs. Michael Wray, vice president; Peter O. Ward, Jr., treasurer; T. George Washington, secretary; and board members Bahman Batmanghelidj, David J. Brown, Mrs. Andrew H. Christian, Douglas Cruickshanks, Christian S. Hutter, Robert B. Lambeth, Jr., Joseph D. Logan III, Mrs. Stuart T. Saunders, George T. Stewart, and Mrs. William O. Thomas.

Others on the staff at Poplar Forest have always been willing to put down their regular tasks whenever I called with yet another request. Among these are Alice Shields, Ann Hos-kins, Susan Phillips, Beverly Mann, and the late Donna Parker Massey.

A number of professionals have joined the Poplar Forest effort since my writing began, and I thank them for being willing and able to take the time to assist me, while at the same time they were having to focus on their new, primary responsibilities. Emily Wright, interpretation coordinator, Dr. Barbara Heath, director of archeology, and William E. Garner, director of development, are among these.

The Corporation has been extremely fortunate in having the services of C. Allan Brown, consulting landscape architect, and Edward Lee Marmon, contract researcher. Brown's *Poplar Forest: the mathematics of an ideal villa* explores and develops ideas that haven't been addressed since Mr. Jefferson first thought of them. His discovery of a plate from an obscure German book that Jefferson owned (figure 20) sheds new light on the possible origins of the plan of the house. Marmon's three-volume *Poplar Forest Research Report* has been invaluable in tying many seemingly loose threads of the Poplar Forest story together. His focus on the history of ownership, farm operations, and the slaves who made it all possible has been invaluable.

Talented volunteer researchers have discovered all sorts of important components of the Poplar Forest story. Special thanks go to Gail Pond, who, in addition to many other favors rendered over the length of the project, researched Andrew Jackson's fascinating and unexpected visit in 1815, and to Sally Williams, who discovered the inventory of one of the builders of the house in the Lynchburg City Courthouse.

Much of the research was conducted at Jones Memorial Library, the mecca for anyone doing research in the Lynchburg/Bedford area. Jones Library is fortunate to have the services of Jeanne Mead, who answered my many questions promptly and fully and often provided supplementary material with which I was totally unfamiliar. I also appreciate the willingness of Edward Gibson, Librarian, in allowing full and free access to the collections at Jones.

The many fellow laborers in the field at Mr. Jefferson's Monticello helped immensely. Under the leadership of Daniel P. Jordan, Executive Director of the Thomas Jefferson Memorial Foundation, they include Susan R. Stein, Lucia ("Cinder") Stanton, William Beiswanger, Ann Lucas, Susanne Olson, Libby Fosso, and Sara Lee Barnes. That they were willing even to consider giving their time and talent while preparing for a major exhibition at Monticello went far beyond the call of duty. A lunch spent with Susan commiserating over our mutual schedules and deadlines was a pleasant and necessary interlude for both of us.

Beyond Poplar Forest and Monticello are countless individuals who, among their other duties, have responsibilities for the Jefferson papers held by their respective institutions. This work could not have been accomplished without the help of John Rhodehamel of the Huntington Library, who always meant it when he ended his letters: "Let me know if I can do anything else." Michael Plunkett and Laura Endicott at the University of Virginia; Peter Drummey and Virginia Smith at the Massachusetts Historical Society; Richard Shrader and John White at the Southern Historical Collection, University of North Carolina, Chapel Hill; James Gilreath at the Library of Congress; and Frances Pollard at the Virginia Historical Society provided help that went far beyond the call of duty.

While most of my research has been conducted within the walls of those hallowed institutions just named, from time to time I had the chance to get outside and follow the pathways that Mr. Jefferson knew. Nathaniel Mason Pawlett, Randolph Byrd, and Irene S. Ellis helped me try and track down the sites of the elusive Flood's and Hunter's taverns, where Jefferson stayed on his journeys between Poplar Forest and Monticello. Dr. James W. Jordan of Longwood College showed me the grave of John Wayles Eppes and the fascinating remains of his house at Millbrook in Buckingham County. Anne Morrill, John L. Morris, Jr., and K. Edward Lay helped in the search for material on the now-destroyed Mount Warren (figure 88), the home of Jefferson's friend, Wilson Cary Nicholas.

Though I have contacted only a fraction of Thomas Jefferson's many descendants, those with whom I have been in touch have been interested and helpful without exception. I would like especially to thank Mary Eppes Turner of Greensboro, North Carolina, who introduced me to Marian Eppes Moss, Athens, Georgia, and her son, Lee Moss, who shared their inherited letters from the Eppes family. Lamar H. Roberts of Atlanta, Dr. Catherine C. Lastavica of Boston, and Mrs. Joseph C. Cornwall of Short Hills, New Jersey, helped in special ways. Thanks to William Lattimore, Edna Eppes Lattimore Clancy, and Harry Hays Lattimore, Francis Eppes's Memoranda is now back where it began, in Bedford County, Virginia, a generous and much-appreciated gift to the Corporation. My meeting in Savannah with Bill Lattimore, when I saw this rare document for the first time, was another of those special moments in this project.

During the course of my work, not only did Francis Eppes's Memoranda surface, so did a note and a letter written from Poplar Forest by Thomas Jefferson. Mrs. William L. Wilson of Lynchburg and Mrs. Frank G. Strachan of New Orleans, their owners, have generously given these to the Corporation. I can take no credit for unearthing them, but take pleasure in thanking Frances Steinheimer of Lynchburg and Mary Denny Wray of Richmond for alerting me to them.

John Catanzariti, editor of *The Papers of Thomas Jefferson* at Princeton, shared his wealth of information on Jefferson's letters and documents. He helped far more than that, when he wrote to Dorsey Bodeman, announcing that "with the blessing of Jim Bear and Cinder Stanton," he was "enclosing five diskettes with the computer files for *Jefferson's Memorandum Books* so that Poplar Forest's architectural and archaeological investigations can proceed without delay." These "files" are

the text for a forthcoming publication from Princeton University Press, and are absolutely invaluable to all of us associated with Poplar Forest. Citations appear throughout my text as evidence of how much they helped me "proceed without delay."

Timothy A. Buehner, whose association with Poplar Forest goes back almost as far as mine, was supervisor of the team of student architects who measured and drew Poplar Forest for the Historic American Buildings Survey in 1985. A number of illustrations from the HABS project are included herein as illustrations. Tim later prepared the drawings shown as figures 21, 28, 95, 108, and 116 especially for this book.

Tom Graves, Jr., was ever willing to go far afield to provide photographs. For his camera artistry and willingness to take on any assignment, I sincerely thank him.

Willie Graham, architectural historian at Colonial Williamsburg, shared in the joy of finding the treasure trove of Poplar Forest material in the Swem Library at the College of William and Mary. He, Ed Chappell, Carl Lounsbury, and Mark Wenger at Colonial Williamsburg have provided assistance at Poplar Forest, as they do throughout Virginia and beyond.

Cynthia H. Foote, of Charlottesville, once again kept me from making many errors, both egregious and otherwise, and I thank her for that.

Over the several years that I have been working on this project, many friends have expressed interest far beyond what I expected. Janie Aldrich, Catherine Bishir, Cinny and Pat Fehr, Francesca and Jon Glassman, Anne Carter and Dick Gravely, Sara and John Hager, Jim Hill, Lib Hodges, Peter Houck, Wendy and Stephen Lash, Betty Gayle and Felix Laughlin, Calder Loth, Sara and Alec Vagliano, Ellen and Larry Walsh, and David and Jack Zehmer are a few of these. I thank them for their indulgence, patience, and interest, and I especially recall Wendy Lash's admonition, given not so long ago, to "just go ahead and write it!" While I don't think that I ever experienced a real attack of writer's block, the words of encouragement Lib Hodges gave, both in person and all too generously in her *Charlie's Children: The Fleets at Home*, came just at the right time. Catherine Bishir's including me as having helped her in her monumental *North Carolina Architecture* was a complete surprise, and I love being able to return the favor here.

Robert H. Garbee, A.I.A., started me off on the right track on this project, just as he had done years ago on another, not entirely unrelated, occasion. Having conducted extensive research on Poplar Forest, he generously shared the information that he and his assistant, Robert Hiller, had uncovered.

I've not yet had the pleasure of meeting all of the members of the regional committees that have been established to assist in the restoration of Poplar Forest, but many of those that I do know have helped in all sorts of ways. Special credit goes to Gene and Lloyd Dahmen, Steve Lash, Catherine Hirsch, and

Mary Denny Wray, the able chairman. I also thank Barbara and Chill Langhorne (who are, more importantly, friends and neighbors as well), Helen Reveley, Val Evans, and Gene and Laura Goley. The Goleys also provided many of the illustrations of houses near Poplar Forest that Mr. Jefferson knew. Nothing of importance in Virginia preservation can be accomplished without the influence of Mary Tyler Cheek, and her assistance at Poplar Forest has been, as always, immeasurable.

Poplar Forest is more than Thomas Jefferson's "other home." In the years following his ownership, it was home to other families as well. Descendants and relatives of the Cobbs-Hutter family have been unfailingly helpful and encouraging, not only in relation to this book, but to the whole restoration effort. Duffy (Mrs. Edwin C.) Hutter of Princeton, New Jersey, is the knowledgeable and appreciative keeper of the family papers. Studying them with her while seated at the table that is in all likelihood the original dining-room table from Poplar Forest was certainly one of the highlights of my research. The late Mr. and Mrs. Beverly S. Hutter, Sr., Chris Hutter, and Ted and Dale Harris, are others of the clan who have helped.

Having known the Watts family while growing up in Lynchburg and having visited them at Poplar Forest, I enjoyed immensely the opportunity of renewing my acquaintance with both Jimmys (senior and junior), Stephen Watts, and Key Watts Giles. The day spent with them at Poplar Forest in late spring 1989 was another highlight, and the donation of their copy of the 1946 deed to the property was a generous and gracious gift to the Corporation.

Before his untimely death, I had the good fortune to meet with Dr. James Johnson, the last private owner of Poplar Forest. As he said, it was a good time "we spent together concerning our mutual friend," Thomas Jefferson. Had he not purchased the property when he did, in all likelihood this book would never have been written.

Jack Zehmer recommended that James B. Patrick, the publisher, of Fort Church Publishers, and Donald G. Paulhus, the designer, of Paulhus Associates, be brought on board. It's entirely due to these two Rhode Islanders, Jim and Don, that the raw material was transformed into the finished product, and that it was accomplished in time to help celebrate Thomas Jefferson's two-hundred-and-fiftieth birthday.

About those computer disks that John Catanzariti furnished. They were Greek to me, but not to my wife, Bettye. As in all my efforts, I couldn't have done this without her, and she helped in far more ways than showing me how to turn the computer on.

In 1943, Edwin C. Hutter gave Norma Cuthbert, who had just published her article on Poplar Forest in the *Huntington Library Quarterly*, something of a backhanded compliment: "There has been more confusion than one would think possible. I have never yet read an article about Poplar Forest that was entirely accurate, in my opinion. Yours was nearly so." With thanks to one and all, I sincerely hope that what I've written on these pages is nearly so.

S. Allen Chambers, Jr.
January 1993

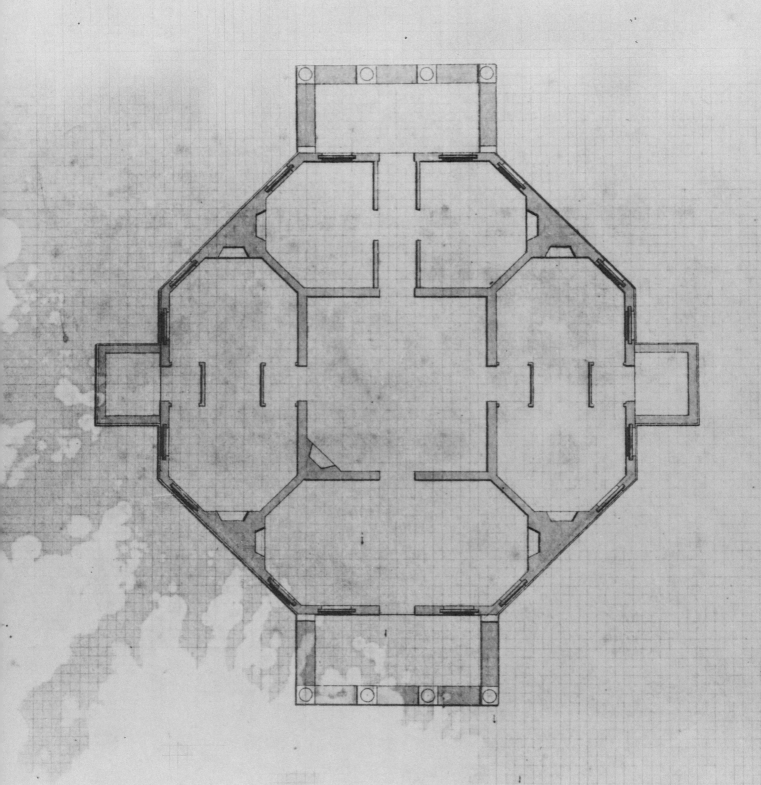